Donia Yetter
Sept. 1983
Madison, Wi

DATE DUE

Withdrawn	

Belinskij and Russian Literary Criticism

Belinskij and Russian Literary Criticism *The Heritage of Organic Aesthetics*

Victor Terras

The University of Wisconsin Press

Published 1974
The University of Wisconsin Press
Box 1379, Madison, Wisconsin 53701

The University of Wisconsin Press, Ltd.
70 Great Russell Street, London

First Printing

Printed in the United States of America

For LC CIP information see the colophon
ISBN 0-299-06350-X

Contents

Preface

This book grew out of several graduate seminars in Russian literary criticism which I conducted at the University of Wisconsin in Madison between 1966 and 1970. It addresses itself to scholars concerned with Russian and comparative literature.

The transliteration system used for transliterating Cyrillic is the one internationally used by Slavic linguists. For a transliteration chart, see J. Thomas Shaw, *The Transliteration of Modern Russian for English-Language Publications* (Madison: University of Wisconsin Press, 1967), pp. 8-9, where the system used in this book is System III.

Dates in the text follow those used in the original works referred to. The thirteen-volume Academy edition of Belinskij's works uses the Julian calendar in Belinskij's correspondence and references to it, and I have left this unchanged.

Translations from all languages are my own throughout, unless otherwise indicated.

It is my pleasant duty to thank those who helped me in my work on this book. Naturally, they are in no way responsible for its shortcomings. The Department of Slavic Languages at the University of Wisconsin greatly helped the progress of my research by allowing me to take advantage of the services of a research assistant for several semesters. Professors René Wellek and J. Thomas Shaw read the manuscript and made many necessary corrections and valuable suggestions which I followed gratefully in almost every instance. My research assistant, Jack Schillinger (now Professor Schillinger), excerpted and catalogued a very large number of passages from Belinskij's works.

Victor Terras

Belinskij and Russian Literary Criticism

All references to Belinskij's works are to
volume and page number in the 13-volume edition
of the Academy of Sciences of the USSR: V. G.
Belinskij, *Polnoe sobranie sočinenij,* 13 vols.
(Moscow, 1953–59).

1
Introduction

ORGANICIST TRAITS IN SOCIALIST REALISM

The Second Congress of Soviet Writers (1954) defined Socialist Realism as "the basic method of Soviet literature and literary criticism, which requires of the artist a truthful, historically concrete representation of reality in its revolutionary development." With some little difficulty the ideological catchwords of Socialist Realist literary and critical practice can be worked into this definition. *Idejnost'* ("ideological awareness") covers the understanding needed to recognize the direction of historical development and to time correctly its revolutionary peaks. *Partijnost'* ("conscious, partisan communist attitude")[1] is implied in a "historically concrete representation of reality," since it means much the same as *idejnost'* applied to the concrete historical situation of the present—only the Communist party of the Soviet Union is presumed to be fully in step with history. *Xudožestvennost'* ("artistic quality") depends on "representation of reality," since a "false" representation of reality or a representation of something that is not a part of reality, as in nonrepresentational art, is denied "artistic quality." Obviously, *idejnost', partijnost',* and *xudožestvennost'* are overlapping concepts expressing different aspects of the same notion.

The same is true of the negative catchwords of Socialist Realism. Its rejection of "naturalism" underscores the importance of ideological awareness, since a mechanical, photographic representation of reality is bound to miss its dynamic essence ("historical development"). "Objectivism" (*ob"ektivizm,*

---

1. The term *partijnost'* is used, in Soviet literary criticism, in the sense given it by Lenin in his article "Partijnaja organizacija i partijnaja literatura" (1905). An incredible amount has been written in the Soviet Union on this short article. See, e.g., Ja. E. Èl's-berg, *Leninskoe nasledie, žizn' i literatura* (Moscow, 1969); V. Gorbunov, "Bor'ba za proletarskuju partijnost' literatury," *Voprosy literatury* (hereafter *VLit*) 15, no. 6 (1971): 42–62; A. S. Mjasnikov, "Lenin i èstetičeskie problemy XX veka," *Izvestija Akademii Nauk SSSR* 29 (1970): 108–27; L. Stolovič, "Lenin i problema xudožestvennoj cennosti," *VLit* 13, no. 10 (1969): 11–30.

more often *psevdo-ob"ektivizm*) is the opposite of *partijnost'*. It is presumed to be camouflaged reactionary bias in almost every instance. Finally, "formalism" means a preoccupation with those elements of the artist's craft which are independent of objective reality. It is condemned as a concession to subjective idealism.

It is largely within this ideological framework that Soviet scholars of undeniable competence present their views on the nature of the work of art, its relationship to its creator, and the relationship of both to the society which produced them.[2] (This is not true of the structuralist school now flourishing in the USSR, even though its exponents will pay occasional lip service to the ideological principles of Socialist Realism. The structuralists, like their predecessors, the "formalists" of the 1920s, are essentially neo-Kantian subjective idealists.[3]) However, the specific doctrines of Marxist aesthetic theory as it prevails in the Soviet Union to this day and as it is taught in Soviet universities[4] may surprise a Western observer who has been familiar only with the political side of Socialist Realism.

To begin with, we find in Soviet aesthetic theory a very high evaluation of the social, cognitive, and prophetic powers of art. In the West, the following opinion could be considered more or less typical:

> We disregard claims about the value or nonvalue of poetry and merely seek to determine what function it fulfills. In areas of life that are not sufficiently

2. As examples of Soviet aesthetic scholarship at its best, see M. Kagan, *Lekcii po marksistsko-leninskoj èstetike*, 3 vols. (Leningrad, 1963–66); Ju. B. Borev, *Vvedenie v èstetiku* (Moscow, 1965); V. V. Vanslov, *Èstetika romantizma* (Moscow, 1966). All three works can be termed Hegelian–or Belinskian.

3. For an example of Soviet structuralism, see Ju. M. Lotman, *Struktura xudožestvennogo teksta* (Moscow, 1970). A spirited polemic between structuralists and anti-structuralists has been in process in the Soviet Union for some time. See M. Kagan, "Itak, 'strukturalizm' ili 'antistrukturalizm,'" *VLit* 13, no. 2 (1969): 113–34; B. Runin, "Toska po iskusstvometrii," *VLit* 13, no. 8 (1969): 104–17; V. Kožinov, "Vozmožna-li strukturnaja poètika?" *VLit* 9, no. 6 (1965): 88–107; P. Zarev, "Ob aktual'nyx voprosax literaturovedenija i strukturalizma," *VLit* 13, no. 12 (1969): 58–72; L. I. Timofeev, "Xudožestvennyj progress," *Novyj mir* 47, no. 5 (1971): 238–42. For a summary, see Hans Günther, "Zur Strukturalismus–Diskussion in der sowjetischen Literaturwissenschaft," *Welt der Slaven* 14 (1969): 1–21. Both the structuralists and their opponents are well aware of the fact that "structuralism" and Belinskian (Hegelian) "organicism" are incompatible. It is fully in character with the debate between these two schools when A. Begiašvili, a structuralist, exclaims as he challenges M. Kagan, a staunch organicist: "Oh, not again this 'organic connection,' this 'organic unity,' etc.! In human language there are probably no greater sinners than these terms which, with their properly respectable appearance, cover up so much that is unclear and undigested in human thought!" ("Predely 'strukturnogo' literaturovedenija," *VLit* 14, no. 6 (1970): 86.

4. See L. I. Timofeev, *Osnovy teorii literatury,* 3d ed. (Moscow, 1966), a standard work the outlook of which is decidedly cautious and conservative.

explored by science, poetry expresses, by means of linguistic forms which have been created for that special purpose, experiences that are present in the consciousness of the poet in the form of moods, feelings, or inspirations, with the aim of communicating these states of consciousness to the reader or listener.[5]

In the Soviet Union, on the contrary, one tends to hear opinions such as the following: "The cognitive potential of art is immense. It was not by accident that Marx remarked that he had learned more about the life of French bourgeois society from the novels of Balzac than from all the works of the political economists of that period, taken together."[6]

Soviet aestheticians have hopes of a superlatively bright future for the aesthetic aspect of the human personality. As man in communist society will have to spend progressively less time on the production of material goods, they believe, he will devote himself more and more to the creation of aesthetic values. Gor'kij's dictum "Aesthetics is the Ethic of the future!" is often quoted. In communist society, says Professor Kagan, "Art will become the principal and special instrument of the organization of the individual's spiritual life."[7] This is a surprisingly old-fashioned utopian socialist position. Even Hegel, with whom Soviet aestheticians otherwise tend to agree, had registered, not without sadness, the impending demise of Art as he knew it.

To be sure, art is conceded to be a "superstructure" (*nadstrojka,* the *Überbau* of Marx) of socioeconomic life. But in general, Soviet aestheticians today refuse to derive from this a utilitarian conception of art. The utilitarian aesthetics of Černyševskij, Pisarev, and other "revolutionary democrats" of the nineteenth century, as well as that of Left-Art in the 1920s, is generally condemned as a mistake of the past.[8] The relationship between art and socioeconomic life is seen as one of dialectic give-and-take through a multitude of different channels.

While often referring back to the "reflection theory" of art (*teorija otraženija*) ascribed to Lenin, Soviet aestheticians, by and large, reject Černyševskij's thesis of the unconditional primacy and superiority of "reality" over its reflection in art. They do so by drawing attention to Lenin's dictum that "human consciousness not only *reflects* the objective world, but also *creates* it." (There exists a genuine division among Soviet aestheticians regarding the question whether the

5. Richard von Mises, *Positivism: A Study in Human Understanding* (New York, 1968), p. 300.

6. Borev, *Vvedenie,* p. 141.

7. Kagan, *Lekcii,* 3:121.

8. It was even so criticized by early Marxist critics, such as Plexanov, Vorovskij, and Lunačarskij. For a contemporary statement of the autonomy of art, based on the postulation of a *sui generis* "aesthetic drive," see P. L. Ivanov, *O suščnosti krasoty* (Moscow, 1967), pp. 166–69. Ivanov quotes Hegel frequently, and usually with approval.

so-called aesthetic categories, and specifically that of Beauty, are objective, as the *prirodniki* [from *prirodnyj*, "natural"] assert, or subjective, as the *obščest-venniki* [from *obščestvennyj*, "social"] believe. It renews the old and hopeless-ly sterile debate between the supporters and the detractors of *das Naturschöne* in post-Hegelian aesthetic literature.[9]

As for the aesthetic fact as such, Soviet aestheticians and critics tend to operate with the familiar polarities of nineteenth-century German idealist aes-thetics: "content" and "form," the "ideal" and the "real," the "universals" ("type") and the "particular" ("individual"), and so forth. Sometimes these polarities are rephrased in slightly different terms, adapted to contemporary ideology. For example, Ju. B. Borev and Ja. E. Èl'sberg, in their introductory paper to a volume of articles on aesthetic and literary theory by leading Soviet scholars and critics, thus define "artistic image" (*xudožestvennyj obraz*, per-haps *the* key term of Soviet aesthetic theory): "This is why the first and fore-most principle (*načalo načal*) of contemporary [Soviet] theory of literature must be recognized in its 'nucleus' (*jadro*): the artistic image as the sphere of the fusion of ideological awareness (*idejnost'*) and artistic quality (*xudožest-vennost'*)."[10]

What is even more important, Soviet aestheticians tend to insist that these are *organic* polarities, where one pole complements the other, rather than mechanical, one-way relationships. A work of art should be concrete in its de-scriptions of reality, yet it should also be the bearer of an ideal. It should pre-sent the truth of individual life, yet not without a certain universal validity. If it fails in the former, it becomes abstract, allegoric, and therefore ineffec-tive. If it lacks the dimension of the ideal and universal, it veers into "natural-ism" and becomes meaningless.[11]

Most Soviet theorists would agree with the poet Maršak, who said: "Every poet, just as every artist, has two sources of nourishment; one of them is life, the other is art itself." Life is the "content," art the "form" of a work of art. A hypertrophy of form leads to "formalism," that is, a separation of art from life. Yet Soviet critics also reject the "factography" once promoted by the Left-Art movement of the 1920s, that is, a literature about "life," but without "art."

To an observer familiar primarily with the practical aspect of Socialist Real-ism, aptly defined as "government naturalism" (*kazennyj naturalizm*) by Georg Lukács, it will come as something of a surprise that Soviet aestheticians operate routinely with the traditional antithetical "aesthetic categories" (so referred to

9. See Borev, *Vvedenie*, p. 29.
10. Ju. B. Borev and Ja. E. Èl'sberg, "Vvedenie: Teorija literatury, istorizm i sovremen-nost'," in *Teorija literatury*, 3 vols. (Moscow, 1962), 1:22.
11. See Kagan, *Lekcii*, 1:122.

by Soviet writers) of the Beautiful (*prekrasnoe*), the Sublime (*vozvyšennoe*),
and the Tragic (*tragičeskoe*). "Beauty" equals "truth," aesthetically represented. "Truth" is historical or, shall we say, "historicized," meaning the manifestation of "true humanitarian ideals" on the highest level which mankind is
capable of attaining during the historical epoch in question. The other aesthetic categories are likewise "historicized." For example, the Tragic is recognized
in the heroic death, at the hands of reaction, of the bearer of a "progressive
ideal." Such death is deeply meaningful, as it presages the future victory of
the hero's ideal. Correspondingly, the Comic, as the antithesis of the Tragic,
is viewed in terms of a light-hearted good-bye to the foibles and absurdities of
a dying class and its ideology.

Discussions of the creative process in Soviet aesthetics tend to move along the
time-honored antithetical lines of "genius" and "talent" (a distinction always
made), inspiration and craftsmanship, the "poet" and the "artist."[12]

Nor is the Soviet aesthetician of today unaware that he is defending what is
essentially nineteenth-century Hegelian aesthetics against a neo-Kantian formalism which prevails in the West and is making inroads even in the Soviet Union.
Thus, the Soviet contributions to the Fifth International Congress on Aesthetics
and the Fifth Hegelian Congress[13] uniformly combat formalism, naturalism, ab-
stractionism, surrealism, pop art, *le nouveau roman*, élitism, Freudianism, and
other trends usually lumped by Soviet writers under the term "modernism" (a
meaningless catchall), largely with quotations from Hegel himself. Soviet aestheticians often do this even on occasions when Hegel's thought, as such, is not
the subject of discussion. There are numerous works in Soviet aesthetic literature which bear a striking resemblance to those of such Hegelian epigoni of the
nineteenth century as F. T. Vischer or H. T. Rötscher.[14]

V. S. Kružkov, one of the contributors to the Fifth International Congress
on Aesthetics, specifies the positions of Soviet aesthetic theory which he feels
are being challenged by contemporary Western trends: "Some of the representatives of West European and American aesthetic thought reject, along with Socialist Realism, the principles not only of socialist but of all realism, such as humanism, the ideal, the "goal-directedness" and the cognitive role of art, the accessi-
bility and intelligibility of art to the broad masses of the people, the artistic
image as an unshakable condition and criterion of the value of every work of

---

12. See Viktor Rozov, "The Process of Creation," *Soviet Studies in Literature* 5,
no. 2 (1969): 3–18.

13. Akademii Nauk SSSR, Institut filosofii, *Bor'ba idej v èstetike: V Gegelevskij i V
Meždunarodnyj kongressy po èstetike* (Moscow, 1966).

14. A perfect example is N. Krjukovskij, *Logika krasoty* (Minsk, 1965). The book is
exactly what the title promises: an attempt to arrive at a kind of aesthetic algebra by way
of Hegelian dialectic and Hegelian aesthetic categories.

art."[15] Obviously, each of these positions is compatible with Hegelian aesthetics.

The concept of the "artistic image" is particularly dear to the Socialist Realist critic. When one of the stalwarts of conventional literary scholarship in the Soviet Union, L. I. Timofeev, recently challenged the structuralist approach of Ju. M. Lotman in Lotman's *Struktura xudožestvennogo teksta,* he stressed the fact that "only a single paragraph was devoted to the concept of the artistic image" in Lotman's book.[16] In his own *Osnovy teorii literatury* Timofeev likewise defends the "artistic image" against some attempts by G. N. Pospelov to curtail its importance (pp. 17–18).

The doctrine of the organic autonomy of art, which Soviet aestheticians accept in theory, has far-reaching consequences which inevitably clash with the political facts of Soviet life. Ideally, the poetic truth at which an artist freely arrives, led by his inspiration and reassured by his aesthetic sense, ought to be in harmony with the historical truth as set down in the program and in the policies of the Communist party. But in practice things are different. The works which seem to follow the Party line are often so weak artistically that even good Communists are disheartened.

In contrast, the Party is far from happy with the ideological side of works which are otherwise artistic and popular successes. So-called modernist art and poetry, suppressed by force in the 1930s, have been gaining strongly since Stalin's death, in spite of vigorous official opposition. It is neither easy nor gratifying for a Soviet critic of the Party persuasion to insist on explaining this as "vestiges of capitalism." Plexanov and other Marxist critics before the Revolution had believed—along with Tolstoj, incidentally—that the esoteric, formalized, alienated, and "dehumanized" art of the twentieth century was meaningful and even aesthetically appealing to the decaying bourgeoisie, as an organic manifestation of the actual historical condition of that class. They also took it for granted that it was historically doomed, along with the bourgeoisie. Today's Soviet aestheticians and literary and art critics share the dilemma of their colleagues in history, political science, and economics: the actual historical developments have failed to bear out the predictions of Marx and Lenin.

Lenin's ideal in the area of literature had been a "party literature," meaning a literature that would support the program of the Party freely, consciously as well as enthusiastically, with conviction as well as talent. Nothing of this

15. I have translated *xudožestvennyj obraz* as "artistic image." "Artistic form" or even "artistic symbol" would be reasonable alternatives. The quotation is from Kružkov's article "Problema xudožestvennoj pravdy v *Èstetike* Gegelja," *Bor'ba idej,* p. 54.

16. Timofeev, "Xudožestvennyj progress," p. 241.

kind ever materialized. Over the years Soviet policymakers, in clear and, no doubt, conscious violation of their professed principles, have accepted the services of bourgeois fellow travelers of dubious sincerity, or of literary hacks devoted to the Party but possessing neither talent nor ideas, while subjecting truly creative writers to a deadening regimentation which at times almost killed Soviet literature. Meanwhile Russian literature kept producing great poetry and prose, much of which, paradoxically, had to be declared inferior, harmful, or irrelevant, and kept from the Soviet reader, since it was blatantly "reactionary."

DESCRIPTION OF ORGANIC AESTHETICS

The germ of the situation which we find in Soviet aesthetic thought is inherent in the organic aesthetics of V. G. Belinskij (1811-1848), whose thinking has dominated much of Russian literary theory and criticism, "left" or "right," for nearly a century and a half, and is still the single most important active influence in this area.

Belinskij owed his aesthetic ideas to the German idealist philosophers of the late eighteenth and early nineteenth century—Kant, Herder, Schiller, Fichte, Schelling, Hegel. This takes nothing away either from his stature as a literary critic or from the historical importance of his life's work. Belinskij was a remarkable man. He took over, largely from the German thinkers just mentioned, a profound and intricate system of aesthetic thought and went on to apply it not only in his practical criticism of Russian literature but also in his effort to integrate that literature into the "progressive" political movement among the Russian intelligentsia, of which he was also a founder.

At the core of Belinskij's aesthetics there lies the so-called organic conception of the work of art, a conception which he consistently and conscientiously applied as a practicing critic and which he tirelessly defended against stubborn rearguard actions of the old "critique of details," whether it be the vestiges of a sentimentalist *critique de beautés,* or a pseudoclassicist quibbling over propriety of diction, *vraisemblance* of plot, or correctness of grammar. In this attitude, Belinskij followed the example of German romantic critics, in particular the Schlegel brothers.[17]

17. On organicism in general, see, e.g., D. C. Phillips, "Organicism in the Late Nineteenth and Early Twentieth Centuries," *Journal of the History of Ideas* 31 (1970): 413-32. For a survey of organic theories in aesthetics and literature, see M. H. Abrams, *The Mirror and the Lamp: Romantic Theory and the Critical Tradition* (New York, 1953), pp. 156-225. For an excellent, concise overview of aesthetic organicism, see G. N. G. Orsini, "The Organic Concepts in Aesthetics," *Comparative Literature* 21 (1969): 1-30. Specifically for German *Organismusästhetik,* see Oskar Walzel, *Grenzen von Poesie und Unpoesie* (Frankfurt-am-Main, 1937).

The organic conception of the work of art is best understood as an empirical notion according to which a successful work of art has certain properties which have a parallel in a living biological organism. It was first developed by Plato (mostly in his *Phaedrus* 264C) and Aristotle (in his *Poetics* 8. 51a32–35). It means, in essence, that in a work of art all the parts should be in keeping with the whole, as well as with each other, in such a way that the alteration of one part causes the alteration of the whole. Plato likens a work of art (the case in point happens to be a rhetorical composition) to a "living being."[18]

Many aestheticians and critics have stopped at this point, recognizing that the "organic analogy" is no more than a metaphor, or a useful working hypothesis. Aristotle and Kant are among these aestheticians. They see the work of art as a structure shaped by an organizing intelligence, either according to patterns found in nature (Aristotle) or according to structural principles generated by the human mind (Kant). The unity of a work of art is then a projection of an organizing scheme (the Aristotelian *logos*), which exists independently of it.

A bolder version of the organic view of art recognizes only those works of art as truly "organic," or "living," the unity of which can be likened to that of a living organism possessed of a soul rather than to that of a mechanical organization or automaton.[19] In abstract language this conception is often stated by the maxim: "The whole is more than merely the sum of the parts" (where "sum" is shorthand notation for "any rational synthesis"). The germ of this proposition is found in Plato's *Theaetetus* 204B where it takes the form: "The all is not the whole."[20] However, it is just as well to see this conception as an actual realization of the organic metaphor; it postulates the presence, in a successful work of art, of some irrational vital force.

For the sake of this conception, Plato rejects what in today's terminology would be called "aesthetic formalism," "aesthetic instrumentalism," as well as "l'art pour l'art." A true poem or oration (unlike Lysias's wretched fabrication, which Socrates demolishes) is possessed of a soul, infused into it by the poet's or orator's inspiration, which is a gift of God. Plato's identification of poetic inspiration (μανία, μανική) with the gift of prophecy (μαντική), which he underscores by pointing out the etymological identity of these terms, leads

18. "I think you will agree that a composition should be like a living being, with a body of its own, so as not to be headless or footless, but so as to have middle and extremities fitting one another, as well as the whole" (Plato *Phaedrus* 264C).

19. A. W. Schlegel in his *Kunstlehre* put it this way: "The works of mechanical art are dead and limited; the works of higher, spiritual art (*Die Werke höherer Geisteskunst*) are living, immanently dynamic, and infinite. The former serve a determinate external purpose and cannot go beyond its attainment, and the reasoning power which devised them can fully comprehend their workings" (August Wilhelm Schlegel, *Kritische Schriften und Briefe,* ed. Edgar Lohner, 4 vols. [Stuttgart, 1963], 2:13).

20. Orsini, "Organic Concepts," p. 17.

to the postulation of the cognitive as well as moral value of poetic creation (*Phaedrus* 245A). German romantic aesthetics (as in the writings of the Schlegel brothers, and Schelling) stresses precisely this vitalistic version of organicism.

As early as in Plato's *Phaedrus* the modern concept of artistic "intuition" or "immediate knowledge" is anticipated in a notion of poetic or mantic "vision" as a recollection (ἀνάμνησις) of divine, eternal ideas. Plotinus, in the eighth chapter of his Fifth Ennead (which concerns how a human soul may join Zeus and the other gods and demons in attaining a vision of the supercelestial space described by Socrates in Plato's *Phaedrus* 246D–247E), gets even closer to a notion which corresponds to what we call "intuition."[21] Plotinus also arrives at what is in effect the romantic conception of the poetic symbol when he praises the Egyptian hieroglyphics—not quite deservedly, let it be said—as an example of expressing an idea as a whole, synthetically rather than analytically (as by letters of the alphabet): "so that each image is cognition and wisdom, as well as a subject and a whole, and not a line of reasoning or a deliberation."[22] This conception is virtually identical with Belinskij's notion of the "artistic image," which he took from the German objective idealists and passed on to his followers in Russia.

An immediate corollary of such belief in the cognitive powers of artistic intuition is a demand for moral earnestness in art. This demand is also made by Plato, who says that an orator should use his inspiration as a road to truth rather than as a means of dissimulation (*Phaedrus* 261A). The important cognitive and moral role assigned to art is characteristic of German objective idealism, as well as of Belinskij and all his followers. It energetically contradicts the notion, as widespread in Plato's Greece as it is today, that poetry is merely more or less frivolous entertainment, and poets either clever imitators of nature or amusing "liars."[23] How serious a point this is, one may learn from the impassioned vehemence with which Gogol', in his dramatic sketch "After the Theater," turns against those in the audience who will take his comedy for mere *pobasenki* ("made-up tales"). The high and serious regard in which art

21. "Everything which is, works of human art as well as of nature, is produced by an intelligence (σοφία), because there is always an intelligence behind creation. Now, granted that creation is guided by intelligence, let us assume that the arts be in that category. But the artist will often rediscover natural intelligence (πάλιν αὖ εἰς σοφίαν φυσικὴν ἔρχεται), according to which things were created, an intelligence not put together from theorems (οὐκέτι συντεθεῖσαν ἐκ θεωρημάτων), but whole and one, not made up of many parts to form a unit, but rather a unit which may be analyzed as having many parts" (Plotinus *Enneads* 5. 8. 5).

22. . . . ὡς ἄρα τις καὶ ἐπιστήμη καὶ σοφία ἕκαστόν ἐστιν ἄγαλμα καὶ ὑποκείμενον καὶ ἀθρόον καὶ οὐ διανόησις οὐδὲ βούλευσις (*Enneads* 5. 8. 6).

23. "Ficta voluptatis causa sint proxima veris" (Horace *Ars poetica* 337).

and the artist are held is one of the cardinal features of German idealist philosophy, the romantic movement, as well as of Belinskij and his school. The extraordinarily close attention paid to art and literature by the Soviet state is an institutionalized version of this tradition.

The "soul" or the "ideal" aspect of the work of art has been associated, ever since Plato, with still another empirical phenomenon: "inner vision" or "inner form" (ἔνδον εἶδος). It amounts to the experience known not only to creative artists but to many ordinary people as well in which the form that the subject will eventually express in words, in colors, or in music is believed to have appeared to his "mental eye" even before the process of expression began. This inner vision may or may not find actual expression. E. T. A. Hoffmann's mad Baron B. hears great music with his ideal, inner sense, while objectively producing screeching, cacophonic sounds. But the ideal music *is* there, as proven by the fact that serious musicians learn a great deal from the Baron's theoretical observations on music.

The theory of "inner vision," though it was apparently a cliché even in the days of Cicero,[24] has been associated with the formulation given it by Plotinus, whose treatise anticipates almost the entire aesthetic system of German idealism, and so Belinskij's. The German idealist philosophers were, of course, familiar with Plotinus, though they did not point out their dependence on him as much as they might have. Belinskij, it seems, did not know how heavily Fichte, Schelling, and Hegel had drawn upon Plotinus. He was, however, familiar with Plato's *Phaedrus*.

Plotinus, a mystic, sees all that is as an emanation of the Absolute. The distinction between things is one of intensity, power, rather than of kind. The artist's inner vision, though often triggered by an object of external reality, is more intense, more beautiful, and nearer to the Absolute than external reality. To Plotinus, Beauty is simply plenitude of being,[25] rather than any particular attribute of being. This conforms with the beliefs of Schelling, Hegel, and Belinskij, to all of whom the truth of life, manifested in the fusion of the real and ideal which is art, equals Beauty. It contradicts assorted psychological theories, popular in the eighteenth century and by no means forgotten in Belinskij's days, which sought to define Beauty as a certain range of physical qualities, proportions, or relations found in the aesthetic object and eliciting a favorable response in the perceiving subject.

24. "Sed ipsius in mente insidebat species pulchritudinis eximia quaedam, quam intuens in eaque difixus ad illius similitudinem artem et manum dirigebat" (Cicero *De oratore* 3, where the subject is Phidias, as in Plotinus).

25. "Where would Beauty be, if it were deprived of existence? And where would existence be, if deprived of Beauty? For in eliminating Beauty, one also takes away from existence. Therefore, existence is desirable because it is the same as Beauty, and Beauty is to be loved, because existence is" (Plotinus *Enneads* 5. 8. 9).

What we would call creative ability today is to Plotinus identical with power (δύναμις) of vision. A man possessed by God or by a Muse has the power to see the Divine in his visions.[26] The concept of power (*Kraft*) is of key importance in the aesthetics of German Romanticism and German objective idealism, as well as of Belinskij. "Talent" and "genius," specifically, are conceived as an ability shared by all men, but raised to a higher power in certain gifted individuals.

An important distinction is to be kept in mind, however: Plotinus describes a vision which is directed inward, while even to Schelling, certainly to Hegel, and almost exclusively to Belinskij, this vision is directed at the external world of human affairs. To Plotinus, this power is the greater, the less material and the more ideal its manifestation. The artist's "inner vision" is therefore inherently superior to its eventual expression in the work of art.[27] Plotinus's example is the beautiful image of a god or hero liberated by a sculptor from the prison of a crude marble block. Plotinus emphasizes, however, that this liberation is never complete; potentially, in the artist's inner vision, the beauty of his creation is far greater.[28] The only law of artistic creation is then absolute and unconditional faithfulness to one's subjective inner vision.

This leads to still another distinction between Plotinus and most romantic aestheticians. To Plotinus, the ideal inner vision is an absolute and has no time dimension—it appears at once and is infinitely superior to its most successful expression; to most romantic aestheticians, the artist's inner vision emerges and grows in the process of creation.

Plotinus explicitly rejects the aesthetic theory of μίμησις: great art creates not copies of nature as perceived by the senses but expressions of ideal visions.[29]

---

26. "But one ought to turn toward oneself and perceive the vision as part of oneself, like a man possessed by Phoebus or one of the Muses, who sees the divine image within himself—if he has the power to see God within himself (εἰ δύναμιν ἔχοι αὐτῷ θεὸν βλέπειν)" (Plotinus *Enneads* 5. 8. 10).

27. Plotinus uses the analogy between inner vision and work of art (the latter being necessarily inferior) to make it plausible that the Maker of our world, beautiful as it is in its very imperfection, must indeed possess absolute Beauty. Here Plotinus follows Plato *Timaeus* 37C.

28. "Certainly this beauty was far greater yet in the artist's art" (ἦν ἄρα ἐν τῇ τέχνῃ τὸ κάλλος τοῦτο ἄμεινον πολλῷ)" (*Enneads* 5. 8. 1). What Plotinus is saying here is that the artist's "art" (τέχνη), as inner potential, striving, and vision, is far superior to even its most successful execution. This notion is corroborated by ample empirical evidence from the biographies of great artists, Leonardo da Vinci, for example.

29. Plotinus's famous passage containing his rejection of μίμησις ends with these words: "Nor did Phidias create his Zeus on the basis of some sense perception, but rather, he created him as he might appear to us if Zeus himself would reveal himself before our eyes" (*Enneads* 5. 8. 1).

The notion that a work of art should express an idea is perhaps the central position of German idealist aesthetics, just as it is of Belinskij's thought. However, Plotinus's ideal vision of Beauty, as reflected in great art, is decidedly intellectual and abstract. It is a region of pure light, absolute rest, unchecked motion. Absolute σοφία, the forever unattainable goal of human wisdom and striving, is identical with absolute being (*Enneads* 5. 8. 4). Schelling's position is not very far removed from Plotinus's. In both Hegel and Belinskij, the "idea" is humanized, concretized, and historicized.

More important than these distinctions is the point on which Plotinus, Schelling, and Hegel, as well as Belinskij and his followers all agree, namely, that the work of art, being the realization of an ideal, is not inferior to nature but rivals it, and can and should surpass it (*Enneads* 5. 8. 1-3). Conversely, the works of nature, too, are in a sense works of art, though on a lower level (a conception emphasized by Schelling and the Schlegel brothers, but not by Hegel and Belinskij).[30]

Plotinus develops the analogy between the macrocosm of divine creation and the microcosm of the work of art (*Enneads* 5. 8. 7). It becomes an outright literary and poetic cliché in Renaissance aesthetics. The analogy between the macrocosm of God's creation and the poetic microcosm becomes of decisive importance when God is no longer considered transcendental to, but rather immanent in, the human spirit. This is the case with Hegel and, of course, with Belinskij. While an all-encompassing "absolute spirit" is recognized *in abstracto* by Hegel, the real concern in his thought is with the structure of and the relationships between its concrete manifestations in the achievements of the human spirit. As regards art, this means that the "idea" which the artist seeks to express and the inner vision which reveals it to him are not reflections of an eternally identical "divine Beauty" but rather concrete hypostases of "living human thoughts."

On the one hand, this secures and in fact greatly enhances art's role in human life. On the other hand, it jeopardizes the very "organic" conception which it thus seeks to protect and to emphasize. It deprives art—and religion, of course— of their privileged status of timelessness, absolute value, and transcendent irrationality. The psychological mechanism, as it were, of "immediate knowledge" —an irrational notion—is retained, but the object of this knowledge is brought down to Earth, is made more rational, tangible, and concrete.

The cognitive function of art, and specifically of poetry, was placed in a synchronic hierarchy by Leibniz: in a continuous scale of cognition which has the steps *obscure:clear* → *diffuse:distinct* → *adequate:inadequate,* what might be

---

30. This particular notion can be detected in Plato *Laws* 10. It is a widespread τόπος in medieval and Renaissance thought. Cf. Anthony J. Close, "Philosophical Theories of Art and Nature in Classical Antiquity," *Journal of the History of Ideas* 32 (1971): 165.

termed "aesthetic cognition" (the term itself was later coined by Baumgarten) is assigned the rung of "diffuse" cognition.[31] Vico gave "poetic wisdom" a place in a diachronic hierarchy as well, pointing out that at a primitive stage of human development it provided man with important insights, many of which were later confirmed by philosophy and science. Vico saw "poetic wisdom," that is, aesthetic cognition, as different from but not inherently inferior to intellectual cognition.

Opinions regarding the cognitive powers of art have greatly varied since Alexander Baumgarten (1724–1762) first argued that there should be a science of "cognition through the senses" (*scientia cognitionis sensitivae*) just as there was logic, the science of cognition through rational thought. Thus, Kant denied art a cognitive role, while Schelling took the opposite view. Belinskij followed Schelling, and Russian aesthetic thought to this day has generally supported the notion that the intuition of a great poet can reveal important social, moral, and historical truths, often before rational scientific thought has achieved the same insights. This position is among the most precarious in all of Belinskij's ideological heritage. Paradoxically, the tendency in Russia has been to demote or ignore a great creative artist who was unwelcome or unsuccessful as a prophet rather than to discard the notion that poetic truth, the mark of great art, must coincide with empirical sociological, psychological, and historical truth. Dostoevskij's fate in Soviet Russia is a case in point.

Once communion with the Absolute is no longer the sole or the main object of "immediate cognition," the human concerns of nationhood, society, morality, and individuality become its targets. Two basic attitudes may be observed. One is the modest, utilitarian one of the Horatian "aut prodesse volunt aut delectare poetae." Here, the poet receives his ideas (moral, political, patriotic, religious) from outside his proper domain, art. It is his job to give them the proper artistic form so that they will attract his pleasure-seeking audience. It is this attitude toward art, often associated with France and French classicism, that the romantics, German idealists, and Belinskij rejected with particular contempt. Belinskij could never forgive Molière his *instruire en divertissant* and stubbornly refused the great Frenchman the title of a poetic genius. The point is, of course, that in classicist poetics the introduction of moral, political, or other ideas into art is "mechanical" rather than "organic."

The other attitude is the "organicist." It takes for granted that a genuine artist's inspiration will unfailingly guide him to the "correct" moral and other ideas of his day and age. Artistic tact is understood to make all censorship or other external control over art and poetry redundant. The artist's prophetic

31. Gottfried Wilhelm Leibniz, "Meditationes de cognitione, veritate et ideis," in *Opera philosophica quae extant latina gallica germanica omnia,* ed. J. E. Erdmann, 2 vols. (1840; reprint ed., Aalen, 1959), 1:79–82.

gifts are believed sufficient to point him in the direction of true human progress. This way of thinking, a corollary of the Neoplatonic identity of the Good, the True, and the Beautiful, is characteristic of German objective idealism and focal to Russian aesthetic thought as founded by Belinskij. Some of Belinskij's successors, notably Grigor'ev and Dostoevskij, were seriously bothered by the possibility of a "Beauty of Sodom" that might coexist with the "Beauty of the Madonna," but ultimately rejected this notion as a ruse of the Devil.

Immoralists such as Konstantin Leont'ev (1831–1891) have been very rare in Russia. Few Russian writers and critics have gone as far as Tolstoj, who in his old age rejected much of the world art and literature, including Shakespeare and his own major works, as "nonart" or "bad art" on the grounds that it was emotionally, socially, and morally irrelevant, or harmful. But a certain moral seriousness and dedication to the moral commitment of the artist has been characteristic of most Russian writers and poets, quite regardless of their political affiliations or ideological persuasions. Belinskij certainly did his share to make it that way.

The belief that a good artist, at least insofar as his work is concerned, must first be a good man is fairly universal. Nor is it limited to organicist aesthetic thought. The analogous notion of the social and historical "organicism" or artistic creation, much less plausible to common sense, is characteristic mostly of the German aesthetic tradition started by Herder. Outside Germany it is usually attributable to German influence, as in Mme de Staël or Hippolyte Taine in France, and in Belinskij and his Russian contemporaries.

It was mostly in France, however, that the notion asserting literature to be both a mirror and builder of society first led to practical action. A poet, by expressing the urgent concerns of his society, by pointing out its ills, and by preaching humane and progressive ideas, would act as society's heart and conscience, much as its philosophers would act as society's brains. This simple, rational, and seemingly irrefutable notion had taken root in Russia even before Belinskij. The Decembrist Ryleev had already exclaimed: "I am not a poet, I am a citizen!" Belinskij's mentor N. I. Nadeždin had defined literature as "the pulse of a nation's inner life."[32]

However, the whole conception of the social role of art remained bland and virtually indistinguishable from the moralism of the eighteenth century so long as it was not put to the test of a conflict of interest between "pure art" and the "social mission of art." (Obviously, in a mechanistic scheme such as that of pseudoclassicist moralism there could be no such conflict.) This conflict originated with Belinskij and is amply reflected in his writings. It has raged in Russian literary criticism ever since.

Belinskij himself clung to the belief that so long as a poet was inspired by

32. *Telescope* 19 (1834): 10.

rational, humanitarian, and progressive ideas, his creative powers—assuming an innate possession of them—would be safe to flourish and bear rich fruit. But if for any reason the poet's ideas became corrupted and perverted, he would be doomed even as an artist. The issue was for Belinskij by no means an academic one. On the contrary, fighting it out with himself, he shed his own life-blood, for the example in point was his beloved and revered Gogol'. On the other hand, an artist of only moderate native talent could accomplish a great deal if in possession of the right ideas.

By and large, Russian aesthetic thought has gravitated toward Belinskij's position, even though it proved to be empirically an untenable one. In the Soviet Union a great deal of energy has been spent on demonstrating that certain great poets and writers were in effect more "progressive" ideologically than would appear on the surface, and a great deal of time devoted to minor figures whose social and ideological position was "right," but whose artistic merits it took some effort to prove.

While the moral function of art, from which its social function is naturally deduced, is a part of the Platonic heritage, the link between art and nationhood is a modern phenomenon. The conception of a nation as the bearer of a specific national ideal or national spirit (*Volksgeist*), closely linked to the conception of the "inner form" of a language (Wilhelm von Humboldt's *innere Sprachform*), is a relatively recent one. The relationship between "human spirit" and "national spirit" is regarded by German romantic and objective idealist thought, and by Belinskij and his followers, as analogous to that between the "ideal" and the "real" or the "infinite" and the "finite." The universal spirit of humanity manifests itself in particular national spirits, each of which realizes one aspect of the human spirit. A national spirit is a finite absolute, much as a great work of art. National literatures relate to world literature (Goethe's *Weltliteratur*) as national spirit relates to human spirit.

Among the younger generation of German romantics, in Hegel and likewise in Belinskij, a conviction takes hold that all great art and poetry are necessarily national and that a poet of genius is a quintessential manifestation of the spirit of his nation. Cosmopolitanism is seen as a mark of sterility and mediocrity.

Belinskij was not the originator of nationalism in Russian literary criticism. A demand for a Russian national poetry had been made by A. S. Šiškov and his followers in the 1800s. This demand had been reiterated by early romantics such as Orest Somov, who urged that "a national poetry, not imitative, but independent of alien traditions" be created in Russia.[33] *Narodnost'* ("nationalism, national spirit, the quality of being national," a term first applied to

___

33. Orest Somov, "O romantičeskoj poèzii," *Trudy Vol'nogo obščestva ljubitelej russkoj slovesnosti,* 24 (1823): 147.

literature by Prince P. A. Vjazemskij in 1817) was so much of a popular slogan by the time Belinskij appeared on the literary scene that the critic frequently felt obliged to combat the indiscriminate application of this term to almost anything that seemed positive and desirable. Yet it is still focal to Belinskij's whole thinking. Even when he had become decidedly a "progressive" and a rebel against the existing order, Belinskij remained a strong Russian patriot, a believer in the national mystique in general and the Russian mystique in particular, as well as a vigorous supporter of a *national* literature.

It is no surprise that he was seconded in this attitude by Grigor'ev, Dostoevskij, and others among his epigoni of the Right, with whom the national spirit, while retaining its identity as a manifestation of the spirit of humanity, tended to rejoin the absolute spirit (= God), as Russian nationalism was fused with the Russian Orthodox religion. Yet the Left, for the most part, also retained this nationalism, down to Stalin and his notorious slogan "Socialist in content, national in form." The idealist and irrational nature of this conception appears more starkly in the writings of the Right, say, in Dostoevskij's famous oration on Puškin, which celebrates the poet first and foremost as a manifestation of the Russian national spirit. It is more unobtrusive in the writings of the Left, where the ambiguity of the Russian adjective *narodnyj* ("national," that is, "of the common people") tends to obscure the issue through the presence of yet another mystique, that of the "common people." Belinskij was not directly responsible for the latter tendency, for he often warned against the dangers of any false involvement, in literature or otherwise, with the subculture of the common people.

History was to show that Russian literature could flourish only if it remained "European," that is, if it remained in incessant, live contact with European literature, sharing its concerns, its technical innovations, reacting to new trends. This was certainly Belinskij's practice.

It was not the Right but the Left that led Russian literature into the cul-de-sac of a narrow provincialism and eventual stagnation. A preoccupation with *Russian* problems, largely social, to the exclusion of everything else, as it was preached by Dobroljubov and his successors, led to a decline of Russian literature during the last third of the nineteenth century. This decline was stopped, temporarily, by the Western-oriented Symbolist movement. In many ways this movement continued the aesthetic and philosophic traditions of the Belinskian Right, specifically of Grigor'ev, but it also went back to the original sources of the organic tradition (Plato, Neoplatonism, and German idealism). While convinced of the historic mission of the Russian people, the Symbolists, much as did Grigor'ev and Dostoevskij, always saw it in a context of occidental civilization. In their creative practice the Symbolists renewed the ties between Russian literature and the literatures of the West, which had been strong in the golden age of Russian poetry and remained so in the novels of Turgenev and Dostoevskij.[34] It is fairly obvious that the decline of Russian literature during the Soviet period has been largely a function of Russia's isolation from the West. Russian literature has continued to be strong and creative even during the Soviet period in those of its authors who were able and willing to remain within the mainstream of world literature. The poetry of Mandel'štam, Pasternak, and Axmatova serves to prove this point.

There is yet another conception to be mentioned here. Like "social" and "national" organicism, it is an integral element of German objective idealist and Belinskian aesthetics, but is not connected with the Platonic tradition. This conception is "historical organicism," or the notion that art and poetry are integrally linked with the historical process and therefore partake of historical progress. In Hegel's aesthetics it led to a historization of the hierarchy of the art forms as well as to the genres of poetry. Belinskij followed Hegel in this matter, as he did in many others.

Art is, in this conception, a quintessential realization of the spirit of an age (*Zeitgeist*). This is how Schelling and Hegel had seen Dante, Shakespeare, and Goethe. This is how Belinskij saw and interpreted his contemporaries Puškin, Lermontov, and Gogol'. This is how Grigor'ev saw Ostrovskij and Turgenev. This is how Dostoevskij saw himself. This is how Lenin saw Tolstoj, whose works he called "a mirror of the Russian revolution." "The poet and his time" (*poèt i vremja*) is a favored theme of literary treatises and dissertations in Russia even today.

Belinskij apparently never became aware of the pitfalls of historical organicism, although in his practical criticism he can be seen struggling with the contradictions inherent in it. There was the empirical phenomenon of the obsolescence of the poetry of the past, which squared with the notion of general historical progress. A mere generation after Deržavin's death his poetry had become irrelevant, boring, barely intelligible. The same was true even of Puškin, who, had he lived, would have been in the flower of his life in the 1840s! But then, there was the equally undeniable and likewise empirical fact that Deržavin and Puškin were great poets, before whom Belinskij's most progressive contemporaries were pygmies. Belinskij tended to sweep the antinomy under the rug by using a "loophole" devised by A. W. Schlegel, who had suggested that the "content" of poetry was subject to the laws of history, while its artistic "form" was absolute, and therefore immortal. But this directly contradicted the organic principle of the unity of "content" and "form." It also contradicted the empirical fact, well known to Belinskij, that great art was eternally young in content as well as in form. Puškin (in one of his unpublished

---

34. Aleksandr Blok, in an essay "Sud'ba Apollona Grigor'eva" (1916), saw Grigor'ev as "the only bridge connecting us with Griboedov and Puškin" and as the last Russian man of letters in the nineteenth century who was capable of thinking in "European" terms.

notes) had once thus commented upon a critic's assertion that the seventh
chapter of *Evgenij Onegin* had had no success because "the times and Russia
had marched forward, while the poet was standing still": "The times can
march forward, science, philosophy, and civic affairs can be perfected and
changed—but poetry stands still. . . . A work of poetry can be weak, unsuccessful, false—but what is at fault is surely the poet's talent, but not the times
which have overtaken him."[35]

When Belinskij said that Puškin's poetry was in many ways "outdated" (he
said so often), he was caught in a simple *quid pro quo*. The interests and pre-
occupations of the Russian intelligentsia, and specifically those of Belinskij
himself, had changed in the 1840s. The new generation of Russian intellectuals, whose mentor was Belinskij, was interested in politics, not art. To a man
still interested in poetry—such as Dostoevskij in the 1840s—not only Puškin
but also Deržavin and Žukovskij were not "outdated" at all, but delightful and
fascinating as ever.

BELINSKIJ'S PRECURSORS

Belinskij was not the first to introduce the principal ideas of organic aesthetics into Russian literary criticism.[36] Russian romantics such as Prince P. A.
Vjazemskij, Orest Somov, Wilhelm Küchelbecker, A. A. Bestužev-Marlinskij,
and Prince V. F. Odoevskij, whenever they theorized on art, poetry, and literature, had employed the organicist clichés which they knew from the writings of
Goethe, Tieck and Wackenroder,[37] the Schlegel brothers, Schelling, Mme de
Staël, Victor Hugo, and others. Schelling in particular had had many knowledgeable followers in Russia ever since the 1820s.[38] There were, first of all, the Moscow "wisdom-lovers" (*ljubomudry*) of the middle and late 1820s: D. V. Veneve-
tinov (1805-1827), V. F. Odoevskij (1804-1869), A. S. Xomjakov (1804-1860),
I. V. Kireevskij (1806-1856), S. P. Ševyrev (1806-1864), and others, some of
whom also represent the "older generation" of the Slavophile movement. V. F.
Odoevskij's *Russian Nights* (1844; but many items in this work were written in
the 1820s and 1830s) is an apology and a treasury of Schellingian thought. A
decade later, the members of N. V. Stankevič's (1813-1840) Moscow circle,
among whom we find Bakunin, Herzen, Belinskij, and some of the "younger

35. A. S. Puškin, *Polnoe sobranie sočinenij*, 2d ed., 10 vols. (Moscow, 1958), 5:546.
36. For a survey of aesthetic theories in Russia in the 1820s and 1830s, see Ju. Mann,
Russkaja filosofskaja èstetika (1820-1830-e gody) (Moscow, 1969).
37. *Ob iskusstve i xudožnikax: Razmyšlenija otšel'nika, ljubitelja izjaščego*, trans.
S. P. Ševyrev, V. P. Titov, and N. A. Mel'gunov (Moscow, 1826) is a Russian version
of *Herzensergiessungen eines kunstliebenden Klosterbruders* (1797) by Ludwig Tieck
and Wilhelm Heinrich Wackenroder.
38. See W. Setschkareff, *Schellings Einfluss in der russichen Literatur der 20er und
30er Jahre des XIX Jahrhunderts* (Leipzig, 1939).

generation" of Slavophiles, were all at one time devotees of Schelling.[39] Simultaneously, scholars such as Belinskij's teacher and employer N. I. Nadeždin (1804–1856) or the Slavophile M. P. Pogodin (1800–1875) studied and taught Schellingian idealism.

The aesthetic pronouncements of the Decembrist poets and writers and their sympathizers bear the familiar traits of romantic aesthetic theory: a belief in the cognitive and prophetic powers of poetry;[40] a conception of poetry as a microcosm symbolic of the macrocosm of the world; the notion that poetry rivals rather than imitates nature;[41] a polarized model of the work of art, which is seen as a fusion of the "ideal" and the "real," the "infinite" and the "finite," etc.;[42] an emphasis on the poet's "inner vision" in the creative process;[43] an

39. See Edward J. Brown, *Stankevich and His Moscow Circle 1830–1840* (Stanford, Calif., 1966).

40. In his programmatic article "Vzgljad na russkuju slovesnost' v tečenie 1824 i načale 1825 godov," A. A. Bestužev-Marlinskij exclaims: "Certainly Fame will not always stay abreast of a genius; often his contemporaries will reject him, failing to understand him. Yet the star of his future fame will warm his zeal and illuminate for him the darkness of the past, which he questions in order to read the present and to teach posterity. . . . And so they [poets of genius] were never led by society, but rather it was they who bore society along with them" (quoted from *Poljarnaja zvezda*, ed. V. A. Arxipov, V. G. Bazanov, and Ja. L. Levkovič [Moscow and Leningrad, 1960], p. 492). Cf. Ignazio Ambrogio, *Belinskij e la teoria del realismo* (Rome, 1963), p. 20.

41. For instance, Bestužev-Marlinskij, in an essay "On Romanticism" (1826), rejects any kind of "aesthetic of reflection" (*otražatel'nost'*): "Poetry, while encompassing all of nature, does not imitate it, but merely uses its means to express the ideals of its own, original creative spirit" (quoted by E. M. Pul'xritudova, "Literaturnaja teorija dekabristskogo romantizma v 30-e gody XIX veka," in *Problemy romantizma: Sbornik statej*, ed. U. R. Foxt [Moscow, 1967], p. 252).

42. Bestužev-Marlinskij defines romanticism as "the striving of the infinite spirit of humanity to express itself in finite forms," which corresponds to Schelling's definition of Beauty: "Beauty is the Infinite, expressed in finite form" (*das Unendliche, endlich dargestellt ist Schönheit*). A. Galič, in his essay "Opyty nauki izjaščnogo," *Moskovskij vestnik* 1825, sec. 3 (also published as a separate booklet in St. Petersburg, 1825), said that a beautiful work of art is created when "the free genius of man, as a morally perfect power, expresses a divine idea which is *per se* important and eternal, and if he does so through an independent, sensually perfect, organic symbol" (*v samostojatel'nom, čuvstvenno-soveršennom, organičeskom obraze*, pp. 75–76; quoted by Vanslov, *Èstetika romantizma*, p. 354).

43. Pul'xritudova quotes the following passage from Bestužev-Marlinskij's *Zurnal Vadimova:* "It is as though I have detached myself from my own soul and, like Dante's shadow, passed through the twilight of the labyrinth of my heart and of my brain. . . . But my inventions and my thoughts, my dreams and my memories, my fears and my hopes—all that of which past, present, and future are textured, all that of which the moral life of a human being is composed, all this appears to me in symbols (*v obrazax*) in which it was either conceived or conjured up by my mind, in marvellous, capricious, sometimes in absurd and monstrous symbols" (Pul'xritudova, "Literaturnaja teorija dekabristskogo romantizma," p. 273).

The romantic "doubling" of the poet's personality is really implied in the Plotinian "inner vision" (cf. note 26 above).

organic and historicist conception of the relationship between art and social life.[44] Also, the Belinskian tendency to draw literature into the orbit of political life and civic action was fully anticipated by the Decembrists.

For example, in a programmatic essay "On the Direction of Our Poetry, Lyric Poetry in Particular, during the Past Decade,"[45] the Decembrist Wilhelm Küchelbecker develops a conception of poetry which can be termed organic to almost the same extent as Belinskij's aesthetics. Küchelbecker defines poetry as a fusion of the "ideal" and the "real" (he is critical of Schiller for being merely "ideal") and rejects the concept of "pure art." He sees the poet as "only a temporal vessel of that divine power which forever renews and regenerates mankind."[46]

Belinskij himself pointed out the active role which N. A. Polevoj (1796–1846) had played in promoting the social role of literature and the idea that history was an organic, monistic process with poetry and the arts an integral part of it.[47] In particular, Polevoj presented the aesthetic ideas of French romanticism, especially those of Victor Hugo, to the Russian public.

It must be stressed, however, that it was Belinskij who became the catalyst of these ideas for the generations of Russian writers and critics after him. It was in the form in which he formulated and applied these ideas that organic aesthetics went on to dominate the Russian literary scene.[48] An important fact to be kept in mind is that the period of Belinskij's activity coincided with the beginning and the peak of Hegel's influence in Russia. Belinskij's predecessors were familiar with French and German romantic thought, and with Schelling, but not with Hegel.

Puškin

Belinskij's aesthetic thought developed independently of the aesthetic views of Puškin and Gogol', the authors to whom Belinskij gave more attention, thought, and love than perhaps to all the rest of Russian and world literature.

44. Pul'xritudova (pp. 287–88) observes the conscious and optimistic historicism of Ryleev, Bestužev-Marlinskij, and Küchelbecker. Characteristically, Bestužev starts his "Vzgljad na russkuju slovesnost' v tečenie 1824 i načale 1825 godov" with this statement: "The literatures of all nations, in describing their circular motion, have always followed the universal laws of Nature" (*Poljarnaja zvezda,* p. 488).

45. *Mnemosyne* 2 (1824): 29–44.

46. Quoted from N. I. Mordovčenko, *Russkaja kritika pervoj četverti XIX veka* (Moscow and Leningrad, 1959), p. 410.

47. See Belinskij's brochure "Nikolaj Alekseevič Polevoj" (1846), 9:671–96.

48. D. S. Mirsky, who had a very negative opinion of Belinskij's role in Russian literature, put it this way: "It was Belinsky, more than anyone else, who poisoned Russian literature by the itch for expressing ideas, which has survived woefully long. It was he also who was instrumental in spreading all the commonplaces of romantic criticism—inspiration,

The following brief summary of the aesthetic views of these two men provides a context for the subsequent presentation of Belinskij's aesthetics. Interestingly, Puškin and Gogol' were antipodal not only as artists but also in their aesthetic views.

Puškin liked to stress his sympathy for and his substantial solidarity with classicism and to dissociate himself from the nebulous teutonic philosophizing of his young friends, the Moscow "wisdom-lovers," in whose journal, the *Moscow Herald,* he published most of the poems that form his famous cycle "on the poet." Puškin often made fun of romantic mysticism and lack of poetic discipline. He appreciated romanticism mainly as a movement that liberated the creative artist from the annoying constraints of the classicistic poetic canon.[49] According to S. M. Bondi, Puškin saw the fundamental difference between classicism and romanticism in romanticism's tendency toward an individualized and even personalized form of the work of art.[50]

Puškin's view of art is best described as Horatian, by which I mean an eclectic position featuring an exalted image of the poet as an inspired creator and a modest view of his work relative to other affairs of men. As far as the divine calling of the poet and the mystique of the creative process are concerned, Puškin agrees with the Neoplatonic conception of the romantics. His cycle "on the poet" and many statements in prose and poetry throughout his works bear witness to this. Puškin's preoccupation with the privilege and the glory of being a poet is as pronounced as Horace's but is accompanied by a simultaneous preoccupation with the burden and the curse of poethood which is quite "romantic."[51] Inspiration and inner vision are taken for granted as a fact of poetic creation, which is seen as an irrational process transcending the poet's everyday personality. The Italian improviser in "Egyptian Nights" is a rather sorry specimen of a traveling performer, seemingly not very different from any magician or ventriloquist. But on stage, when he "senses the god's approach" and launches into his inspired improvisation he is completely transformed—even physically—and the audience whose money he had so obsequiously pursued is suddenly quite unworthy of his noble and beautiful effusion.

When it came to establishing the relationship of poetry to life at large, Puškin was at a loss for a rational and consistent answer. "The Prophet," perhaps his

---

sincerity, genius, and talent, contempt for work and technique, and the strange aberration of identifying imaginative literature with what he called 'thinking in images'" (D. S. Mirsky, *A History of Russian Literature from the Beginnings to 1900* [New York, 1958], p. 174).

49. See the chapter "Puškin's romanticism" in B. Tomaševskij, *Puškin,* 2 vols. (Moscow and Leningrad, 1956), 1:603–15.

50. S. M. Bondi, "Istoriko-literaturnye opyty Puškina," *Literaturnoe nasladstvo* 16–18: 425.

51. Cf. Victor Erlich's essay on Puškin's conception of the poet in his *The Double Image: Concepts of the Poet in Slavic Literatures* (Baltimore, 1964).

most famous poem, would suggest, in the interpretation of those who would like to claim Puškin for their "cause," that the poet's prophetic and visionary gifts should be in the service of a great idea. But "The Prophet" is very clearly a paraphrase of Isaiah 6:1-10, and, in my opinion, should be seen as the treatment of a poetic theme, that of a visionary getting the call, rather than as an allegory on the poet's mission. In those instances where Puškin explicitly speaks of the poet's calling while referring to himself, he does not go beyond half-hearted assertions that "in a cruel age, he sang of freedom, and pleaded mercy for the fallen" (meaning his Decembrist friends who were languishing in their Siberian exile) or "exposed enthroned vice." Puškin's "Exegi monumentum" does not go very far beyond that of Deržavin,[52] who prided himself on having "told monarchs the truth, with a smile."

Mozart and Salieri, where the ethical and the aesthetic planes meet, is ambiguous; certainly, Salieri's ability to commit a heinous crime confirms what we, and Salieri himself, knew all along, namely, that Salieri is a nongenius. But then, too, Mozart, while innocent and incapable of great evil, lacks the serious moral virtues which one would expect in a high priest of divine Art—as Salieri observes with bitterness. Mozart seems shallow, casual, even frivolous.

In "A Feast during the Plague," the ethic ambivalence of aesthetic experience is made explicit in the song of the Master of Revels:

> All, all that threatens to destroy us
> Affords the hearts of mortals
> An inexplicably voluptuous pleasure—
> A pledge of immortality, perhaps!

There seems no way to escape the impression that Puškin saw no organic two-way relationship between poetry and history,[53] poetry and society, or poetry and *narodnost'*. His essay "On *narodnost'* in Literature" (1825) takes a moderate position. Puškin shows himself a believer in the "national spirit" and expects the poet to partake of it: "Climate, the form of government, religion give each nation a particular physiognomy which is reflected, more or less, in its poetry." But he does not think that *narodnost'* is an end in itself which the poet should actively pursue (for example, by purging his language of foreign expressions). Nor does Puškin totally reject the Karamzinian notion of a literature of "high society."

Belinskij soon observed that Puškin viewed the world almost exclusively with the eyes of an artist, in terms of poetic themes and aesthetic possibilities.[54]

---

52. The interpretation of Puškin's "Exegi monumentum" is still under debate, as scholars cannot agree on what is meant seriously in this poem and what is ironic. See M. P. Alekseev, *Stixotvorenie Puškina,* "Ja pamjatnik sebe vozdvig . . ." (Leningrad, 1967).

53. See Puškin's pronouncement on this subject quoted earlier in this chapter.

54. See Erlich, *Double Image,* pp. 22-23.

Puškin's poet does not expect to be a teacher or leader. He brusquely rejects the crowd's invitation to enlighten and to edify: "Go away! What does/The peaceable poet have in common with you?/Fear not to become hardened in your depravity:/The voice of the lyre will not regenerate you" ("The Poet and the Crowd"). The poem "Arion" is a parable of Puškin's own fate:

> There were many of us on board,
> Some spread the sails,
> Some pulled, together,
> The Mighty oars. The sea was calm.
> Bent over the rudder, our wary helmsman
> Was steering the heavy ship in silence.
> Meanwhile I, full of carefree faith,
> Sang to the crew ... Suddenly a howling whirlwind
> Broke loose, stirring up the bed of the sea ...
> The helmsman and his crew were lost!
> Only I, mysterious singer,
> I was carried ashore by the storm.
> I sing the hymns which I sang before
> And dry my wet clothes
> In the sun, under a rock.

The poet stands by himself. For a while he may believe that he is involved in the affairs of this world, but life itself teaches him that his art stands apart and is independent from other human concerns ("The Poet and the Crowd"):

> Not for the cares and troubles of life,
> Not for gain, not for battles:
> We were born for inspiration,
> For sweet sounds and for prayers.

Belinskij, to whom such utter rejection of "social organicism" was alien, said unfairly (though without rancor) that "Puškin thus forever locked himself in behind the proud majesty of the misunderstood and hurt artist."[55] The fact of the matter was that Puškin, in his *poetry* (he was also a journalist, a historian, and a man of letters), refused to be the organ of anyone but his Muse.

While proud and self-assured in some respects, Puškin's image of the poet and his work was modest in others. He recognized poetic imagination and its vehicle, inspiration, for a narrowly defined phenomenon and believed that it should not trespass beyond the limits of its domain. In a letter to Prince Vjazemskij, 1826, Puškin writes: "Your verses . . . are too clever. Poetry, may the Lord forgive me, must be a little stupid (*glupovata*)."[56] This is exactly what Goethe

---

55. The quotation, from Belinskij's Fifth essay on Puškin (1844), belongs to the critic's late, socially oriented period. See Belinskij, 7:347.

56. Puškin, *Polnoe sobranie sočinenij*, 10:207.

had demanded of poetry in a letter to Schiller, 6 March 1800: "a certain good-natured narrowness, enamored of reality (*eine gewisse gutmütige, ins Reale verliebte Beschränktheit*), behind which the Absolute is concealed."[57] Toward the other end of the scale of human faculties, poetic inspiration has nothing to do with powerful emotions. Inspiration (*vdoxnovenie*) should not be confused with enthusiasm (*vostorg*), Puškin writes in a note occasioned by Küchelbecker's essay in *Mnemosyne*. "Inspiration," says Puškin, "is a disposition of the soul to a ready reception of impressions, and therefore to a quick grasp of concepts."[58]

Gogol'

Puškin's pronouncements on aesthetic and literary theory do not form a consistent system—nor was it a concern of Puškin's to rationalize what he knew intuitively. The contrary is true of Gogol'. His aesthetic pronouncements are many; they are often interesting *per se* and revealing of the genesis of his fiction.

All his life Gogol' searched for an aesthetics which he could integrate into his general *Weltanschauung* and *Weltgefühl*. In many ways he anticipated both Belinskij and those who came after him: Grigor'ev, Dostoevskij, and even Solov'ev and the Symbolists. Zen'kovskij has aptly described the evolution of Gogol' 's aesthetic views as a movement from "aesthetic romanticism" to "religious romanticism," a development also often encountered in the West.

Gogol' 's earlier writings show him not only well versed in the clichés of romantic aesthetics but also eager to realize them in his critical essays as well as in his fiction. Some of his essays show extraordinary critical acumen and synthetic ability. His view of Puškin, in particular, is most perceptive and largely anticipates Belinskij's. The conception of Puškin as Russia's "national poet" was originated by Gogol' as early as 1835.

Gogol' 's *post factum* interpretations of his own works, specifically *The Inspector-General* and *Dead Souls*, while considered far-fetched and wayward by many critics, are extremely intriguing and reflect his profound thinking on the nature of the creative process. His essay "On the Ukrainian Folk-Song" (1834), a panegyric to *narodnost'* in general and to the genius of the Ukrainian people in particular, was epoch-making in its own field. Gogol' 's essays on other art forms, such as "Sculpture, Painting, and Music" (1834) and "The Architecture of our Age" (1833) repeat the familiar romantic clichés, both organic and historicist. But they also contain many interesting thoughts, some of which may well be original.

57. Quoted from Ernst von Bracken, ed., *Briefwechsel zwischen Schiller und Goethe,* 2 vols. (Berlin, 1938), 2:376–77.
58. Puškin, *Polnoe sobranie sočinenij,* 7:41.

Gogol' 's aesthetics was different from Puškin's in that Gogol' insisted on integrating his philosophy of art with his general philosophy of life, and specifically with his religious ethics. From the very outset, he had a romantic, exalted view of the importance of art. His search for an integrated world view in
which art might retain this exalted position led him to the Neoplatonic notion
that explains the sacredness of art (to Puškin, an empirical fact that required
no further explanation) in terms of its representing glimpses of the Divine.[59]
Eventually, this took Gogol' to a pointedly "Christian" (his contemporaries,
and Belinskij in particular, said "ascetic") conception of art, where the proof
of a work of art was no longer in art *per se*, but in its moral effects, where
"true works of art" were "invisible steps toward Christ." Tolstoj, too, arrived
at this position in *What Is Art?* Belinskij and his followers of the Left performed a similar reversal of priorities with the social role of art.

Gogol' was a more consistent and conscious "organicist" than Puškin. In an
early essay "On the Development of Journal Literature" (1836), he joins
forces with Belinskij in combating criticism à la Senkovskij, which refuses to
treat a work of art as a whole. Gogol' demands that a critic should at first ask
what the author's intent was, then, how he has realized his intent, or if not,
how he should have realized it. Very definitely, too, Gogol' sees a successful
work of art as a fusion of the "ideal" and the "real." In a famous passage in
the seventh chapter of *Dead Souls* Gogol' says, in defending his own "naturalistic" creations, that it takes "much spiritual depth to illuminate a picture taken
from the despised low-life and transform it into the quintessence of a pearl of
creative art." The metaphor *vozvesti v perl sozdanija* suggests a process of
idealization and intensification (*vozvesti* literally means "to raise to a higher
power") which does not, however, reduce the reality or the concreteness of its
subject. It corresponds exactly to A. W. Schlegel's Schellingian definition of
art as "nature, passed through the medium of a perfect spirit, illuminated and
intensified."[60]

59. The sacredness of art is a focal motif in "The Portrait" (1835) and in the late story
"Rome" (1842). In a letter to his friend S. P. Ševyrev, 28 February 1843, Gogol' explains
why the second part of *Dead Souls* will not appear soon: "I may die of starvation, yet I
shall never publish a thoughtless, hasty creation. Do not condemn me. There are things
which one cannot explain. There is a voice which commands us and before which our
wretched reason is powerless. There are many things which can be sensed only in the
depths of our souls, in moments of tears and prayers, but not in moments of practical, rational deliberation!" (N. V. Gogol', *Polnoe sobranie sočinenij*, 15 vols. [Moscow, 1940–
52], 12:145). And in his famous letter to Žukovskij, 29 December 1847, Gogol' writes:
"It is not for me to decide to what extent I am a poet. I only know that before I ever
got to understand the meaning or the purpose of Art, I already felt, with all my soul, that
Art must be sacred" (ibid., 14:33–34).

60. "Man könnte die Kunst daher auch definieren als die durch das Medium eines
vollendeten Geistes hindurchgegangene, für unsere Betrachtung verklärte und

In a letter to Žukovskij, 29 December 1847, which Gogol' originally planned to include in a projected second volume of *Selected Passages* (under the title "Art Is Reconciliation with Life"), he develops the idea that a true work of art has something soothing and conciliatory about it. "When a poetic creation lacks this property," says Gogol', "it is only a noble and ardent impulse, the fruit of a temporary condition of the author's soul—it will stand as a remarkable phenomenon, but will not earn the name of a creation of art."[61] This conception bears a strong resemblance to Belinskij's opinions during the critic's period of "reconciliation with reality." It also squares with Gogol''s own philosophy of humor, as developed earlier in his dramatic sketch "After the Theater" (1842), in his "Dénouement of *The Inspector-General*" (1846), and in his "Author's Confession" (1847, published posthumously, 1855). In the first of these pieces we find Gogol''s famous eulogy of Laughter, "the real hero of *The Inspector-General*":

> Not that laughter which is born of a passing irritation . . . not that light laughter either, which serves the idle diversion and amusement of people — no, that laughter which wholly emanates from man's brighter nature, which emanates from it because that eternally flowing spring of laughter is hidden at its bottom. . . . There are many things which can raise a man's indignation, once they have been presented in their whole nakedness; yet when illuminated by the power of laughter, they bring reconciliation to the soul, even as they strike it. . . . No, only a kind soul can break into a kind, bright laughter.[62]

This particular conception of humor was popular among the German romantics, specifically Jean Paul and E. T. A. Hoffmann, whom Gogol' knew well. A famous passage on humor found in Hoffmann's *Prinzessin Brambilla* says much the same thing as Gogol' in the passage just quoted. This conception was later canonized by post-Hegelian aestheticians such as Vischer.[63] Belinskij was never able to accept it. To him, the highest form of comic art was that which sustained the ideal by presenting it in its negation (a routine Hegelian formula). Belinskij's debate with K. S. Aksakov regarding the interpretation of *Dead Souls* touches upon this point. Aksakov saw in the humor of *Dead Souls* precisely that epic acceptance of an imperfect reality of which Gogol' speaks in his eulogy of Laughter. Belinskij, on the other hand, saw *Dead Souls* as a bold revelation of the negative sides of Russian reality, without any "reconciliation."

---

zusammengedrängte Natur" (A. W. von Schlegel, "Über das Verhältnis der schönen Kunst zur Natur" [1802], *Sämtliche Werke*, 12 vols. [Leipzig, 1846–47], 9:308).

61. Gogol', *Polnoe sobranie sočinenij*, 14:33–34.

62. Ibid., 5:169–70.

63. See Friedrich Theodor Vischer, *Aesthetik oder Wissenschaft des Schönen,* 4 vols. (Reutlingen and Leipzig, Stuttgart, 1846–57), 1:452–54. Vischer, in a veritable apotheosis of Humor, defines it as "das absolut Komische."

On many other points Gogol''s aesthetics largely coincides with Belinskij's. Gogol' shared with Belinskij a firm belief in the "national spirit," with the inner form of language its direct expression (there is a famous passage to this effect in *Dead Souls*, at the conclusion of Chapter 5) and a conception of art as an organ of national life. Much as for Belinskij, this was for Gogol' a matter not only of theory but also of practical and personal concern. Much as in Belinskij's case, but with more immediately and more spectacularly disastrous results, such concern with the social mission of art led to unresolvable aporias.

Gogol''s aesthetic philosophy developed along a line which ran parallel to Belinskij's. In his earlier years Gogol' had been confident that autonomous and independent art would, in its free creations, fulfill its moral and didactic role without any help from the outside. Under the impact of the shock received from the violent public reaction to *The Inspector-General* Gogol' momentarily retreated to a Puškinian position of *odi profanum vulgus*.[64] But after Puškin's death his concern for the moral and prophetic role of art in general, and his own mission in particular, rose steadily. It reached a peak in *Selected Passages from a Correspondence with Friends* (1847), where Gogol' explicitly condemned the unlimited autonomy and self-sufficiency of art (*against* Puškin, whom he continued to admire): "New tasks stand before poetry . . . it must call us to a more exalted battle—not for temporal freedom, rights, or privileges, but for our souls."[65] Gogol''s creative genius, his soul and, toward the end, his very physical existence were poisoned by the antinomy involved in this position. Belinskij, not himself a creative genius, did not have to pay for his own very similar error all this dearly.

The antinomy was, in Gogol''s case, the following. The leitmotif of Gogol''s fiction had been the beauty and, more often, the banality (*pošlost'*) of life. As Zen'kovskij has emphasized, *pošlost'* is an aesthetic concept no less than "beauty" is. In exposing the *pošlost'* of life, Gogol' gave expression to his longing for beauty. (The concept of the "negative ideal" was well known to him.) In his Schillerian, optimistic "aesthetic humanism," Gogol' had been convinced that such pursuit of beauty—and persecution of banality—were even morally rewarding. We read, in "After the Theater": "In the hands of a skillful physician both hot and cold water treat the same disease with equal success. In the hands of a

---

64. In a letter to M. P. Pogodin, 28 November 1836, Gogol' writes: "The die is cast. Having left my country, I have also abandoned all my contemporary strivings (*sovremennye želanija*). . . . It is not the poet's business to meddle in the marketplace of this world. Like a taciturn monk, he lives in the world not being himself a part of it, and his pure, innocent soul knows only how to talk with God alone" (*Polnoe sobranie sočinenij*, 11:77).

65. Ibid., 8:408. Cf. V. Zen'kovskij, *N. V. Gogol'* (Paris, 1961), p. 123. Zen'kovskij has brilliantly grasped the essence of the conflict between ethics and aesthetics in Gogol''s thought.

writer of talent everything may serve as an avenue to Beauty, if only he is guided by the exalted idea to serve Beauty."[66] By that token, exposing and ridiculing human banality was as meritorious an undertaking as castigating human vices. The prostitute in "Nevskij Prospect" is not only depraved but also terribly banal, and so are Gogol' 's negative characters in general.[67] Gogol' had believed that aesthetic education and the example of living beauty in art could have immediate and tangible moral results. After having read Žukovskij's splendid translation of the *Odyssey,* he expressed a hope that it would have an immediate effect on the spirit of Russian society. Incredible as it may sound, he sincerely expected a similar effect from his own works.

When disappointed in these hopes, Gogol', rather than accepting the fact of the incompatibility of aesthetic, moral, and practical values, decided that something was wrong with his works. His attempts to create something that would satisfy both his intuitive aesthetic sense and his moral and religious convictions failed utterly. Belinskij managed to avoid a showdown with this antinomy, although it was staring him in the face during the last years of his life. It has remained a chronic malady of Russian literary criticism to this day.

Gogol' was much bolder in facing up to the possibility, largely swept under the rug by Belinskij but later focal to Dostoevskij's aesthetic thought, that Art and perhaps Beauty, too, could be in the service of Good as well as Evil. This idea is pivotal to the Künstlernovelle "The Portrait."

There is one important point on which Gogol' and Belinskij are in total agreement. They are both in favor of a democratization of art in every possible way: overcoming the last vestiges of the theory of genres as well as all other restrictive literary conventions; choosing subjects from contemporary everyday reality and presenting them in simple, unadorned fashion; using simple language, ignoring the rules of pedantic grammarians and "well-bred ladies." Gogol' 's famous, though rather naïve, apology of the realistic writer in the seventh chapter of *Dead Souls* fully agrees with Belinskij's thinking on this subject. Gogol' sees the distinction between the romantic writer who presents "the few exceptional" ideal characters that can be found in life, and himself, the writer who presents "boring, repulsive, and sadly real characters" (the vast majority of all people) in terms of a positive accomplishment: since it is a far more thankful task to create beautiful, idealized figures, the artist who produces a "pearl of creation" from ordinary, "real-life" material deserves special recognition.

The two notions expressed here, and shared by Gogol' and Belinskij, are, first, that dealing with unadorned everyday reality is *per se* a virtue, and second,

---

66. Gogol', *Polnoe sobranie sočinenij,* 5:143–44.

67. Cf. V. V. Gippius, "Tvorčeskij put' Gogolja," in *Ot Puškina do Bloka* (Moscow and Leningrad, 1966), p. 80.

that one will learn more about the truth of life from a treatment of ordinary types than from a treatment of exceptional characters. Both Gogol' and Belinskij had moments when they knew better, to wit, that there could be more "living truth" in a fairy tale by Hoffmann than in a physiological sketch by Dal', and that Hamlet, a highly exceptional character, was at least as revealing of human nature as Gogol' 's Pirogov, the epitome of triviality.

2

Belinskij's Idiosyncrasies as a Critic

HIS THEORY OF LITERARY CRITICISM

It is characteristic of Belinskij and the critical tradition which he established not to be satisfied with any kind of impressionist or formalist interpretation of literature, but to judge it on the basis of a philosophy which would create a distinct pattern of relationships between the work of art, its constituent parts, its creator, and the world at large. Belinskij knew that a critic must have talent, just as a poet must.[1] But he believed that the critic should approach a work of art armed with native aesthetic sense, as well as good taste and erudition, and with certain general ideas. "The subject of criticism is the application of theory to practice," he writes in a programmatic essay of 1836,[2] and four years later he says:

> The task of true criticism is to seek out, in the works of a poet, the general and not the particular, the human and not the personal, the eternal and not the temporal, the necessary and not the fortuitous, and to define, on the basis of the universal (of the idea, that is), the value, the worth, the place, and the importance of a poet. ("Sketches on Russian Literature: The Works of Nikolaj Polevoj" ["Očerki russkoj literatury: Sočinenija Nikolaja Polevogo"], 1840, 3:509)[3]

A similar conception is developed, in considerable detail, in Belinskij's longest work devoted specifically to criticism, a review of A. V. Nikitenko's "Discourse on Criticism" (1842, 6:267–334). To be a critic, Belinskij says here, means "to seek and to discover in a particular phenomenon the universal laws of reason, according to and through which a living, organic relationship exists between the particular phenomenon and its ideal" (6:270).

At the beginning of his Fifth essay on Puškin (1844) Belinskij gives yet

1. See, e.g., Belinskij, "Mencel', kritik Gete" (1840), 3:419. "To be a critic one needs talent, taste, knowledge, erudition, mastery of language," Belinskij writes in "Russkaja literatura v 1843 godu," 8:73.
2. "O kritike i literaturnyx mnenijax *Moskovskogo nabljudatelja*" (1836), 2:124.
3. Cf. 5:344; 7:143, 302–3.

another outline of his theory of literary criticism (7:302–12). Again he stresses that only a happy combination of intuitive grasp and theoretical analysis can produce good criticism. He suggests that a critic's first step should be a careful study of the poetic work in his charge, followed by an intuitive grasp of the poet's creative personality. Once he has come to understand the poet, the critic seeks to establish just how well the poet's idea has been expressed in his creation. The degree to which a poet's spirit is realized in his work is the measure of its artistic value. Finally, the critic determines the universal validity, import, and value of the poetic idea under his scrutiny. Thus, as a theorist, Belinskij is in 1844 as strong an exponent of "philosophic" and "organic" criticism (both terms are used by Belinskij) as he had been during his early, Schellingian period (1834–37).

Belinskij has often been charged with inconsistency, and with good reason. He knew very well himself that he had often changed his opinion—less so regarding the aesthetic value of any particular work than regarding the merit of certain schools of philosophic and critical thought. Nor did he hesitate to admit this in print.[4]

For Belinskij, a work of art consists of its *form*, the excellence of which depends on the talent of its creator and is recognized by the critic's intuition, and its *content*, the value of which lies in its objective historical importance and reveals itself to the philosopher-historian's understanding. As regards aesthetic judgment, Belinskij trusted his intuition:

> When it comes to judging art, and particularly its immediate understanding, i.e., that which is called aesthetic sense or receptiveness to beauty, I am bold and self-assured, and in this area my boldness and self-assurance extend so far that even the authority of a Hegel could not restrain them. (letter to M. A. Bakunin, 12–24 October 1838, 11:313)[5]

HIS IDEOLOGICAL DEVELOPMENT

Belinskij rarely had to change his judgment regarding the aesthetic merits of any work of contemporary Russian literature. A number of times, however, he substantially changed his philosophical premises, as well as his opinions on political theory and the course of history. Along with these ideological meanderings, Belinskij's estimation of the historical role and absolute value of certain literary figures (Goethe and Schiller, for example), changed drastically more than once.[6] Often Belinskij had to regret opinions expressed in print a short

---

4. See, e.g., 10:263.
5. Cf. letter to V. P. Botkin, 27–28 June 1841, 12:50.
6. Belinskij was much more consistent as regards Russian authors. The only major work about which he changed his opinion significantly was Griboedov's comedy *Woe from Wit.*

time earlier. For example, in a letter to V. P. Botkin, 11–12 December 1840 (11:574–78), he remorsefully berates himself for having only recently called that great poet and honest patriot Mickiewicz "a loudmouth and a poet of rhymed pamphlets," for having wrongly denounced the great French nation, and for having failed to recognize Russian reality for what it was—all because of having embraced the now-abandoned notion that "all that is rational is real, and all that is real is rational."[7]

In the same letter, Belinskij calls Heinrich Heine "such a marvellous, such a wonderful personality . . . whom we once viewed with contempt, carried away by our childish, one-sided convictions" ((11:577). A few months later (letter to Botkin, 1 March 1841, 12:24) we hear that Wolfgang Menzel (a "progressive" German critic whom Belinskij had demolished in an essay of 1840) is, in a certain sense, wiser than Hegel, "and as for Heine, this goes without saying" (that he is wiser than Hegel). Two years earlier, Belinskij had had this to say about Heine:

> Infected by the noxious spirit of the most recent literary schools of France, he embraced its frivolity, superficiality of judgment, and shamelessness which, for the sake of a casual witticism, is willing to distort a sacred truth. Living himself in Paris, he gives vent to his bile about why it should be cold in winter and hot in summer, or why China should be in Asia rather than in Europe, and other such defects of this imperfect world, which positively refuses to turn itself upside down, convinced by Mr. Heine's wisdom. (review of vol. 10 of *The Contemporary* [*Sovremennik*], 1838, 2:504)

The question is not whether Belinskij possessed a consistent philosophy which may have served as a basis for his critical pronouncements; it is safe to say that he did not. Some would assert that the theoretical views held by Belinskij during a certain period of his life represent the "true" Belinskij, while opinions held by the critic at other times are to be either disregarded or challenged as aberrations. Thus, the critic's right-wing followers, especially Apollon Grigor'ev, pro-

---

Belinskij values it very highly in "Literary Reveries" (1834), is rather critical of it in "Woe from Wit" (1840), where it suffers from comparison with Gogol' 's *Inspector-General,* and is much more positive again in later references. Cf. A. N. Pypin, *Belinskij, ego žizn' i perepiska,* 2d ed. (St. Petersburg, 1908), pp. 92–93, who points out the peripeties in Belinskij's attitude toward Schiller.

7. The passage on Mickiewicz is found in Belinskij's essay "Mencel', kritik Gete," 3:403. According to Lebedev-Poljanskij, it was really Bakunin who was responsible for Belinskij's faulty interpretation of Hegel's dictum. Bakunin, in an introduction to his translation of Hegel's "Gymnasial-Reden" in *Moskovskij nabljudatel'* (March 1838, fasc. 1 and 2), had interpreted it to mean that "accepting reality (*primirenie s dejstvitel'nost'ju*) in every respect and in every sphere of life is the great task of our age." See P. I. Lebedev-Poljanskij, *V. G. Belinskij* (Moscow and Leningrad, 1945), pp. 68, 168. Cf. also Belinskij's letter to N. V. Stankevič, 29 September 1839, 11:387–88.

claimed themselves disciples of "Belinskij up to 1844," while the radical Left would conveniently ignore the Belinskij of the 1830s and draw their image of him from the writings of his last few years. Such selective use of Belinskij's heritage is dishonest. It is also self-defeating, for even a cursory study of Belinskij's writings will reveal that he often expresses the "wrong" view in the same breath with the "correct" view. Thus, in his last major article, "A Survey of Russian Literature in 1847" ["Vzgljad na russkuju literaturu 1847 goda"] (1847–48),[8] we see him preaching the autonomy of Art (10:302–3), yet also defending the blatantly utilitarian "physiological sketches" of the Natural School.

The question is: Was Belinskij at all times merely the advocate and popularizer of whatever philosophic or aesthetic doctrine had most recently caught his fancy, or was the intricate development of his theoretical views an organic process with a constant basis in the critic's own intellect? In other words, is Billig right in saying that "Belinskij was ruled by his ideas, he never ruled over them,"[9] or was Belinskij a truly creative thinker, seeking to work out his own philosophy, albeit with external stimulation? Belinskij's opponents, even in the critic's lifetime, suggested the former. The following opinion, quoted in full by Belinskij, is expressed by the Slavophile Ju. F. Samarin in 1847:

> Mr. Belinskij is the exact opposite of Mr. Nikitenko. Almost never is he just himself, and he rarely writes using his own free initiative. Although by no means devoid of aesthetic sense (evidence his articles, especially the earlier ones), he seemingly makes light of it, and, while possessing his own capital, constantly chooses to live on credit. Ever since he has been following a critic's calling, he has invariably been under the influence of some alien thought. His unfortunate receptiveness, his ability to grasp ideas easily and superficially, as well as to reject them quickly and resolutely even when they were his only yesterday, his tendency to be carried away by a novelty and to carry it to extremes have kept him in a condition of continuous excitement, a condition which has finally become permanent with him, and have checked the development of his faculties. ("A Rejoinder to *The Muscovite*" ["Otvet *Moskvitjaninu*"], 1847, 10:261)

Belinskij resolutely rejects Samarin's opinion as unfounded, and there is reason to believe that he was sincerely convinced that Samarin was wrong.

Belinskij's conception of the creative mind was a dynamic one. In his early, very Hegelian refutation of Wolfgang Menzel's criticism of Goethe (1840, 3:385–419), Belinskij points out that true humanity is always in a state of flux, that true life is constant movement, steady development, and that the

8. During the years 1841–47, Belinskij published annual surveys of Russian literature under slightly varying titles. References to these surveys are hereafter cited as "1841" . . . "1847."

9. Joseph Billig, *Der Zusammenbruch des deutschen Idealismus bei den russischen Romantikern (Bjelinski, Bakunin)* (Berlin, 1930), p. 3.

advance toward Truth is strewn with errors, contradictions, and negations. And, the greater and more profound a human mind, the more prone it is to error (3:418-19). Belinskij retained this view until the end of his life. A passage from his Second essay on Puškin (1843) is typical:

> We do not envy those *ready-made natures* that recognize everything at once and, having once recognized it, continue to hold the same opinion for the rest of their lives, boasting about the constancy of their views and their unfailing judgment. That is right, we do not envy them, for we are deeply convinced that only he who does not seek the truth will never err, and that only he who has no need and no thirst for conviction never changes his convictions. (7:106)

The opinion expressed here can be projected upon Belinskij's image of himself. The question is then whether the corpus of Belinskij's aesthetic thought, full of changes, reversals, and contradictions, indeed mirrors the organic growth of an aesthetic philosophy which should rightfully bear his name.

One is not surprised to have Černyševskij say that Belinskij's articles, if read in chronological order, show no breaks or turning points in the critic's ideological development and that, rather, each article develops quite logically from the one preceding. Nor is one surprised to have Plexanov confirm this opinion.[10] But one is impressed to see no less an authority than Grigor'ev—and what is more, toward the end of that critic's career—also agree with this opinion: "His contradictions and changes of opinion could appear as contradictions and changes only to the really narrow-minded men of his epoch. To him, to his disciples, that is, to practically all of us, these were stages of a development, stages of an advance toward Truth."[11]

I believe that there is a great deal to be said in favor of Grigor'ev's view. Belinskij's aesthetic theory is anchored in certain constants which he never questioned. To use a mathematical simile, Belinskij's conception of the work of art and its relationship to objective reality is like a differential equation, where the variables may assume quite different values both absolutely and relatively, yet within definite limits.

Among Belinskij's constants we find an organic and dialectic, rather than mechanistic or formalist, conception of the genesis and structure of the work of art, as well as of its relation to life at large; the notion that a work of art is the realization of an idea, a dialectic fusion of the "real" and the "ideal"; and hence, the notion that a work of art has two aspects—an ideal content which

10. See Lebedev-Poljanskij, *Belinskij*, p. 186; and G. V. Plexanov, "Literaturnye vzgljady V. G. Belinskogo," *Sočinenija*, 24 vols. (Moscow, 1923), 10:278.

11. Apollon Grigor'ev, "Famous European Writers before the Tribunal of Our Criticism" ("Znamenitye evropejskie pisateli pered sudom našej kritiki"), *Time* (*Vremja*) 1861, no. 3; quoted by N. N. Straxov, *Bor'ba s zapadom v našej literature*, 3 vols. (Kiev, 1897-98), 3:288.

coincides with the historical life of the artist's nation and of mankind, and a concrete form which is a manifestation of the aesthetic sense and a product of the artist's genius. In the ideal aspect, Art is free, autonomous, and absolute; in the concrete form, it is determined by the laws of history. There is the belief that aesthetic intuition parallels and even anticipates the teleology of history, and, in connection with the last point, an extremely high opinion of the social role of the artist. Finally, Belinskij's love and respect for art must be considered an important factor in any evaluation of his theoretical views. Unlike some of his successors, he was biased in favor of great art, in fact, of anything that deserved the name of art.

Within this framework, spectacular shifts occur in Belinskij's views. During his Hegelian period (ca. 1838–40) Belinskij favors objective over subjective art. Thereafter, in his famous review of Gogol' 's *Dead Souls* (1842, 6:209–22), for example, he begins to make concessions to the subjective element, meaning an ideological tendency or social message, in art. In his last years, he much prefers the ideologically committed Herzen to the "objective artist" Gončarov. And yet, Belinskij never relinquishes the notion that art must possess both an *ideal* content and a *real* form: rhetoric, abstract philosophizing, preaching, allegory, on the one hand, and photographic naturalism, contentless entertainment, uncontrolled effusions of emotion, on the other, are nonart, as far as Belinskij is concerned, useful perhaps, and deserving of a place in life and in literature, but nonart.

The shift in Belinskij's theoretical views is illustrated by his attitude toward French and German thought. Until about 1840 Belinskij favors German idealism over French positivism:

> Experience [*opyt*] leads not to truth but to error, for facts are infinitely varied and contradictory to such an extent that a truth developed from one fact can be instantly refuted by another fact. Only in the human spirit can we find the inner continuity and unity underlying this variety and contradictoriness of facts. Consequently, a philosophy based on empirical experience is an absurdity. . . . And so, the devil take the French: their influence has brought us nothing but harm. We went out to imitate their literature— and killed our own. (letter to D. P. Ivanov, 7 August 1837, 11:152)[12]

A few years later we find Belinskij thoroughly disappointed in German idealism, mainly for the reason that its ideals have failed to find an adequate

12. Belinskij was not the first to develop this image of French and German national characters. H. J. Hunt, *Le Socialisme et le romantisme en France: Étude de la presse socialiste de 1830 à 1848* (Oxford, 1935), p. 187, quotes Victor de Laprade's comments on the French national character, made at about the same time, to the effect that the French genius is distinguished by "*le sens vulgarisateur et pratique,* while lacking *la faculté de la spéculation et de la contemplation du beau et du vrai.*"

expression in the sociohistorical reality of German life. He now admires the French for their ability to transform ideas into action, for their having developed such a dynamic, intense, intellectually active society, for their enthusiastic espousal of new ideas.[13] Toward the end of his life Belinskij once said that he loved only two nations: the Russians, of course, and the French.[14] He loves them for their good common sense and their practical approach to life, for their "positivism," in short!

Yet, Belinskij never abandoned the basic premises of German idealism, his serious concern with German philosophy, or, for that matter, his respect for the German nation.[15]

In his next to last survey of Russian literature (1846), Belinskij devotes a number of pages (10:23-29) to one of his many definitions of "reality," arriving at what is in essence a perfectly good Hegelian, idealist formulation. He accepts the notion that the *ideas* of Truth, Virtue, Love, and so forth, are eternal and absolute (10:23). Likewise, he concedes that "that what we call spirituality (*duxovnost'*), that is, man's feelings, his reason, and his will, in which his eternal, imperishable, and necessary essence is revealed" represent "the highest and the noblest reality of man" (10:26). Furthermore, Belinskij stresses the distinction between what is fortuitous (*slučajno*), relative, and therefore insignificant in man (his external appearance, his manners, his voice), and what is substantial, absolute, and therefore truly "real" (*ego dejstvitel'nost', ego real'nost'*)—his intellectual and moral qualities (10:27). Finally, Belinskij expressly states that the greatest individual genius stands immeasurably below the collective mind of humanity (ibid.).

At the same time, however, Belinskij seeks to demonstrate that ideal entities reveal themselves only in concrete, individual, national, and temporal forms. And he lets it be known that he is interested in the reality of phenomena more than in their ultimate ideal essence.

And yet, to give the screw still another turn, Belinskij, in the above discussion (and elsewhere), is engaged in a polemic with opponents (the Slavophiles, in this case) whose views were to the right of Hegel. On the rarer occasions when Belinskij clashes with the nascent positivism of his age, his emphasis may sometimes be placed in the opposite way.

Another point to be kept in mind when dealing with Belinskij's lack of consistency is that he, even by virtue of being a Hegelian, is a dialectic thinker. He does not fear contradiction and sees in the negation of a given thesis not so much its cancellation, the reduction of a truth to a nontruth, as an advance to a new truth. Moreover, the old truth just challenged and declared invalid will

13. Letter to V. P. Botkin, 10–11 December 1840, 11:576–77.
14. Letter to Botkin, 2–6 December 1847, 12:451.
15. Ibid.

some day return on a higher level of understanding, and its negation in turn negated. It is quite characteristic of Belinskij to exclaim: "The crowd won't understand that everything living differs from what is dead precisely in that it contains in its very essence the principle of contradiction" ("The Works of Deržavin" ["Sočinenija Deržavina"], 1843, 6:588). For Belinskij this is not a mere phrase, but a methodological principle which he actually applies in his criticism.

On a more mundane level, Belinskij was, at least most of the time, a practitioner of *la critique du jour,* a literary critic and a publicist at the same time. Certain inconsistencies in his writings and some outright logical and factual blunders, irrelevancies, and unsupported assertions must be seen in the light of these extrinsic circumstances. One cannot fairly hold Belinskij to the letter of his writings the way one can and should do in treating a scholar's literary criticism.

HIS SEMANTICS

Belinskij's critical vocabulary is not always consistent. He explicitly distinguishes three different meanings of the word *romantizm* ("romanticism"). In the narrowest sense, it is a literary movement of the late eighteenth and early nineteenth centuries, essentially a reaction against French classicism and its normative poetics (for example, 9:684). In a broader historical perspective, it is Christian, spiritual art, as opposed to the more sensuous art of pagan Greece, or Catholic, medieval, and mystical art as opposed to the realistic art of enlightened Protestantism and of Belinskij's own age (9:685–86). Finally, on a universal, anthropological scale, "romanticism" stands for that aspect of art which reflects "man's inner world, the world of the soul and of the heart, the world of feelings [*oščuščenija*] and beliefs, the world of strivings for the infinite, the world of mysterious visions and intuitions, the world of heavenly ideals" ("1841," 5:548).[16] In addition, Belinskij will often use the words "romantic" and "romanticism" pejoratively to suggest melodrama, affectation, sentimentality, and the like.

A marked evolution can be observed in Belinskij's attitude toward romanticism. The early Belinskij is himself a romantic. The later Belinskij sees his age as one of sober thought and practical activity in the face of challenging but not hopeless reality, and he tends to downgrade romanticism as outdated and actually harmful. He often makes fun of elderly or middle-aged romantics who refuse to leave the literary scene, but does not deny either the historical merits of romanticism as a literary movement or the fact that as an attitude of the human spirit romanticism continues to have deep roots in human nature.

16. Cf. 7:145; 9:684–86.

However, there undeniably remains an untidy residue of semantic confusion between the different meanings of this term.

Belinskij seems to have been less aware of the ambiguity of the terms "objective" and "subjective" in his writings, an ambiguity connected with a shift in the relative value he placed on these aspects of artistic creativity. To the early Belinskij, objective art, as exemplified by Shakespeare, is vastly superior to subjective art, and "subjective" is necessarily a negative term. Thus, when Belinskij must note the fact that Schiller (according to the poet's own observation, let it be said) is a subjective poet, he adds that "Schiller's subjectivity is the subjectivity of a genius" ("A Journal Note" ["Žurnal'naja zametka"], 1838, 2:465).

By 1841, when Belinskij's thinking had become quite "historicized," only art which expresses substantial historical developments deserves, in his opinion, the epithet "objective," and suddenly Goethe becomes "largely a subjective and lyrical poet, who fully expressed the contemplative, ascetic aspect of the German national spirit" (review of *Goethe's Works,* 1842, 6:182). Yet at the same time Belinskij has words of the warmest praise for the new "subjectivity" which he detects in Gogol''s *Dead Souls* (a few years earlier, in an essay on I. I. Lažečnikov in 1839, 3:15–16, he had admiringly registered the "objectivity" of *The Inspector-General*):

> Here we do not mean that subjectivity which, through its narrowness or one-sidedness, distorts the objective reality of the subjects depicted by the poet; rather, we mean that profound, all-embracing, and humane subjectivity which reveals in the artist a human being possessed of an ardent heart, a sympathetic soul, and a spiritual and personal individuality—that subjectivity which will not allow him to view the world with apathetic indifference, or to remain alien to the world depicted by him, but rather, will force him to let the phenomena of the external world pass through his *living soul*, thus breathing a *living soul* into them. . . . This prevalence of subjectivity, which permeates and gives life to Gogol''s entire poem, at times attains to high lyric pathos. (review of *Dead Souls,* 6:217–18)

From this time on, "subjective" tends to mean "actively engaged in historical progress," and an absence of this element is seen as a defect:

> Simplicity and a sense of reality are an inherent quality of Count Sollogub's stories. In this respect, he is now second only to Gogol' in Russian literature. The weakness of his works lies with an absence in them of a personal (pardon the expression: subjective) element, which would permeate and give a direction to the whole, so that these truthful descriptions of reality might possess, in addition to their truthfulness, the extra value of an ideal content. ("1842," 6:536)

No wonder, then, that Belinskij begins to detect in himself "a certain hostility toward objective works of art" (letter to V. P. Botkin, 8 September 1841, 12:73). This tendency becomes more pronounced toward the end of Belinskij's life. In one of his last letters, he regrets that Dickens is "so little *personal,* so little *subjective*" (letter to Botkin, 2–6 December 1847, 12:446).

Nevertheless, Belinskij continues to be capable of appreciating objective art, or "mere art" (*tol'ko iskusstvo*), as he now tends to call it. Belinskij had neither love nor respect for Gončarov, but of this writer's purely objective art he said: "You read it and feel as if you were eating a cool, twenty-pound watermelon on a hot summer day" (letter to V. P. Botkin, 4 March 1847, 12:347–48).

In the above examples and elsewhere Belinskij uses the terms "objective" and "subjective" now in the conventional psychological sense, referring to the creative process, and then within the broader framework of a Hegelian historical teleology, that is, with reference to the artist's participation or nonparticipation in the affairs of the world and in the course of history. In effect, by being "subjective" in the first sense, Gogol' becomes an "objective" poet in the second sense, while Goethe is called "subjective" in the second sense on account of his objectivity in the first sense. Yet Belinskij could always intuitively distinguish a poet who was subjective by virtue of his active and partisan commitment to the problems of his age from one who was subjective because of a lack of creative imagination.

"Reality" is perhaps the key word in all of Belinskij's aesthetics.[17] Perhaps unbeknownst to Belinskij himself, his search for reality is essentially an effort to establish a hierarchy of values. The terms "real" and "illusory" (*dejstvitel'nyj* as against *prizračnyj*) have for him, as they have for Hegel, a strong axiological connotation.[18]

To the early Belinskij, "reality" is the metaphysical, "higher" reality of Schellingian Neoplatonism: "Thought, or the idea, in its absolute, universal meaning, this is what a man should pursue in his studies. Outside of thought, everything is but an illusion, a dream; only thought is substantial and real" (letter to D. P. Ivanov, 7 August 1837, 11:146).

When Belinskij becomes converted to Hegelianism his concept of reality expands. He now sees the adjective "real" as an antonym of (a) "imaginary" (*voobražaemyj*) and (b) "illusory" (*prizračnyj*). The world created by a Homer, a Shakespeare, or a Puškin is "imaginary-and-real" (*voobražaemyj dejstvitel'nyj*),

---

17. For an excellent presentation of the concept of reality in Belinskij, see Herbert E. Bowman, *Vissarion Belinski 1811–1848: A Study in the Origins of Social Criticism in Russia* (Cambridge, Mass., 1954), pp. 100–139. I agree with Bowman when he says that "a systematic exposition of what Belinski meant by 'reality' is out of the question" (p. 101).

18. This interpretation forms the basis of Bernhard Schultze's book *Wissarion Grigorjewitsch Belinskij* (Munich, 1958).

that is, "as indubitable as the world of nature and of history," while the world
of a Ducray-Duminil or of a Sumarokov is "imaginary-and-illusory" (3:85).[19]
This Hegelian concept of reality is still emphatically idealistic, since ideas—substantial, fertile, rational ideas, that is—are considered to be more "real" than
the irrational and fortuitous trivia of day-to-day living: "A man drinks, eats,
clothes himself—this is the world of illusion, because his spirit does not have
any part in it; a man feels, thinks, is aware of himself as an organ of the spirit,
as a finite particle of the universal and the infinite—this is the world of *reality*"
("Woe from Wit" ["Gore ot uma"], 1840, 3:436).

Hegel's insistence that art should spring not from any abstract idea but from
the plenitude of life (*Überfülle des Lebens*), and that the aesthetic idea should
be concrete and incarnate, is reflected in Belinskij's move toward a more realistic conception of art. Belinskij himself explains this shift in his own thinking
as the result of Hegel's influence (ibid., 3:432). In good Hegelian fashion, too,
Belinskij's demand for realism in art is now "historicized"; it is declared a necessary trait of the new age of which the critic feels himself to be the herald: "*Reality* is the password and the slogan of our age, reality is everything—in one's beliefs, in science, in art, in life. A vigorous, courageous age it is, suffering nothing
which is false, counterfeit, feeble, vague, and loving only that which is potent,
firm, substantial. . . . the most recent poetry is *the poetry of reality*, the poetry of life" (ibid., 3:432–33).

During the last few years of Belinskij's life this Hegelian demand for what was,
after all, "realism in a higher sense" not infrequently lapses into an insistence
on the presentation, in literature and in the other arts, of simple and unadorned,
empirical, contemporary social reality. Belinskij's defense of the pedestrian
products of the Natural School, in which the ideal aspect of art is often eclipsed
by a preoccupation with realistic detail, comes close to calling "real" that
which he had earlier called "illusory," namely, the incidental trivia of everyday
life. This is an important and real contradiction in Belinskij's aesthetic thought.

The terms "reality" and "real" may denote, in Belinskij's writings, anything
from an ontological concept ("real" as against "ideal") to a concept of value
("real," that is, "substantial," as against "illusory," meaning "fortuitous, fleeting"), as well as a moral and practical one ("real" as against "false, affected,
fantastic"). Belinskij does not always have full control over the various connotations of these, his favorite philosophic and critical terms.

We will observe similar semantic shifts in other key terms of Belinskij's aesthetic theory, and, correspondingly, similar inconsistencies in the frame of
reference in which they are used. The three examples cited here serve the purpose of suggesting, in a preliminary way, that Belinskij's aesthetics is (1) not a
static, but a dynamic system, and (b) that it is not free of illogicalities, equivocations, and contradictions.

19. Cf. 3:439.

3

The Sources of Belinskij's
Aesthetic Ideas

Belinskij's philosophic and aesthetic ideas were borrowed from Western sources, a fact which Soviet scholars have attempted to minimize. Their assertions to the effect that "Belinskij's aesthetic theory was organically linked with his revolutionary-democratic convictions"[1] or that "Belinskij created his own aesthetics, departing from the social and literary practice of his country"[2] are true, to a limited extent, of the later Belinskij. Belinskij's dependence on the aesthetic thought of Schelling, Fichte, Hegel, and Feuerbach was emphasized by Plexanov, who also pointed out when and where Belinskij departed from his examples.[3] Soviet scholars, with some noteworthy examples, limit themselves to generalities when it comes to establishing the relationship between Belinskij and these foreign influences.[4] Thus, in a 60-page survey article on Belinskij, Lavreckij mentions Schelling only once, in parentheses, and in a rather irrelevant connection.[5]

Belinskij knew French fairly well (he did some translations from the French and often uses French phrases in his writings). His German was not good enough to read philosophy in the original language. He knew no other foreign languages. He learned his German philosophy largely from the accounts of his friends Stankevič, Bakunin, Katkov, Turgenev, Botkin, Annenkov, and others, as well as from translations by one or the other of these writers. However, every observer seems to agree that Belinskij readily made these second-hand

1. N. A. Guljaev, *V. G. Belinskij and the Foreign Aesthetics of His Time* [*V. G. Belinskij i zarubežnaja èstetika ego vremeni*] (Kazan', 1961), p. 36.

2. A. Lavreckij, *Belinskij's Aesthetics* (*Èstetika Belinskogo*) (Moscow, 1959), p. 11.

3. G. V. Plexanov, "Belinskij i razumnaja dejstvitel'nost'" and "Literaturnye vzgljady V. G. Belinskogo," *Sočinenija*, 10:237–39, 259.

4. Cf. Guljaev, *Belinskij*, p. 6; Lavreckij, *Èstetika Belinskogo*, pp. 9–10. But V. S. Nečaeva, in her excellent 4-volume work *V. G. Belinskij* (Moscow, 1949–67), takes care to point out every source that can be identified.

5. A. Lavreckij, "Belinskij," in *Istorija russkoj kritiki*, ed. B. P. Gorodeckij et al., 2 vols. (Moscow and Leningrad, 1958), 1:369–429.

borrowings his own, that he understood his Schelling and his Hegel as well as anyone among his more learned friends, and that he used the tools placed into his hands by others independently, intelligently, and creatively.[6] P. V. Annenkov, to whom Belinskij owed a great deal, put it this way:

> Belinskij had the talent to develop quickly every corollary of a given idea, the talent to apply that idea perceptively to contemporary phenomena, taking into account the needs of a developing Russian society, or actually causing these needs to arise, and, finally, a talent to establish aesthetic-philosophic positions applicable to the day-to-day developments in Russian literature, often on the spur of the moment.[7]

Nevertheless, Belinskij's ideas originated in the West, and it is necessary to identify their sources. Belinskij never hesitated to do so himself. The names of such major figures as Herder, Kant, Schiller, Goethe, Fichte, Schelling, Hegel, and Victor Hugo appear frequently in his writings, and other authorities, for example, Friedrich and August Wilhelm Schlegel, Jean Paul, Heinrich Theodor Rötscher, Friedrich Theodor Vischer, Wolfgang Menzel, François Guizot, and many others, are mentioned here and there. The names of Left-Hegelians, such as Feuerbach, Bruno Bauer, Stirner, and Ruge, and French utopian socialists, such as Saint-Simon, Barrault, Leroux, Buchez, and Fourier, appear only in Belinskij's correspondence, if at all. The censors would have struck out any explicit reference to them, no matter what the context. For the same reason, the names of some more liberal French writers and critics (Sainte-Beuve and Sue, for example) appear in nonideological contexts only, though Belinskij was familiar with their political ideas and, specifically, with the *socialisant* drift of their aesthetics.

6. I. S. Turgenev put it this way: "In this matter nobody was his teacher or his advisor: he had gathered virtually all of his knowledge, his familiarity with the achievements of science and scholarship, in his contacts with the circle of his Moscow friends; he owed them a great deal, for they had given him the tools which he would use; but nobody could ever tell him how to use them, and whom to attack with them" (I. S. Turgenev, "Vstreča moja s Belinskim" [1860], *Polnoe sobranie sočinenij,* 15 vols. [Moscow and Leningrad, 1960–67], 14:209. Cf. also Turgenev's "Vospominanija o Belinskom" [1869], ibid., 14:22–63).

Turgenev's reminiscences of Belinskij were challenged by N. N. Straxov, among others. In an article, "Zametki o Belinskom" (1869), Straxov took Turgenev to task for the frivolous tone and light content of his reminiscences. Straxov said, among other things, that Turgenev had not bothered to point out Hegel's true influence on Belinskij but had limited himself to generalities. See Straxov, *Bor'ba s zapadom,* 3:275–96.

Prince V. F. Odoevskij, himself a knowledgeable student of Schelling, expressed a similar opinion: "I could not fail to be amazed how he [Belinskij], from only a superficial knowledge of *Naturphilosophie,* developed a whole organic philosophical world *sui generis*" (quoted by Pypin, *Belinskij,* p. 466).

7. Quoted by Lebedev-Poljanskij, *Belinskij,* pp. 95–96.

Still, as René Wellek has pointed out, it is often difficult to pinpoint the specific origin of a given thought in Belinskij's writings. It is usually wiser to tag it with an adjectival form, such as Schellingian, Hegelian, or Saint-Simonian, than to claim direct borrowing.

Belinskij himself refers to the time around 1836 as the "Fichtean" period of his career. Yet, as Pypin first suggested, it is still difficult to identify the sources of Belinskij's early idealist philosophy.[8] Inasmuch as Fichte's philosophy was only peripherally concerned with aesthetics, and Belinskij's aesthetic thought during the years 1834–37 is saturated with Schellingian ideas, I prefer to call this entire time the Schellingian period of the critic's life.

In some instances Belinskij's own evidence facilitates identification. On 1 March 1841, Belinskij writes to Botkin: "K[atko]v let me use his notebooks [which contained Hegel's lectures on aesthetics]—I took whole passages from them and put them into my article" (12:24). The article in question was "The Division of Poetry into Kinds and Genres" ["Razdelenie poèzii na rody i vidy"] (1841, 5:7–67).

Belinskij's essay on the idea of art borrows rather heavily from Rötscher's essay on criticism of a work of art, which had appeared in Russian translation in *The Moscow Observer.*[9] After paraphrasing Rötscher's interpretation of the "Mothers" scene in Goethe's *Faust II*, Belinskij says in a footnote: "This entire passage, containing references to *Faust,* is an excerpt from Rötscher's article 'On the Philosophic Criticism of a Work of Art,' prepared by the translator of said article, Mr. Katkov, and quoted here in full. V. *Moscow Observer,* vol. XVIII, pp. 187 and 188."

These instances are the exception rather than the rule. Usually, the tracing of Belinskij's sources must follow circumstantial evidence. The ideas that move Belinskij appear almost simultaneously, though in a somewhat different form, in Germany and in France. (Belinskij and his Russian contemporaries had relatively little direct contact with England.)

Thus, the early Belinskij's cosmic pantheism is generally identified as a Schellingian trait. But many of the Saint-Simonians and Fourierists were also cosmic pantheists, and this fact is reflected in their conception of the nature of the creative process and the artist's calling. Belinskij's historicism, one of the focal traits of both his general philosophy and his aesthetic theory, is tacitly taken for a Hegelian feature of his world view. Yet some of the French utopian socialists, Pierre Leroux, for example, also had a distinct notion of

8. Pypin, *Belinskij,* pp. 147–48.

9. Belinskij's essay was untitled, written early in 1841, and published posthumously in 1862, 4:585–602. H. T. Rötscher, "Das Verhältnis der Philosophie der Kunst und der Kritik zum einzelnen Kunstwerke," in *Abhandlungen zur Philosophie der Kunst* (Berlin, 1837), pp. 3–72. "O filosofskoj kritike xudožestvennogo proizvedenija," *Moscow Observer* 18 (1838): May (sec. 2) and June (secs. 1, 2).

historical continuity and historical progress in literature, along with an understanding that a true poet would express the quintessential "reality" of his particular epoch.[10]

The conception of the dialectic nature of historical evolution and, specifically, an understanding of the necessity of negation for the sake of progress, so important to Belinskij's aesthetic theory, are commonly felt to be Hegelian. Yet, Saint-Simon's conception of alternating "organic" and "critical" epochs in world history (it appears under different labels, such as "admirative" versus "satirical," in the writings of other utopian socialists) expresses much the same notion. But then, too, Vischer uses the term "critical epoch" in exactly the same sense.

Hegel's optimistic historical determinism is paralleled by the French utopian socialists' firm faith in progress toward a new golden age of mankind. Even more important, as far as Belinskij is concerned, the French utopian socialists generally share the beliefs of German objective idealism as regards the cognitive and prophetic powers of art, giving the artist a leading position in the forefront of historical progress.[11] Furthermore, the notion, so characteristic of Hegel, that civilization had arrived at a point where art, in the old sense, was about to expire, giving way to a new form of the creative human spirit, is also found in Saint-Simonian thought: "Nous sommes revenus à la nullité poétique de l'école d'Alexandrie," exclaims Buchez.[12] (This is one notion which Belinskij was not eager to adopt.)

Nevertheless, circumstantial evidence suggests that Belinskij owed most of his ideas to German idealism. His formulations, terminology, and examples tend to coincide with those of German idealism. Also, the direct evidence of Belinskij's explicit references to German sources makes it quite certain that the origins of Belinskij's more interesting and meaningful aesthetic ideas are to be sought there. According to the index of *Polnoe sobranie sočinenij,* Hegel is mentioned in Belinskij's writings at least a hundred times, Schelling somewhat less frequently; Goethe and Schiller hundreds of times, though in many instances as poets rather than as philosophers or critics. The later positivist and utilitarian strain in Belinskij's writings no doubt owes a great deal to the French theoreticians of the Left.

Many of the positivistic and utilitarian precepts of the French utopian socialists are difficult to distinguish from similar ideas current in the eighteenth-century Enlightenment and much earlier, specifically in Aristotle and in Horace's *Ars poetica.* As regards Belinskij, one rarely has the impression that he was ever in any way an aesthetic reactionary—an impression one cannot escape when

10. Hunt, *Le Socialisme et le romantisme,* p. 95.
11. Ibid., p. 34 (Barrault), p. 44 (Sainte-Beuve), p. 85 (Buchez).
12. Ibid., p. 87.

reading Černyševskij—or that he had simply abandoned his earlier "organic" ideas. Rather, Belinskij's returns to a position which might smack of the Enlightenment can be seen as a case of a new synthesis ("realism") resurrecting certain aspects of an old thesis ("classicism") over its more recent antithesis ("romanticism"). Belinskij himself certainly saw it that way.

KANT, HERDER, AND SCHILLER

It can be taken for granted that Belinskij was familiar with the classicist aesthetics of Boileau, Batteux, and La Harpe, which, along with the principles of classical poetics and rhetoric, was then taught in Russian secondary schools and universities. The names of these authors, as well as their doctrines, come up frequently in Belinskij's writings, but almost invariably only to be refuted. The first positive influence to be mentioned is that of Immanuel Kant (1724–1804).

Kant is mentioned about 25 times in Belinskij's writings, and some of these references suggest that the critic was familiar with the principles of Kant's philosophy and aesthetic theory. In Belinskij's time Kant was no longer a living, controversial thinker. Rather, he was the author of a number of dicta which had become axiomatic positions of all advanced aesthetic thought. Puškin wrote in 1830: "While aesthetics has been developed with such clarity and on such a broad front since the time of Kant and Lessing . . . we [Russians] keep repeating that *the Beautiful* is imitation of beautiful nature and that the principal virtue of art is *utility*."[13] Puškin had not read Kant, of course, but he knew that the German philosopher had defended the autonomy of art.

There was, first of all, Kant's hypothesis according to which the aesthetic idea (*die ästhetische Idee*) is distinct from the intellectual idea (*die Vernunftidee*) on the one side, and from sense impressions (*Sinnenempfindung*) on the other.[14] Belinskij, along with the entire aesthetics of German idealism, firmly rejects both the intellectualist aesthetics of the earlier, rationalist Enlightenment of France and Germany, and the sensualist aesthetics of British empiricism. The concept of the "aesthetic idea" (it usually appears as the "poetic idea") is a focal one in Belinskij's thought.

The aesthetic idea is generated by creative imagination (*Einbildungskraft*), a faculty possessed by all humans, but in varying degree, the highest of which Kant calls genius. The creations of genius are no mere reproductions of specific natural objects, but are of a higher order: creative imagination has the power to create, from material provided by Nature, a "second nature," as it were.[15]

13. Puškin, *Polnoe sobranie sočinenij*, 7:211.
14. Immanuel Kant, *Kritik der Urteilskraft*, ed. Gerhard Lehmann (Stuttgart, 1966), par.45.
15. Ibid., pars. 46 and 49.

Originality and creative power are the principal characteristics of genius. Like Kant, and all German idealism, Belinskij consistently rejects aesthetic "naturalism" (a term first applied to literature by Schiller) and often puts stress on the criterion of originality.

Kant's hypothetical postulation of a *sui generis* intuitive intelligence (Kant speaks of *anschauende Urteilskraft*) which can overcome the antinomies of discursive human intelligence (such as the antinomy of the universal and the particular) was developed by Schelling into the conception of a mystic organ of dialectic synthesis. The latter conception prevails in Belinskij's early writings and never disappears entirely. In his later articles, Belinskij generally follows Hegel in breaking down the walls between the different compartments of the human mind, which Kant had established, and in assuming that intuitive and discursive cognition cooperate in the poet's mind.

The central thesis of Kant's aesthetics reads that Art and its product, Beauty, appeal to man in a "disinterested way" (*interesseloses Wohlgefallen*), or "objectively," that is, independently of sentiment (*Rührung*), sensuality (*Reiz*), economic, political, or moral interest. Like Kant, and German idealism in general, Belinskij rejects out of hand, not only aesthetic sensualism, but also aesthetic emotionalism, as well as moralism and didacticism—all of which had been characteristic of pre-Kantian eighteenth-century aesthetic thought. A corollary of the disinterestedness of artistic creation is its freedom, which is simply taken for granted by the aesthetics of German idealism, just as by Belinskij. Like Kant and all of German idealist aesthetics, Belinskij rejects rhetoric as nonart, because it is neither "disinterested" nor "free."[16]

There are important differences between Kant's subjective idealism and the objective idealism of Schelling and Hegel. These differences are borne out by their respective aesthetic theories. In these instances Belinskij invariably follows Schelling and Hegel rather than Kant.

Kant considers that "the laws of Art" are given in the creative subject. In other words, art is the subjective product of individual genius.[17] In objective idealism, and very strongly in Belinskij, the laws of Art are organically linked to the spirit of an epoch, to the national spirit, and to the course of history: the age of Catherine the Great could produce a Lomonosov and a Deržavin but not a Puškin or a Gogol'.

Consistent with his subjectivism, Kant is cautious about ascribing to the poetic genius any cognitive, visionary, or prophetic faculty (which would give his creations objective validity and greatly enhance his social and historical stature), and draws a definite line between art and science, assuming that art "has a limit which it cannot transcend, a limit which, one may assume, was reached a long

16. Ibid., pars. 43 and 53.
17. Ibid., par. 46.

time ago," while science continues and will continue to make progress.[18]
Schelling and Hegel, on the contrary, ascribe to Art a definite cognitive function as well as an inherent ability to advance with the general development of
civilization. On this point, Belinskij tends to be even more optimistic than
Hegel, who envisaged the eventual end of art as a manifestation of the Absolute Spirit. Kant's aesthetics is "anthropological" rather than "historical."
Belinskij embraces the historicism of German objective idealism, while his
successor Černyševskij returned to an "anthropological" aesthetics.

Lastly, Kant's "organic" conception of the work of art is essentially a metaphor. To Kant, the biological organism is in a sense an analog of the work of
art, but there is a fundamental difference: the work of art is a "living organism" only by virtue of the fact that there exists a rational being (its creator, or
viewer, or reader, etc.) who breathes the spirit of life into it.[19] In objective
idealist aesthetics, the work of art is seen as an organic phenomenon in a more
immediate sense, and its creator as a catalyst through whom the Absolute
makes itself manifest. Again, Belinskij follows objective idealism in that we
hear him speak of works of art, of literary styles and epochs, of national literatures and their trends rather than of creative subjects and their working models,
designs, devices, and tools.

Many of Belinskij's ideas can be ultimately traced to Johann Gottfried Herder (1744-1803). Belinskij's understanding of folk poetry in particular, as expressed in his articles on Russian folk poetry (1841, 5:289-450) and in some
of his other essays,[20] is largely Herderian in its outlook. However, Herder was
no longer a living source of knowledge or of inspiration even in Belinskij's
youth. Many of his ideas had become accepted commonplaces, others were
being rediscovered in the new formulations given them by the romantics. Nevertheless, occasional references to Herder in Belinskij's works suggest that he was
aware of Herder's historical importance and had a distinct image of his philosophy. For example, in refuting V. F. Odoevskij's notion that in *Boris Godunov*
Puškin had somehow "divined the character of the Russian chronicler," Belinskij suggests: "Did he divine it, really? Didn't he rather let him—according to
Herder, though in the Russian style—perform an apotheosis of history, that is,
say things which could not have possibly entered the mind of any chronicler,
European or Russian?" (review of *Sočinenija knjazja V. F. Odoevskogo,* 1844,
8:319).

It has been suggested that the nucleus of Herder's aesthetics is to be found in

18. Ibid., pars. 47 and 49.
19. Ibid., par. 65.
20. See, e.g., "A General View of Folk Poetry and Its Importance" ["Obščij vzgljad na
narodnuju poèziju i ee značenie"] (written 1842-44, published posthumously in 1862,
5:654-59) and his essay on the Russian folk tale (no title, written 1842-44, published in
1860, 5:660-77).

the statement that "every human perfection is national, temporal (*säkulär*) and, if viewed very closely, individual."[21] The relativism implicit in this position is balanced by Herder's strong insistence on the presence of absolute values in all true art and on the continuity of the vital principle which manifests itself in the art and poetry of all peoples and all epochs. Herder is very much a Platonist in his belief that the three fundamental manifestations of the vital principle, the Good, the True, and the Beautiful, are substantially identical. Therefore, Herder tends to take for granted that a work of genius will, even without extrinsic pressure, satisfy the principles of morality.

Herder's historicism lives on in Hegel, where it assumes that particular form in which it appears in most of Belinskij's writings. The same is true of Herder's nationalism. In Belinskij, Herder's conception of the nation as a concrete manifestation of the spirit of mankind appears without the German philosopher's partiality to folk cultures, and with a Hegelian emphasis on the creations of "historical," that is, civilized nations.

The third member of Herder's triad, individuality, is neglected by Belinskij, as it is by Hegel. Belinskij always tends to see the individual poet as an expression of the spirit of his nation, his age, and his ideas. Rarely, if ever, will he shift his focus to the poet as an individual, so that nation, society, history, and ideas would become the medium in which the poet realizes his creative potential.

Herder was a strong proponent of the organic conception of the work of art. "Like the human soul, the work of art is an inseparable whole," he once said.[22] Therefore, "content" cannot be separated from "form." Belinskij is, in this respect, an equally determined organicist, as is every major figure whose influence he experienced. The notion of the analogy between the human microcism, as presented in art, and the macrocosm of the world, characteristic of Herder and subsequent romantic thought, appears prominently in Belinskij, especially during his earlier, Schellingian period:

> The entire art of the poet should consist of placing the reader on a vantage point from which he can perceive all Nature in a compressed form, in miniature, like the globe of the Earth on a geographic map, and so, in letting him sense the breeze, the breath of that life which animates the cosmos, in imparting to his soul the fire which warms it ("Literary Reveries" ["Literaturnye mečtanija"], 1834, 1:34)

Accordingly, Belinskij assigns an all-important role to human intuition, to the bond which makes this analogy possible. It had been Herder's particular merit

21. J. G. Herder, "Auch eine Philosophie der Geschichte," *Sämtliche Werke,* 33 vols. (Berlin, 1877–99), 5:505. Regarding Herder, I follow, by and large, Armand Nivelle, *Kunst- und Dichtungstheorien zwischen Aufklärung und Klassik* (Berlin, 1960).
22. Quoted by Nivelle, *Kunst- und Dichtungstheorien,* p. 164.

to have extended the area of aesthetic intuition from expressions of the movements of the human soul to all artistic creation. Belinskij does not fall short
of Herder in this respect. Today, Belinskij's faith in the artist's intuitive powers (as compared with the scholar's painstaking labors) would seem extravagant.
On the other hand, the Neoplatonist, religious, revelationist, and mystic aspect
of Herder's aesthetics will be encountered only in Belinskij's earliest writings,
specifically in his "Literary Reveries" (1:20–104) and in Schellingian formulations.

Belinskij's connections with Friedrich Schiller (1759–1805) are more direct
than those with Kant or Herder. It is quite obvious that Belinskij was familiar
not only with Schiller's poetry (which he quotes often), but also with his more
important theoretical writings.[23] But Schiller the poet and tribune of humanity
was always more important to Belinskij than Schiller the epistemologist and
aesthetician.[24]

Schiller, himself a poet of genius, while a good Kantian in his epistemology,
tends to ascribe to Art far greater powers and importance than does Kant. He
is also a great deal more concrete in his formulations than Kant, knowing his
subject from active, firsthand experience. Some of Schiller's observations on
the creative process and on the ontology of the work of art have remained living thoughts to this day.

Schiller's idea that Art is the one possession of man which makes him human
and that the evolution of *homo aestheticus* (*die ästhetische Erziehung des
Menschen*) is also the history of mankind[25] is not very important for Belinskij,
who shows little interest in speculative anthropology. The same is true of
Schiller's speculations on the ontology of art. To him, art is an exercise in human freedom following either of two basic drives (*Stofftrieb* and *Formtrieb*—
roughly, the will to grasp and take possession of what the senses point out to
one, and the will to organize and to understand the world), and Beauty is the
achievement of a precarious yet perfect balance between them. This theory is
hardly reflected in Belinskij's aesthetic thought. But its corollary, the conception of the inherently dual nature of art and its mediatorship between different

23. For a detailed account of the stormy peripeties of Belinskij's relationship with Schiller, see Edmund K. Kostka, *Schiller in Russian Literature* (Philadelphia, 1965), pp. 81–116.

24. Here is a typical passage from a letter to Botkin, 4 October 1840, written just
after Belinskij had overcome his Hegelian period of "reconciliation to reality," during
which he had been extolling the objective poet Goethe, and downgraded the more
subjective Schiller: "I curse my vile reconciliation to a vile reality! Long live Schiller,
that noble advocate of humanity, that bright star of salvation, that emancipator of
society from the bloody prejudices of tradition! 'Long live Reason, let darkness flee!'
as the great Puškin exclaimed!" (11:556). Cf. 6:122; 7:165; 12:38.

25. See Schiller's Fifteenth letter "Über die ästhetische Erziehung des Menschen,"
Schillers sämtliche Werke: Säkular-Ausgabe, 16 vols. (Stuttgart, 1904–5), 12:59.

spheres of the human spirit,[26] is very much in evidence throughout Belinskij's writings.

Schiller's deep-rooted and eloquently defended idea of the civilizing and educational value of the *free play* of art as a check against the one-sided development of any one human drive does not appear in Belinskij, who viewed the civilizing role of art in more general and straightforward terms: the direct action of the "human" side of man counteracting the animal in him.[27] It stands to reason that Schiller's notion of "a happy realm of play and illusion, where man is allowed to shed the shackles of his circumstances and be free of all that has the name of force, whether it be in a physical or in a moral sense"[28] would not appeal, at least not in the long run, to the *objective* idealist and man of *action* Belinskij: it smacked too much of escapism, of turning one's back to "reality." But Schiller's conception of art as a synthesis of freedom and necessity was such, in its general formulation, that all of German idealism and virtually the entire Russian tradition, from Belinskij to Socialist Realism, could *mutatis mutandis* subscribe to it:

> Human beings lack the quality of perfection, which natural objects possess. But they partake of the Divine, in which natural objects fall short of man. Man is free, while natural objects are bound by necessity. Man changes, while they remain the same. But only when both are united, when human will freely follows the Law of Necessity, and Reason, in spite of all the changeability of fantasy, still follows its own rules, then the Divine, or the Ideal, is born. ("Über naive und sentimentalische Dichtung," *Säkular-Ausgabe,* 12:163)

The formula "when human will freely follows the Law of Necessity" (*wenn der Wille das Gesetz der Notwendigkeit frei befolgt*), in particular, admirably serves all "organic historicism," German as well as Russian, and is a convenient key to Belinskij's aesthetics no less than to that of a Dobroljubov, a Grigor'ev, or, for that matter, to that of Socialist Realism.

Of equal importance to Belinskij's aesthetic thought is Schiller's conception— it reappears, with slight modifications, in Schelling and in Hegel—of art as a fusion of the "ideal" and the "real." Schiller calls it "the elevation of reality to the level of the ideal, or, what amounts to the same, the representation of the ideal." It is perhaps the most clearly Neoplatonic trait of Schiller's—and Belinskij's—aesthetics (ibid., 12:188). A striking and important corollary is Schiller's conception of the "negative ideal":

26. "Das Schöne veredelt die Sinnlichkeit und versinnlicht die Vernunft" ("Aus den ästhetischen Vorlesungen," *Säkular-Ausgabe,* 12:356). Cf. the Eighteenth letter "Über die ästhetische Erziehung des Menschen," 12:67.

27. See, e.g., ibid., 10:370.

28. See the Twenty-seventh letter "Über die ästhetische Erziehung des Menschen," *Säkular-Ausgabe,* 12:117.

In satire, [common] reality as a condition in which the ideal is lacking is juxtaposed to the ideal as the highest reality. By the way, it is not at all necessary that the latter be made explicit, provided that the poet succeeds in awakening it in our minds. However, the latter effort he absolutely must achieve, or his work will remain quite unpoetic. [Common] reality is then, in this case, necessarily an object of disaffection; however, what is exceedingly important here is that such disaffection should necessarily spring from the presence, on the other side, of the [positive] ideal. (ibid., 12:194)

The conception of the "negative ideal" plays a key role in Belinskij's (and Grigor'ev's) interpretation of Gogol'. It is still important in the aesthetics of Socialist Realism.

Schiller's most famous contribution to aesthetic theory, his postulation of two distinct types of poets and of poetry, which he calls the "naïve" and the "sentimental," is amply reflected in Belinskij's criticism. Naïve poetry is, according to Schiller, basically realistic, objective, and "plastic," while sentimental poetry is essentially reflective, self-conscious, and "musical." Naïve poetry attains a limited goal, sentimental poetry strives for an unattainable ideal. Obviously, no poet and no poetic work represent either type in a pure form. Rather, these are basic tendencies present in every poet and in every work of poetry. Schiller's conception was largely psychological and anthropological. The Schlegel brothers, following some leads present in Schiller's essay, almost immediately gave it a historical dimension, as they identified "naïve" with "classical," and "sentimental" with "romantic" art. In Belinskij, the Schillerian dichotomy appears mostly under the label of "objective" versus "subjective" poetry, a conception that he must have gotten from Friedrich Schlegel's *Geschichte der alten und neuen Literatur,* which he read in Russian translation.[29] A historicized, Hegelian version of the dichotomy is also very much in evidence in Belinskij. For example:

In our day, poetry in the sense of the ancient poets, a poetry which views the phenomena of life without any regard to the poet's person (objective poetry) is hardly possible . . . but on the other hand, in our day and age, the absence in a poet of the inner (subjective) element is a shortcoming. ("The Poetry of M. Lermontov," 1841, 4:520)

Schiller's most ambitious venture was his attempt to bring about a fusion of the Good and the Beautiful in the concept of "ethic-aesthetic humanity" or *Kalokagathie.* It is believed by many to have been a misconception.[30] Schiller

29. See René Wellek, *A History of Modern Criticism,* 4 vols. (New Haven, 1955–65), 3:245. For a description of a copy of this work, owned and annotated by Belinskij, see *Literaturnoe nasledstvo* 60 (1948): 512-13.

30. See Käthe Hamburger, "Schillers Fragment *Der Menschenfeind* und die Idee der Kalokagathie," in *Philosophie der Dichter* (Stuttgart, 1966), pp. 83-128.

himself, in his Tenth letter "On the Aesthetic Education of Mankind," admits
that in a concretely historical perspective there seems to be a great deal of
truth to the notion that Beauty may serve evil as well as good ends, since the
flowering of the arts often coincides with the beginning of political and moral
decadence.[31] Belinskij, in theory as well as in practice, largely dispenses with
the concepts of the Good and the Beautiful, his interest belonging mainly to
the third member of the triad, the True. There is hardly a trace of Schiller's
noble but all too abstract conception to be found in Belinskij's writings. In
Belinskij's thinking, a work of art is beautiful *because* it is true. He was always
suspicious of any reversal of this proposition. It is, of course, important for
Dostoevskij.

Schiller's most felicitous and profound thoughts in the area of aesthetic theory stemmed from his personal experience as a creative genius who had, at the
same time, a rare gift of critical introspection. Thus, he will observe time and
again that Art is a distinct presence in a work of art, rather than its predicate,
that Art is always serene, pure and tranquil, no matter what the subject matter
of the work of art, and that Art has a close affinity with "power," or is in effect identical with it.[32] These insights anticipate romantic aesthetics. Such irrational intuitions were generally alien to Belinskij.

SCHELLING

The influence of Friedrich Wilhelm Schelling (1775-1854) is more tangible
than that of Schiller, even though Belinskij does not mention Schelling nearly
as often as Schiller. Belinskij had his Schellingian period (1834-37), and Schelling remained a factor in Belinskij's aesthetic thought even after the explicit rejection of his philosophy.

Among Belinskij's close friends, Bakunin, Herzen, and especially Stankevič

---

31. But then, Schiller was too much a man of the Enlightenment to take this thought
too seriously. "To the honor of human nature," he writes in his essay "Über den morali-
schen Nutzen ästhetischer Sitten" (1793-96), "it may be assumed that no man could
sink so low as to prefer Evil merely because it is evil; that, rather, any man without exception would prefer the Good—unless, by accident, it excluded pleasure or had displeasure
for its consequence" (12:152).

32. In his essay "Gedanken uber den Gebrauch des Gemeinen und Niedrigen in der
Kunst" (1793), Schiller points out that, paradoxically, a theft, morally the lesser evil,
is aesthetically harder to justify in a work of art than a murder. He explains this
phenomenon by the fascination of "power" (*Kraft*): "Any cowardly and base action
is repulsive on account of the lack of power [*Kraftmangel*] which it reveals; on the
other hand, a diabolic action may appeal to us aesthetically, so long as it gives the impression of power" (12:287). In his Twenty-second letter "Über die ästhetische
Erziehung des Menschen" (12:83) and in his essay "Über naive und sentimentalische
Dichtung" (12:192-93) Schiller very clearly states his understanding of the absolute
and most specific nature of the aesthetic fact: Beauty is an absolute which remains a

were, at least during one period of their association with the critic, more or less confirmed Schellingians, as were many of their opponents in the Slavophile camp. Thus, Belinskij's career began in a philosophical ambiance of Schellingianism. In a general sense, Schelling's transcendental idealism, with its underlying principle of the identity of the "objective" world and the "subjective" human consciousness, as well as the corollary of this principle, which is that the human mind can know the world *absolutely,* not just *relatively,*[33] always remained the guiding light of Belinskij's critical thought.

In the early Belinskij the identity of the epistemological subject and object still appears in a Neoplatonic formulation. Thus, he accounts for the phenomenon of the poet's "inner vision of truth" (*vnutrennee jasnovidenie istiny*) in these terms: "The reason for such *insight (ponjatlivost')* lies in the affinity, or better, in the identity of the cognizing and the cognized (*v toždestve poznajuščego s poznavaemym*)" ("A Hero of Our Time, 1840, 4:201). Here, "inner vision of truth" is, of course, the Plotinian ἔνδον εἶδος and, as in Plotinus, the assumption is that such inner vision may reveal the objective, absolute truth of being. The later Belinskij, while he has by no means relinquished his belief in the cognitive powers of poetic intuition, is no longer inclined to follow Schelling in drawing the logical consequences from the quasi-empirical fact of the artist's inner vision and to formalize this mystic view of the creative process and of all cognition.

The treatment of works of literature as microcosms, symbolic of the macrocosms of society, nation, and mankind, is based on a Neoplatonic notion which was popular even in the aesthetics of the Renaissance.[34] Schelling and Hegel

---

constant regardless of its context (genre, age, national traits, etc.) and even its psychological effect on man is always the same.

33. The difference between Schelling's objective and Fichte's subjective idealism lies in Schelling's notion that the human mind can know the world *absolutely,* not just *relatively* ("Nicht 'das Ich ist Alles,' sondern 'Alles ist Ich' ").

34. For instance, Tasso in his *Discorsi del poema eroico,* III, describes the infinite variability of God's world, only to liken it to the microcosm of the poet's world and to exclaim proudly regarding the poet's work: "Who is said to be divine for no other reason than because he participates in the divinity of the supreme artificer (*supremo artefice*), whose works his own resemble." Tasso goes on to point out that the work of art is, nevertheless, one single whole: "if a single part were removed, or displaced, the whole would be destroyed." And finally, he produces a clear statement of the "identity" of macrocosm and microcosm: "And if this is true, the art of composing a poem ought to be analogous to the rational order (*ragion*) of the universe, which is composed of contraries, much as the harmony of music (*ragion musica*); for if it were not multiple, it could not be whole, nor would it present a rational order, as says Plotinus [the reference is to Plotinus *Enneads* 2. 3. 16]" (Torquato Tasso, *Prose,* ed. Ettore Mazzali [Milan, 1959], pp. 588–89. Cf. Arthur O. Lovejoy, *The Great Chain of Being* (Cambridge, Mass., 1966), pp. 85–86, where examples of this conception of art are quoted from St. Augustine, Dante, and Giordano Bruno.

put great emphasis on it. It is a key trait of Belinskian criticism. It has dominated much of Russian literary criticism ever since and is firmly established in
Socialist Realism, though under the label of a "theory of reflection."

Another corollary of Schelling's identity principle—also anticipated by Plotinus and by Renaissance aesthetics—is the notion that the artist creates freely,
competing with Nature, as it were, rather than "imitating" her, and that he
produces works which are themselves "nature." This notion is reflected not
only in Belinskij's literal statements to this effect[35] but also in the critic's un-
wavering faith, echoed by his epigoni in the nineteenth and twentieth centuries, in the active social and historical role of Art. Along with it there comes
an exalted opinion of the artist's calling: the artist creates not an image of life,
but life itself; he is not a recorder of history, but a maker of history. Belinskij,
and even more so his epigoni, were often mindless of the original premise of
this position: Schelling's *Identitätsprinzip* and its Neoplatonic source, the notion that works of art and works of nature spring from the same spiritual
source.

Belinskij defined Art as "the *immediate* contemplation of truth, or thinking
in *images*" ("The Idea of Art," 1841, 4:585).[36] This famous definition, which
is still a cornerstone of Socialist Realism, squares with the identity principle as
well as with the conception of Art developed by Schelling and Hegel. Here, for
comparison, is Schelling's definition of Art: "Art can be defined as the real representation of the forms of things as they are in themselves—their proper, native forms, then." Or more concisely: "Art is the real representation of the
Absolute."[37] A. W. Schlegel defined poetry as "an expression of thought in

35. For example: "The poet does not imitate Nature, but rather competes with her;
and his creations flow from the same source, and by the same process as do the phenomena of nature, with the sole difference that on the side of the poet's creative process there
also stands consciousness, which Nature lacks in her creative action" ("The Poetry of M.
Lermontov," 1841, 4:499). Cf. 5:237–38, 557; 10:318.

36. The Russian term *obraz* has the dictionary meanings of (1) shape, form, appearance,
(2) image, (3) mode, manner, (4) icon, sacred image. Hence, the Russian term has the
connotation of "something that is formed, or shaped," and also more or less inevitably
that of "symbol, symbolic image." Hegel uses the German equivalent, *Bild,* in the narrower sense of English "image" or "picture." However, Belinskij's usage of *obraz* coincides
with that of Friedrich Theodor Vischer, who devotes a full chapter of his *Aesthetik* to the
concept *Bild* (1:93–116), emphasizing that it implies the meaning of *Gebilde* ("shape,
form, appearance") as well as that of "symbol" (as opposed to "allegory"). Furthermore,
A. W. Schlegel and Schelling often use *Sinnbild* as a synonym of *Symbol.* The term *obraz,*
specifically in conjunction with the adjective *xudožestvennyj,* is a key term of all Russian
aesthetics and plays as great a role as ever in Socialist Realism. It has no equivalent in
English aesthetic and critical thought. Cf. Vischer, *Aesthetik,* 1:93.

37. F. W. Schelling, *Philosophie der Kunst,* in *Schellings Werke,* ed. Manfred Schröter,
14 vols. (Munich, 1927), 3:407, 478. All quotes from Schelling are from this edition,
where the essay *Philosophie der Kunst* (1802) is found in vol. 3, pp. 375–507, the treatise

sense images" (*bildlich anschauender Gedankenausdruck*) as early as 1798.[38]

Belinskij himself eventually described Schelling's aesthetics as "mystical." Actually, Schelling, no less than but not as persistently as Hegel, stressed the *real* aspect in Art's fusion of the ideal and the real.[39] Thus, while Schelling's— and Hegel's—aesthetics is mystical in the sense that it embraces the notion of immediate, intuitive cognition, this is in effect a mysticism which it shares with Belinskij and most of his epigoni.

Schelling insisted that the nature of art is, by definition, *symbolic* rather than *schematic* or *allegoric*. According to Schelling, a schematic representation is one in which "the general signifies the particular," an allegoric representation one in which "the particular signifies the general," and a symbolic representation "a synthesis of both." This means that in a symbolic representation neither the particular signifies the general nor the general the particular, but that both are fused to form a single representation: "We wish an object of absolute artistic representation to be so concrete, so much alike itself, as only an image can be, yet as general and meaningful as a concept; hence the excellence of the German rendering of 'symbol' as *Sinnbild*" (*Philosophie der Kunst,* 3:432). German *Sinn* is "meaning, sense," and *Bild* is "image." This is a particularly clear and emphatic statement of Schelling's symbolic view of art. It is, in effect, also Belinskij's view of art.

Even at his most utilitarian, Belinskij will still reject "allegories" as well as "dissertations" (that is, schematic representations) as nonart. At the same time, Belinskij to the very end refuses to admit the literary daguerreotype (his own metaphor) to the realm of art. His theory of type demands that literary "types" be well-rounded human individuals, not abstract schemes "bearing

---

System des transzendentalen Idealismus (1800) in vol. 2, pp. 327–634, and the essay "Über Dante in philosophischer Beziehung" (1803) in vol. 3, pp. 572–84. References to these works are subsequently cited only by title and volume number in the *Werke.* Schelling's *Philosophie der Kunst* did not appear in print until 1856. However, the ideas expressed in this work were widely known. Dmitrij Tschižewskij points out that some of Tjutčev's poems "actually echo Schelling's *Philosophie der Kunst,* although this work appeared only later" (*Russische Literaturgeschichte des 19. Jahrhunderts,* 2 vols. [Munich, 1964], 1:134). Cf. Wellek, *Modern Criticism,* 3:360 n.4.

38. Another formulation of A. W. Schlegel's is: "Poetry is, if I may say so, the speculation of imagination" (A. W. Schlegel, *Sämtliche Werke,* 1:292). Likewise, Hegel: "The content of art is the Idea, its form being sensual representation in images (*ihre Form die sinnliche bildliche Gestaltung*). Art must unite both of its aspects to form a free, reconciled totality" (Georg Wilhelm Friedrich Hegel, *Ästhetik,* 2d ed., 2 vols. [Frankfurt-am-Main, n.d.], 1:77.

39. "Mysticism then = subjective symbolism. . . . Mysticism as such is unpoetic—for it is the opposite pole of poetry, which realizes the unity of the Infinite and the Finite in the *Finite*" (*Philosophie der Kunst,* 3:476).

little tags with legends of their virtues and vices on their foreheads," yet also that they have some inherent universal validity, importance, and interest.

This leads to an organic conception of the work of art. According to Schelling, "in a genuine work of art, there are no particular beauties, only the whole is beautiful" (*Philosophie der Kunst,* 3:379). Therefore, a critic "who is incapable of grasping the idea of the whole is totally incompetent to pass judgment on a work of art" (ibid.). This particular point is one that Belinskij also never tired of stressing.

Schelling took up Schiller's conception of the dual nature of the creative process and developed it in a number of directions. "The work of art is a reflection of the identity of *conscious* and *unconscious* activity" (*System des transzendentalen Idealismus,* 2:619). Its creator is a conscious *artist* as well as an inspired *poet* (ibid., 2:618). The creative process starts out from "a feeling of irresoluble contradiction" and ends in "a feeling of infinite harmony" (ibid., 2:617). Furthermore, the creative process represents a fusion of "freedom" and "necessity," in that the artist creates consciously and freely, yet has no control, and in fact no awareness, of the ultimate product of his creativity: the work of genius contains more than the artist consciously planned to put into it, something that transcends his consciousness. Schelling liked to illustrate this position by likening the artist—and, in fact, man in general—to an actor who plays his role imaginatively and with his own improvisations; in the long run, and in the things that really matter he must submit to the text provided by "the Absolute." All of these positions are of the utmost importance for Belinskij and, in fact, for much of Russian literary criticism after him.

Some aspects of Schelling's aesthetics found little or no echo in Belinskij's writings, except perhaps at the earliest stage of his career. This applies especially to the more blatantly Neoplatonic elements in Schelling's aesthetics. Belinskij, passionately involved as he was in "real life," had little use for divine Beauty shining through the creations of genius. Schelling's idea that the world made sense as a work of art—as a structure, we would say today—and that human language was in that sense a work of art and a symbol of the divine *logos* (*Philosophie der Kunst,* 3:378, 503-4) is hardly reflected at all in Belinskij's thought.

More importantly perhaps, Belinskij took little advantage of Schelling's profound conception of myth and mythology, specifically "modern myth" (Schelling actually admitted the possibility that modern speculative physics might create a new mythology) and its historical role. Belinskij saw in Peter the Great a "mythical figure" (*mifičeskoe lico*), "the Russian Achilles" and a "perfect expression of the Russian spirit," whose idea was "the abnegation of the accidental and the arbitrary in favor of the necessary, the rejection of the crude forms of a nationhood falsely developed in favor of a rational content of national life" ("The Works of Deržavin," 1843, 6:618-19). But he failed to extend this

notion of a modern mythology to Russian literature. The Slavophiles were
more perceptive, realizing, for instance, Gogol' 's myth-creating role in Russian life, something which Belinskij refused to see.

The "divine" nature of creative genius is underplayed, in comparison with
Schelling, even by the early Belinskij, as is the connection between art and religion. Schelling had a very strong sense of Art as a "miracle," and was always
aware of the fact that his conceptions of art as a fusion of the finite and the infinite, the real and the ideal, and so on, were irrational. Consistent with this,
he rejected the application of empirical, "scientific" psychology to art. Belinskij, little concerned as he was with metaphysics or even with individual psychology, largely overlooked these subtleties. All together, the more rational
aesthetics of Hegel was more congenial to Belinskij and his age.

HEGEL

Georg Wilhelm Friedrich Hegel (1770-1831) was probably the single most
important influence experienced by Belinskij, certainly as far as his aesthetic
thought was concerned. We know that Belinskij was thoroughly familiar with
Hegel's aesthetics.[40] M. N. Katkov had a conspectus of Hegel's lectures on aesthetics and let Belinskij use it in 1840-41. Belinskij had been familiar with
Hegel's philosophy even earlier. In 1838 his friend M. A. Bakunin published
an introductory essay to his own Russian translation of Hegel's "Gymnasial-
Reden." Bakunin's essay became programmatic for a new trend in Russian,
and in Belinskij's, thought. It was at the same time that Stankevič began to
concentrate on Hegel, even though he had begun to study his philosophy as
early as the winter of 1835-36. On 10 November 1835, Stankevič, then still a
confirmed Schellingian, had written to Ja. M. Neverov: "I am as yet not familiar with Hegel."[41] But as early as 24 November of that year he tells Bakunin
that he is translating, for *The Telescope*, an article on Hegel's philosophy from
the *Revue germanique,* and that he was "joyed to meet in Hegel some of his
own favorite thoughts."[42] Belinskij's correspondence with Bakunin suggests
that they were both confirmed Hegelians by the fall of 1837.[43] Belinskij's long

40. For Hegel's influence on Belinskij, see the chapter "Hegel in Russland" in Dmitrij
Tschiževskij, *Hegel bei den Slaven,* 2d ed. (Darmstadt, 1961), pp. 145-387. Tschiževskij,
certainly no admirer of Belinskij's, is willing to concede that the critic had a fairly good
grasp of the principles of Hegel's philosophy. Cf. also Malcolm V. Jones, "Some echoes of
Hegel in Dostoyevsky," *Slavonic and East European Review* 49 (1971): 500-520. For some
significant passages in Belinskij's works in which the principles of Hegel's philosophy are expounded, see 3:330-34; 4:586-87, 599-601; 5:315, 654-59; 6:92-94, 419-20, 582-85;
7:58; 8:271-77.

41. Aleksej Stankevič, ed., *Perepiska Nikolaja Vladimiroviča Stankeviča, 1830-1840*
(Moscow, 1914), pp. 338-39.

42. Ibid., pp. 594-95.

43. See Belinskij's letters to Bakunin, beginning with letter 1 November 1837, 11:184-202.

essay on Shakespeare, "*Hamlet*, a Drama by Shakespeare: Močalov in the Role of Hamlet" (1838, 2:253–345), started late in 1837, shows him to be a good Hegelian:

> Every manifestation of the Spirit, as a given stage of its consciousness, is beautiful and great; but the phenomenal world, being infinite, lives dynamically and mechanically, without being aware of itself, and only in man—that reflection of the Divine—does the Spirit manifest itself freely and consciously, and only in him does it find its subjective personification. Having passed through the entire chain of organic particularization and having attained the stage of Man, the Spirit begins to develop in mankind, and each moment of history is a given stage of this development. Each moment, in turn, has its proper exponent. Shakespeare is one of these exponents. The world is the prototype of his creations, and his creations are a replica of the world, but one arrived at consciously and therefore freely. (2:288)

We have here a particularly clear and literal statement of the Hegelian "organic" conception of the microcosm of the work of art as a symbol of the macrocosm of the world. The Kantian metaphor of the work of art as an "organism" has been hypostatized and, in fact, realized in Schelling's aesthetics, and realized as well as historicized in Hegel's aesthetics. Just as a biological organism is, in relation to its constituent parts, both a *universal* (it determines that which the parts have in common) and a *particular* (it also determines that which differentiates these parts), so the work of art is, in Hegelian aesthetics, a *concrete universal:* concrete as an assemblage of individual entities (forms, devices, characters, descriptive detail, specific events), universal as the expression of an idea. The idea, in turn, is a concrete manifestation of the self-revealing Absolute Spirit. It is this conception that is before Belinskij's eyes as he creates his seminal interpretations of *Evgenij Onegin, A Hero of Our Time,* and *The Inspector-General.*

From this time on, Hegelian formulations and Hegelian terminology (specifically, a peculiar meaning attached to such terms as "rational," "real," "concrete," "substantial," and so forth appear frequently in Belinskij's writings.[44]

In Soviet scholarship, Belinskij's "Hegelian" period is commonly identified with the critic's "reactionary" streak extending from autumn 1837 to summer 1840.[45] The essays and reviews of this period—some of them are among Belinskij's best efforts—display an outspoken willingness not only to accept the Russian social and political *status quo* as a necessary stage in the historical development of the country, and consequently a "rational" phenomenon, but also to encourage Russian literature to act as its loyal organ. Some of Belinskij's writings of this period, for example, the reviews of "The Anniversary of Boro-

44. For examples, see 3:230, 247, 330–31, 427–28; 4:237, 493, 586–87, 599–601; 5:315, 654–59.
45. See, e.g., Lebedev-Poljanskij, *Belinskij,* p. 186.

dino" (1839, 3:240–50) and "Sketches of the Battle of Borodino" (1839, 3:325–56), are unctuously loyal, patriotic, and monarchist effusions. They are also strongly Hegelian in their emphasis on the subordination of the "subjective principle" (that is, the individual) to the "objective principle" (that is, the power of the state).

The most important theoretical article of this period is "Menzel, a Critic of Goethe" (1840). It rejects virtually every notion with which Belinskij's name—in a broader, historical perspective—will be commonly associated: social *engagement* of literature, its concern with the specific issues of the contemporary scene, its role in the forming of public opinion. It defends socially and ideologically neutral "objective" art in general, and Goethe's detached "Olympian" attitude in particular. In each of these traits, Belinskij follows Hegel scrupulously, if not always intelligently.

The question has been raised, How correctly did Belinskij interpret Hegel, especially during his period of "reconciliation with reality"? He certainly understood Hegel correctly when Hegel insisted that every individual, and so a philosopher, a poet, or an artist, was inevitably a son of his age—in the sense that any substantial and noteworthy creation of his would have to be no more and no less than the spirit of that age, expressed in thought, in verbal symbols, or in images, while any merely imaginary ideal would exist only abstractly "in a soft medium which could receive the imprint of no matter what impression."[46] When Belinskij says that the theories of Boileau, Batteux, and La Harpe are nothing but "a distinct [intellectual] understanding of that which was immediately expressed (as a phenomenon, as reality) in the works of Corneille, Racine, Molière, and La Fontaine" ("Discourse on Criticism," 6:271), he shows that he has understood Hegel perfectly.

Belinskij temporarily misunderstood Hegel's famous dictum, "What is rational is real, and what is real is rational."[47] Hegel meant by this statement that philosophy "is the study of the rational, and therefore of the *present* and *real,* and not the postulation of anything transcendent."[48] In modern parlance this would mean that philosophy is the study of the structured aspect of things, much in the sense in which grammar is the study of the structured aspect of

46. "As far as the individual is concerned, each is, moreover, whether he would or not, *a son of his own age;* so that philosophy, too, is *its own age captured in thought.* It is just as foolish to assume that any philosophy could transcend the present world of which it is a part as it is foolish to think that any individual could leap across his own time, leaping farther than Rhodes. If his theory actually transcends it, if he builds himself a world *as it ought to be,* it exists, to be sure, but only in his assumptions, that is, in a soft medium which can receive the imprint of no matter what impression" (G. W. F. Hegel, *Grundlinien der Philosophie des Rechts,* ed. Johannes Hoffmeister, 4th ed. [Hamburg, 1955], p. 16).

47. "Was vernünftig ist, das ist wirklich; und was wirklich ist, das ist vernünftig" (ibid., p. 14).

48. Ibid.

language. Obviously it is quite wrong to gather from this position that philosophy or literature should support and perpetuate *any* existing condition of things. On the contrary, Hegel specifically challenges such thinking and likens it to the despotism of imperial Rome which made everything equal: nobility and slavery, virtue and vice, honor and dishonor, knowledge and ignorance.[49] It was here that Belinskij erred: Russian despotism and the condition of Russian life were precisely of the kind Hegel would have considered irrational (meaning "structureless"), fortuitous, "unreal," and thus unsuited to be the subject of philosophy, poetry, or art. Čaadaev had arrived at precisely this notion. It appears quite routinely in Belinskij as well.

Belinskij abandoned his political conservatism rather quickly,[50] but philosophically he remained a Hegelian to the end of his life,[51] as even Plexanov pointed out. As far as Belinskij's aesthetic theory was concerned, the Hegelian strain remained dominant to the end. For example, according to Hegel, the epos is possible only under the conditions of what he calls *der epische Weltzustand* ("the epic condition of the world"), meaning the presence of a well-developed, stable way of life and an integrated world view.[52] "Epic totality" is impossible without these conditions. Belinskij, along with other Westernizers, believed that Russian life was as yet unformed, that Russia was yet to become a "historical nation" in the same sense as the great nations of Western Europe. Under these conditions, the birth of a great epos was impossible in Russia. The Slavophiles (K. S. Aksakov, in this case) felt

49. Ibid., p. 13.
50. "I have been suspecting for a long time that Hegel's philosophy is only a moment, albeit a great one [in the history of thought], but that in an absolute sense its results are not worth a damn, and that I would rather die than acquiesce in them. . . . These fools are wrong, saying that Hegel changed life into dead schemes; but it is true that from the phenomena of life he has created mere shadows, dancing, their bony hands linked up in the air over the graveyard. The subject is for him not an end in itself, but a means toward the momentary expression of the universal, which is in his philosophy, with regard to the subject, a Moloch, because, having shown off in it for a time (in the subject, that is), he casts it off like an old pair of pants. I have particular reason to be angry in earnest with Hegel, because I feel that I was loyal to him (in my own feelings) at the cost of reconciling myself to Russian reality, praising Zagoskin and other such abominations, and hating Schiller" (letter to V. P. Botkin, 1 March 1841, 12:22).
51. As Ščukin and others have pointed out, Belinskij's involvement with French utopian socialism never changed the critic's basic, strongly Hegelian philosophy. Belinskij, says Ščukin, had too strong a sense of reality and knew Russian reality too well to consider the utopian ideas of Saint-Simon or Fourier as anything but pleasant pipedreams. Belinskij was pursuing real goals (freedom of the individual; a bourgeois, not a socialist idea), which Černyševskij termed "extremely modest." See S. E. Ščukin, *V. G. Belinskij i socializm* (Moscow, 1929), pp. 45, 130, 144, and *passim*.
52. Hegel, *Ästhetik*, 2:406–7.

otherwise and greeted *Dead Souls* enthusiastically as "the Russian epopoeia."[53]

In his essay on Deržavin (1843, 6:582–658), Belinskij sketches the historical development of the "aesthetic ideal" entirely according to Hegel's lectures on aesthetics: from Indian pantheism as outright "deification of nature," to Egyptian mythology where the Man-Animal makes his appearance, on to Greek anthropomorphism,[54] and so on, until he reaches the age of Deržavin. About this age Belinskij comments: "Any true poetry is an ideal mirror of reality, and the rational aspect of reality as it existed during that period found expression only in a few individuals in the retinue of the Monarch" (6:656). This is very suggestive of Hegel's statements concerning the Prussian state.

No wonder, then, that as late as 1846, Botkin, who had by that time discovered and to some extent embraced socialism and Left-Hegelianism, complained to their mutual friend Annenkov that Belinskij, having almost rid himself of Hegelian theories, was still firmly stuck in "art as such (*xudožestvennost'*). As a result of this, Botkin felt, his friend's criticism lacked "that freedom, that originality, and that simple and down-to-earth approach of which he was by nature capable."[55]

During the last few years of Belinskij's life, strictly Hegelian judgments and formulations appear side by side with positivist, utilitarian, and simply rhetorical violations of Hegel's aesthetic principles. Belinskij did not live to resolve these contradictions. Nor were they resolved by his followers.

Hegel, even more than Schelling, stressed that activity is the very essence of the Spirit and that the Spirit can be known only through its concrete manifestations. The younger Hegel actually used "life" in lieu of "idea," and even in his mature works "life" and "idea" are usually synonymous. His philosophy is clearly vitalist, with strong emphasis on the concrete, dynamic, and vigorous manifestations of the life spirit. Hegel's particular concern is with the "objective spirit," that is, that spiritual entity which we know from its manifestations

53. "An Explanation in Response to an Explanation" (1842), 6:416. The exchange between Aksakov and Belinskij was occasioned by Aksakov's anonymous brochure "A Few Words regarding Gogol' 's Poem *The Adventures of Čičikov, or Dead Souls*" (Moscow, 1842). Belinskij reviewed it, rather condescendingly rejecting its central thesis that *Dead Souls* was a "Russian epopoeia" (see 6:253–60). Aksakov responded with an "Explanation" in *Moskvitjanin* 5, no. 9 (1842): 220–29. Belinskij concluded the exchange with his "Explanation in Response to an Explanation" (6:410–33). Today it would seem that the naïve Aksakov was more right than the "sensible" Belinskij. Aksakov had said: "Before us, there emerges a new type of poetic creation; a whole sphere of poetry, long held in contempt, finds its justification; the ancient epos is resurrected before our eyes." Significantly, Belinskij rejects Aksakov's notion by using the Hegelian argument which says that the epos is impossible in the modern world (6:414).

54. Hegel, *Ästhetik*, 1:438, 580.

55. Quoted in Nečaeva, *Belinskij*, 4:412.

in the areas of morality, social institutions, language, forms of thought, material culture, and the fine arts. This concern led him to a thoroughgoing historicism, a treatment of the evolution of the Spirit in terms of concrete historical developments.[56] Belinskij followed Hegel wholeheartedly and intelligently on this point. It is remarkable that Černyševskij, apparently under the influence of Feuerbach, abandoned this concrete and historical approach to aesthetic phenomena in favor of an old-fashioned "anthropological" line of thought—a circumstance duly noted by Plexanov.

Belinskij's concern with "Russian literature," rather than with specific writers and poets, and his tendency to see a given literary figure in the context, and as a necessary product, of his age, are Hegelian traits. Belinskij invested Lomonosov, Deržavin, Žukovskij, Puškin, Gogol', and Lermontov with distinct historical roles, not only in the development of Russian literature but in the very development of the Russian national consciousness.

An important trait of Hegel's philosophy of history which appears in Belinskij's thought is a distinction (implying a value judgment) of varying degrees by which the "objective" (or "national") spirit is realized, depending upon the measure of concreteness, that is, the inner as well as external organization attained by it. There are "historical" and there are "ahistorical" peoples. It is in conjunction with this Hegelian conception that Belinskij keeps reiterating that pre-Petrine and even eighteenth-century Russia was too amorphous, too much lacking in well-defined, substantial forces, social institutions, and ideas, to have produced a poet of world-historical stature: no matter how great Deržavin's talent, and it was immense, the lack of national substance in the Russia of his age prevented him from becoming a universal genius. Only with the emergence of truly substantial social and ideological forces in the Russia of Belinskij's own age, Belinskij believed, could a universal genius such as Puškin emerge and realize his full potential.

Hegel's historization of the poetic genres deeply affected Belinskij's evaluation of Russian literature. His devastating refutation of K. S. Aksakov's notion that *Dead Souls* was the great Russian epopoeia has already been mentioned. The epopoeia, Belinskij says time and again, is possible only during a specific stage of historical evolution. Thus the epics of Tasso, Milton, and Klopstock, and even Vergil's *Aeneid*, as well as the best Russian efforts, such as Puškin's *Poltava*, not to speak of Xeraskov's *Rossiada*, were doomed beforehand to become pseudo-epopoeias, more or less successful in their details but failures as wholes. Specifically, the condition of the Russian nation was such as to allow the manifestation of its ideal only in the negative—while the epic attitude must be fundamentally a positive one. Both of these assumptions about

---

56. The early Hegel used the term *Volksgeist* in lieu of the later "objective spirit."

the nature of epic poetry, along with Belinskij's examples—except the Russian ones, of course—were taken from Hegel.[57]

The same is true of Belinskij's conception of the novel as the "modern" art form, organically linked with the modern way of life.[58] Also, Hegel's prophecy of the demise of the romantic art form and the advent of an entirely new era of human creativity is often echoed by Belinskij, even though the Russian critic's remarks on this point are simplistic compared with the German philosopher's subtle and sensitive formulations.[59]

Belinskij's conception of romanticism entirely coincides with Hegel's.[60] It is to Belinskij's credit that he was willing to appreciate romantic poetry and fiction even while assigning the romantic movement as such to a historic past, overcome and disclaimed by his own age. Hegel, a contemporary of the great German romantic poets, was singularly intolerant and unappreciative in his comments about them.

Hegel was a strong proponent of realistic and objective art. The fantastic, extravagant, and whimsical so frequently found in the art of his romantic contemporaries he disliked heartily. Nor had Hegel any use for romantic irony, or for any other manifestation of a subjective or aestheticizing attitude toward art. Belinskij's taste certainly agreed with Hegel's in this matter. Furthermore, Hegel was most intolerant of aesthetic naturalism. He wanted art to concentrate on the substantial, "natural" (we would say "normal"), and "rational" phenomena—and conflicts—of life. For this reason he disapproved of such themes as a servant's love for his mistress or a despot's arrogance of divine power, considering them "unaesthetic." Belinskij showed a similar tendency when he seriously criticized Dostoevskij for the "fantastic" quality of his novel *The Double*, a work which he otherwise admired. Likewise, Belinskij consistently rejected any "mechanical" or indiscriminate reproduction of nature, since it lacked the cohesive force of an organic idea—the *conditio sine qua non* of a true work of art.[61] This particular notion amounts to a demand for "typicalness" (*tipičnost'*), a concept characteristic of Russian criticism to this day.[62]

Belinskij's interpretation of Gogol''s *Inspector-General* is built around the notion that the world of the Skvoznik-Dmuxanovskijs is a "phantom world" or "phantom reality" (*prizračnaja dejstvitel'nost'*), a negative reality flowing

57. For Hegel's definition of the epos, see *Ästhetik,* 2:406–7, 428–29, 438. For his negative evaluation of Vergil, Milton, Klopstock, et al., see 2:434–36.
58. For Hegel's view of the modern novel, see *Ästhetik,* 2:452.
59. For Hegel's remarks on the "end of art," see *Ästhetik,* 1:110; 2:335, 570, 577–78.
60. For Hegel's view of the romantic art form, see *Ästhetik,* 1:500 ff.
61. Hegel, however, does not use this term.
62. For examples of "naturalism" rejected by Belinskij, see 2:342; 3:415; 5:567; 9:56; 10:42, 303–4.

from the irrational, chaotic principle of life, with the negative reality struggling against the emergence of a higher, rational reality. Hence Gogol''s comedy is seen as a statement of the ideal through its negation. The entire conception is Hegelian.[63]

Equally important corollaries of Hegel's demand for objective, realistic, and substantial art are the criteria of social universality and national specificity. Hegel rejected esoteric, "erudite" art: "For Art exists not for a small, segregated circle of a few preferentially educated people but rather for the whole nation at large" (Hegel, *Ästhetik*, 1:268). Simultaneously, Hegel asserted that Art, while ultimately an expression of the spirit of all humanity (*Weltgeist*), "is destined to find artistically suitable expressions in the spirits of individual nations" (ibid., 1:577). Art must be "either of universal human interest or have at its base a pathos which is, for the nation for whom it was created by the poet, a valid and a substantial one" (ibid., 1:530).

Both of these notions are equally characteristic of Belinskij. The first is implicit in his lifelong concern with the social role of art. The second is expressed in his just as consistently positive attitude toward "nationalism" (*nacional'nost'*) and "populism" (*narodnost'*) in literature. Even late in his career, Belinskij stood up for the idea that Russian literature, in order to fulfill its historical mission on behalf of its people and mankind, would have to be "national" (*narodnyj*) rather than cosmopolitan.

In "A Survey of Russian Literature in 1846" (1846, 10:7–50), Belinskij polemicizes with V. N. Majkov (1823–1847), who had claimed that "the true greatness of a man is directly proportionate to his independence from external circumstances, and consequently, from national and local traits."[64] Belinskij arrives at the following, very Hegelian formulation of "nationality":

> What *individuality* is with regard to the *idea* of Man, *nationality* (*narodnost'*) is in relation to the *idea* of mankind. In other words, the various nationalities are the individuals of mankind. Without nationalities, mankind would be a dead logical abstraction, a word without a content, a sound without a meaning. In this question, I am prepared to join the Slavophiles rather than to stay on the side of certain humanistic cosmopolitans. . . . (10:28–29)

The last point is of particular importance, since it shows Belinskij defending a Hegelian position against Majkov's more "progressive" view which was advo-

---

63. Belinskij's brilliant Hegelian interpretation of *The Inspector-General* is found in his essay "Woe from Wit" (1840, 3:420–86). An echo of this interpretation can be seen in his "Survey of Russian Literature in 1847" (10:294). For Hegelian passages to this effect, see Hegel's *Ästhetik*, 1:191; 2:552, 571–72.

64. V. Majkov, "Stixotvorenija Kol'cova," *Otečestvennye zapiski* 49, nos. 11–12 (1846): 43.

cated by some Left-Hegelians in Germany and by some utopian socialists in France.

An important coincidence between Hegel and Belinskij is their identical use of the term "pathos." Hegel defines "pathos" as "the substantial content of a situation and the rich, powerful individual quality in which the substantial movements of the Spirit are brought to life, achieving reality and expression" (Hegel, Ästhetik, 1:273). This perfectly describes Belinskij's usage of the term.[65]

Belinskij certainly takes notice of Hegel's dialectic method, accepts it as a guiding principle of his own thought, and apparently seeks to put it to use. Not infrequently the adjective "dialectic" is applied to the critic's own method as well as to the attitude underlying it.[66] Evidently Belinskij found in Hegel's dialectic model of a world in constant, creative flux a conception which appealed to his own temperament. Crude, mechanistic positivism and subjective idealism were both uncongenial to him:

> Failing to see that nothing but that very same free necessity of a dialectically evolving idea, which is the content of history and of philosophy, is also the content of Art, the empiricists reduce the creations of art to mere objects, designed to relieve boredom in an agreeable fashion and to entertain indolent inactivity—meaning that these creations are of the same order as elegant furniture or that pretty bric-a-brac with which fashion decorates our fireplaces, tables, and bookstands. The idealists [Belinskij means "subjective idealists," as the context shows] arrive at a similarly extreme position, only from the opposite direction. According to their teaching, life and art must each go their own separate ways, without interfering with one another, without depending on one another, nor having any influence on one another. Giving a literal interpretation to their premise that art is an end in itself, they arrive at a position where art is not only without any purpose but also without any meaning. ("The Works of Deržavin," 1843, 6:587)

Such sharp rejection—and in one breath, too—of both a positivist and a subjective idealist ("formalist") aesthetics is, on the one hand, most Hegelian.

65. For another definition of "pathos" by Hegel, see Ästhetik, 1:229. Vischer's usage of the term also coincides with Belinskij's; see Vischer, Aesthetik, 1:316-17.

66. For example, in the essay on the idea of art (1841), we are told that "thought consists of a dialectic movement, or of the development of thought from itself" (4:587), that this process is made possible by the existence of two aspects of the Spirit, the subjective and the objective, and that history is the dialectic evolution of their synthesis, the Absolute Spirit (4:587-88). In his essay "The General Idea of Folk Poetry" (1841), Belinskij once again describes the dialectic process, this time as an introduction to his proposition according to which romanticism and classicism, as well as nationality and universality (narodnost' and obščnost'), are thesis and antithesis of one and the same idea (5:293-94). Cf. 5:80, 549; 6:22, 137, 275, 457-59, 488, 582-88, 602; 10:195.

On the other hand, it points toward Grigor'ev, Dostoevskij, and Marxist aesthetics.

All in all, Belinskij's aesthetics is, like Hegel's, what the Germans call a *Gehaltsästhetik*, one focused in the content rather than in the form of art. And, like Hegel's, it is rather excessively "organic," emphasizing the inner unity of the work of art, its deep roots in the life of its age, and its strong and inevitable connections with the course of history—all of this at the expense of the individual and accidental, or even playful, aspects of art. We are dealing with a characteristically Hegelian attitude when Belinskij insists on seeing Gogol' as "a result of the whole past development of Russian literature, and an answer to the contemporary demands of Russian society" ("A Rejoinder to *The Muscovite*," 1847, 10:243), and chooses to ignore the fact, strongly suggested by his opponents, that Gogol', even by virtue of his Ukrainian background, was a highly irregular and unique phenomenon in Russian literature. As Ambrogio has pointed out, Belinskij, whose aesthetics is "romantic" in many points, never had much use for the three notions, characteristic of romantic aesthetics: art as play, art as irony, and art as revelation.[67] And neither did Hegel.

Hegel's disciple Vischer, who had moved away from his master's *Gehaltsästhetik* toward a Kantian *Formästhetik*, felt that Hegel had overemphasized content (*Gehalt*) so much that the spheres of art and religion would tend to overlap.[68] Simultaneously, Vischer defends Hegel against the much more energetic criticism of Wilhelm Theodor Danzel, who had charged that Hegel had seen art "merely as a specific form of the expression and representation of the True, as an incidental surrogate of thought."[69] Those traits which distinguish art from the pursuit of truth, Danzel had asserted, played a secondary role in Hegel's aesthetics, so that art turned out to be nothing but diffuse, second-rate thought and "Hegel's whole aesthetics nothing but a refined version of Baumgarten."[70] (Alexander Baumgarten was the rationalist founder of aesthetics as an independent discipline which he defined as *scientia cognitionis sensitivae* or *gnoseologia inferior*.)

Belinskij's eventual disaffection toward Hegel was caused by different considerations which had, however, the same roots: Hegel's excessively abstract rationalism. To Belinskij's pragmatic thinking, Hegel showed insufficient concern for the concrete social and political detail. To Vischer and Danzel, the philosopher had paid insufficient attention to the concrete detail of artistic form and individual imagination. To put it schematically, Vischer and Danzel presented a shift from objective idealism toward subjective idealism, while

67. Ambrogio, *Belinskij*, pp. 54–56.
68. Vischer, *Aesthetik*, 1:50.
69. W. T. Danzel, *Ueber die Aesthetik der Hegelschen Philosophie* (Hamburg, 1844), quoted in Vischer, *Aesthetik*, 1:60.
70. Ibid.

Belinskij stood for a shift from objective idealism toward objective materialism.

LEFT-HEGELIANS AND UTOPIAN SOCIALISTS

During the last six or seven years of his life Belinskij was experiencing the growing influence of two ideological trends which, to a not inconsiderable extent, ran contrary to his earlier philosophy: German Left-Hegelianism and French utopian socialism. Owing to censorship conditions, representatives of neither group, except "fellow travelers" such as Eugène Sue and George Sand, are ever mentioned in those of Belinskij's writings which were meant for publication. But Belinskij's correspondence suggests that he was avidly assimilating their ideas.

Regarding the Left-Hegelians, the following passage in a minor review written late in 1844[71] shows Belinskij's attitude toward this group, even though it does so largely by omission:

> Hegelianism has now split into three factions: the Right, which has come to a standstill at Hegel's last word and refuses to go on; the Left, which has departed from Hegel and makes its progress through a dynamic synthesis (*v živom primirenii*) of philosophy and life, of theory and practice; and the Center, presenting something in between the dead stagnation of the Right and the driving forward movement of the Left. If we said that the Hegelian Left has departed from the position of its teacher, this does not mean that it has rejected his great merits in the sphere of philosophy or declared his teaching an empty or sterile phenomenon. No, it merely means that it wants to go on, and, its respect for the great philosopher notwithstanding, place the authority of the human spirit above that of the spirit of Hegel's authority. (8:502)

Obviously, Belinskij has understood that the future of Hegelianism could only lie with the pragmatic sociopolitical application of its revolutionary principles: the conception of practical activity as the essence of the Spirit, the denial of any transcendence (Hegel's Absolute Spirit, that is, God in no way transcends Man, but is immanent in him, Man being himself "spirit"), its evolutionary teleology which made change an immanent condition of being, its historical determinism, and, last but not least, its belief that negation is a necessary aspect of progress.

We know from Belinskij's correspondence that he was familiar with some of the writings of the Hegelian Left. Several of his friends, notably A. I. Herzen,

---

71. The subject of the review is *Rukovodstvo k poznaniju teoretičeskoj material'noj filosofii,* by Aleksandr Petrovič Tatarinov (St. Petersburg, 1844). For another, similar statement, see Belinskij's review of *Istorija Malorossii* by Nikolaj Markevič (1843), 7:49–50.

P. V. Annenkov, V. P. Botkin, and M. A. Bakunin, had some close connections with the Hegelian Left and kept the critic informed, orally as well as by translating important articles and passages for him. Belinskij must have known Feuerbach's *Das Wesen des Christentums* (1841) as early as 1842, because Botkin, in a letter of 23 March 1842, takes for granted that his friend is familiar with that work.[72] However, it appears that Feuerbach's sensualist aesthetics had little or no influence on Belinskij. It went on to have a strong impact on Černyševskij. But then, the materialization (or "socialization") of the ideal component of art in the later Belinskij may well be due, at least in part, to Feuerbach's influence. In his last major article, "A Survey of Russian Literature in 1847," Belinskij writes this about Gogol':

> To these works a different definition of Art applies—that of "a representation of reality in its whole truth." Here, the matter rests entirely with *types*, and the *ideal* is understood not as an embellishment (and consequently, a lie) but as the relationships into which the author has placed the types created by him, according to the idea which he is endeavoring to develop in his work. (10:294–95)

As Lebedev-Poljanskij has pointed out,[73] this somewhat obscure passage (the Russian original sounds just as awkward as my translation) seems to suggest that Belinskij has replaced abstract "ideals" with concrete social relationships.

It would seem that a more tangible positivist influence on Belinskij's aesthetic views came from French utopian socialists, whose works the critic could read in the original.[74] We know from Herzen's reminiscences that Saint-Simonism was known to students of Moscow University in the 1830s. In a letter to Botkin, 27–28 June 1841, Belinskij exclaims (after having reported that he has just read Plutarch's *Lives*):

> Men must be brothers, and they must not offend one another, not even with a shadow of any kind of external or formal superiority. What about these two nations of antiquity that were born with this idea! What about the French who, without any German philosophy, have understood what German philosophy does not understand to this day! The devil knows, I ought to get acquainted with the Saint-Simonists. I see women with their eyes. Woman is a victim, a slave of modern society. (12:53)

72. Botkin's essay "German Literature," *National Annals* 1841, fasc. 1, reports on the Young-Hegelian movement with obvious sympathy (pp. 1–4). Cf. Pypin, *Belinskij,* p. 418; Lebedev-Poljanskij, *Belinskij,* pp. 77–78.

73. Lebedev-Poljanskij, *Belinskij,* p. 75.

74. For an analysis of the influence of French utopian socialism on Belinskij, see Harry B. Weber, "Belinskij and the Aesthetics of Utopian Socialism," *Slavic and East European Journal* 15 (1971): 293–304. My own remarks follow Weber's to some extent. Cf. also the chapter "Belinskij i utopičeskij socializm" in Nečaeva, *Belinskij,* 4:35–67, and V. Komarovič, "Idei francuzskix social'nyx utopij i mirovozzrenie Belinskogo," in *Venok Belinskomu,* ed. N. K. Piksanov (Moscow, 1924), pp. 243–72.

Belinskij's subsequent correspondence, as well as reports of his contemporaries, Dostoevskij among others,[75] suggests that he realized his intention and learned a great deal about French utopian socialism.[76] Nor was it very difficult, in the Petersburg of the 1840s, to become conversant with its ideas. *La Revue indépendante* (started by Leroux in 1841) and other publications of the utopian socialists were avidly read and discussed at the house of I. I. Panaev (1812-1862), a good friend of Belinskij's, and Panaev's articles in the *National Annals* (*Otečestvennye zapiski*) were in part inspired by utopian socialist ideas. We learn from Belinskij's correspondence that, after a period of great enthusiasm for utopian socialism, he grew rather cool toward it during the last two or three years of his life.[77]

The aesthetic thought of French utopian socialism presents anything but a homogeneous picture. There is a great deal of disagreement among those of its exponents who wrote on art and literature, and each of them, in turn, tends to be unsystematic, eclectic, and easily swayed by the influences of the moment.

It would seem that Pierre Leroux's was the single most important utopian socialist influence on Belinskij. As Evans has demonstrated in a monograph on Leroux,[78] Leroux's symbolist aesthetics (he is credited with having coined the term *symbolisme* and to have anticipated Baudelaire's famous *Correspondances*), as developed in his essays "Du style symbolique" (1829) and "De la poésie de notre époque" (1831), as well as elsewhere, was inspired by German sources. These were, specifically, an item entitled "Pensées de Jean-Paul" in *Le Globe*, 29 March 1829, and a French translation (1825), entitled *Religions de l'Antiquité*, of Georg Friedrich Creuzer's *Symbolik und Mythologie der alten Völker* (Leipzig, 1810-12). Creuzer was a follower of Schelling's, and so Leroux's symbolist aesthetics bears the traits of the German philosopher's *Identitätslehre*.

A comparison of Belinskij's writings with Leroux's shows that the Russian critic was vastly more familiar with German philosophy and its issues than Leroux. Thus, in the early forties Leroux sided with Schelling against the growing influence of Hegel's philosophy, believing Hegel to be reactionary and Schelling progressive.[79] Belinskij knew better, of course, as his acid comments on the stand taken by Leroux show (letter to Botkin, 17 February 1847,

---

75. For Dostoevskij's reminiscences, see *A Writer's Diary*, 1877, January, chap. 2, sec. 3. Also, Dostoevskij's letter to N. N. Straxov, 18–30 May 1871. And Dostoevskij's notebooks: *Zapisnye tetradi F. M. Dostoevskogo*, ed. E. N. Konšina (Moscow and Leningrad, 1935), pp. 116–117, 154; and *Literaturnoe nasledstvo* 77: 69.

76. See Belinskij's references to Pierre Leroux in his correspondence with Botkin (12:100, 330, 332).

77. See, e.g., letter to V. P. Botkin, 17 February 1847, 12:329–32.

78. David Owen Evans, *Le Socialisme romantique: Pierre Leroux et ses contemporains* (Paris, 1948), pp. 133–34, 147–54.

79. Ibid., pp. 72–73.

12:330). Nevertheless, the general outlines of Leroux's aesthetics resemble
those of Belinskij's. Like Belinskij, Leroux believed that all great art is inspired
by and addressed to Life. But unlike most of the French socialists of his time
he was not a partisan of *l'utilité directe de l'art*. His aesthetics, like Belinskij's,
is "organic" in principle. The vitalist phraseology found in Leroux also appears
in German objective idealism, and Belinskij uses it, somewhat more in the 1830s
than in the 1840s. There are also some important differences between Leroux
and Belinskij. For instance, Leroux's cosmopolitanism makes him seek out,
for approval, the supranational quality of great poetry, with Goethe a case in
point.[80] Belinskij, on the other hand, always believed in the national quality of
great art.

Saint-Simon's conception of history as humanity's advance toward perfection
through a succession of alternate *époques organiques* and *époques critiques*,
echoed in the aesthetic writings of his followers Barrault and Buchez, resembles
the Hegelian model of history. One might find a reflection of Saint-Simon's
dichotomy in statements of the later Belinskij, such as the following:

> We have tended to believe that poets make their appearance during periods
> of a strong inner development in a nation's life, that is, in effect during its
> happiest epochs, and that we Russians are living precisely in such an epoch,
> this being the reason why we have had, in the course of such a brief time, so
> many outstanding poets. We have also tended to think that poets could not
> be external, accidental phenomena with regard to the life of a nation, being
> necessary manifestations of its inner development. . . . (review of *The Mos-
> cow Literary and Learned Almanac for 1847* [*Moskovskij literaturnyj i
> učenyj sbornik na 1847 god*], 1847, 10:194)

Belinskij's diction here is ironic: of course these are still his most cherished
beliefs. One can gather from this passage that Belinskij identifies his own age
as an "organic" period, apparently its very beginning. The author of the essay
under review had expressed the strange thought that Russia had no need for
poets at the present time precisely because she was experiencing a "happy"
period of her history.

However, the same notion occurs even in the writings of the early Belinskij,
before he seems to have become familiar with French utopian socialism. In a
review of Baratynskij's poetry (1835), Belinskij writes: "In literature every nation has its epochs of enchantment and disenchantment. At first there reigns
uncritical admiration: everything seems beautiful, great, immortal. . . . Then,
there follows an epoch of disenchantment, bringing about a spirit of reaction,
criticism, and analysis" (1:323). Here Belinskij's language is reminiscent
of Goethe's famous passage on alternating periods of "faith" and "loss of

80. Ibid., p. 156.

faith" (*Glauben* and *Unglauben*) in one of the notes to his *West-Oestlicher Divan*.[81]

Like Hegel, the French utopian socialists saw a link between the historical progress of society and that of the arts and literature. Like Hegel, too, they tended to view their own age as one during which poetry and the arts—at least in the form mankind had known them for millennia—were destined to disappear, or to undergo a radical transformation.

When it came to understanding and appreciating the Russian literature of the past or to formulating aesthetic judgments concerning more recent works, Belinskij was at least the equal, in philosophical preparation, literary erudition, and critical talent, of any of the "progressive" French critics, including even the great Sainte-Beuve. What Belinskij could and did learn from the progressive French critics of the 1830s and 1840s was to see literature as a means of creating and organizing a society, and of giving it a certain direction. In the last years of his life Belinskij was convinced that the main object of literature was, certainly in his day and age, to create a powerful social consciousness—"progressive," of course.

As late as 23 August 1840, Belinskij had complained, in a letter to K. S. Aksakov, that Russia was still a nation without a society, a nation with "no political, no religious, no learned, no literary life" (11:546). Yet in the same breath he had suggested that Russia was "a country where ample elements for [the creation of a social] life exist, but which is at present like an infant swaddled in an iron vise and suffering from rickets" (ibid.). But then in his review of Nikitenko's "Discourse on Criticism" (1842) Belinskij sketches the history of Russian poetry as "the history of its endeavors, beginning with Kantemir and Lomonosov, to become natural and original, instead of artificial and imitative, of its striving to overcome its own bookishness and to become instead a living and a social entity, of its tendency to get nearer to life and to society" (6:295). A year later, in his Second essay on Puškin, Belinskij declares that it is the critic's job "by way of analysis, to transform public opinion into a conscious awareness, and to demonstrate the import, the meaning of a talent or a genius, to determine that vital [read "socially progressive"] element which constitutes the exclusive quality of his works and with which he has enriched the literature of his country and the life of its society" (7:143).

The later Belinskij defines the function of contemporary literature more and more as one of pointing society toward social progress, specifically toward improving the lot of the underprivileged. It is here that the influence of French socialism is most strongly in evidence. When Belinskij reviews the Russian

81. See Hill Shine, *Carlyle and the Saint-Simonians: The Concept of Historical Periodicity* (New York, 1971), pp. 23–24 and *passim*.

translation of Eugène Sue's novel *Les Mystères de Paris* in 1844, he distinctly recognizes the aesthetic weaknesses of this *roman-feuilleton,* but wholeheartedly agrees with the author's "sincere and noble" intent: "to present to a depraved, selfish society, whose only god is the Golden Calf, the spectacle of the sufferings of those unfortunate ones who are condemned to ignorance and poverty, to vice and crime" (8:170). This is the language of the Fourierist journals, which had greeted Sue's mediocre (at best) novel with vociferous enthusiasm.

From this time on, Belinskij consistently defends the interest of the Russian Natural School in "the insulted and the injured" on social and moral grounds, countering the opposition's contention that such interest had nothing to do with humanitarianism, but was no more than a literary fad, born of idle curiosity, which the exotic and lurid qualities of life in the slums of the big city were apt to arouse. His tone and his arguments are entirely those of the French socialists.

Saint-Simonian thought recognized three basic forms of *l'art social:* pure propaganda (of the Saint-Simonian or Fourierist doctrines); Art as a part of the vanguard of political and scientific progress, with the artist's imagination in an exploratory and pathfinding role; and, third, Art in its revelatory and inspirational role as a replacement of some of the functions of the old religion. The question which of these three roles Art ought to fulfill primarily was the subject of heated debates among the French utopian socialists. Saint-Simon apparently leaned toward a utilitarian view of art. But his disciple Barrault had an extremely high opinion of the artist as a prophet and leader of society. Buchez recognized the cognitive as well as the prophetic role of art.[82] And, of the many poetic effusions of the Saint-Simonians and Fourierists at least some deserve to be called "hymns" of the new cosmic religion, for example, Leconte de Lisle's "Ode à Fourier" (1846).

By and large, the French utopian socialists seem to have held the position that literature ought to be socially involved (*socialisante*) but not frankly utilitarian, and that it ought to fulfill its historic mission freely. This position is admirably stated in Leroux's article "De la poésie de notre époque":

> And therefore I shall say to the artist: you are free: express the life that is within you, realize it poetically; yet I shall add: if instead of being inspired by your own epoch, you make yourself the representative of another age, allow me to place your works among the products of the earlier epoch to which you address yourself. Or if you forget that Art is Life, and produce art solely for the sake of so doing, allow me to refuse to see in you the prophet, the *vates* whom mankind has always sought in its poets.[83]

82. See Hunt, *Le Socialisme et le romantisme,* p. 34 (Barrault), p. 85 (Buchez).
83. Quoted by Hunt, ibid., p. 95.

These words could have come from Belinskij—certainly after 1842 when he first became directly acquainted with utopian socialist thought. In fact, one seems to recognize the very tone of Leroux's rhetoric in many of Belinskij's later articles. Belinskij, too, displays the same, rather facile confidence that the free artist will, "by expressing the life in himself," become a vehicle and a prophet of progress, and the same tendency to make light of the contingency that some artists just might happen to be reactionaries.

Leroux's statement is remarkable for the "organic" view which it takes of the artist and his work. And this, precisely, is also true of the later Belinskij. Mordovčenko puts it very well when he says, after having correctly pointed out that in 1847–48 Belinskij was very much in favor of a conscious, ideological tendency in literature:

Yet at the same time Belinskij warned against pressuring a writer into taking a certain "direction," against embracing a social tendency artificially rather than organically. For Belinskij, the struggle for a progressive world view, for the presence in literature of conscious thought was simultaneously a struggle for true freedom of artistic creativity. This is why Belinskij stood up against didactic art, cold and lifeless, just as he stood up against "pure" art.[84]

It seems almost as if Mordovčenko, a fine scholar of considerable learning and understanding, were looking toward Belinskij for aid and comfort from the vicissitudes of his own age (his book on Belinskij appeared during the darkest period of Stalinist control over literature and scholarship) and for an indirect affirmation of the freedom of the creative individual.

It must be stressed, then, that Belinskij never embraced the uncompromising utilitarianism which we find in Černyševskij and in some of the articles in the Fourierist journals of the 1840s. And it must be understood that the thinking of the French utopian socialists was also commonly "organic," often in an entirely idealistic and even mystical sense. A definition such as "l'art, c'est la réalité reproduite au point de vue du beau, mise en présence de l'ideal,"[85] quite typical as it is of French utopian socialist thought, is one to which not only Belinskij could have freely subscribed but also Vischer or Rötscher.

The later Belinskij shares many of the more specific preferences, sympathies, and antipathies of the French utopian socialists: their disapproval of any return to the classical or medieval past (note, however, that even Herder warned against the use of subjects and settings remote from the poet's own life); their emphasis on contemporary life and its problems; their downgrading of the individual hero in favor of social tendencies; their admiration for Shakespeare and their

84. N. Mordovčenko, *Belinskij and the Russian Literature of His Age (Belinskij i russkaja literatura ego vremeni)* (Moscow and Leningrad, 1950), pp. 275–76.
85. *La Démocratie pacifique,* 13 February 1847, quoted by Hunt, *Le Socialisme et le romantisme,* p. 137.

total rejection of classicism (if a choice had to be made, both Belinskij and the French utopian socialists would choose romanticism over classicism); their preference for Schiller, the tribune of humanity, over the pantheist Goethe, indifferent to the affairs of his time.[86]

Utopian socialism may well have had something to do with Belinskij abandoning some of the most cherished beliefs of his earlier days. For a long time, Belinskij was an uncompromising opponent of moralism in art but was later inclined to make some concessions to it. For example, in "Thoughts and Notes on Russian Literature" (1846), Belinskij suggests that "it would be ridiculous to expect that a satire, a comedy, a short story, or a novel might reform a depraved man" (9:434–35). But in the same breath he proposes that while a satire will not reform a corrupt official, it may well leave an indelible impression on his son. "And so," the critic exclaims, "literature acts not only educationally but actually effects an improval in public morality" (9:435). A strong moralist strain is characteristic of French utopian socialist criticism. Proof that the statement just quoted was in a serious vein (knowing the earlier Belinskij, one is tempted to assume that it was made tongue-in-cheek) is contained in Belinskij's letter to Botkin, 2–6 December 1847:

> You, Vasen'ka, are a sybarite, you have a sweet tooth. You say, "give me poetry and artistic quality," and then you'll taste it and smack your lips. Whereas I need no more of that artistic quality than is enough to make the story ring true, that is, that it won't fall into allegory or smack of dissertation. What I care about is the business part of it. First and foremost, it should raise questions and have a moral effect on society. (12:445)

Heavily as Belinskij leans toward the "business part" (ideological "content" as against artistic "form") of literature, he still refuses to give up his organicist position: the story must "ring true," and allegoric or schematic representation is still unacceptable.

Belinskij's frequent excuse for tolerating a certain amount of utilitarianism in contemporary literature is that "this is the order of the day," the implication being that there are periods in the history of a nation when aesthetic values have to be sacrificed to overriding social concerns. This notion, widely current in Russia in the middle of the nineteenth century (even the aesthete Turgenev assented to it), conforms with the thinking of the French utopian socialists.

86. Hunt, p. 89.

4

Art and Objective Reality

THE EVOLUTION OF BELINSKIJ'S AESTHETICS

Belinskij's world view always remained "organic." To the end of his life, he never doubted the unity and interrelatedness of all that is: one universe, one life, one mankind, one historic process. His "Survey of Russian Literature in 1847" contains an example: "Certainly life is divided and subdivided into a multitude of aspects, each of which possesses a certain independence; however, these various aspects are fused with one another in a living pattern (*živym obrazom*), and there is no clear demarcation line separating them. No matter how hard you try to split up life, it will still remain an integral whole" (10:304–5).

As a corollary of this view, Belinskij—along with German objective idealism, and romantics everywhere—saw all art as one. He and most of his epigoni liked to refer to works of literature as "works of art," and to writers as "artists." There was a strong presumption shared by virtually everybody with this trend of thought—and Belinskij was no exception—that a critic who had proven himself as a connoisseur of one branch of art, usually poetry, was therefore entitled to an authoritative opinion in matters relating to other art forms, painting, for example, and other branches of literature such as the drama. At any rate, Belinskij was always a strong defender of the essential unity of all art forms: "To define poetry means to define art in general, that is, it means just as much as to define architecture, sculpture, painting, music, as well as poetry, because the last mentioned is distinguished from the aforementioned not by its substance, but by its means of expression" (review of *Opyt istorii russkoj literatury* by A. Nikitenko, 1845, 9:158).

It has been pointed out that Belinskij's entire career represents a search for a definition of "reality" (*dejstvitel'nost'*). That art was to represent the reality of life Belinskij never doubted for a moment:

When poetry is the living word of reality it is a great thing here on Earth; but when it strains to bring into existence that which is nonexistent, or to make possible the impossible, when it glorifies the trivial and praises the false, then it is no more than a game for children who like their hobby horse better than a real horse. . . . Nor is he a poet who is deprived of all tact of reality, of all instinct of truth; not a poet is he, but a juggler who can dance blindfolded between eggs without breaking them. ("1844," 8:469)

Belinskij always took for granted that art and literature were serious things, as serious as anything in life. He scornfully rejected any suggestion that the purpose of art might be to entertain, to amuse, to help to forget "real life." He would associate this approach to art with the frivolous and immoral eighteenth century: it was simply passé, not worthy of a refutation. Belinskij refused to concern himself with a writer like Alexandre Dumas (*père*), in spite of his wide popularity in Russia. The point is that such refusal stemmed not from Dumas's inferior craftsmanship (alleged or real) but from the absence in his works of any connection with "reality."[1] Belinskij was willing to discuss at length works which, from a literary and artistic viewpoint, were inferior to Dumas's but were in some way concerned with "real life."[2] The novels of Eugène Sue were examples. This particular position of Belinskij's has been held by most Russian literary critics ever since. It was seriously challenged only by the Formalists of the 1920s.

Belinskij's reasoning as he rejects Gogol''s *Selected Passages from a Correspondence with Friends* (1847) is characteristic. In that book Gogol' had said many things that Belinskij believed to be false and insincere. Also, the book apparently was not a literary masterpiece. From these two premises, Belinskij jumps to the conclusion that "nothing that is false, affected, unnatural can ever be masked; rather, it is always mercilessly cut down (*kaznitsja*) by its own banality (*pošlost'*)" (10:60). In other words, Belinskij is convinced that by virtue of having departed from the truth of life, Gogol' had *eo ipso* ceased being an artist.

Belinskij's attitude toward the autonomy of art (he actually uses this term: *avtonomija iskusstva*, 4:482) is not as ambivalent as it might appear from a casual juxtaposition of his many seemingly conflicting statements on this matter. Belinskij's basic position, never abandoned, is that art, while an autonomous and *sui generis* function of the human spirit, and an end in itself, is organically linked with moral, intellectual, social and national life. Any attempt to set it apart from the other areas of human life is either illusory or sterile. By the same token, any tampering with the autonomy of art, any attempt, no matter how well-intentioned, to give art a "direction" from without is bound to fail.[3]

Belinskij rejects as equally "bad extremes" (*durnaja krajnost'*) both "didactic, doctrinaire, cold, arid, dead art, the products of which are nothing but rhetorical exercises on given themes" ("1847," 10:303) and "pure art," which

1. See "1847," 10:297–98. Cf. 10:114 on Dumas in particular.
2. Belinskij says so explicitly, too. See, e.g., 9:397.
3. See 1:222; 3:397; 4:482, 496; 5:221; 6:582; 7:330; 10:93, 235, 257, 303–4.

he sees as a kind of "intellectual China, with sharply defined boundaries separating it from everything that is not art in the strictest sense of that word" (ibid., 10:318). Often Belinskij expresses the opinion that pure art has in fact never existed, though "the ancient Greeks approached it" (10:92–93): in actuality, true art is and always has been organically embedded in life. Belinskij supports this thesis by pointing out the religious connections of ancient Greek and of Renaissance art, the civic, historical, psychological, and philosophical message in Shakespeare's plays, the *Zeitgeist* and German national spirit in *Faust*.[4]

In the heat of polemic, Belinskij may sometimes overstate either side of his position. In challenging Menzel's social and national utilitarianism (in "Menzel, a Critic of Goethe," 1840), Belinskij will sound like a proponent of "pure art." In combatting the Kantian tendencies of Nikitenko in his discussion of Nikitenko's "Discourse on Criticism" (1842), he will say that "our age is decidedly opposed to art for its own sake, or to beauty for the sake of beauty: art without a rational content which has a historical meaning as an expression of the *Zeitgeist* can satisfy only inveterate lovers of art after the old fashion" (6:277). There are enough passages where Belinskij sounds like a utilitarian critic. But, on balance, the following statement from "A Survey of Russian Literature in 1847" seems to describe Belinskij's position best:

> Without a doubt art must be, first and foremost, art—and then only can it be an expression of the spirit and of the direction of social life during a given epoch. No matter how excellent the thoughts which might fill a poem, no matter how strongly they might respond to topical questions, if there is no poetry in it—why, there won't be any excellent thought, nor will there be any questions, and all that one will be able to find in it will be a good intention, poorly executed. (10:303)

The really crucial notion about this position is not made explicit, but is implied: Belinskij is confident that genuine art will indeed "be an expression of the spirit and of the direction of social life during a given epoch." This is, of course, the pivotal position of Hegelian objective-idealist (as opposed to Kantian subjective-idealist) aesthetics. A natural corollary of it is Belinskij's (and Hegel's) lack of sympathy and understanding for the fantastic in art and poetry and for stylized art.

At the root of Belinskij's conception of the analogy between art and reality lies the assumption, usually tacit, but sometimes explicit, of a cognitive capacity inherent in artistic creation. Needless to say, this is one of the principal traits that links Belinskij with the Neoplatonic "organic" tradition. Lavreckij mentions that Belinskij's notion of art as a "special kind of cognition"

4. See 10:92–93, 307.

(*osobyj vid poznanija*) is taken from Hegel but fails to point out its broader Neoplatonic background.[5]

In discussing Gogol' 's "Diary of a Madman," Belinskij asserts that this work contains not only a wealth of poetry but also "a wealth (*bezdna*) of philosophy," and that "this case history of mental illness, presented in poetic form, is amazing in its truth and profundity" ("On the Russian Short Story and the Short Stories of Mr. Gogol' " ["O russkoj povesti i povestjax g. Gogolja"], 1835, 1:297). Modern psychiatrists have tended to see little, if any, psychiatric verity about Gogol' 's tale.[6]

We see here that Belinskij takes for granted that artistic intuition is "a sudden breakthrough to the truth," as he himself puts it.[7] Statements that reflect this view can be found throughout Belinskij's writings.

In an early polemic with the scholarly S. P. Ševyrev ("On the Criticism and Literary Opinions of *The Moscow Observer,*" 1836), Belinskij claims that "inspiration does not need learning (*nauka*), for it knows more than learning does, and is never wrong" (2:139).

A few years later, when Belinskij has mastered Hegel's historical approach, the cognitive function of art is properly historicized:

> The truth was revealed to mankind first of all in *Art,* which is *truth made sensible* (*istina v sozercanii*), that is, truth expressed not in an abstract idea but in an image (*obraz*), and moreover, in an image which is not a conventional symbol (as was the case in the East),[8] but an *idea-turned-flesh,* a full, organic, and immediate manifestation [of the idea] in the beauty of its form, with which it is fused as inseparably as the soul is with the body. ("Woe from Wit," 1840, 3:423)

Art (specifically poetry) and learning (*nauka*) were for Belinskij always two different approaches to the same goal: the truth of objective reality. Time and again, art and learning are mentioned in one breath:

> Poetry and learning are identical, if we are to understand by "learning" not mere schemes of knowledge but an understanding of the ideas implicit in it.

5. Lavreckij, *Èstetika Belinskogo,* p. 12.

6. See N. E. Osipov, *"Dvojnik, Peterburgskaja poèma* F. M. Dostoevskogo," *O Dostoevskom,* ed. A. L. Bem, 3 vols. (Prague, 1929), 1:47.

7. "Like every artist, an actor creates under the influence of inspiration (*po vdoxnoveniju*), and inspiration is a sudden breakthrough to the truth (*vnezapnoe proniknovenie v istinu*)" (essay on *Hamlet,* 1838, 2:307).

8. This follows Hegel's conception of the "symbolic art form," in which "spirit" and "form" remain separate. Symbolic art, according to Hegel, at best only divines their ultimate identity. At worst, it degenerates into arbitrary ornamental art. See Hegel, *Ästhetik,* 1:419. Except in his early, Schellingian articles, Belinskij uses *simvol* either with reference to primitive, preclassical art, or, when referring to modern poetry, as a synonym of "allegory."

Poetry and learning are identical, being grasped not by any particular faculty of our psyche but by the whole plenitude of our spiritual being, which is expressed in the word "reason" (*razum*). In this respect, they are divided by a sharp line from the so-called exact sciences, which require merely intelligence (*rassudok*), and perhaps some imagination. ("The Poetry of M. Lermontov," 4:480)[9]

Like the German idealists, Belinskij consistently draws a line between *rassudok*, by which he means a narrow "rational faculty," and *razum*, the integral whole of man's spiritual powers. Poetic intuition, while only one aspect of *razum*, is often rated higher than *rassudok*, especially by the early Belinskij.[10]

Belinskij goes as far as to suggest that poetic intuition can discover important truths just as the scientist Cuvier, "who, from a single bone dug up from the ground, would correctly establish the genus, species, size, and shape of an animal" ("*Roman Elegies* by Goethe," 1841, 5:234–35).

Belinskij often repeated verbatim, as well as less directly, his definition of art as "the *immediate* contemplation of truth, or thinking in images," with which he introduced his essay on the idea of art (1841). There is no doubt that he stood by it until the end of his life. That poetry was "thinking in images" was a notion first developed by A. W. Schlegel and very popular in Germany subsequently.[11] The general conception is found as early as Vico and is ultimately Neoplatonic. Guljaev's contention that "Belinskij was the first in world aesthetics to put, and give a solid foundation to, the question of a firm connection between learning and art" is quite unfounded.[12] Both Schelling and Hegel had asked the question and had answered it in the way Belinskij did, following their lead. In discussing the difference between art and science, Schelling observed that a scientific problem could be solved both mechanically, with the aid of the intellect alone, and intuitively (*genialisch*), whereas art worked by intuition alone.[13] Hegel, on his part, said that art "becomes true art and achieves its highest goal only when it joins religion and philosophy, representing yet another way by which the Divine, the most profound interests of Man, and the most far-reaching truths of the Spirit enter human consciousness and are expressed."[14]

9. Cf. Belinskij's review of *An Outline of the History of Russian Literature* by A. Nikitenko (1845), where virtually the same assertion is made once more (9:157). The Russian word *nauka* covers "scholarship, learning, humanistic erudition" as well as "science." Similarly, German *Wissenschaft* (which is translated by *nauka*), while it also means "science," may also include "philosophic speculation," as it does in Hegel's usage.

10. See Rolf Lettmann, *Die Abstracta* um *und* razum *bei Belinskij: Semasiologische Untersuchungen* (Munich, 1971).

11. See Wellek, *Modern Criticism,* 2:42.

12. Guljaev, *Belinskij,* p. 98.

13. Schelling, *System des transzendentalen Idealismus,* in *Werke,* 2:623.

14. Hegel, *Ästhetik,* 1:19.

It follows from Belinskij's realization of the specificity of aesthetic cognition that "poetic truth" (Belinskij tends to say "artistic truth"—*xudožestvennaja pravda*) must not *formally* coincide with empirical truth as revealed by science, scholarship, and historiography. "Doesn't the esteemed author know that there are works of art which, while unnatural, unreal, and absurd in a factual sense, are poetically true nevertheless?" the critic demands as he discusses the work of a singularly obtuse scholar.[15]

Belinskij, like Hegel, refuses to follow Kant and many of Kant's followers who derive, from a belief in the *sui generis* character of the aesthetic process, a special realm or independent domain of "art for art's sake."[16] A truth derived by way of intuition is not, for Belinskij, of a different order than one arrived at through scientific investigation or logical deduction.

On the other hand, at least toward the end of his career Belinskij (unlike Hegel) tended to derive aesthetic merit directly from the alleged objective truthfulness and social relevance of a work of literature. He felt that Herzen's "correct" ideas helped that writer's work immeasurably even in an artistic sense (10:319–20). Belinskij seriously considered *Whose Fault?* a novel of great artistic merit, while conceding, in the same breath, that its author lacked true imagination.

The logical error in Belinskij's judgment becomes obvious when one compares it with the critic's comments on Gončarov's first novel, *The Same Old Story,* discussed in contrast to *Whose Fault?* Gončarov, according to Belinskij, has no "correct" ideas, but his native talent nonetheless leads him to correct conclusions. Works of art may (or perhaps always do) express the truth of life, but it does not follow that a work of literature which expresses the truth of life is *eo ipso* a work of art, or even that "correct" ideas have any bearing upon the artistic quality of a work of literature. The fact that the truth of life can be arrived at in several different ways accounts for this circumstance, and Belinskij shows that he is well aware of these routes. Belinskij's error was repeated by his followers over and over again. It crops up frequently in contemporary Socialist Realist criticism.

As pointed out earlier, Belinskij's conception of objective truth, with which "poetic truth" is inseparably linked, undergoes an evolution. "Reality" does not mean the same thing to Belinskij the Schellingian, the Hegelian, and the "revolutionary democrat."[17]

---

15. Review of *O xaraktere narodnyx pesen u slavjan zadunajskix* by Jurij Venelin (1836), 2:66–67. Cf. 3:9–10, 132; 6:591; 7:329; 10:343.

16. Cf. Ambrogio, *Belinskij,* pp. 287–88.

17. Here, Western scholars (e.g., Wellek, *Modern Criticism,* 3:247–48) are in agreement with Soviet scholarship (e.g., Gorodeckij et al., eds., *Istorija russkoj kritiki,* 1:375). Generally, three distinct periods are seen in Belinskij's search for true "reality." Berdjaev distinguishes: "(1) moral idealism, heroism; (2) Hegelian acceptance of the rationality of

To the early Belinskij truth is "essential truth," spiritual reality. It is that intensity of thought and emotion which one encounters in great art. At this stage there exists for Belinskij a hierarchy of reality in which the truly artistic representation of a character, or an event, or of a landscape expresses the essence of the subject more truthfully than nature itself can: "Reality is beautiful in itself, but it is beautiful in its essence, in its elements, in its content, but not in its form. In this respect, reality is pure gold, but as yet unpurified, in a pile of ore and dirt. Learning and art purify the gold of reality, smelting it into beautiful forms" ("The Poetry of M. Lermontov," 1841, 4:491).

Having produced some examples from history and literature, Belinskij concludes by claiming that in learning and in art, "reality is more like reality than in actual reality." A work of art created by a great poet's imagination is superior to any correct account of an actual event. Belinskij crowns his demonstration by stating flatly that a historical novel by Sir Walter Scott is a more reliable document concerning the spirit of a given epoch than any work of pragmatic historiography, and that a landscape created by a painter of talent is superior to the most picturesque sights of nature (4:491).[18]

That peculiar intensity and plenitude of life, that appearance of the life force raised, as it were, to a higher power, which one meets in great art, the earlier Belinskij likes to call "poetry." He finds poetry in nature, in history, in the individual human life, and, of course, in works of art. "Poetry," Belinskij exclaims in the essay just quoted, "is an expression of life, or even better, it is life itself; and even this is not enough: poetry contains more life [literally: in poetry, life is more life] (*žizn' bolee javljaetsja žizn'ju*) than reality itself" (4:489).[19] Still in the same essay, Belinskij goes on to produce the following archromantic definition of poetry (which, incidentally, greatly resembles Boris Pasternak's famous "Definition of Poetry" in *Life, My Sister*):

> Poetry, then, is life par excellence, is its very essence or, so to speak, the most rarefied ether, the triple extract, the quintessence of life. . . . Poetry is the innocent smile of an infant, its clear gaze, its bright laughter, its vivid joy. Poetry is the bashful blush on the cheeks of a beautiful maiden. . . . Poetry is the fiery gaze of a youth, seething with overflowing strength. . . . Poetry is the concentrated, self-controlled power of a man fully mature. . . . Poetry is the tranquil luster of an old man's colorless eyes. . . . Poetry is a

---

reality; (3) rebellion against reality toward its radical change in the name of man" Nikolaj Berdjaev, *Russkaja ideja: Osnovnye problemy russkoj mysli XIX veka i načala XX veka* (Paris, 1971), p. 60. In Belinskij's critical practice, there is some overlap of these three stages.

18. Cf. 2:132–33; 5:300; 7:54–55; 8:281. It is conceivable that Belinskij's strange overestimation of the poet's historical intuition was inspired by Rötscher. Vischer, *Aesthetik*, 2:364–65, criticizes Rötscher on that score.

19. Cf. Lavreckij, *Èstetika Belinskogo*, p. 47. Other examples: 1:258; 4:354, 493.

brilliant triumph of existence, it is that bliss of being alive which will, unexpectedly, visit us in rare moments; it is intoxication, trepidation, thrill, the tenderness of passion, the excitement and the storm of emotions, the plenitude of love . . . it is a thirst, perennial yet never satisfied, to embrace all and to be fused with all; it is that divine pathos which makes one's heart beat in unison with the cosmos . . . that divine pathos through which the terrestrial shines divine, the divine merges with the terrestrial, and all Nature appears in the brilliance of her wedding finery, an unriddled hieroglyph of the Spirit, now reconciled to her. . . . " (4:493–94)

This eloquent passage shows Belinskij far removed from a mimetic type of aesthetics. Art is here not derived from Nature, but is itself nature, nurtured by the same ideal life force. It is, in brief, not an *Abbild* but a *Gegenbild* of nature.[20] And so one is not surprised to hear, a little farther in the same essay, that "the poet does not imitate nature, but rivals it, and his works stem from the same source, are created by the same process as all phenomena of nature" (4:499). Nor does Belinskij conceal the Platonic origins of his thoughts. The hieroglyphic image, popular in romantic aesthetics, ultimately goes back to Plotinus.[21] Toward the end of the theoretical part of his essay, Belinskij quotes a long passage from Plato's *Phaedrus,* recently translated by Ševyrev. It is the passage (sec. 244) in which Socrates points out the sacred and God-given nature of holy (prophetic) madness, then goes on to identify the poetic gift as such madness. It appears that Belinskij was not aware of the direct historical connection between the ideas used by him in this context: Plato's *Phaedrus* is the basis of, and the occasion for, Plotinus's treatise on divine Beauty in *Enneads* 5. 8, the foundation of Neoplatonic aesthetics, of which Schelling, Belinskij's principal source in this instance, was a leading exponent.

It is also here that Belinskij comes closest to the Neoplatonic notion that the essence of all true art, inasmuch as art is a reflection of the Absolute, is eternally the same and is narrowly defined, even though it expresses itself in an endless variety of forms: Béranger, in so far as he is a true poet, is Shakespeare's equal (4:501–2). Belinskij's analyses of particular poems during this period of his career suggest that he had himself experienced the impact of the power of great poetry:

Read it [A. N. Majkov's poem "Kogda ložitsja ten' "], and you will understand for yourself, without any explanation, that poetry is an expression of the inexpressible, a revelation of the mysterious, a mute emotion, lost in its own vagueness, stated in clear and definitive (*opredelitel'nyj*) language! ("*Roman Elegies* by Goethe," 1841, 5:257)

20. Cf. Schelling, *Philosophie der Kunst,* 3:388–89. The distinction is all-important. Its corollary is, in objective idealism, that artistic intuition is a "shortcut" to objective truth. In subjective idealism it leads to "formalism," opening the way to nonrepresentational art.
    21. Plotinus, *Enneads,* 5. 8. 6.

Even in the early Belinskij these mystic moods are not the general rule. And even his mysticism tends to have an undertone of humanism rather than religion. Of the various mystiques toward which Belinskij leans, that of "human nature," or "the human spirit," is the most constant and the most prominent. Belinskij shares the idealistic and optimistic anthropology of the eighteenth-century *philosophes,* the French utopian socialists, and German idealism.

After Belinskij's conversion to Hegelianism, his conception of "reality" becomes more concrete. As early as in a letter to Bakunin, 12–25 October 1838, Belinskij says that he prefers a man who lives in reality, albeit with his emotions, to one who lives in an illusory world, even if it be with his thoughts, and that he likes best the man who lives in reality with his thoughts. His respective examples, aptly chosen, are Peter the Great, Fichte, and Hegel (11:315).[22] The reality that opens itself to the poet's intuition is now "historical reality," the particular reality of an epoch and of a people.

At this stage, Belinskij's concept of historical vision is beginning to be linked with a concern for "substantial" (*substancial'nyj*) and "rational" (*razumnyj*) reality. While to Belinskij the Schellingian reality has been a function of spiritual power, it is to Belinskij the Hegelian a function of reason—meaning, in historical and critical practice, life in the presence of those rational ideas which determine the fate of a nation and the course of history. A typically Hegelian definition of reality appears in Belinskij's essay on E. A. Baratynskij (1842):

> Reality?—But what is reality, if not the realization of the eternal laws of Reason? Any other reality is a temporary eclipse of the light of Reason, a pathological vital process. . . . One must know how to distinguish rational reality, which alone is real, from nonrational reality, which is illusory and transitory. Faith in the idea saves us, while faith in mere facts is our undoing." (6:477)[23]

In this sense, Russian literature before Puškin had not been the expression of any reality, Belinskij thought. Deržavin, whose gifts were quite extraordinary (Belinskij never tired of repeating that), could not become a poet of world-historical stature, because there did not exist, in his time, a Russian reality worthy of being expressed by a poet of genius. Only in the age of Puškin did Russia finally develop a historical reality, meaning a modicum of social organization and civilization based on certain more or less definite ideas. These Puškin expressed with an artistic perfection rarely met in world literature.

It is in this context that one can understand Belinskij's interpretation of Gogol' as an artist who expressed his—and Russia's—ideal through a negation, by exposing the "illusory" world of the Ivan Ivanovič's and Ivan Nikiforovič's

22. Cf. 4:170; 6:9.
23. Cf. 6:100–101.

for what it was, "a world of accidental trivia, of unreason . . . a negation of life, a banal, sordid reality" ("Woe from Wit," 3:441). Also, one can understand why Belinskij, in the same essay, voices such an exceedingly high opinion of Gogol' 's historical novel *Taras Bul'ba:* he sees the "substantial," positive, meaningful world of Taras Bul'ba as an ideal expression of concrete historical reality. Patriotic Russian and Ukrainian critics agree with Belinskij's judgment of *Taras Bul'ba* to this day.

Belinskij's overestimation of the potential of poetic intuition in the presentation of historical reality, remote or contemporaneous, is one of the worst blemishes on his record. Although there is little historical truth in *Taras Bul'ba* (it is actually impossible to place the action within any particular century), it reflects some of the main ideas which have dominated the history of the geographic region in question. But can flagrant religious intolerance, a revolting antisemitism, and a rabid chauvinism be classified correctly among Hegel's "rational" ideas which move the life of civilized nations? To see Taras Bul'ba as the bearer of an idea ("this man had an idea, by which and for which he lived") is extravagant, and so is the statement with which Belinskij concludes his discussion of *Taras Bul'ba:* "Every nation's essence of life is a great reality, and in Taras Bul'ba this essence has found its fullest expression" ((Woe from Wit," 3:441). Gogol' 's short novel is much too tenuous to support such a momentous statement.

It is also in this Hegelian context that one can understand Belinskij's stubborn insistence that Gogol' 's works were an expression of contemporary Russian reality,[24] while many of his contemporaries, such as Ševyrev, Polevoj, and Senkovskij, distinctly saw the elements of caricature, hyperbole, and the grotesque in Gogol'. Ševyrev in particular emphasized that Gogol' was a great poet of the "absurdity of life" (*Bessmyslica žizni*)—a sensible and perceptive view. But Belinskij would have no part of this.

Soviet scholars, such as G. A. Gukovskij,[25] have revived Belinskij's notion that, if Gogol' 's world seemed unreal, fantastic, and absurd, this was not Gogol' 's fault, but rather the fault of the world which he depicted in his art. A similar notion, incidentally, was decidedly popular among the German roman-

---

24. *Dead Souls,* says Belinskij, is "based on the pathos of reality as it exists" (review of *Dead Souls,* 6:219). Nečaeva, *Belinskij,* 4:79, points out that during Belinskij's last years *Dead Souls* became for him "something like a social and aesthetic Gospel," which he would quote to corroborate his revolutionary and democratic ideas. It must be said that Belinskij's acceptance of Gogol' as an authority on Russian reality was duplicated by other honest and knowledgeable men. Herzen, for instance, saw Gogol' 's work as "a scream of horror and of shame, emitted by a man who has gone to seed under the pressures of life and who suddenly sees his bestially degraded face in a mirror" (quoted by Nečaeva, *Belinskij,* 4:78).
25. G. A. Gukovskij, *Realizm Gogolja* (Moscow and Leningrad, 1959).

tics. E. T. A. Hoffmann, for example, often speaks of the "ghostlike" (*gespenstisch*) quality of the Philistine's world.

In his Hegelian stage, Belinskij still speaks of "ordinary reality" and "poetic reality." The representation of ordinary reality can be achieved by "daguerreotype" (Belinskij's own term) reproduction. Poetic reality, if captured by art, manifests the idea of a certain sphere of life in its whole truth and plenitude. Poetic intuition captures the "typical," the quintessential, the truly important traits of reality.[26] In a sense, then, "poetic truth" is a purer, a more intense, or, one might say, a more ideal analogue of the reality of life, and this reality exists in various degrees of concreteness, substantiality, and plenitude:

> Every period has its innermost thoughts, joyous or sorrowful; and it has its needs and its interests, and therefore its proper poetry. The longevity of the poetry of each epoch depends on the ideal significance of that epoch, on the depth and universality of the idea expressed by its historical life. Those works of art live longest of all which convey, in its whole plenitude and power, what was truest, most substantial, and most characteristic about that epoch. (Second essay on Puškin, 1843, 7:214)

Hegel had been an armchair philosopher, or, as Lev Šestov once put it, a "public philosopher," to whom the conflict between the irresistible development of substantial historical forces and the life and happiness of private individuals was an inevitable, in fact, a necessary philosophical antinomy.[27] Belinskij's position in this matter is ambivalent. On the one hand, he was a "political" man no less than Hegel but, on the other hand, he was not so naïve as to believe that progress—in which he also believed, and passionately so—could be achieved without a great deal of private suffering. Belinskij's interpretation of Puškin's *The Bronze Horseman* (Eleventh essay on Puškin, 1846, 7:542–48) suggests not only that he understood this work as a clear statement of this antinomy but also that he was inclined to accept it as Hegel would have: "And with a humble heart, we recognize the triumph of the universal over the particular, without, however, refusing our compassion to the suffering of this particular individual" (7:547). Ironically, the Bronze Horseman, a phantom, is assigned by Belinskij a higher degree of "reality" than the fate of Evgenij, the phantom's all-too-real human victim. One cannot help thinking that Belinskij will condone private suffering whenever the universal good which entails it has his strong approval. We know that Belinskij was a lifelong admirer of Peter the Great and his idea, of which Petersburg was the symbol.

On other occasions Belinskij expressed quite different ideas. In several letters

26. See, e.g., Belinskij's remarks on the Korobočka episode in *Dead Souls,* "A Literary Conversation Overheard in a Bookshop" ["Literaturnyj razgovor, podslušannyj v knižnoj lavke"] (1842), 6:359.

27. Lev Shestov, *Athens and Jerusalem* (New York, 1968), p. 371.

to Botkin, and specifically in the famous letter of 1 March 1841, Belinskij vehemently protests giving up one's concern for the human individual and his
happiness in favor of any abstract historical teleology. In a spirited tirade,
which reminds one of Ivan Karamazov's "return of his ticket" to the Creator
of this world,[28] Belinskij returns his ticket to Hegel, saying:

> With due respect to your philosopher's cap, I have the honor of reporting
> to you that even if I succeeded in climbing to the very highest step on the
> ladder of evolution, I would still ask you to give me an account of all the
> victims of living conditions and of history, of all the victims of accidents,
> superstitions, inquisitions, Philip II, etc., etc.—or else I shall throw myself off
> that highest step, head first. I do not want happiness even gratis, unless I be
> assured regarding the fate of each and every one of my blood brethren—bones
> of my bones, and flesh of my flesh. (12:22)

When it comes to facing the antinomy concretely, with regard to Belinskij's
own age, Belinskij ultimately goes against Hegel. He is able to take a broad, historical view of the period of Peter the Great, of the Napoleonic wars, even of
the fate of Puškin's Evgenij in *The Bronze Horseman.* But for his own age and
its literature, "reality" is reduced to the miseries of everyday living as presented in the works of the Natural School and to the critic's concerns with a plea
for immediate and tangible social reforms—instead of any long-range historical
vistas.

Belinskij, like Hegel, had been from the beginning a staunch defender of realistic art. He had always felt that art should deal with contemporary reality.
But the earlier Belinskij had displayed a lively concern and indubitable talent
for grasping and formulating the "ideas" which were apparently moving that
reality, what Apollon Grigor'ev would later call the "drift" (*vejanie*) of an
epoch. During the last few years of his life Belinskij seems to have lost his grip
on these "ideas," or perhaps his faith in their reality. For example, he had immediately sensed the drift of Lermontov's *Hero of Our Time,* recognized Pečorin as a new social type, and correctly understood his historical significance.
But when faced with Dostoevskij's equally significant novels *Poor Folk* and *The
Double*, Belinskij, even though he actually called *Poor Folk* "the first Russian
social novel," was unable or unwilling to speculate on their broader social and
historical significance, producing what was essentially a psychological interpretation.

Instead, the later Belinskij pays more and more attention to naked, empirical
reality. He now perceives the history of Russian literature as a long struggle,
once unconscious and now conscious, "to get closer to life, to reality, and consequently, to become original, national, Russian" ("1846," 10:10). There
emerges in Belinskij's writings of his last years the conception of a struggle be-

28. Berdjaev, *Russkaja ideja,* p. 78, points out the similarity.

tween a "satirical" and a "rhetorical" tendency in eighteenth-century Russian literature, with Kantemir initiating the satirical and Lomonosov, of course, the pervading influence in the rhetorical direction. It may well be that this dichotomy was derived from Saint-Simonian thought.

Belinskij also believed that this process had found its completion in the works of Gogol' and the Natural School, in which ordinary Russian life was dealt with directly and in Russian terms. In the critic's later writings one will find many instances in which he commends relatively mediocre authors for their devotion to simple and unadorned truth, or actually suggests that even a writer of modest talent can achieve excellent results if he is determined to make his works an honest mirror of reality.[29] The following passage on a minor Russian writer is characteristic of Belinskij's thought along these lines:

> In our opinion, Mr. Butkov has no talent for the novel or the short story, and he does very well to stay always within the limits of that special genre of daguerreotype tales and sketches which he has himself created. This is not art (*tvorčestvo*), this is not poetry, yet there is a peculiar kind of art, a peculiar kind of poetry in them. Mr. Butkov's tales and sketches relate to the novel and short story in the same way as statistics relates to history, as reality relates to poetry. They show little imagination but, instead, a great deal of wisdom and feeling; little humor but, instead, much irony and wit, the source of which is a sympathetic soul. ("1846," 10:39)

The question is: What stands in lieu of the missing ideal content of these naturalistic sketches, and what might be their "peculiar kind of poetry"? It is rather obvious that Belinskij must resort to Aesopian language to put this across, for the *pafos*—to use Belinskij's own term—of the sketches lies in their social protest, in their call for social change. Dostoevskij's first novel, *Poor Folk* (1846), had gone very far not only in taking the poor and downtrodden to a point at which an angry outburst of protest and a vigorous assertion of abused human dignity seemed inevitable, but also in venting the poor man's resentment in very poignant and articulate words. This was exactly what Belinskij expected of literature in 1845 (when he first read Dostoevskij's novel). Of course, he was disappointed when Dostoevskij's ensuing works showed less and less of that tendency—which, it may be added, had been presented under a cloud of ambiguity even in *Poor Folk*.[30] The following fiery passage in Belinskij's Third essay on Puškin (1843) quite explicitly states this particular conception of the ideal aspect of poetry, which the critic had embraced during the last few years of his life:

29. See 2:78, 109, 221, 288; 10:35, 96, 105, 317.
30. See Victor Terras, *The Young Dostoevsky (1846-1849): A Critical Study* (The Hague and Paris), 1969), pp. 57–62, 165.

> Praised be he who, refusing to remain satisfied with the present reality, bears in his soul the ideal of a better life, who lives and breathes to only one thought: to help, according to the strength given him, in the realization of that ideal on Earth; who leaves early in the morning to join the common cause, whether it be with his sword, his word, his spade, or his broom, whatever his capacities may be, and who joins his brethren not only in gay festivities, but in sorrow and lamentation, too. . . . (7:195)

This is the phraseology of Lamennais or Leroux. We have, then, in the later Belinskij a conception of reality which derives its ideal aspect not from any Hegelian "mystique of time" (to use René Wellek's term) but from a social ideal which, at this stage in the development of Russian society, does not seem to be immanent either in the empirical Russian reality of the times or in the naturalistic literature dealing with it. In other words, the later Belinskij is intent upon turning Russian literature into the bearer of a progressive social, or even socialist, ideology, while there is still no basis for such a tendency in Russian reality. Thus, he has in effect a dialectic conception of the relationship between literature and reality. On the one hand, his insistence on "realism" in literature means that realism depends, for much of its content, on the condition of the society which it mirrors. But on the other hand, the role of literature as an active factor of social change makes society depend on literature. What is even more surprising, Belinskij often enough seems to see things exactly in these dialectic terms, and quite consciously so. What was wrong with German literature, he would often say, was that it had refused, this far, to become a social factor. French literature, on the contrary, had a tradition of close interaction with social and political life, in which it played an ever-increasing role.[31] In amazingly unequivocal terms, Belinskij welcomes the active part which Russian literature was destined to play in the "progressive" movement in Russian society:

> Could it have been possible for this new social movement not to be reflected in literature, which is always an expression of society? In this respect, literature has actually done even more: it has, rather, stimulated and aroused this new direction in society instead of being merely its reflection; it has, rather, moved ahead of it, instead of merely keeping pace with it. ("1847," 10:302)

This and many other such passage were actually passed by the censor in 1848. There is no denying that in this and similar pronouncements Belinskij is saying what Maksim Gor'kij would say, *mutatis mutandis,* at the First Congress of the Union of Soviet Writers in 1934. Yet even in the 1840s Belinskij was not the only Russian critic to voice such a view. V. N. Majkov, in a review

---

31. See, e.g., "Thoughts and Notes on Russian Literature" (1846), 9:453.

of V. F. Odoevskij's works in the *National Annals* (1847), explicitly stated that the history of a work of literature did not end with its completion and publication, but that it continued through its influence on the society in which it had appeared.

And so Belinskij had described a full circle, or spiral, in his conception of the relationship between "art" and "reality." He had begun by crediting art with the expression of the ideal inherent in reality, without paying much attention to the fact that art was itself largely responsible for the very existence of these ideal values. He had then gradually expanded the range of art's contacts with reality to a point where it embraced even those aspects of reality that are least congenial to art: sordid, trivial, "everyday" life. But in so doing he reached a point where he had to transcend this reality and introduce ideal values from the outside in order to breathe life into the art which represented it. Belinskij's initial metaphysical conception of art ultimately becomes an ideological one.

ART AND INDIVIDUALITY

Belinskij's reality is determined nationally, socially, and historically much more than individually, psychologically, and anthropologically. Religion and metaphysics, not to speak of the supernatural or even the fantastic (which in Belinskij's parlance covers the socially exceptional, pathological, perverse, or otherwise abnormal), are largely ignored or actually rejected in contemporary literature.

Belinskij is, of course, aware of human individuality as such. Specifically, poetic individuality is a concept which we encounter regularly in his writings.[32] But nonetheless Belinskij's emphasis, in good Hegelian fashion, is generally on the human individual as a particular expression or manifestation of the universal values of nationality, society, and humanity: "In order to be a real man, and not a phantom, a man must be the particular expression of the universal, or the finite manifestation of the infinite" ("Sketches of the Battle of Borodino," 1839, 3:340).

To the very end, Belinskij accepts the Hegelian hierarchy of "individualities," where the human individual as a biological organism is the lowest and mankind as a spiritual entity the highest form of organization. A human individual's highest merit is to be as nearly perfect as possible an incarnation of his age, his society, his nation, and what is best and highest about them.[33]

Belinskij's interpretations tend to derive the poet's creative individuality from

32. See 6:656; 7:309–10; 10:27–30, 208–10.
33. For example: "What *individuality* is to the *idea* of Man, *nationality* is to the *idea* of mankind. In other words, nationalities are the individualities of mankind" ("1846," 10:28–29).

certain universal trends of his age, his nation, and his society. Quite consistently, Belinskij—like Hegel—likes to formulate his observations regarding dramatic
and fictional characters in terms of social phenomena and historical trends
rather than in terms of individual psychology. This is true of his interpretation
of Hamlet (1838) no less than of that of Pečorin (1840) or Herzen's Bel'tov
(1847).

Furthermore, Belinskij's critical practice shows a pattern of negative evaluations of literary characters who stand for individualism, egocentrism, and what
we would today call "inner-directedness." In his famous analysis of Puškin's
Tat'jana, Belinskij says that "the very attempt to develop independently, away
from the influence of society, gives one a certain strangeness, a certain deformi-
ty (*čto-to urodlivoe*)." Any person who, like Tat'jana, was formed by books
rather than by society will tend to be "strange" and "deformed" (Ninth essay
on Puškin, 1845, 7:485).

ART AND NATIONALITY

The positive terms in which Belinskij seeks to approach "reality" and its
representation in art are "nationality" (*narodnost'*), "sociality" (*social'nost'*),
and "historicity" (*istoričnost'*).

Contrary to the accusations of some of his antagonists, Dostoevskij, for example, Belinskij was a good Russian patriot from beginning to end. The mystique of nationhood is a focal element of his philosophy and of his aesthetics.[34]
Belinskij's conception of a nation (*narod*) is decidedly "organic": "A nation
is not an abstract concept, but rather a living entity, a spiritual organism whose
manifold functions serve a single end; a nation is an *individuality* in the sense a
man is just that" (3:325). This quotation is from one of Belinskij's "reactionary" Hegelian pieces, his review of F. Glinka's "Sketches of the Battle of Borodino" (1839). But there is no reason to assume that Belinskij ever changed his
mind on this point,[35] as illustrated in his review of Smaragdov's history text
(1844): "A nation, too, is an individual, just as a man is. Mankind is an individual, too, in the same sense that a nation is, only higher yet. So then, if it is
the goal of the life of every man as an individual to develop a consciousness, is
it not necessarily the goal of every nation, and of mankind, to do likewise?"
(8:279).

The Herderian idea (fully endorsed by German objective idealism) that a nation expresses, in its national life, a particular aspect of humanity, is found as
early as 1834 in "Literary Reveries" (1:35). It is noteworthy that Belinskij
says, in the same breath, that nations in whose life this is not the case merely

34. Billig, *Der Zusammenbruch,* pp. 19–21, gives a concise review of Belinskij's conception of nationhood.
35. Cf. 2:552–53; 3:266; 5:193, 643; 7:45, 443; 10:29–32.

"vegetate" rather than "live" (ibid.)—a very Schellingian conception of "intensity" and "power" even in the spiritual aspect of nationhood. In the same essay, language is seen as the organic creation of a people, and the most direct and profound expression of its spirit—another Herderian idea. The works of a truly national literature are, likewise, an inspired and spontaneous manifestation of "the innermost depths and pulsations of a nation's inner life" (ibid., 1:24). Again, there is reason to assume that Belinskij never abandoned this notion.

Belinskij always believed in national individuality and originality as a precondition of genuine artistic creativity. Therefore, all attempts of eighteenth-century poets and writers to create a Russian literature by imitating Western examples were bound to fail: "One does not create a literature," says Belinskij, "it creates itself in the same way as the language and customs of a people create themselves, without the people being consciously aware of it" (ibid., 1:87). The heroes of a Sumarokov, an Ozerov, or a Kukol'nik may bear Russian names, they may wear Russian costumes, they may speak the Russian vernacular, but they are still not Russians, just artificial transplants from Racine, Voltaire, or Schiller—one of Belinskij's favorite thoughts, which he repeated many times (cf. "The Russian Theater in Petersburg," 1841, 5:498–99).

Belinskij always believed that a true genius was necessarily national, "a son of his age," and "a citizen of his society." The great Goethe's *Hellenism* is inherently suspect, Belinskij surmises, while his claim to being a *German* genius is unquestioned ("Literary Reveries," 1:93).[36]

In another early essay, Belinskij produces a definition of *narodnost'* in literature which will remain valid to the end of his life and which is still widely accepted in Russia today:

> What is *narodnost'* in literature? It is a reflection of the individuality, of the character of a nation, an expression of its inner as well as of its external life, with all of its typical nuances, colors, and birthmarks—right? If this is so, it seems to me that there is no need to make such *narodnost'* mandatory for a true talent, for a true poet, because it will inevitably and spontaneously manifest itself in any creative work. ("Nothing about Naught, or a Report to the Publisher of *The Telescope* on the Past Half Year [1835] in Russian Literature" [Ničto o ničem, ili Otčet g. izdatelju *Teleskopa* za poslednee polugodie (1835) russkoj literatury"], 1836, 2:23–24)

Belinskij then goes on to corroborate this assertion by drawing a parallel to another necessary trait of artistic creation, namely, individuality. Is not a poet's nationality as much of a real factor as his individuality? Could any poet

---

36. Apollon Grigor'ev would develop the notion of the national determinateness of all artistic creation in his essay "On Truth and Sincerity in Art," *Russkaja beseda* 1856, no. 3. It was also one of Dostoevskij's favorite notions.

conceal the fact that he is a German, a Frenchman, or a Russian? Belinskij chooses Puškin's *Evgenij Onegin* to make his point. Could anyone deny, he says, that all its characters, while typical, human, and universal, are also uniquely Russian? Would not their whole meaning be destroyed if Evgenij and Vladimir became Adolphe and Ernest, if Ol'ga and Tat'jana were transformed into Henriette and Amalia? To a possible rejoinder that this merely proves a good poet's familiarity with the society which he has chosen to describe, Belinskij responds that this fails to take into account the fact that such knowledge can be found only in a person who deeply sympathizes with a society, who is initiated into all its secrets, who is, in short, himself a part of it. Anticipating still another rejoinder, namely, that Russian poets are known to be perfectly capable of expressing "European" concerns, Belinskij adds that this only proves that modern Russians have a vital share and a legitimate interest in European life (2:25).

In the same essay, Belinskij draws an important distinction which, again, will remain a part of his critical inventory until the very end, namely, that between *narodnost'* and *prostonarodnost'* (from *prostoj narod,* "the plain people"), the "national" as against the "popular" element in Russian literature. A true talent, says Belinskij, cannot help being "national," just as he cannot help being true to life. Such is the case with a Puškin or a Gogol'. A poet of no talent who seeks to be national will instead be merely popular and trivial (2:25–26).[37] Even in his later writings Belinskij always stresses that a truly national poet of Russia could not possibly anchor his work in the language, the customs, and the thinking of the plain people (*prostoj narod*), but would have to focus it in the life of the educated classes.[38] Belinskij assigns a relatively minor role to the popular poetry of Kol'cov, a much-admired personal friend, and shows very little sympathy for the great Ukrainian poet Taras Ševčenko. Belinskij's refusal to identify his ideals with the viewpoint of the Russian *mužik* was so pronounced that progressive and populist critics who had otherwise the highest opinion of Belinskij felt that an apology or even mild censure was in order on that score.[39]

During his Hegelian period, and even later, Belinskij put great stock in a further distinction, that of *narodnost'* versus *nacional'nost'*. It was based on a Hegelian distinction between "historical" and "ahistorical" nations. Those nations are "historical" that have developed substantial national traits, that can boast original national achievements in one area of human endeavor or another, and that stand for a specific "idea" of life which is of some import with regard to the general movement of mankind toward its ultimate goal.[40] An "ahistorical"

37. Cf. 2:349; 5:131, 302; 7:443; 8:457.
38. See, e.g., Belinskij's Eighth essay on Puškin (1844), 7:439.
39. See, e.g., Pypin, *Belinskij,* pp. 415–16.
40. E.g., 5:96, 307, 541, 632, 638–39, 658; 6:458, 618–19.

nation, or the ahistorical aspect of a nation's life, can produce *narodnost'* only, whereas a "historical" nation generates *nacional'nost'* as well.

Belinskij's ideas on this subject, which recur often in his writings after 1838, are summarized in a major essay on pre-Petrine Russia, technically a review of several works dealing with that period, including Grigorij Kotošixin's *On Russia during the Reign of Aleksej Mixajlovič* (1841, 5:91-152). The essence of *nacional'nost'* is defined as "substance" (another Hegelian term), the permanent and immutable aspect of a nation's spirit, which remains intact through all the peripeties of its history. *Narodnost'* is the first stage of *nacional'nost'*, its initial manifestation. *Nacional'nost'* implies dynamic movement, since a historical nation possesses ideals which it seeks to realize. *Narodnost'*, on the other hand, is static. *Nacional'nost'* implies a certain amount of universality, a positive contribution to the growth of human civilization.[41] Pre-Petrine Russia is seen by Belinskij as having had *narodnost'*, but not *nacional'nost'*, because Russia was then a nation without a world-historical mission, without ideal substance, and stagnant in its Byzantine ways. These opinions are of course debatable, or perhaps simply incorrect, but they conform with Belinskij's evaluation of Russia's indigenous literary tradition.

Belinskij was the first Russian critic to treat folk poetry extensively in theoretical terms. He used a framework of Hegelian aesthetics to assign to Russian folk poetry a definite slot in a Hegelian historical scheme. Belinskij's four essays on Russian folk poetry appeared in the *National Annals* in 1841. Technically, they were reviews of several collections of folk tales and folk poetry which had recently appeared. The title of the first essay (the others were untitled), "The General Idea of Folk Poetry" ("Obščaja ideja narodnoj poèzii," 5:289-310), describes their content well.

Folk poetry, according to Belinskij, is at best only *narodnyj*. In a historical perspective it is the preparatory stage of national literature (*nacional'naja literatura*). Belinskij observes that with a people who have not yet reached real historical stature "folk poetry" is invariably superior to *Kunstdichtung*, because "literary poetry" requires a certain universality which, under such conditions, can be acquired only through direct borrowing and a resultant lack of originality. Contemporary Czech literature is mentioned as a case in point ("The Russian Folk Tale," 1841, 5:308).

Folk poetry, in Belinskij's opinion, can appeal to an educated audience only through its form, while its content inevitably lacks historical substance. Time and again, Belinskij emphasizes that the *Kunstdichtung* of his own age is vastly superior to Russian folk poetry. For example, he believes that Lermontov's "Song of the Merchant Kalašnikov" (1838), a romantic imitation of the Russian folk epic, stands high above it ("The Poetry of M. Lermontov," 4: 516-17).

41. E.g., 4:197; 5:305-6, 579; 8:571.

Consistent with this view, Belinskij generally discourages Russian poets from any attempts at imitating the style or the spirit of Russian folk poetry.[42] Such a negative attitude toward folk poetry is met even in German romanticism, specifically in Friedrich Schlegel, and is characteristic of Hegel.

Belinskij's opinion of Russian poetry before Puškin is also a low one. Lomonosov and Sumarokov, not to speak of lesser talents, are seen as unoriginal, slavish imitators of Western originals. Poets who, like Deržavin in some of his incidental verse or Krylov in his fables, would turn their eyes toward Russia's native ways, are given the predicate *narodnyj* when at their best.[43] At worst they are merely *psevdo-narodnyj*, like M. N. Zagoskin in his famous historical novel *Jurij Miloslavskij* (1829, see "The Russian Folk Tale," 5:299). Belinskij is invariably harsh on poets and writers who take external traits of Russian life, such as beards, peasant garb, and uncouth manners, for the essence of *narodnost'*. He also denounces the fashionable tendency of his own day to put the label of *narodnost'* on a variety of qualities, such as "creativity," "inspiration," and "originality," which per se have nothing to do with the Russian people.[44]

According to Belinskij, Puškin was the first truly national poet of Russia. The critic never tires of reiterating this thesis (first stated by Gogol').[45] Puškin, Belinskij felt, was fully a "Russian poet" whose works reflected not only Russia's landscape and climate, the customs and habits of her people, but also the very heartbeat of Russian life, the vital concerns of the whole Russian nation.[46] Yet at the same time, Belinskij also insisted, Puškin's works had a universal meaning and were immediately comprehensible to every educated European.[47] Certainly Belinskij anticipated the myth, later developed by Grigor'ev and made famous by Dostoevskij in the latter's "Oration on Puškin" (1880), according to which "universality," an ability to identify in spirit with all European nations, was a peculiarly Russian trait, first manifested in the poetic genius of Puškin.

The appearance of poets of national, and therefore universal, stature, Belinskij believed, was a function of the emergence of Russia as a great nation, equal to the French, the British, or the German. It was for this reason, Belinskij observed, that Gogol', in order to realize himself as a great poetic genius, had to

42. E.g., 3:143; 10:13.
43. See 7:140; 8:569; 10:290. The whole essay "Ivan Andreevič Krylov" (1845, 8:565-91) deals extensively with the concept of *narodnost'* in literature.
44. See 5:127, 289, 299-302, 654. In the introductory section of his first essay on Russian folk poetry (1841), Belinskij debunks the use of the adjective *narodnyj* as "a magic word, a mysterious symbol, the sacred hieroglyph of some deeply significant, immeasurably broad idea" (5:289-90).
45. Gogol' first developed this idea in his essay "A Few Words on Puškin," which was included in his *Arabesques* (Moscow, 1835), pp. 213-25.
46. See 4:427; 5:318, 357-58; 7:34-36, 333.
47. See 4:425; 5:308.

write in Russian rather than in Ukrainian ("The Russian Folk Tale," 5:330). In *Dead Souls,* a work in which he had altogether freed himself from any ties with his native Ukraine, Gogol' was a great national poet (review of *Dead Souls,* 6:217). With Gogol', Belinskij said, Russian literature began to deal with Russian life to the exclusion of everything else. As a result, it became more one-sided than it had been before, but at the same time more original, more "organic," and richer in "the truth of life" ("Thoughts and Notes on Russian Literature," 9:438).

Time and again Belinskij asserts that it takes two things to produce greatness in any area of human endeavor: native genius and the substantial reality presented by the life of a truly historical nation. This is why Russia produced no "historical personages" before Peter the Great (Ninth essay on Puškin, 1845, 7:485–86). In literature, a talent to re-create reality is no help, Belinskij said, so long as there is no reality worth re-creating. In an essay on A. I. Poležaev (1842, 6:119–60), Belinskij brings up the hypothetical possibility that Schiller might have been born a Chinaman: he would never have become the great poet he was simply because the Chinese nation could not have provided him with the substance of his poetry. For Belinskij, as for Hegel, China was the epitome of a stagnant, ahistorical, vegetable existence. Russia before Peter the Great appeared to Belinskij as something similar to China.

Any truly great poet, Belinskij repeats over and over again, is also a national poet.[48] By the same token, a great nation is bound to produce great historical personages, mythological figures, and poets ("The Works of Deržavin," 6:618–19).

Belinskij's assumption that a poet's greatness depends not only upon his personal genius but also upon the genius of his nation—an inevitable corollary of "national organicism"—has important consequences for the critic's evaluation of his great Russian contemporaries, Puškin and Gogol'. "A great Russian poet whose natural gifts are equal to those of any great European poet," says Belinskij, "still cannot, at the present time, attain the same importance" ("Thoughts and Notes on Russian Literature," 9:441), because Russia's development as a historical nation has just only begun.

Belinskij will unhesitatingly place such Western poets and writers as Byron, Schiller, Walter Scott, and George Sand *above* Puškin and Gogol'. Only in the future, when the Russian nation will have become a truly equal member of the European community of nations, will her poets be compared with European poets of the first magnitude (ibid., 9:442).

Such reasoning is, of course, easily refuted. For one thing, Belinskij overlooked the fact that Elizabethan England was not exactly in the forefront of European civilization—yet it produced Shakespeare. On the other hand, during its unquestioned political, cultural, and literary hegemony in the

48. See 6:694; 7:267; 8:569; 9:438; 10:9.

eighteenth century, France produced no poets of truly universal stature.

An important point, sometimes overlooked, is Belinskij's lifelong belief that the progress of humanity is realized in national endeavors and not in any cosmopolitan movement. This is one matter in which Belinskij, to the end of his life, sides with the German Herderian tradition, accepted by Schelling and Hegel, against some of the Left-Hegelians and "progressive" thought in general.

In 1846–47 we find Belinskij engaged in a polemic with V. N. Majkov, who was then spreading the Left-Hegelian idea that human progress lay with a gradual elimination of *particular* (that is, national), and the emergence of *universal* traits of human civilization. Majkov was claiming that all true human greatness was inversely proportional to man's dependence on external circumstances, such as national and geographic particulars, and that men were "great" insofar as they were able to break out of the narrow world of local and national traditions and to realize in their various activities a universal human essence. The life of every nation was an eternal struggle between the particularism, regionalism, and conservatism of the majority, and the efforts of a small progressive minority to overcome these inertial and disjunctive forces. Majkov's anthropological interpretation of this state of the human condition was, however, optimistic: along with Fourier (whose theories he knew well), he felt that human vices, inertia, and narrow-mindedness were induced by the physical environment (in the broadest sense of that term), whereas man's virtues, such as creativity, reason, and an ability to cooperate with other humans, were innate to him.

In his "Survey of Russian Literature in 1846," Belinskij sets out to refute what he calls Majkov's "fantastic cosmopolitanism" (10:25–32). He challenges Majkov by asserting that "to split the national and the human into two entirely alien, even hostile principles is to resort to the most abstract, the most bookish sort of dualism" (10:26). Belinskij prefers to see the relationship between these two forces as positive, constructive, and creative: the national, the particular, and the individual being the concrete manifestations of the universal. This means that Belinskij is staying with the old Hegelian formula. Furthermore, Belinskij feels that Majkov puts excessive trust in the creative powers of an elite. He points to the corrupt and effete *ancien régime* of France as an example of what can happen when an elite is *opposed* to the popular masses rather than being the bearer of the ideals of the whole nation. As for great men, Belinskij concludes, they are in most cases typical children of their country: "A great man is always just as national as his people, for he is great precisely because he represents his nation" (10:31). What Majkov believes to be the struggle of a genius's universality against a national inertia of the masses is "simply the struggle between old and new, between idea and empiricism, between reason and prejudice" (ibid.).

There is a rather deep and basic difference between the views of the two

Russian critics. Belinskij, still very much the "organicist," believes that the seeds of the positive ideas which move nations and mankind are present in the minds of *all* people and are merely brought into the open by great men. Majkov, inclined toward a more mechanistic form of thinking, sees the people as a largely passive, inert mass, to be acted upon by individual "doers."

As far as art is concerned, Belinskij is convinced to the end that there can be no such thing as cosmopolitan art. Art, to him, is national by its very essence, as he says in an article, "Notes on the Contemporary Scene" ["Sovremennye zametki"] (1847, 10:92–93). In one of his last reviews, that of *The Moscow Literary and Learned Almanac for 1847,* Belinskij once more states his Russian nationalist position very clearly and rejects cosmopolitanism as "a false and, in fact, a suspect feeling, for its source is the head much more than the heart" (10:198).

We have, in this instance, complete agreement between Belinskij's views and those of the *počvenniki* (Grigor'ev, Dostoevskij, Straxov) of the 1860s. In particular, Belinskij clearly expresses the notion, which we know so well from Dostoevskij, that while the foreign can never *replace* the native, either in life or in literature, nor serve as a substitute for a missing national substance, it certainly can be assimilated and transformed into a part of the native, much as nourishment is transformed into flesh and blood ("1846," 10:9).

Belinskij's Herderian nationalism triumphed, in the long run, over every cosmopolitan tendency in Russian literature, including even Marxism.

There is still another element in Belinskij's conception of *narodnost'* which makes him a precursor of a later trend. With all his keen sense for the aesthetic pitfalls of a false populism, Belinskij occasionally falls prey to that strange mystique of "the people" (*narod*) which began to dominate the Russian literary scene in the 1840s and which was never to leave it again. Belinskij's pronouncements about the intuitive wisdom, primeval strength, and moral integrity of the common people of Russia are certainly not focal to his thought. And almost invariably they are made with some reservations, for example: "What an amazing creature—the people! Almost always ignorant, crude, narrow-minded, blind —yet infallibly true and right in its instincts" (Tenth essay on Puškin, 1845, 7:521).[49]

49. Cf. 7:345 and 9:140 for similar statements. And below is an example of Belinskij's attitude toward the uncritical cult of "the people" found in the writings of the Slavophiles. In his polemic article "A Rejoinder to *The Muscovite*" (1847), Belinskij quotes this statement made by the Slavophile Ju. F. Samarin concerning Turgenev's sketch "Xor' i Kalinič": "Here you can see what it means to get a touch of the soil and of the people: you get strength immediately! While Mr. Turgenev kept talking about his boring loves and all kinds of apathy, about his egoism, everything came out limp and feeble; but the moment he touched the people, touched it with sympathy and compassion, look what a fine story he has written!" (10:269).
Belinskij does not deny that Samarin is right. His point is that the same Samarin who

In one of his very last reviews (*Readings for Country Folk,* ed. V. F. Odoevskij and A. P. Zablockij, 1848), Belinskij dwells on the character and the calling of the common people of Russia (10:367-71). His analysis is sober and dispassionate. He agrees with the Slavophiles that the common people are "the guardian of the essence, of the spirit of national life" (10:367) and that they are a "conservative force" (*sila oxranitel'naja, konservativnaja*) (ibid.). He also says, with some fervor, that "the Russian people are among the most gifted, the most talented in the world" (10:371). But, on the other hand, Belinskij very firmly asserts that the so-called middle and upper classes are the bearers and propagators of progress, and specifically of intellectual and artistic creativity. "Therefore," he says, quite resolutely, "such division into classes has been necessary for the development of mankind," and continues: "Creative individuality apart from the people is an illusion (*prizrak*), but the people apart from the individuality are also an illusion. One depends upon the other. The people are the soil (*počva*) which conserves the vital juices of all development, while individuality is the flower and the fruit of this soil" (10:368). Belinskij then goes on to explain that progress is accomplished through the achievements of individuals, and that men of genius have often "understood better than the (common) people themselves what was needed for the (common) people," oftentimes overcoming the people's resistance in the process. And finally, he points out that while many great scholars and artists came from among the people (he may be thinking of Lomonosov), it was not the people to whom they addressed themselves but the "upper classes."

A populist mystique had to be in conflict with Belinskij's consistent Westernism and general tendency toward rationalism. Although Belinskij asserted, in his famous "Letter to Gogol'" (1847), that the Russian people were "by nature, deeply atheistic" (10:215), it was clear to him nonetheless that it was difficult to see the Russian peasantry as a progressive social and cultural force. By and large, Belinskij cannot be made directly responsible for the populist fixation of his epigoni, either of the Right or of the Left. A Dostoevskij, on the one side, and a Dobroljubov, on the other, went far beyond anything ever said by Belinskij on this score. From his own vantage point of a mystical faith in the soul of the Russian people, Dostoevskij was not altogether wrong in claiming that Belinskij had had no love for the Russian people.[50]

---

praises Turgenev's story—which is, after all, nothing but another "physiological sketch" in the style of the Natural School—downgrades similar works printed in the same issue of the *National Annals,* because they do not live up to his sentimentally idealized image of the Russian people (10:269).

50. Belinskij never concealed his disgust with the brutishness, cruelty, drunkenness, and filth prevalent in the life of the Russian peasantry. In polemicizing with his Slavophile opponents about the truthfulness and merit of Grigorovič's naturalistic stories of peasant life, Belinskij does not hesitate to quote from a document published by the *Journal of the*

But then, Belinskij accorded a warm reception to D. V. Grigorovič's *Anton Goremyka* ("1847," 10:347) and to other works in the same vein. Such critical approval, together with the critic's strong and virtually single-handed defense of the Natural School, certainly contributed a great deal to the emergence of what might be called a school of "populist utilitarianism" in Russian literature, a rapidly growing and never-ending flow of sketches, short stories, novels, and plays, all concerning the plight of the common people and offering suggestions as to how their condition might be bettered.

ART AND SOCIETY

Although the early Belinskij was not the apostle of *social'nost'* he would become in the 1840s, a distinct awareness of the social role of art is present in his "Literary Reveries" of 1834.[51] Belinskij's ideal, even at this early stage, is a literature which expresses the life of the entire nation. One of the many faults which he sees in the French classicists and their eighteenth-century Russian imitators is that they mirrored only the life of a narrow upper stratum of the nation (1:28-29, 47). In his first great essay on Gogol', "On the Russian Short Story and the Short Stories of Mr. Gogol'" (1835), Belinskij calls S. P. Ševyrev's suggestion that the author of *Mirgorod* should try his hand at describing the upper strata of Russian society[52] "a terrible anachronism" (1:307).

Belinskij's general tendency is, then, to move away from the class-oriented French concept of society and toward the German, Herderian concept of a nation as a homogeneous whole. Basically, Belinskij retained this attitude until the end of his life. It is significant that the Russian radicals (and later the Soviet leadership) never accepted the Marxist concept of a class literature, but retained the Belinskian concept of a national literature.

The following statement, made in a review of 1839, will remain substantially valid even for the later Belinskij:

All of what we have said was designed to show that society, or a nation, is not an abstract concept, but a living individuality, a single body and a single soul; that it is born not by any accident, not by any human contract or arbitrary decision, but by the will of God; that it is a necessary phase in the

Ministry of Internal Affairs 19 (1847): 201-67, which reveals the commonness of brawling, wife-beating, and child abuse among the Russian peasantry ("A Rejoinder to The Muscovite," 10:251-52). When travelling in southern Russia, Belinskij compares the Ukrainian peasant with his Great Russian counterpart, much to the latter's disadvantage. "The Russians," Belinskij writes to his wife, "are worse and filthier than swine" (letter, 14-15 June 1846, 12:288).

51. For a detailed study of this aspect of Belinskij's criticism, consult Herbert E. Bowman's accurate and well-documented study (see Chap. 2, n. 16).

52. S. P. Ševyrev, review of *Mirgorod* by Gogol', *Moscow Observer* 1 (1835), sec. 5.

development of mankind, that its causes are not found in people's needs and advantage, but that it is an end in itself, being its own *raison d'être;* that it develops not mechanically but dynamically, that is, through the action of its own vital force, which is its essence, rather than through anything that is attached to it or grafted upon it from the outside, growing immanently from its own resources, organically, like a tree from its seed. . . . ("Sketches of the Battle of Borodino," 3:338)

When Belinskij discusses the dialectic tensions which account for the dynamics of human societies, the opposing poles which he discerns are "society" and the "individual," not social classes at war with each other. With but a few exceptions, Belinskij's searchings for a formula of the relationship between "art" and "society" deal with the individual artist facing society, not with a class-conscious artist expressing the ideals of his social class.

However, Belinskij's opinions regarding this relationship undergo an interesting development. In the—still "reactionary"—essay "Menzel, a Critic of Goethe" (1840), Belinskij strongly suggests that art cannot serve society other than by serving its own ends. He writes:

Whenever we demand that art serve social goals, and view the poet as a caterer with whom we may, one day, place an order to sing for us the sanctity of marriage and, on the next day, the good fortune of those who give their life to their country, and, on the third, the obligation to pay one's debts punctually, then, instead of creating works of art, we will inundate our literature with rhymed dissertations on abstract and reasoned subjects, arid allegories, expressing not any living truth, but dead ratiocinations; or, ultimately, with the poisonous fumes of petty passions and partisan ravings. We have both in French literature. (3:397–98)

At the same time, Belinskij assures his readers, and himself, that it does not follow from all this that the poet should be, or that Homer, Shakespeare, and Goethe were, indifferent to contemporary events, to the needs, the problems, and the passions of the society which had produced them. Quite to the contrary, Belinskij is confident that there exist necessary, firm, and organic ties between the microcosm of the poet's world and the macrocosm of society. All he wanted to say by his assertion on the autonomy of art, Belinskij assures his reader, was that an artist's inspiration cannot be guided "by the calendar." In other words, Belinskij accepts as granted by nature what a utilitarian aesthetics seeks to safeguard by its prescriptions to, and pressures upon, the poet.

In his articles on Lermontov (1840–41), Belinskij reaffirms in explicit and eloquent terms both his conviction that "society is, like any individuality, something live and organic, something that has its stages of growth, its periods of health and of sickness" ("The Poetry of M. Lermontov," 4:488), and his equally strong belief that a truly *living* man (*živoj čelovek*) lives the life of his society with all his mind and with all his heart. Since a poet is, virtually by definition, a *living* man, a man who lives life more intensely than most men do, it follows inevitably that this is especially true of him: he is pained by his society's failures, feels tormented when it suffers, blooms when it is healthy, is blissful when it is happy (ibid.).[53]

Consistent with this view, Belinskij rationalizes his negative evaluation of eighteenth-century Russian literature by the argument that its poets failed to identify with the society of their age: they did not suffer its ills, nor did they express its ideal strivings. Sumarokov's resentment of a society which failed to appreciate his "genius" was, in effect, the clearest proof that Sumarokov had failed to grasp the meaning of his age ("1841," 5:526).[54]

In this context, the notion that any "living man" is, and every poet should be, rooted in "the soil" (*počva*) is very much in evidence in Belinskij's writings of this period:

> Our favorite (and sensible) thought has always been to elevate our whole life to the level of reality, and consequently, our mutual relationships as well; and so then what? A dream is a dream and will always remain one; we were phantoms and we shall die phantoms, but this is not our fault. Reality arises from the soil, and the soil of all reality is society. (letter to V. P. Botkin, 8 September 1841, 12:66)

Here as elsewhere, Belinskij's conception of society, and of literature as its projection, is both organic and holistic. Literature, he stresses time and again, receives its content from *all* of national life. It expresses, in a conscious and artistically formed manner, the ideal strivings of a *whole* society ("1841," 5:570). The subject of art is therefore *man*, not *barin* or *mužik* (but if the question were raised, a poet would find more "life" in the life of the educated, than in that of the uneducated classes). It is quite absurd, says Belinskij, to prefer the *mužik* simply because he is a *mužik*, that is, crude, uncouth, and ignorant ("The Russian Folk Tale," 1841, 5:303-4).

This view is by no means limited to Belinskij's writings of the early 1840s. In his essay on *Evgenij Onegin* (1845), he makes it very clear that social class has nothing to do with virtue or other absolute human values: the fact that Onegin is a member of high society does not affect his stature as a human being in any important way. All social classes have essentially the same human vices, though in a somewhat different form (7:448-50).

53. Cf. 4:502; 9:77, 436; 10:106, 109, 302, 311.
54. In his essay on Deržavin (1843), Belinskij repeats this observation: "Every great poet is great because the roots of his suffering and of his bliss are planted deeply in the soil of social consciousness (*obščestvennost'*) and history, because he is an organ as well as a representative of his society, his age, and of mankind. Only small poets are unhappy or happy by and through themselves" (6:586).

Belinskij felt that class antagonism was on the wane in Russia. He undoubtedly saw the awakened concern of the educated classes (specifically his own concern, and that of many men he knew) for the welfare of the masses as one positive sign, and the slow yet undeniable increase in the general level of literacy and civilized ways as another.[55] Russian literature, ever growing and gaining in social importance (another indubitable fact), was apparently a powerful cement which would glue different strata of society together, giving them a common consciousness.[56]

Belinskij liked to point out that French classicism and its Russian imitators had seen art as an extension not of the whole people but of "society" (meaning "high society"), and, as a consequence, it had idealized life as a whole. In contradistinction to this school (which Belinskij calls the "rhetorical"), those tendencies in Russian literature which strove for more reality were also "national," and to some extent "popular."[57] The German romantics had made a similar comparison between French (and German) classicism and the trend in German literature which they themselves represented.

When Belinskij outgrows his period of "reconciliation with reality," his everlouder clamor for *social'nost'*[58] expresses not so much a new conception of the structure of Russian society as a broader understanding of the role of literature: in addition to its positive role of expressing the life and the ideals of society, it now assumes the negative task of exposing its ills. The poet is now asked to be not only the oracle but also the physician of society ("The Poetry

55. "The hostility between the estates is disappearing, and they are becoming reconciled in a realization of their mutual need for each other and their common importance for the whole of society" (review of *A Manual of Universal History* by F. K. Lorenz, 1842, 6:92).

56. See "Thoughts and Notes on Russian Literature," 1846, 9:435–36; "1847," 10:306.

57. See, e.g., "1847," 10:289–91.

58. The following is a famous passage from Belinskij's letter to V. P. Botkin, 8 September 1841: "Sociality, sociality, or death! That is my motto. What is it to me that the universal lives, while the individual suffers? What is it to me that the genius here on Earth lives in heaven while the crowd wallows in filth? What is it to me that *I* understand the idea, that the world of the idea is open to me in art, in religion, in history, when I cannot share this with all those who should be my brothers in humanity, my neighbors in Christ, but who are alien and hostile to me in their ignorance? What is it to me that there is bliss for the select few while the majority does not even suspect its existence: Away with bliss for me, if I am to possess it alone among a thousand! I want no part of it unless I can share it with the lowliest of my brothers!" (12:69).

Bowman rightly observes that "sociality" (*social'nost'*) here might be interpreted as a principle of humanitarian concern for the welfare of one's fellowman (Bowman, *Belinskij*, p. 144). Belinskij's notion of *social'nost'* is close to the *socialité* of the French utopian socialists in that the element of enlightenment is very strong in it. With later Russian socialists, concern for the material welfare of the exploited lower classes takes precedence over all other considerations.

of Apollon Majkov," 1842, 6:9). Social analysis and social critique are now the order of the day, Belinskij asserts in his programmatic essay occasioned by Nikitenko's "Discourse on Criticism" (1842).

To Belinskij's credit, he always stresses that the "social" aspect of the new literature must not be confused with conventional satire. This is particularly true of Gogol'.[59] Unlike satire (which, Belinskij always felt, never produces that organic fusion of the "ideal" and the "real" which is the mark of true art),[60] Gogol' 's art is not only true to life, but is "life itself."

Belinskij had a simple explanation for the prevalence of negative characters and descriptions in the works of Gogol' and the Natural School: Russian reality was like that. Of course, he could not say this in print (he said so often in private and in his letters), at least not directly. But the implication was there, and his readers saw it. Belinskij also had an explanation for the dearth of convincing, poetically truthful positive characters in contemporary Russian literature; it, too, could not be printed. But we find it in Belinskij's correspondence. In a letter to K. D. Kavelin, 7 December 1847, Belinskij says that there must be as many positive types in Russia as in any other country, perhaps more. But Russian reality is such that natural virtue, humanity, and goodness must of necessity be engaged in a constant feud with the existing social order. Censorship being what it is, conflicts of this type cannot easily be introduced into literature. Therefore, it becomes nearly impossible to present a positive type in its natural condition, that is, with poetic truthfulness (12:460).

In the later Belinskij, emphasis on social critique becomes progressively stronger. He does not hesitate to censure even a Goethe or a Puškin when compelled to register their "practical and historical indifferentism" ((Fifth essay on Puškin, 1844, 7:346). When he speaks, in the same breath, of Puškin's "lack of an up-to-date European education" (which calls to mind Černyševskij's equally preposterous criticism of Gogol'), he must mean the poet's disregard of contemporary, largely French, "progressive" thought. In another of his essays on Puškin, the Ninth (1845), Belinskij is close to a Marxist interpretation of the absence of social criticism in *Evgenij Onegin:* in spite of his indubitable humaneness, Belinskij says, the poet shows at every step that he is himself a Russian landowner, and that there can be no question as to his full solidarity with his class. And thus, the critic concludes, "in Puškin's very satire, there is so much love, and his very censure often resembles approval and fondness. . ." (7:502).

59. See, e.g., Belinskij's review of *Dead Souls,* 6:212, 220.
60. See 3:309, 442; 4:414-15; 8:89; 9:642-43. Belinskij's exclusion of satire from the domain of poetry allies him with the aesthetics of German idealism, and Hegel in particular.

The possibility of social critique "from within," as a sign of a society in decline, also occurs to Belinskij. In an essay on the works of Zeneida R——va (pseudonym of Elena Andreevna Hahn [Gan]), written in 1843 (7:648-78), Belinskij discusses contemporary French literature and in particular the huge success of Eugène Sue's novels *Mathilde* and *Les Mystères de Paris*, both bitter indictments of French society, and both received with enthusiasm by the very class whose moral decay they exposed. Belinskij explains this reaction of the French public by the fact that French society no longer believes in the rectitude of its own way of life or in its professed moral principles ("to which M. *de* Balzac still clings") and is ready to applaud an author who, though himself a part of that society, nevertheless denounces it (7:649). This thought clearly anticipates similar statements by Marxist critics, especially Plexanov, regarding comparable tendencies in the literature of their time.

Belinskij's most unequivocal statements regarding the sociopolitical role which he wishes Russian literature to play are found in his correspondence. One must agree with Pypin[61] that the following statement made in a letter to V. P. Botkin, 2-6 December 1847, presents Belinskij's "mature and broad" view regarding this subject:

> Of course, if a story does raise questions [Belinskij means sociopolitical questions] and has a moral effect on society, while also being of high artistic quality—the more I like it; but what really matters, as far as I am concerned, is still the business side of it rather than a showing off of brilliance. Let a story be a million times worth of high artistic quality, if it has nothing businesslike to say, *je m'en fous.* I know that I am stuck in a one-sided position, but I refuse to abandon it, and I feel rather sorry for those who do not take this position. This is why I did not see any drawn-out passages in *Anton Goremyka,* or rather, enjoyed them as though they were ambrosia. . . .
> (12:445)

This apology of social utilitarianism is preceded by an important reservation, important especially because it makes a point which Belinskij takes for granted. He says that "a story ought to have only as much poetry and artistic quality as is necessary for it to be true, that is, so it will not veer into allegory or smack of a dissertation" (ibid.). That a story be "true" is, in this context, a very strict requirement which in effect leaves intact the early Belinskij's conception of the free and "organic" way in which art is to serve society.

By 1846, the world-wise Botkin had resigned himself to the fact that the practical social role of literature was independent of its aesthetic qualities (*xudožestvennost'*), and he virtually taunted Belinskij for his continued belief in

---

61. Pypin, *Belinskij,* pp. 553, 579. What to us may look like an incomprehensible misunderstanding of the nature of art by both Belinskij, a fine critic, and Pypin, an excellent scholar, had for them the fascination of a breakthrough to a great and simple truth.

the possibility of a synthesis of both.[62] While Belinskij's interests were veering more and more in the direction of social action and political propaganda, those of his thoughts which were reserved for art continued along the old organicist lines of his early period. Time and again, he reiterates his belief that true art will always take care of its own living truth. Thus, in a polemic with Ju. F. Samarin ("A Rejoinder to *The Muscovite*," 1847, 10:221-69), Belinskij rejected the Slavophiles' demands that the Natural School introduce some positive characters, descriptions, and observations in their pictures of Russian life; he argues that this prescription would yield to the precise charge of the Slavophiles against the Natural School: it would mean a concession to an extraneous, political and moralist, tendency.

To the end, Belinskij was willing to admit that his own side was not immune to this danger. In "A Survey of Russian Literature in 1847," Belinskij points out that "even poets of genius, carried away by their desire to solve social problems, have recently surprised their public by producing works the artistic merit of which in no way equals their talent, or at least shows up in details only, while the whole work is weak, drawn out, limp, and tedious" (10:306-7). The writer in question is George Sand, whom Belinskij admired not only as a writer but especially as a champion of social progress.

I. A. Gončarov's reminiscences contain the following passage, which would seem to describe Belinskij's position during the last years of his life:

> At times he would seem to tear into me for my not having that anger, irritability, and subjectivity. "To you it is all the same whether you run into a scoundrel, a fool, a monster, or a decent, kindly person—you'll describe them exactly alike: no love, no hatred toward any of them!" And he would be saying this (and he said it more than once) with a kind of good-natured anger. But once he put his hands tenderly on my shoulders after having said it, and added in a whisper: "And it is good this way, that's what is needed, that's the mark of an artist!"—as though he were afraid that someone might hear him and accuse him of sympathizing with a writer without a tendency.[63]

ART AND HISTORY

Belinskij's conception of history is entirely "organic." In a review of S. Smaragdov's history text (1844, 8:270-93), not to mention an earlier, purely Hegelian review of Friedrich Lorenz's *Manual of Universal History* [*Rukovodstvo k vseobščej istorii*] (1842), he shows an undisguised scorn for pragmatic historiography which, he thinks, tends to contain less historical truth than philosophically oriented studies, "even if the more philosophical studies are actually guilty

62. See Nečaeva, *Belinskij*, 4:412.
63. I. A. Gončarov, "Zametki o ličnosti Belinskogo" (1874), *Sobranie sočinenij*, 8 vols. (Moscow, 1955), 8:50-51.

of intentional distortion of facts to suit a one-sided and biased view" (8:272). During his entire career, Belinskij clung to the belief that historical evolution is an organic process which can be described and understood in terms of certain fundamental ideas. A nation's history should therefore be viewed as an integral process, ruled by those ideas which make up the nation's national spirit (of which pragmatic political, social, military, and economic developments are a concrete manifestation). Historical knowledge is for Belinskij primarily an understanding of these fundamental ideas. Once they are understood, the social institutions, the laws, the religion, the philosophy, and the art of a nation, or of a historical period, all become clear.[64] The pragmatic details, those which lack an ideal basis, are considered fortuitous and of little consequence.[65]

This understanding of history reveals itself in two basic concepts. The first of these is the concept of the *epoch* (the Latin word *saeculum* might actually give a better idea of Belinskij's Russian usage of *vek*) as a distinct entity, defined by the ideas which rule it. The other is that of historical *continuity* and historical *progress*, also defined in terms of the life of ideas.

Belinskij's terminology is inconsistent, but he apparently has a clear intuitive conception of *saeculum* and *Zeitgeist*. He certainly hypostatizes "epochs" in the history of Russian literature with great facility. As early as "Literary Reveries" (1834), he speaks of the "Puškinian period of Russian literature" (a period ending about 1830). In the same breath, he speaks of Karamzin and others as representing the eighteenth century, while living and writing in the nineteenth (ibid., 1:67; cf. 9:318). Here, and throughout his writings, Belinskij uses *vek, vremja* ("time"), *èpoxa,* and *period* as virtual synonyms.

Belinskij believes that all the different aspects of human life during a given *saeculum* are manifestations of a single, integral *Zeitgeist*. The literature of an age is necessarily animated by the same spirit as its social institutions, its laws, its art, and its religion. In his portrayals of earlier ages, Belinskij follows either the clichés, largely Hegelian, which he found in contemporary German historiography, or literary *topoi* which he met in the literature of his day. When Belinskij describes the Middle Ages as "that religious period of mankind, when glory, courage, love, and everything, everything was religion" ("A Literary Chronicle," 1838, 2:351), he is simply repeating a cliché. It is significant, however, that he is referring here to Puškin's ballad "The Poor Knight" ["Žil na svete rycar' bednyj"] (1829), which he takes to express the spirit of the Middle Ages with great power. The implication is that Puškin, who had never studied

---

64. "A belief in the idea is the sole foundation of all knowledge. One must search for ideas in learning. If there is no idea, there is no learning! The knowledge of facts is valuable *for the only reason that* behind facts ideas are concealed; facts without ideas are so much trash for your head and for your memory" (review of Smaragdov's history text, 8:276).

65. See, e.g., Belinskij's review of Lorenz's work, 6:100–101.

the history of the Middle Ages, was nevertheless able to grasp their very essence through his poetic intuition.

The same goes for the eighteenth century, described as "that hypocritical, debauched, sugary age" ("Literary Reveries," 1:68).[66] The following passage from Belinskij's essay on Deržavin (1843) is significant in that it credits Puškin with a better statement of the "spirit" of the eighteenth century than Deržavin himself:

> The eighteenth century is mirrored only in the magnates of that age, as we have already observed. But since Deržavin, through his talent, became a member of the aristocracy, it was inevitable that the eighteenth century should be mirrored, more or less, in him also. However . . . all the works of Deržavin taken together do not express the eighteenth century with even remotely the same plenitude and plasticity as does Puškin's excellent poem "To a Magnate." (6:620–21)

Belinskij liked to make similar observations concerning his own age. "Our age," he says in his review of Lorenz's *Manual of Universal History,* "is first and foremost a *historical* age" (6:90). By this he means that the thinking of his age in all spheres of life is characterized by a "historical" attitude, that is, an awareness of the progress of mankind and a belief in the existence of universal historical laws which govern it (ibid., 6:95).

In his essay on Deržavin, Belinskij calls the latter's famous last poem, "The River of Time" (actually the first stanza of an ode, "On Perishability"), a typical expression of eighteenth-century thinking, which was incapable of understanding that "individuals pass and change, while the spirit of human life lives forever" and that "what is drowned in the river of time are forms, not ideas" (6:632). If nothing else, this comment demonstrates Belinskij's ability to apply Hegelian models to concrete works of Russian literature. Belinskij's observation of the fundamental distinction between the classicist and the romantic time percept seems both apt and profound.[67] Deržavin's attitude had been one of gracefully resigned acceptance of the immutable and inscrutable law of inexorable time. Belinskij's own age, he felt, had developed a quite different sensibility. It was an age of bold critical analysis, of tireless search for the causes of things, of audacious belief in the power of the human spirit and its ability to shape the world after its own free will. The great herald of this new age was Byron, whom the Russian critic venerated. In Russia, Belinskij thought, this new *Weltgefühl* was first announced in Puškin's poem "The Demon"

66. This image of the eighteenth century seems inspired by literature more than by anything else. I am thinking specifically of Puškin, *Evgenij Onegin,* chap. 4, stanzas 1–7.

67. Cf. Victor Terras's articles "The Time Philosophy of Osip Mandel'shtam," *Slavonic and East European Review* 47 (1969): 344–54, and "Grifel'naja oda O. Mandel'štama," *Novyj žurnal* 92 (1969): 163–71, dealing with Mandel'štam's reaction to Deržavin's ode.

(1823).[68] But ultimately, Puškin was unable to become its chosen organ, and it became Lermontov's lot to be its principal exponent in Russian literature (First essay on Puškin, 1843, 7:105).

Although Belinskij never made it quite explicit (on account of censorship, no doubt), it is easily gathered from many of his essays after 1841 that he believed the time had come for yet another age, characterized by rapid social progress, with literature its standard-bearer. In this, as in so many other things, Belinskij was proven by history to have been a good prophet. It is impossible not to credit him with a very definite "sixth sense" for the drift of time.

The idea of historical continuity is central to Belinskij's whole thinking. He always viewed history as a monistic process consisting of certain determinate stages which form a continuous, dialectic chain, much like the various biological forms of life.[69]

During his Schellingian and earlier Hegelian period, Belinskij saw history essentially as the evolution of the Idea, that is, a rational process by which the manifestations of the Absolute in the human spirit were approaching the ultimate goal of identity with the Absolute. At this stage Belinskij believed that under the philosopher's gaze, "millions of fortuitous phenomena change into units of necessary phenomena, each of which is a moment in the embodiment of the evolving divine idea, stopped forever in its flight" ("The Idea of Art," 1841, 4:589).[70]

In Belinskij's later years, this notion of continuity persists, but there is less emphasis on the absolute value of each particular stage of evolution, and "progress" is seen largely in concrete social and scientific, rather than in abstract intellectual terms:

> All organic development is achieved through progress. Only that develops organically in which each particular phenomenon is the necessary result of a preceding phenomenon and is explained in terms of the latter. If one might imagine a literature in which, from time to time, some admirable works appear, which are, however, in no way connected with one another by any inner bonds, but which owe their appearance to external influences, to imitation [of foreign examples], then, such a literature would have no history. Its history would be reduced to a mere bibliography. The word "progress" cannot be applied to such a literature. ("1847," 10:283)

Belinskij's conception of progress is dialectic.[71] He knows well that progress means not only building the new but also tearing down the old. In the passage, a part of which is quoted just above, he also very boldly says that "there are,

---

68. "The Poetry of M. Lermontov," 4:524.
69. See 6:95; 7:221; 8:282; 10:164.
70. Cf. 1:192, 214; 5:95, 316–17; 6:611.
71. See 5:549; 6:22, 137, 275, 459, 583.

in the life of nations, epochs during which whole generations are sacrificed, as it were, to the coming generations" (10:283). And on different occasions he expresses the thought that his own age may be just such an age, a period during which mankind is gathering the material means toward a new and mighty forward leap in the spiritual sphere (review of Smaragdov's history text, 1844, 8:283-84). This particular notion coincides with French utopian socialist thought. In the early 1840s, Belinskij had some legitimate reason to assume that artistic creativity in Russia was on the decline, while political and economic forces were on the upswing in Russian life. The French utopian socialists had some reason to think likewise. Both they as well as Belinskij were proven wrong in that periods of great artistic achievement were to follow in their countries.

Belinskij's notion of the role of "genius" (*genij*) in history is Hegelian. The genius (Hegel's "world-historical personage") must inevitably clash with established traditions and with the masses. Such clash is like an "examination": if the genius prevails he has won the right to alter the course of history.[72] Belinskij defends Ivan the Terrible precisely on these grounds. He was the exponent of a new current in Russian life and prevailed over the old appanage system, which he defeated in a cruel, merciless struggle (review of *The Moscow Literary and Learned Almanac for 1847*, 10:195). Boris Godunov, on the other hand, was a pseudo-genius who failed his examination.

It goes without saying that the sanction given to the destructive role of "world-historical personages" in history collides with Belinskij's belief in the individual's right to happiness. But in this there is also an important implication for literature. By and large, Belinskij seems to be of the opinion that "no one can stand above his age or his country" and that "no poet will ever express a content which was not prepared and worked out by history" (review of Gogol''s *Dead Souls*, 6:259). But a genius, by definition, transcends his age as well as his country, and it is implied that a great poet should be not just an observer, but also a mover of history. Belinskij's later essays suggest that he would very much like to believe that this is actually true. He felt that Lermontov, if he had lived, might have become a great spiritual leader of his nation. And if he rejected Gogol''s claims to such leadership, this was not because he thought that an artist should stay within the confines of his art. Belinskij's comment, often repeated by him, that Puškin was "an artist, and nothing but an artist" expressed not approval, but regret. In the absence of the revolutionary

72. "A reaction on the part of the masses against the genius is inevitable; in this way, they subject the genius to an examination. If he will take his own in spite of everything, he is in fact a genius, i.e., he bears within himself the right to affect the fate of his country. If it were otherwise, any *raisonneur,* dreamer, or philosopher, any petty great man would treat the people like a horse, directing it to one or the other side according to his own arbitrary whims or fantasies. . ." ("1846," 10:31).

leadership of a great genius, Belinskij was willing to accept a literature moved less spectacularly, but steadily, by the collective efforts of a number of strong talents who, while not capable of giving direction to history, would at least stay abreast of it.

This leads to what is perhaps the crucial point not only in Belinskij's but in all of Russian aesthetic thought, namely, Belinskij's belief that the historical development of a literature shares the historical teleology of the nation to which it belongs. This belief implied that "true art" could not possibly be reactionary or out of touch with the times, even if the artist's conscious concerns were purely aesthetic and had little to do with politics or ideology.[73]

At the height of his Hegelian period, and especially in his essay "Menzel, a Critic of Goethe" (1840), Belinskij quite consciously and systematically postulates the existence of an identical teleology governing both history and art. The will of great men always coincides with the will of God (3:393). An individual, insofar as he represents but a small part of the whole, may err and embrace false beliefs, "but a poet, being the organ of the general and the universal, and a direct manifestation of the Spirit, cannot err or tell a lie" (3:397). A genius will always have an intuition (*instinkt*) for that which is true and real. Therefore, Belinskij mentions as a matter of course the calm prediction of Puškin, a true genius, that "the Slavic streams would all flow together into the Russian sea,"[74] while the more narrow Mickiewicz angrily and fruitlessly rebelled against the inevitable course of history (ibid.). Belinskij would soon regret such denigration of Mickiewicz's image. However, he did not change his theoretical position.

In a major article on the poetry of A. I. Poležaev (1842, 6:119-60), Belinskij seeks to account for the failure of this talented poet and in the process delivers a whole essay on poetic failure in general. In typically Hegelian fashion, he minimizes the importance of subjective factors, such as a lack of "formal" talent or of education, disadvantageous external circumstances, or a lack of sympathy and recognition on the part of the poet's contemporaries. Proceeding, then, to analyze the greatness of truly great poets, Belinskij quickly comes to the conclusion that it occurs only when produced and nurtured by the life of a great historical nation and its culture. In fact, only he is a great poet who reflects and enhances in his art that powerful movement of the life forces of which his own spirit is a quintessence. Even a poet of mediocre formal talent, but able to maintain strong organic ties with the life of his nation, will make a contribution to its literature. He will be remembered longer than a gifted rhymester whose flashy but empty verses may deceive a frivolous audience for a brief

73. For a detailed statement of the organic unity of art and life at large, see, for instance, Belinskij's essay on Deržavin (1843), 6:583-85.
74. In his poem "To Those Who Slander Russia" (1831).

moment. Finally, there will always be poets who, like Poležaev, simply cannot come to terms with life and, in spite of considerable talent, cannot but present "a melancholy and instructive spectacle" (6:127).

That Belinskij never relinquished his belief in a mystical analogy between poetic creativity and the course of history, is shown by many explicit statements in his later writings. For example, in a review of Nikolaj Markevič's *History of Little Russia* (1843), Belinskij points out that "in the movement of historical events there exists, besides external causality, an inner necessity which gives these events a deep inner meaning" (7:53). Then he goes on to demand that a true historian be able to see this inner necessity, or "in other words, the idea behind the facts" (ibid.). Finally, he says quite unequivocally that it takes poetic flair (*poètičeskoe čut'e*) to grasp the meaning and to penetrate to the "living" core of historical facts (ibid.). Belinskij then proceeds to say—not for the first time, nor the last—that Sir Walter Scott's historical novels contain more living historical reality than many pragmatic historical works which read "like a bad fairy tale, where everything happens not according to the laws of rational necessity but as though by some strange magic" (ibid.).

Belinskij the critic draws a logical corollary from this conception when he believes to have discovered that in *The Gypsies* Puškin's spontaneous and unconscious intuition produced a much more truthful and historically relevant poetic idea than was the poet's conscious intention (Seventh essay on Puškin, 1844, 7:386). The belief in a synchronized teleological movement of history and artistic creation is found even in Belinskij's last articles. In his "Survey of Russian Literature in 1846," we read:

> The writers in whom the progressive movement involving the liberation of Russian literature from Lomonosov's influence found its expression did not give this any thought whatsoever; it all happened unconsciously; it was the *Zeitgeist* (*dux vremeni*) which was working for them, and they were its organs. (10:13)

Such a view has specific consequences for the actual evaluation of works of literature. If it is true that a genuine work of art marches along with the times and will never contradict history, it ought to be possible for a critic of talent to demonstrate that a work which is historically false, that is, reactionary, is also inferior as a work of art. It is precisely this argument that Belinskij adduces as he defends the Natural School against Samarin's attacks: if the works of the Natural School are indeed painting as false a picture of Russian reality as Samarin would have it, Samarin ought to subject these works to thorough aesthetic criticism and prove that they are in violation of the basic principles of art ("A Rejoinder to *The Muscovite*," 1847, 10:257). The notion that a true work of art might be historically indifferent, reactionary, or in outright opposition to all social and historical reality, hardly occurs to Belinskij—he simply takes the analogy of life and art for granted.

To do justice to Belinskij the thinker (as opposed to Belinskij the historical figure of far-reaching influence) on this and other important points, we should note that Belinskij had his moments of doubt and "private" as opposed to "public" thoughts. In 1840 Belinskij began to assume the ideological stance in which he is generally recognized. But his correspondence during that year suggests that he was continually struggling with thoughts that were in sharp conflict with his "public" organicist conception of literature.

In a letter to V. P. Botkin, 14 March 1840, Belinskij makes it quite clear that he has decided to sacrifice his love for art to his historical mission, and that it has not been an easy decision:

> No, let all these higher aspirations and goals go to the Devil! We live in terrible times. Fate is forcing us to take monastic vows [*nalagaet sximu*, a metaphor suggesting an involuntary renunciation of worldly concerns], and we must suffer so that our grandchildren may have a better life. Let us all do not what we want, but what we must, and what we can do. If you're not destined to carry a field marshal's baton, why, grab a rifle, and if you haven't got one, get yourself a spade and start scraping the shit off the Russian public. . . . I am a writer, so I am saying this with pain, yet also from a joyous and proud conviction. (11:494)

In a letter to the same correspondent, written a month later (16 April 1840), Belinskij expresses his conviction that he has been chosen to be a tool of history—"though it be only a broom, a spade, or a shovel"—and is satisfied and happy with that role: he will be used until he breaks, and then thrown away (11:503–4). He who speaks here is not Belinskij the "public critic" (who eats his cake and has it, too) but a lover of art who has decided to sacrifice art to something more important. It is significant that in another letter of that year (to Botkin, 30 December 1840) Belinskij states to his distinct satisfaction that there are three kinds of poetry: "artistic (higher poetry—Homer, Shakespeare, Walter Scott, Cooper, Byron, Schiller, Goethe, Puškin, Gogol'), religious poetry (Schiller, Jean Paul, Hoffmann, even Goethe), and philosophic poetry (*Faust, Prometheus, Manfred* to some extent, etc.)." As an afterthought, he adds that "there is also social poetry, the poetry of current life" (11:582). Victor Hugo is mentioned as a worthy practitioner of social poetry. It is difficult to imagine anything farther removed from the "public" Belinskij, even the "public" Belinskij of the same period.

At the time when he was writing, Belinskij faced no very striking examples, at least not in Russian literature, that might have disproved his "organic" conception. Virtually every major figure in Russian literature could be considered either in tune with his age or actually "progressive." One notes, nevertheless, a recurrent element of discord in Belinskij's essays on Puškin: the critic cannot

help voicing his disappointment at the poet's relatively conservative views and
—just like Soviet textbooks to this day—tries to "save" the poet whom he
loves by asserting that he was, inevitably, a child of his age and of his class.
When Gogol' "betrays" progress, Belinskij reacts as will any man who sees the
very foundations of his world view put in question: he rationalizes the situation by trying to convince himself that Gogol' had ceased being a great artist
because he had turned reactionary (or vice versa). No doubt, Belinskij's almost
frantic efforts to minimize the talent of his former protegé Dostoevskij
stemmed from the same thought: since Dostoevskij was turning reactionary,
he had to cease being a great artist. From here on, much of Russian literary
criticism will be vitiated by the belief, shared by Left and Right alike, that "poetic truth," and consequently artistic greatness, depends on the "truth" or
"falsehood" of the poet's or artist's ideological position.

Belinskij's organic historicism had yet another important side effect. Belinskij was so much fascinated by continuity in a broad historical perspective
that he tended to disregard continuity on a pragmatic, purely literary level.
He saw the dynamic continuity between Onegin, Pečorin, and Bel'tov, but
failed to register the important and obvious antithetic relationship between
Dostoevskij's first heroes and their Gogolian prototypes. Only twentieth-century Formalist scholars bothered to state that Makar Alekseevič Devuškin was
a definite "antiparody" of Gogol' 's Akakij Akak'evič Bašmačkin and to draw
the literary and ideological consequences from this circumstance.

The Formalists of the 1920s were right in charging that Belinskij and his entire tradition substituted a broad history of Russian society and ideology for
actual *history of literature.* The Formalists also corrected some erroneous opinions launched by Belinskij as a result of his disregard for the pragmatic facts of
literary connections. Belinskij tended to treat Gogol' as though that writer had
emerged out of nowhere, creating his chefs d'oeuvre entirely from the resources
of Russian reality and his own imagination. This was quite wrong: Gogol' 's art
was intimately connected with specific trends, aesthetic concepts, and works of
contemporary and older literature, Russian as well as Western. Belinskij's contemporaries, such as Ševyrev, Senkovskij, and Polevoj, pointed out Gogol' 's dependence on Hoffmann, the French *école frénétique,* West Russian chapbooks,
and other sources, but Belinskij would not listen to them.

Belinskij consistently distinguishes between the relative (historical) and the
absolute (artistic) importance of a writer or poet: "In the history of literature
the names of some mediocrities are immortal . . . but in the sphere of art they
are inconsequential" (review of *The Theater in France from the Sixteenth to
the Nineteenth Century* by Nikolaj Jakovlevskij, 1841, 4:573).[75] Nor will
Belinskij hesitate to apply this principle to his practical criticism:

75. Cf. 5:195, 523–24, 544.

As far as artistic execution is concerned, there can be no comparison between Onegin and Pečorin. But just as Onegin tops Pečorin in an artistic
sense, so Pečorin stands above Onegin in his idea. However, this advantage
belongs to our age, and not to Lermontov. ("A Hero of Our Time," 1840,
4: 266)

The matter is complicated, however, by Belinskij's insistence on making value judgments regarding both the historical and the artistic merits of an artist
and his work. Thus, in discussing the *Igor' Tale*, Belinskij praises its poetic
qualities but feels obliged to remark that its content is rendered insignificant
by the fact that it deals "not with a battle of two nations but with a raid by
one tribe on another" ("The Russian Folk Tale," 1841, 5: 348). Obviously,
says Belinskij, these shortcomings of the *Igor' Tale* derive not from the poet's
lack of talent but from the dearth of historical substance with which the life
of his nation was able to provide him. Analogously, Belinskij blandly asserts
that it is the fault of Russian history, not of Puškin, that there is no "drama,"
no real passion, struggle, or action in *Boris Godunov* (Tenth essay on Puškin,
1845, 7: 505–8).

The same reasoning leads Belinskij to deny the desirability of "Ukrainian poetry" on the grounds that it would severely limit a poet's possibilities. Ukrainian being spoken only by peasants, the use of that language would greatly curtail the content of a poet's work. It would take quite exceptional talent, such
as Gogol' 's, to impart an ideal content to poetry based on the life of the
Ukrainian peasantry (review of *The Swallow*, a Ukrainian anthology, 1841,
5: 177).

In trying to weigh the relative merits of Deržavin and Žukovskij, the critic is
caught in a veritable net of equivocations. On the one hand, he feels obliged
to establish the great and highly beneficial role which Žukovskij's poetry
played in the moral and aesthetic evolution of Russian society ("1841," 5: 546).
Deržavin's historical role, on the other hand, had to be much more limited, because in his day Russian society was practically nonexistent. But Belinskij
knows intuitively, and he admits it, that Deržavin is a much greater poet than
Žukovskij (ibid., 5: 547). How is he to explain this, particularly since, "as
verses go, Žukovskij's are much better than Deržavin's"? (Here Belinskij is
guilty of a flagrantly careless formulation, mistaking *regularity* for *excellence*,
but he still has a valid question.) He tries to extricate himself by claiming that
"as a *poet*, Deržavin was incomparably superior to Žukovskij," meaning that,
while a mediocre craftsman, Deržavin was moved by a true Russian spirit, had
a lofty, inspired soul, and genuine creative power—all of which Žukovskij
lacked. But then, rather surprisingly, Belinskij comes back to claim that "the
superiority of Žukovskij's poetry lies in its *content*" (ibid., 5: 547). He means
"historical content," of course.

Again measuring an artist's greatness against the greatness of his age, Belin-skij says (in the same article) that Batjuškov, if only he had lived *after* Puškin when life could offer a poet some substance for the content of his creations, would have no doubt become a poet of great stature (5:551-52). Finally, turning to Puškin himself, Belinskij is ready to acknowledge that "Puškin as an artist had creative powers equal to those of any poet in the world" (5:558). Yet, on the other hand, the depth and content of his poetry could not stand comparison with the creations of the great European poets. The content of Russian life during Puškin's lifetime simply lacked the substance worthy of a poet of Puškin's genius (ibid., 5:569).[76]

The Hegelian conception of history as a monistic process means, in the his-torian's usage, that certain nations, developments, and ideas are left by the wayside as "ahistorical," irrelevant, or actually contrary to the irreversible for-ward movement of mankind.[77] In literature, this means that certain poets, genres, types, and ideas can be, and often are, out of step with, or lagging be-hind, history. Thus, for a decade Puškin was one of those fortunate poets ful-ly in harmony with the spirit of their age (Fourth essay on Puškin, 1843, 7:269). During the last years of his life, however, he and Russian society grew apart (ibid., 7:295). Such a development may not be fatal to a great talent, but it will certainly harm it, as it harmed Puškin. Belinskij's relatively low esti-mation of the works of Puškin's late period, especially his prose, is explained by this historicist bias.

Belinskij uses this conception in various other contexts. The following is an example of its application to "type":

> The idea of Don Quixote does not belong to the age of Cervantes alone: it is an eternal, universal idea, like every "idea." Don Quixote has been possi-ble ever since human society came into existence and will remain possible so long as people will not return to the state of savages. Don Quixote is a noble and wise man who is devoted to his cherished idea with his whole being, with his whole ardent, energetic soul. The comic aspect of Don Quixote's charac-ter lies in the contradiction between his beloved idea and the demands of his age. It lies in the fact that his idea cannot be realized, that it cannot be put to action. (review of *Kuz'ma Petrovič Mirošev* by M. N. Zagoskin, 1842, 6:34)

Belinskij's emphasis on the *historical* aspect of this "type" is quite character-istic of his thinking. Turgenev's conception of the same type (in his famous

---

76. Cf. 6:123.
77. Poležaev, for example, is identified as such an aborted phenomenon in Russian literature (6:127-28).

essay "Hamlet and Don Quixote" [1860] and elsewhere) virtually ignores this aspect.[78]

Belinskij's organic historicism leads to the inevitable conclusion that most, if not all, works of literature sooner or later become dated and outdated. All eighteenth-century literature, even including the poetry of Deržavin, is relegated to the category of "works of merely historical interest." It took courage to say the following things about Deržavin in 1843:

> Reading Deržavin's poems, one can hardly understand anything about them without a historical commentary about the manners of the age of which he was the organ . . . The language, the way of thinking, the feelings, the interests—everything is alien to our age. . . . But Deržavin is not dead, just as the age which he celebrated is not dead: the age of Catherine paved the way for the age of Alexander, which in turn prepared ours. And so, between Deržavin and the poets of our age there exists the same historical blood-bond that exists between these three periods of Russian history. ("The Works of Deržavin," 6:582)[79]

In other words, Deržavin is banished to the historical limbo of "precursors." The same applies for Batjuškov. "Who reads Batjuškov's poetry today? Everything about him belongs to his age, almost nothing to our own," Belinskij observes, rather casually (Third essay on Puškin, 1843, 7:241). Žukovskij is not exempt from the same verdict, nor is Puškin.

To Belinskij, *Evgenij Onegin* is first and foremost "a poetic representation of Russian society, seen at one of the most interesting moments of its development" (Eighth essay on Puškin, 1844, 7:432). But that moment has passed, and Onegin has long since become a type out of the historical past. He was superseded by Pečorin who, in turn, has since become outdated (Eighth essay on Puškin, 1844, 7:447).

We are dealing here with a strange visual defect in the perceptive Belinskij. To be sure, times were changing rapidly in Russia, and because Belinskij, who was only a decade younger than Puškin, belonged to an entirely different and, one might say, "new" social class, these changes looked even more spectacular to him. But a glance at any of the great foreign literatures could have told him that great poetry never grows old. In fact, in other contexts Belinskij fully acknowledges this. It is not that Belinskij did not believe that great works of

78. Belinskij's interpretation is very close to that given by Hegel, *Ästhetik*, 1:565–66 and 2:466. The Hegelian Vischer stresses yet another element of tension in *Don Quixote*, which Belinskij does not notice. The ironic chorus of Sancho Panza's replications to his master's noble ravings makes *Don Quixote* a *Volksroman*, which attacks the outdated aristocratic ideal of chivalry from the viewpoint of the common people (Vischer, *Aesthetik*, 3:1316).

79. Cf. 6:651, 657; 7:268; 9:297; 10:9–10, 182.

art have an absolute value. His entire criticism suggests that he never doubted this. But unlike Hegel who, all his "historicism" and "contentualism" notwithstanding, had made sure that there would be a place in his system for the absolute value of great art, Belinskij was never really concerned about this problem. That the problem is a real and a difficult one can be seen, for instance, in Dostoevskij's valiant attempt to solve it in "Mr. —bov and the Question of Art" and elsewhere.

Belinskij's point of view in the above, as well as in a number of other statements about Puškin, is virtually that of the "sociological school" of the 1920s. In the light of such passages, there seems to be justification for Berdjaev's remark that Belinskij was, among other things, also the first Russian Marxist (without having read Marx, of course).[80]

A certain hypertrophy of historicism is not solely characteristic of Belinskij's Leftist epigoni, as is sometimes assumed. The "organic historicism" of a Grigor'ev or a Dostoevskij all too often operates with much the same arguments. When Dostoevskij criticizes Gončarov's *Precipice* or Turgenev's *Smoke,* his principal point is that these authors are out of touch with contemporary Russian reality. When Gončarov presents the gentlemanly indolence, the dilettantism, the endless talking (without ensuing action) of his hero Rajskij, as though these were *the* fateful Russian vices, he is, so says Dostoevskij, simply whipping a dead horse. Times have changed.

The Left and the Right would disagree, of course, about precisely what should be called "new" and "old." Thus, Dostoevskij and his many epigoni felt that the future belonged to the Russian "religious revolution," which their opponents felt was a reactionary anachronism. The point is that both would introduce this question in an argument regarding the aesthetic merit of a novel.

LITERATURE AND SOCIOHISTORICAL REALITY

Belinskij's conception of "literature" (in the sense of its being art, *xudožestvennaja literatura*)[81] is "organic" in every respect. He sees it as a function of both nationality and society, on the one hand, and as "a living whole," on the other. The national function of literature fully emerges even in the early Belinskij:

> Literature is national self-awareness, and where no such self-awareness exists literature is either a premature fruit or a "way to make a living" for a certain group of people. Even if such a literature will produce beautiful and refined creations, these are exceptions rather than positive phenomena,

80. Berdjaev, *Russkaja ideja,* p. 61.
81. Belinskij is well aware of the variety of meanings in which the term *literatura* is used. See, e.g., 4:21–22, 148–49; 5:620–22.

and there is no rule for exceptions. . . . ("Nothing about Naught," 1836, 2:50)[82]

It appears that Belinskij never abandoned this conception.[83] His organic conception of literature becomes well defined during his Hegelian period when he begins to view Russian literature in a determinate historical context, like every other "substantial" fact of national life. In his article "Russian Literature in 1840" (1841, 4:408–47), Belinskij uses the terms *literatura* and *slovesnost'*, which he had previously used almost indiscriminately, to denote the distinction between the verbal creations of a historical and those of an ahistorical nation. Only a historical nation can have a literature (*literatura*), or, vice versa, the presence of a literature vouches for the historical existence of a nation (ibid., 4:414).

A national literature has its distinct individuality. The presence of a number of excellent works does not in itself constitute a literature. What creates a literature is the presence of a vital, "organic" bond between the different authors and schools which together make up a nation's literary life (ibid., 4:431–32; cf. 10:283). This, in turn, is explained by the fact that literature is the expression of the life of a society. Where no society exists there can be no literature—only more or less talented writers and poets (ibid., 4:434–35). By "social life" Belinskij means an abundance of common intellectual, aesthetic, and spiritual interests, the presence of a distinct world view, the regular exchange of living ideas, and a certain movement, variety, and direction in all of these phenomena. In Belinskij's opinion, Russia had, in his age, finally reached the point in her history where a society in the above sense was beginning to develop, so that the nation would soon be able to boast its own literature, as an expression of a newly won social awareness (ibid., 4:447).

Belinskij's lengthy essay on the general meaning of the word "literature" is of considerable theoretical interest.[84] It was a preliminary step to a major work, never written, in which he meant to determine how Russian literature measured up to the concept. Belinskij distinguishes three distinct layers of Russian literature (in the widest application of that term): *slovesnost'*, the oral tradition which, through folk poetry, extends to the present; *pis'mennost'*, in a broader sense simply "the written word" and thus a medium for *slovesnost'* as well as *pis'mennost'* in a more narrow sense, with *pis'mennost'* embracing the whole homiletic, hagiographic, polemic, annalistic, and other ecclesiastic literature of pre-Petrine Russia; and *literatura*, literature proper, as the

---

82. There is the following even earlier statement: "And so, literature must absolutely be the expression, the symbol (*simvol*), of the inner life of a nation" ("Literary Reveries," 1834, 1:29). Cf. also 1:24.

83. Cf. 9:152; 10:283.

84. An untitled manuscript written between 1842 and 1844, published posthumously in 1862, 5:620–53. Cf. a similar discussion in "Russian Literature in 1840," 4:417–21.

organic expression of Russian national life in creative works of the imagination.

When Belinskij says that "an organic consistency of its development is what determines the specific character of *literatura* as opposed to *slovesnost'* and *pis'mennost'*" (ibid., 5:623), he flagrantly underestimates the actual social and historical role of both *slovesnost'* and *pis'mennost'*. He visualizes pre-Petrine Russian culture and literature as static and noncreative and is quite unaware of the fact that in Old Russian culture and literature, too, there existed different periods, with different world views, ideas, and styles, as well as conflicts of ideas and styles, and therefore a historical evolution as well. It must be said in Belinskij's defense that even experts in the field held a view similar to his at the time.

Belinskij's failure to appreciate the creative and artistic aspect of Russian medieval art and literature is less easily excused. It must have had something to do with his anticlericalism, on the one hand, and his altogether present- and future-oriented outlook, on the other. The view toward the future appears plastically in Belinskij's opinion regarding the loss of much of Russian *slovesnost'* through medieval Russia's neglect to make written records of it: "They were ultimately right," says Belinskij, "for only that perishes in the river of time which lacks a robust seed of life, and therefore does not deserve to be left alive; so that, while we should not hold in contempt those remnants of our folk poetry which have been preserved, we should not lament excessively the loss of what has perished" (ibid.).

Slovesnost', says Belinskij, is meaningful and interesting mostly through its verbal form, while its ideal content tends to be indifferent. Thus, *slovesnost'* has a history only insofar as its verbal form is concerned, while literature expresses, in its types and in its ideal content, the various moments in a nation's historical progress (ibid., 5:637). Therefore, works of *slovesnost'* and *pis'-mennost'* (songs, tales, legends, annals, and so forth) can originate from monastic cells, from banquet halls, from the wide plains and dark forests of Russia, while society (Belinskij only implies "urban society"), with its lively intercourse of ideas, opinions, mutual criticism, applause, and censure, is the true laboratory of literature (ibid.). Again Belinskij's opinion is based on erroneous factual information. A work of *slovesnost'*, with its successive generations of authors and audiences, is a product of social selection, and therefore a collective achievement. Nor does Belinskij know that medieval Russian chronicles were consistently reworked and rewritten to suit a new political situation. If historical, political, and social identity is the criterion of "literature," much of what Belinskij calls *slovesnost'* and *pis'mennost'* meets his requirements very well. But this was established only by later scholars.

Belinskij is really in his element when he discusses literature as he knows it in his own day: as the "living pulse of society," as a sure indicator of a society's health in all of its vital functions, as a nation's consciousness (*soznanie naroda*) (ibid., 5:626; cf. 9:432-33). In good Hegelian fashion, Belinskij defines such a national consciousness as the presence of an intellectual life, of moral principles, and of a historical purpose. And again he seems to be in conflict with the facts. A feeling of moral and ideological unity and an awareness of having a world-historical mission were strong in medieval Russia and were vigorously stated in her literature. For all we know, the Kievan state of Jaroslav the Wise or the Muscovite state of Ivan the Terrible "existed morally, rather than only empirically" (ibid., 5:646-47) as much or more than did Belinskij's Russia.[85]

At any rate, for Belinskij, the greatness and world-historical significance of Russian literature lie in the future. Russian society and Russia's national identity are still being formed. Belinskij, a good patriot throughout, often expresses his belief in the extraordinary giftedness of his people.[86] Russia, he says, can be likened to a gifted child who gives promise of becoming a great man some day, but whose features and talents are as yet only vaguely outlined (ibid., 5:649).[87] In spite of Russia's great political power, Belinskij feels that even in his own age Russian literature is still lacking in world-historical significance.[88] This admission comes somewhat unexpectedly from a man whom we know for a Russian patriot and who, moreover, had great love and admiration for the genius of a Puškin or a Gogol'. Nor was Belinskij alien to the notion, later made popular by Dostoevskij, that in Puškin the Russian genius had already found its incarnation.[89] However, Belinskij finds a way to reconcile all this with his notion of Russia's historical "immaturity." Contemporary Russian civilization and literature, he observes, are different from other civilizations and literatures in that they arose not of themselves and from Russian soil but rather as a result of the "artificial" (rather than "organic") reforms of Peter the Great, who quite arbitrarily transplanted a foreign civilization into Russian soil. It is therefore the task of the Russian people to make the new life style forced upon them truly their own. It is the task of Russian literature to convert sterile rhetoric and slavish imitation into true art. Puškin was the first Russian poet who was wholly successful in doing this.

Belinskij's high appreciation of Puškin's greatness as an artist is tempered by important reservations. The essence of Puškin's poetry, says Belinskij, is that of pure, objective art: "Puškin is a poet and artist par excellence . . . the first in Russian literature to introduce art as art, poetry as artistic creation"

85. On the ideal meaning of *Rus'* in the Middle Ages, see Henryk Paszkiewicz, *The Making of the Russian Nation* (London, 1963), *passim*.

86. E.g., 3:221-22, 231; 5:399, 426.

87. Cf. also 4:422.

88. See 4:423-24; 5:297, 648.

89. See 3:222-23; 4:425; 5:318, 557-58, 651; 7:336.

(*iskusstvo kak iskusstvo, poèzija—kak xudožestvennoe tvorčestvo*) (ibid.,
5:650–51). Belinskij will make it quite clear in later essays that he means Puškin's poetry is lacking in social *pafos* and historical substance.

In his discussion of Nikitenko's "Discourse on Criticism", Belinskij develops
the same ideas even more explicitly. The reforms of Peter the Great are again
called "artificial." Eighteenth-century literature is said to have developed "not
out of the needs of society but out of blind imitation of foreign literature"
(6:289). Its evolution was therefore conditioned by a natural striving for more
freedom from the strictures of alien forms. The first goal of Russian literature
was to become genuinely artistic. It was brilliantly achieved by Puškin, whom
Belinskij calls "the *first* Russian poet, even chronologically speaking" (6:294).
And again a reservation is added:

> Puškin is an artist in the full sense of that word; this is his overwhelming
> importance, his highest merit and, perhaps, his failing, because the more he
> became an artist, the more he also moved away from contemporary life and
> its interests and embraced an ascetic tendency which in the end alienated
> him from the society that had earlier admired him without any reservation.
> (ibid., 6:295)

Here, "ascetic" is of course Aesopian language for "reactionary, removed
from real life." Without a doubt, this passage (and a number of others in which
Belinskij said much the same thing) did more damage to Belinskij's reputation
than almost anything else he ever said. It is also quite wrong even in its own
narrow terms, for Puškin was just then beginning to come into his own as a
"social" and "historical" factor of immeasurable importance, a civilizing, myth-
making, and nation-building force rarely paralleled in the history of any nation.
But it is to Belinskij's partial exoneration that he knew only a severely censored
version of Puškin's writings.

Belinskij's insistence on the value of national originality and his assumption
of an absence of it in much Russian literature are justified in some respects,
misplaced in others. Belinskij ignores the fact that much about the greatest
works of English, French, and German literature was also "borrowed" in one
way or another. He also ignores the indubitable and by no means trivial fact
that Russian versification had fully adapted itself to the language and was firmly established even in the poetry of Lomonosov. Finally, he underestimates
the excellence of Russian poetry before Puškin. On the other hand, Belinskij
was right in that the myth-making process in modern Russian literature had
only just begun. It was simply too early to recognize in *The Bronze Horseman*
or *Dead Souls* the germs of a Russian national mythology. And of course Belinskij's optimistic prognosis of the future of Russian literature was quite correct.

There is some vacillation in Belinskij's evaluation of Russian literature after

Puškin. Most of the time he is optimistic and feels that it has taken firm roots in the soil of Russian national life, that it plays a vital role in the continued development of Russian society, that it is, by and large, a strong progressive force, and that its negative and reactionary elements are invariably defeated in the long run.[90] But there were times when Belinskij recognized the fact that this might be the biased impression of a professional littérateur whose very lifeblood was literature, while to a majority of even the educated, literature was "still merely a pleasant and profitable, innocent and noble pastime to fill the leisure hours of writer and reader alike" (review of the works of Zeneida R—va, 1843, 7:650).

On occasion, Belinskij also becomes conscious of the fact (ever present in the minds of his successors, such as Černyševskij and Dobroljubov) that the whole educated class, to which he belongs, is only a small part of the nation. In a letter to V. P. Botkin, 8 September 1841, he flatly says that the Russian educated class, with all its undertakings and strivings, is like a cancerous growth in the body of a nation which simply is not yet a nation. Other nations have common interests, goals, and activities shared by all. Their social life has some substance. In Russia things are different: "We are men without a country—or worse yet, we are men whose country is a phantom. Little wonder, then, that we ourselves become phantoms, that our friendships, our loves, our strivings, our activities are phantomlike. . . . We are men for the boundless content of whose life no ready form whatsoever is provided by our society and our age" (12:66–67). This very Čaadaevian thought keeps recurring to the end of Belinskij's life.

In Belinskij's "Survey of Russian Literature in 1846," we find some remarks on this subject which are decidedly reminiscent of the later Herzen, or of Dostoevskij. Belinskij starts by challenging the relative historical chronology of the Slavophiles. Their mistake is, he says, that they project Russia's world-historical life into the past and present rather than into the future. They take the early formative stages of a young nation for the flower of its historical life. Russia, says Belinskij, simply cannot be compared to the old and established nations of Western Europe. Rather, Russia ought to be compared with the United States of America, whose whole life lies in the future. Russia is still an embryo, an enigma, something as yet only vaguely outlined. Human nature being what it is, Belinskij proceeds, many Russians are impatient with such a state of affairs, and are either scornful of their country's lack of originality, identity, and character, or overestimate the virtues of Russia's pliability and "universality." Belinskij himself takes a cautiously optimistic stand. Russian literature, he says, has been in existence for a little over a hundred years, but has nevertheless produced works which even a foreigner will find original, different from anything he may have met elsewhere, in short, "national,"

90. See 5:652; 6:514, 674–75; 10:302, 314.

Russian. So there is such a thing as "Russian national life." On the other hand, it is still impossible to define "Russian nationality." Only the future will reveal its character in full. At present, its elements are beginning to take shape as they break through the colorless imitative forms produced in the wake of the reforms of Peter the Great.

A little farther in the same article, Belinskij states quite unequivocally that Russia's problems are not at all the same as those of the West. Russia ought to take some interest in Western trends and problems but never get involved in them to the point of neglecting her own interests: "Here, in our own country, in our own minds, in our own environment, that is where we must look for our problems as well as for their solution" (ibid., 10:32).

These thoughts are very close to the ideas of the *počvenniki* (from *počva,* "soil") Grigor'ev, Dostoevskij, Straxov, and others (who were all influenced by Herzen) in the 1860s. Belinskij, like the *počvenniki,* steers a middle course between uncompromising Slavophilism and uncompromising Westernism in an attempt to salvage the idea of Russia's "organic" development without rejecting the reforms of Peter the Great.

Belinskij's conception of the organic growth of Russian literature makes good sense in a broad historical perspective. Belinskij's prediction of future Russian writers of a truly universal stature was fulfilled much sooner than he had expected. Belinskij's scheme also accounts well for the fact that Puškin, the most important figure in Russian literature from a "national" point of view, lacks the universal stature of even a Gogol'. Some of the flaws in Belinskij's scheme are factual, while others relate to his overemphasis of the "national" and "universal" aspects of literature at the expense of the "individual" aspect.

Belinskij underestimates those traits of eighteenth- and nineteenth-century literature which are connected with the pre-Petrine epoch and with the folk tradition, for example, the important influence of liturgic poetry and ecclesiastic rhetoric on Lomonosov. On the other hand, he overestimates the originality of Gogol', failing to realize how much that writer owes to world literature. Belinskij conceives of world literature not so much as an aggregate of specific works and authors relating to other authors and works, as an ideal corpus of universals expressed in various form in the national literatures of the world. In his essay on the general meaning of the word "literature," he measures the importance of a particular literature to world literature not in terms of specific borrowings, influences, genres, forms, or types but rather in terms of the degree to which "the substantial idea which fertilizes a nation's life is universally human" (5:632). This means, in other words, that "the more the life of a nation represents that of all mankind and the more it affects the fate of humanity, the more the literature of such a nation will fall under the concept of 'universal literature'" (ibid.). This Hegelian conception, while it will not account for many facts relating to strictly literary relationships, seems to have withstood the test of history rather well. Dostoevskij, a writer who insisted at all times that he was a Russian writer who tackled universal problems entirely in Russian terms, became the most universally influential of all Russian writers. His universal success was largely due to the fact that the *Russian* problems which his creative intuition had so admirably grasped eventually turned out to be full-fledged *universal* problems after all—proving that Russia had certainly joined the mainstream of historical development.

The fact that Gogol', too, has become firmly established in world literature does not quite follow Belinskij's "model." History has shown that even Belinskij underestimated Gogol'. Of course, Gogol' has not become a great figure in world literature because he exposed the inefficiency and corruption of the imperial bureaucracy under Nicholas I. Rather, the sad, mad, absurd, and hyperbolically banal world which he created has been found to be deeply symbolic of the modern existential experience—not just in Russia but in the world at large.

Belinskij sensed and correctly diagnosed the greatness of a writer whose spirit was kindred to Gogol''s—E. T. A. Hoffmann. In a letter to V. P. Botkin, 16 April 1840, he writes: "I have been reading Hoffmann's *Serapion Brothers*. This Hoffmann is a wondrous and great genius! For the first time I now understood [the meaning of] the fantastic in his works. It is the poetic incarnation of mysterious hostile forces concealed in the depths of our spirit. With this point of view, Hoffmann's morbidness has disappeared for me, and only poetry has been left" (11:508) A similar interpretation, *mutatis mutandis,* would have been in order in approaching Gogol''s works. Belinskij misinterpreted Gogol', having been thrown off the scent (picked up by less perceptive critics) by his own fixation on social and historical organicism.

5

The Work of Art

Belinskij's conception of the work of art is organic from beginning to end. The "form" of a true work of art is the "living and organic body" of its "idea" (which is its "soul").[1] The comparison of a work of art to a living organism occurs innumerable times in Belinskij's writings. It is, of course, a cliché of German idealist aesthetics.[2]

Belinskij is very much aware of the work of art as an independent *sui generis* entity, a complex structure, and an ontological problem. In his essay "Woe from Wit" (1840), he makes it clear that a work of art may be viewed as a function of social life—from *les intérêts du jour* to history in the broadest sense—or as an absolute, as something with an immanent worth. As an absolute it is also an immediate manifestation of the Spirit, to be judged not by any temporal and relative, but by universal, rational laws. The first approach, according to Belinskij, is the "French," and the second the "German" view.[3]

The basic model of the work of art used by Belinskij is consistently dualistic rather than monistic or pluralistic. His fundamental conception of the work of art is that of an objective "idea" realized in a concrete "form," often referred to as "artistic image" (*xudožestvennyj obraz*). This, of course, is the notion of German objective idealism, as in Schelling's "Art as the real representation of the Absolute" (*Kunst als reale Darstellung des Absoluten*).[4] This model is opposed, on the one hand, to the subjective-idealist ("formalist") conception, according to which the work of art is a structure created by a craftsman to achieve

1. "On the Criticism and Literary Opinions of *The Moscow Observer*" (1836), 2:152.
2. According to Hegel, "every true work of poetic art is an organism, infinite in itself" (Hegel, *Ästhetik,* 2:361).
3. Belinskij is saying that only the "German" is relevant to the work of art as such, whereas the "French" approach deals with its historical importance. In this particular case, Belinskij states that he will avail himself of both approaches to Griboedov's comedy ("Woe from Wit," 1840, 3:473).
4. Cf. chap. 3, n. 36. Schelling, *Philosophie der Kunst,* 3:478.

a preconceived effect (which is immanent in the craftsman's mind). On the other hand, it is opposed to the mimetic conception, according to which a work of art is a representation of a part of nature. In the subjective-idealist approach, the "organic" connection with objective reality is absent, in the mimetic conception the objective reality presented by a work of art lacks an "idea" to animate it.

The polarity of "idea" and "form" appears in a great variety of formulations, all of which can also be found in German idealist aesthetics. The work of art is described as a fusion of the ideal and the real, of the abstract and the concrete, of thought and feeling, of the conscious and the subconscious, of freedom and necessity, of the rational and the irrational, of the infinite and the finite, the universal and the particular, the eternal and the temporal, of "creation" and "craft," of poetry and art, of content and form, of nature and history.[5] Belinskij's emphasis is always on the organic unity of these two poles, at least whenever their relationship is discussed. A typical statement would be: "One of the main conditions for any work of art is a harmonious correspondence between idea and form, form and idea, as well as the organic wholeness of its creation" (*organičeskaja celostnost' ego sozdanija*) ("The Works of Deržavin," 1843, 6:592). In the course of his career, Belinskij shifted his emphasis from the ideal toward the real aspect of this polarity. However, the fundamental postulate of their unity in the work of art remains intact to the end.[6]

THE IDEA IN ART

Belinskij took for granted the existence of what Plotinus had called "inner vision" or "inner form" ($\check{\epsilon}\nu\delta o\nu$ $\epsilon\check{\iota}\delta o\varsigma$). He considered its presence a prerequisite of artistic creation.[7] For example, in "Literary Reveries," Belinskij explains

5. References to these polarities are scattered throughout Belinskij's works. For examples of the ideal and the real, see 5:300; 8:89; 10:291, 317. For the abstract and the concrete, see 10:23. For thought and feeling, see Belinskij's observation, in speaking of Schiller's poem "Die Grösse der Welt," that "thought is dissolved in feeling, feeling in thought, and of this mutual annihilation, great art is born" (essay on V. G. Benediktov, 1835, 1:365); cf. 1:223; 6:270–71. On the irrational in Shakespeare, there is an interesting passage in Belinskij's letter to V. P. Botkin, 1 March 1841 (12:25). For the infinite and the finite, see 2:288, 420; 3:425. For the eternal and the temporal, see 5:562; 6:284, 585; 7:101. For "creation" and "craft," see 3:321, 364. For poetry and art, see 2:441–42. For nature and history, see 6:122–23, 601.

6. For a lengthy discussion of this point, see Belinskij's review of the poetry of A. Grigor'ev and Ja. P. Polonskij (1846, 9:591).

7. In Hegelian aesthetics the Plotinian $\check{\epsilon}\nu\delta o\nu$ $\epsilon\check{\iota}\delta o\varsigma$ is very much a psychological reality. In the creative process, says Hegel, "objectivity exchanges its earlier external reality for an inner reality, as it comes into existence in [the artist's] consciousness as a spiritually hypostatized and envisaged entity. Thus, the Spirit objectivates itself on its own grounds, using language only as a means of communication or immediate externalization . . ."

the fascination exerted by Balzac's Ferragus (in *Histoires des treizes: Ferragus*) by the fact that "Balzac did not invent, but rather created him, because he would appear to him before the first line of the story was ever written, because he tormented the artist until he transformed him from [a creature of] the world of his own soul into a phenomenon accessible to all" (1:84). Similar references to inner vision are frequently found in Belinskij's criticism. The Russian term for it is either *vnutrennee videnie* (1:48; 4:118) or *vnutrennee sozercanie* (4:201).

Plotinus's original image of the sculptor who liberates his inner vision from its captivity in an unhewn block of marble is well known to Belinskij. In an essay on Benediktov's poetry (1838), he expresses his appreciation of the deep truth conveyed by the myth of Pygmalion and exclaims: "Yes, fortunate is that artist who has communicated to marble that breath of life, that *something* which I cannot even name. . ." (2:421).

The Generative Idea

Belinskij's critical analysis invariably begins with a search for the generative idea (variously called *ideja, tvorčeskaja mysl', tvorčeskij razum, pafos*) and only then proceeds to an analysis of the logical and poetic structure of the work. The following passage from Belinskij's essay "Woe from Wit" (1840) is characteristic: "Every work of art is born of a single general idea, to which it owes the artistic quality (*xudožestvennost'*) of its form as well as the inner and external unity which makes it a distinct, closed, and complete world in itself" (3:473). Belinskij then proceeds to deny Griboedov's comedy recognition as a work of art precisely because it lacks such a "single general idea."

It is quite clear that Belinskij believed to the end of his life that a work of art, in that it is the realization of an idea, is quintessential reality and in a sense more real than real life itself. The following passage from a minor review of November 1845 contains a clear statement to this effect: "Today's Russian novel and short story no longer invent or make up stories; rather, they express facts of reality which, having been raised to an ideal level (*vozvedeny v ideal*), that is, freed of all that is fortuitous and particular, are truer to reality than reality is true to itself" (9:351).

If an "idea" must be the basis of a true work of art, mere representation of empirical reality, without an underlying and organizing idea, cannot be genuine art. Even outside the realm of aesthetic theory, Belinskij is generally opposed to positivism, empiricism, and relativism. In a review of an edition of Plato's works in Russian translation (1842), Belinskij defends philosophy, and

---

(Hegel, *Ästhetik*, 2:331). Similarly, Vischer speaks of "the transformation of the object into an inner image (*inneres Bild*), which is both sensual and not sensual, independent of the object's presence—and yet a hypostatized form, created by the Spirit" (Vischer, *Aesthetik,* 2:320-21; cf. 2:311, 330, 358; 3:1165, 1170).

specifically philosophic idealism, against the empiricism and relativism of O. I. Senkovskij and asserts that man strives for *ideal* truth, "because every empirical truth is a lie" (6:389). During the last few years of his life, Belinskij became acquainted with the positivist philosophy of Auguste Comte and rejected it, mainly because he believed that Comte "did not see historical progress, that living bond which, like a live nerve fiber, goes through the entire living organism of the history of mankind" (letter to V. P. Botkin, 17 February 1847, 12:331). Belinskij's general philosophic outlook always remains organicist and idealist, as does his philosophy of art.

However, Belinskij's notion of the essence of the "idea" in art undergoes an evolution and is at times rather ill-defined. Until about 1841, Belinskij frequently speaks in terms of absolute, hypostatized ideas. His untitled essay on the idea of art (1841, 4:585-602) shows him to be almost a better Platonist than Hegel.[8] The Poet, he believes, through his poetic intuition, partakes of the absolute Idea, of ideal truth, and of divine Beauty.[9] It is understood that the poet's striving for the absolute and the infinite is inherent in human nature.[10] The following passage from his Second essay on Puškin (1843) is quite characteristic:

> There is present in man a sense of the infinite; it is the very foundation of his spirit, and the striving for it is the mainspring of all spiritual activity. Without a striving for the infinite there is no life, no development, no progress. The essence of development lies in *striving* and *achievement*. But whenever man has achieved something, he will not stop there, nor will he be fully satisfied with it; rather, the triumph of achievement tends to be brief in his soul and is soon replaced by new strivings. (7:180–81)

Belinskij also believes that the striving for certain moral ideals, such as courage, truth, and love, is universal in all men and is expressed by the poets of all nations (review of Tegnér's *Frithiofssaga,* trans. Ja. Grot, 1841, 5:286).

There are moments when Belinskij, like so many artists and critics before and after him, senses that the ideal content of poetry is a very narrowly defined "something," called "beauty," "poetry," or "art," which a great artist possesses in an infinitely higher degree than is given to ordinary mortals, and which he can communicate to the common people. Instances of such thinking can be found in Belinskij's writings during all stages of his career, though they are more common in his earlier years.

8. To be sure, this essay shows a particularly strong influence of Heinrich Rötscher's essay "Das Verhältnis der Philosophie der Kunst und der Kritik zum einzelnen Kunstwerke" (1837), whole passages of which Belinskij paraphrases. And there was a tendency among right-wing Hegelians, such as Rötscher, to revert to the pre-Hegelian, more openly Neoplatonic thought of Schelling (or to the subjective idealism of Kant and Fichte).

9. See 1:30–32; 2:250–51; 4:74–77; 11:146.

10. See 4:485–86.

In a rather melancholy letter to M. A. Bakunin, 1 November 1837, Belinskij discusses Puškin and genius in general, and eventually expresses the following notion of the essence of poetic creation:

> But he was a genius, and so minutes of his life would contain whole ages; he was a poet, and his ability to express himself, to demand and to receive as his due the sympathy of his fellowmen, rewarded him for minutes bereft of the eternal Spirit. In him, there was an inexhaustible spring of Love, which could never run dry, no matter what; and, from the cradle to the grave, Love was smiling at him. (11:191)

Here, Belinskij very acutely senses the difference between "merely living" and "really living," a distinction which he makes quite routinely: "There are two kinds of people," he writes in his essay on *Hamlet* (1838), "people who vegetate, and people who live" (2:256). In this context, poetry is "living life" (*živaja žizn'*), life with a very high degree of intensity. When Belinskij exclaims, "Where there is life, there is poetry!" (review of *Dawn*, an almanac, 1839, 3:68), he means "living life," life in an intense, particularly vigorous form.[11]

In his essay on Deržavin (1843), Belinskij observes that "in a true poet, even an old thought will become new, for a true poet makes one sense the living essence of a thought which the crowd will repeat senselessly, like a dead letter" (6:593). And returning to Deržavin two years later, Belinskij tartly corrects Polevoj who had, in his own discussion of Deržavin, drawn a line between "true" and "false" poets. A "false poet," says Belinskij, is a contradiction in terms, like cold fire or dry water. A poet can be very great, or somewhat less great, and so on, in infinite variations. But no matter how minor, so long as he is a poet, he cannot be a "false poet" (9:299–300). The implication is that the quality of being "a poet," "a work of poetry," or "poetic" is an absolute— like the quality of being alive. The essence of poetry lies not in its subject, or the thought expressed by it, but in a mystic quality—*élan vital*, intensity, or power—associated with it. The conception of great art as "life in a higher power" is specifically Schellingian. It appears in a variety of different metaphors throughout romantic poetry and criticism.[12]

The Historical Idea

Beginning with his Hegelian period, Belinskij tends to look for specific

11. Cf. 3:438; 4:106.
12. It would not be devious to say that in romantic aesthetics "power" (German *Kraft*) equals "poetry." *Kraft* as an attribute of the poetic word is the key concept of Friedrich Schlegel's *Gespräch über die Poesie*. According to Novalis, "to romanticize [=to poeticize] is to raise qualitatively to a higher power" (*Romantisieren ist nichts als qualitative Potenzierung*).

"historical" ideas, or rather, for universal ideas manifesting themselves in the particular form of their nation and age. Quite consistently, Belinskij begins his critical reviews with a search for the "historical idea" of the work under review. Whenever such an idea is found missing, the work in question is refused the title of a "true work of art." Such denial is accorded Griboedov's *Woe from Wit* (in an essay of that title, 1840, 3:473-86), the *Igor' Tale* (5:344-45), Deržavin's poetry (5:529-30), Zagoskin's novels (5:199), and Baratynskij's poetry (6:485).

Shakespeare's tragedies are analyzed accordingly, each being assigned its proper "basic idea," from which everything else follows. Here, Belinskij follows rather closely the canon of interpretation established by German romantic criticism. H. T. Rötscher, with whose works Belinskij was familiar, practiced precisely this kind of exegesis of Shakespeare. To give an example, the idea of *Hamlet,* as defined by Belinskij in his essay on that play (1838, 2:253-344) is "the idea of disintegration (*ideja raspadenija*), as a result of doubt, which in turn is the result of leaving the domain of natural consciousness" (2:257).

Belinskij's interpretations of works of Russian literature are intelligent attempts to identify the historical ideas underlying them. His philosophical interpretations of Puškin, Gogol', and Lermontov quickly acquired canonic status and can still be found, substantially unchanged, in Soviet college texts. The "idea" of Puškin's *Gypsies,* for example, is, according to Belinskij, the tragicomedy of the absolute egoist who finds the conventions of society to be an unbearable insult to his human dignity and therefore chooses the freedom of life outside civilization, then proves himself to be the worst enemy of freedom, as he murders his beloved and her young lover in a jealous rage. Belinskij concludes his analysis with this almost-triumphant observation: "Note this line: *You want freedom only for yourself*—it contains the whole meaning of the poem, the key to its basic idea" (Seventh essay on Puškin, 1844, 7:398). Very clearly, this was a moral which could be applied to the Russian intelligentsia— a circumstance which Dostoevskij later made quite explicit in his "Oration on Puškin."

The "idea" in Puškin's *Bronze Horseman* is seen "in these continuous clashes of the unfortunate hero with 'that giant on a horse of bronze,' and in the impression which the Bronze Horseman makes on him" (Eleventh essay on Puškin, 1846, 7:545). As was pointed out earlier, Belinskij, in spite of censorship, managed to convey the conflict in *The Bronze Horseman* very well: it is the conflict between Czar Peter, the "world-historical personage" and the great historical idea which he promotes, on the one side, and the life and happiness of the private individual sacrificed to this idea, on the other.

In his analysis of Puškin's *Boris Godunov,* Belinskij reaches the conclusion that the poet failed to conceive an artistically and historically correct "idea" of Godunov's tragedy. Puškin should have, says Belinskij, presented it as the dismal failure of a capable, well-meaning, but ordinary man who ill-advisedly chose to play the role of a great reformer and a master of his country's fate— in a word, the role of a great genius, of a "world-historical personage." Instead, Puškin let himself be influenced by Karamzin's eighteenth-century moralizing view of history, and made his Godunov a melodramatic villain who in the end humbly accepts his deserved punishment (ibid., 7:508–34). Belinskij's interpretation has merit, but a rather similar interpretation and criticism had been suggested earlier by Polevoj. Today Belinskij's interpretation of Puškin appears one-sided, as successive generations of critics have discovered other "ideas" and some ambiguities of which Belinskij was not aware. However, in every case Belinskij's conception continues to serve as an initial thesis—even if the emphasis is on aspects of interpretation antithetical to his.

In similar fashion, Belinskij approaches the works of Gogol' and Lermontov. The "idea" in *The Inspector-General* is as follows: "*The Inspector-General* is based on the same idea as 'The Story about How Ivan Ivanovič Quarreled with Ivan Nikiforovič.' In both instances the poet has expressed the idea of the negation of life, the idea of an illusory existence which, under his chisel, has taken the shape of objective reality" ("Woe from Wit," 1840, 3:452).[13]

Belinskij never explicitly defined his conception of the "idea" in Gogol''s *Dead Souls*. In his review of that work (1842), he speaks of the "*pafos* of subjectivity" (by then, Belinskij used the term *pafos* more often than the term *ideja*), paired with a complete penetration of and empathy into Russian "reality." The context, as well as some of Belinskij's other pronouncements on *Dead Souls*, suggests that the "*pafos* of subjectivity" is Aesopian language for "living social idea" (*živaja obščestvennaja ideja*) (review of the 2d edition of *Dead Souls*, 1846, 10:51). It is safe to say that Belinskij saw the "idea" in *Dead Souls* in a bold presentation of Russian reality "as it was," coupled with deep sorrow and honest indignation at its disgraceful condition, as well as sincere faith in a better future and great love for the Russian people. For Belinskij, the very "lowering of genre" performed by Gogol' and the Natural School was a "living idea." Belinskij never tired of pointing out Gogol''s faithfulness to Russian reality ("that terrible faithfulness to reality," he calls it in his review of *A Petersburg Almanac* [*Peterburgskij sbornik*], 1846, 9:544); it was challenged rather superficially by his contemporaries, and then soberly and systematically by a number of scholars and critics around the turn of the century.[14]

13. Cf. 3:441 and 6:661 (concerning *Taras Bul'ba*), and 6:574 (concerning *The Marriage* and its hero, Podkolesin).

14. Andrej Belyj, in his book *Masterstvo Gogolja: Issledovanie* (Moscow and Leningrad,

The "idea" in Lermontov's *Hero of Our Time* is seen by Belinskij as the presentation of "that state of the mind where every thought that emerges in our consciousness keeps disintegrating into its own moments, until the spirit is ready for the great act of rational reconciliation of opposites" ("A Hero of Our Time," 1840, 4:262). In less philosophical language, Belinskij felt that Lermontov's hero was the image of a man whose deep dissatisfaction with the condition of his society appeared, for the moment, as an acute inner conflict, a futile probing of his own consciousness for an escape from this impasse.

The Ideal

During the last few years of Belinskij's life, the static "idea" gives way to a dynamic "ideal." Belinskij has described a full circle. Having issued from the Fichtean ideal of spiritual self-realization and the Schellingian ideal of participation in a universal cosmic spirituality, Belinskij had arrived at his Hegelian (or pseudo-Hegelian) "reconciliation with reality," the ideal of being in harmony with the pulse of time and the heartbeat of one's nation. He had then begun to put more and more emphasis on the active, dynamic, progressive aspect of sociohistorical consciousness. And finally, from this sense of the movement of time, there emerged a new ideal—the social ideal of justice, equality and brotherhood, happiness for all. Belinskij's conception of the "ideal" is defined in "Russian Literature in 1843" (1843):

> Ideals are contained in reality; they are not the arbitrary play of fantasy, not idle fancy, nor dreams; yet at the same time, ideals cannot be copied from reality, as they mean the potential existence of a given phenomenon, divined by reason and expressed by the imagination (*fantazija*). . . . Poets who depend on imagination alone always look for their subjects in all kinds of exotic countries or in the remote past, while poets who, in addition to creative imagination, also possess profound reasoning power find their ideals in their own environment. (8:89)

In such a context, the aesthetic "ideal" cannot be static, but must be something eternally new. And so Belinskij follows Hegel in seeing an evolution from the sensual ideal of classical antiquity to the indistinct spiritual ideal of the Middle Ages, and on to a rational ideal of humanity being realized in his own age, the ideal of a society in which "there will not be any more struggle between the strivings of the heart and the organization of society, with these two tendencies reconciled to one another rationally and freely" (Second essay

---

1934), demonstrates with many examples how Gogol' creates an illusion of solid reality with a minimum of hard facts. Cf. S. A. Vengerov, *Pisatel'-graždanin Gogol'* (Petersburg, 1913), pp. 117–42 (a chapter entitled "Gogol' Had No Knowledge Whatsoever of Real Russian Life").

on Puškin, 1843, 7:159-60). In 1843 the *political* message in this statement
is to be understood in utopian socialist, not in Hegelian, terms.

It is in this connection that Belinskij fails to find in Puškin all that he expects of contemporary poetry. In his Ninth essay on Puškin (1845), Belinskij
quite explicitly characterizes the poet as a conservative by nature, whose beau-
tifully idealized expression of Russian life, especially in *Evgenij Onegin,* was
set entirely within the ideas and beliefs of his age and his social class:

> Everywhere you see in him a man who, body and soul, belongs to the fun-
> damental principle which stands for the essence of the class whose life he
> describes . . . in brief, all along you see in him the Russian landowner. . . .
> He will attack everything about this class that is against humanity; yet the
> class principle itself is for him an eternal truth. . . . (7:502)

In this passage, Belinskij comes amazingly close to a Marxist view of Russian
literature. What Belinskij resents about Puškin is the poet's basic acceptance
of life as he knows it, his ability to create great poetry within the ideological
and social premises of Russian society as it existed in his day. In other words,
Puškin's conservative "ideal" is unacceptable to Belinskij.

It is not surprising that Belinskij found Lermontov so much closer to his own
sensibility, and therefore overestimated him in relation to Puškin. Lermontov
appealed to Belinskij because, albeit for quite different reasons, they both felt
alienated from contemporary Russian life and rather sweepingly rejected the
status quo. Belinskij realized only too well that Lermontov lacked a positive
ideal. But he was searching for one, and Belinskij found this encouraging.[15]

Gogol' was, to Belinskij, the most forward-looking poetic spirit of his age.
But he found that even Gogol' had been unable to create a positive poetic ideal
of Russian life. Whenever Gogol' tried it, Belinskij felt, it was either a false
ideal, and therefore artistically a failure, or it was not organically Russian, and
so equally a failure.[16] However—and Belinskij never tired of stressing this point
—Gogol' expressed Russia's need for a new ideal by boldly rejecting her present
reality. Good Hegelian that he was, Belinskij welcomed the wrecking job
which—so he thought—Gogol' was doing on Russian society. Gogol' 's negativism, he felt, was superior, in a sense, to Puškin's positive attitude toward life:

> All of Gogol' 's works are devoted exclusively to the depiction of Russian
> life, and he has no equal in representing it in its whole truth. He softens

15. In a letter to V. P. Botkin, 16–21 April 1840, Belinskij reports on a visit he paid
Lermontov at the St. Petersburg guardhouse where the poet was confined for his latest
duel: "He is himself Pečorin, of course. I argued with him, and I was joyed to see in his
intellectual, cold, bilious view of life and of people the seeds of a deep faith in the dignity
of both. I told him so—he smiled and said: 'By God, I wish this will come true!' " (11:509).
Belinskij was clearly overwhelmed by the poet's powerful personality.

16. See, e.g., 6:425-26.

nothing, embellishes nothing on account of a love for certain ideals, preconceived ideas, or habitual prejudices, as did, for instance, Puškin, who in his
Evgenij Onegin idealized the life of the Russian landowner. To be sure, the
prevalent mode of his works lies in the negative. A negation, in order to be
alive and poetic, must be made in the name of an ideal. Nor is this ideal in
Gogol', or in any other Russian poet, his own, that is, a native ideal, because
the life of our society still lacks the shape and the stability to provide literature with such an ideal. ("1847," 10:294)

This somewhat cryptic passage, if interpreted in the light of what we know
about Belinskij in 1847–48, means just about what Lenin meant when he called
Tolstoj "a mirror of the Russian revolution": Gogol' had amply demonstrated
the total bankruptcy of Russian society under the present regime; the negative
aspect of his message was true and well stated; however, his "positive ideal,"
that is, his suggestions as to how conditions might be improved (Gogol' suggested religion, higher moral standards, steady self-perfection), was a false, reactionary, and irrational one, and was impracticable. Someone else would have to
come up with a historically correct and practicable ideal.

The notion of a "false idea," or "false ideal," occupies a place in Belinskij's
thinking. In his "Survey of Russian Literature in 1846," Belinskij explains
how Ševyrev distorts the facts of Old Russian literature by "that awesome
power which the spirit of a system, the fascination of a ready-made idea assumed to be immutably true even before a study of the facts, will have over a
man's reasoning ability" (10:46–47). Belinskij is convinced that Ševyrev's
Slavophilism is a "false idea" which runs contrary to the logic of history. It
makes fools out of sensible, brilliantly educated, and well-meaning men, such
as the Aksakovs, Xomjakov, and Samarin. Belinskij is also convinced that a
false idea will inevitably ruin a work of art aesthetically as well as morally—another Hegelian notion.[17]

After about 1842 the term "pathos" (*pafos*) often replaces the term "poetic
idea" in Belinskij's writings, as noted above. Belinskij's usage of *pafos* definitely coincides with Hegel's.[18] The emphasis in *pafos* is necessarily on the dynamic and "other-directed" aspect of the "poetic idea." *Pafos* is a "poetic idea"
which asks for passionate involvement and for action.

17. For an eloquent statement of this belief, see Vischer, *Aesthetik,* 2:386. Vischer
uses the image of a young, beautiful woman from whose mouth a little red mouse would
suddenly spring (from the *Walpurgisnacht* in *Faust*) to characterize the inner rottenness
of some dazzling romantic works.
18. Cf. Billig, *Der Zusammenbruch,* p. 44. The following examples of Belinskij's usage
of *pafos* show that the term is virtually synonymous with "poetic idea": "The *pafos* of
Dead Souls is humor, viewing life *through laughter visible to the world,* and tears, *unseen
and unknown to it*" (6:255). Or, still speaking of *Dead Souls:* "True criticism must un-
cover the *pafos* of the epopoeia, which consists of a contradiction between the social

Belinskij's conception of *pafos* is developed at some length in his Fifth essay on Puškin (1844, 7:311–14). "Every poetic work," says Belinskij, "is the fruit of a powerful idea (*mysl'*) which has taken possession of the poet." However, the poetic idea is distinct from the intellectual idea in that it can be described as "living passion" (*živaja strast'*), or *pafos* (7:311–12). Belinskij then goes on to describe *pafos* in detail. Creation, like child-bearing, being connected with care, labor, and suffering, some powerful force, some invincible passion, must move the poet toward the act of creation. This force, or passion, is *pafos*. It is distinct from sensuous passion in that its content is moral and ideal rather than physical and carnal: "*Pafos* is always a passion which is kindled in a man's soul by an *idea,* and which itself always strives toward an idea, and so it is a passion which is purely spiritual, moral, divine" (7:312). For example, in Hamlet's *pathetic* soliloquies the whole *pafos* of the tragedy is revealed and "that eccentric inner force manifested which made the poet take his pen in order to unburden his soul of the burden weighing heavily upon it" (7:313). Any truly poetic work must be the fruit of *pafos*, must be wholly penetrated by it. Without *pafos*, it will remain cold and cerebral.

By 1842 (and sometimes even earlier) Belinskij conceived of the poet as a man possessed by the same powerful feelings (indignation, outrage, compassion at the sight of social injustice in Russia) as were then moving his own heart. He tends to recognize *pafos* in a work whenever it is motivated by a strong social tendency, as in Herzen's short novel *Whose Fault?* or in Elena Andreevna Hahn's feminist short stories.[19]

The conception of the ideal aspect of the work of art in terms of *pafos* places art squarely into the magnetic field of life at large. It means that artistic creation is moved by the forces (ideas and passions) which also create historical movement. Belinskij's conception of *pafos*, though it somewhat overemphasizes the emotional side of artistic creation, is substantially consistent with Hegel's philosophy of history and of art. It has reigned in most of Russian literature and literary criticism ever since.

FORM IN ART

The other pole of Belinskij's conception of the work of art is "form," or "poetic form." It is often denoted by the term *poètičeskij obraz*, which covers the meanings of both "form" and "image," as it has a connotation of "shape, structure" as well as "picture." The German term *Bild,* of which Russian *obraz*

---

forms of Russian life and its profound, substantial principle (*substancial'noe načalo*), as yet mysterious, unrevealed to our own consciousness, and eluding the grasp of any definition" (6:431). Cf. 4:523; 5:563; 6:82, 218–19, 290; 7:227, 314, 350, 410, 657.

19. See 7:656, 666; 10:319–26.

is the translation, has the same connotations. On the one hand, it is connected with *bilden* ("to shape, to form") and on the other, it means "image, picture." Moreover, Plotinus's ἔνδον εἶδος is often translated as *inneres Bild*.[20] In Hegelian aesthetics the work of art is "the aesthetic unity of idea and image" (*die ästhetische Einheit von Idee und Bild*).[21]

As has been already observed, art is to Belinskij "the immediate contemplation of truth, or thinking in images."[22] Also, Belinskij liked to repeat, over and over again, that "the poet must *show* rather than *prove*, for in art what is *shown* is already *proven*" ("Menzel, a Critic of Goethe," 3:413). This is a position which Belinskij held from beginning to end. In his last major essay, "A Survey of Russian Literature in 1847," he once more states this position very clearly:

> A philosopher thinks in syllogisms, a poet in forms and images (*obrazami i kartinami*),[23] yet both say one and the same thing. The political economist *proves* . . . through his statistical data that the condition of such-and-such class in a given society has greatly improved, or greatly deteriorated, for such-and-such reasons. A poet, armed with live and colorful representations of reality, *shows*, in truthful pictures acting upon his reader's imagination, that the condition of such-and-such class in a given society has in fact greatly improved, or greatly deteriorated, for such-and-such reasons. The one *proves*, the other *shows*, and both seek to *convince*, except that the one does it by logical argument and the other by pictures. (10:311)

Belinskij's definition is a great deal more elegant than the English translation might indicate, since *dokazyvat'*, "to prove," and *pokazyvat'*, "to show," are neatly polarized by being derived from the same verb, but formed with a different prefix. At the same time, Belinskij always makes it clear that a poetic image is by no means the same thing as a mere faithful description, or copy, of reality. A "poetic image" is of course distinct from a mere representation of reality by virtue of its union with the "poetic idea" (ibid., 10:304).

"Poetic form"—unlike a mere picture or copy of reality, which can be constructed piece by piece—is associated with the quality of "immediacy" (*neprosredstvennost'*), even in Kant's aesthetics a *sine qua non* of the genuine work of art. Belinskij's lengthy discussion of this term in "The Idea of Art" (4:593–96)[24] makes it clear that he means "immediacy" to include the quality of being expressed and perceived intuitively rather than intellectually. Poetic form, by virtue of its being "immediate" (*neprosredstvennyj*), is "whole" (*celyj, celostnyj*) and "definite, specific" (*opredelennyj*). It is never "put together, manufactured" or "abstract, indefinite."

20. Vischer, *Aesthetik,* 3:1163.
21. Ibid., 3:1205.
22. Cf. 2:476; 3:423, 481; 4:37, 106, 585; 5:557, 583; 6:591; 7:389.
23. This distinction shows that, at least in some contexts, *obraz* is to Belinskij not simply "image, picture," but anything created by the imagination.
24. Cf. 1:33–34; 6:287; 7:389; 10:23; 11:386, 473–74.

Even when he embraces utilitarianism, Belinskij will energetically reject schematic and abstract works of fiction and poetry ("dissertations," as he calls such works), no matter how "correct" their message.[25] A work of art must be conceived as a living whole by the artist's mental eye, so that it may come to life before the reader's or listener's eyes.

Belinskij's conception of the polarity inherent in the work of art is quite different from that of modern structuralism, which treats the work of art in terms of material (acoustic, visual, verbal) and structure (imparted to it by the artist). Belinskij's polarity is the organicist one of an incorporeal idea versus its incarnate image. His observations regarding composition, characterization, descriptive details, imagery, symbolism, versification, and style invariably point toward the one question: How do these details relate to the idea of the work? One will find very little structural analysis in Belinskij and only occasional, unsystematic observations on the poet's or writer's craft.

POLARIC FORMULATIONS OF IDEA AND FORM

The Ideal and the Real

Underlying Belinskij's understanding of the polarity inherent in the work of art is the notion of the "concreteness" (used in the Hegelian, etymological sense of that word)[26] of poetic idea and poetic form:

> Concreteness (konkretnost') is derived from concrete, which in turn is formed from the Latin word concresco, "I grow together." This word belongs to the most recent philosophy and is of considerable importance. Here we are using it as an expression of the organic unity of idea and form. The idea is concrete when it has penetrated the form and the form has expressed the idea, so that if the idea were destroyed the form would be destroyed also, and vice versa. In other words, concreteness is that mysterious, inseparable, and necessary fusion of idea and form which creates all life and without which nothing can be alive. (review of Nikolaj Polevoj's Ugolino, 1838, 2:438).[27]

Here, the analogy between "living organism" and "living artistic creation" is taken quite literally: they are both "concrete" in the same sense. The concreteness of the work of art is a focal point of Belinskij's entire theory of literature and literary criticism.

In Belinskij's most direct and most common formulation of the polarity inherent in the work of art, he conceives of it as a fusion of the "ideal" and the "real." It is precisely in the use of these two terms that Belinskij runs into all kinds of contradictions and equivocations.

25. See, e.g., Belinskij's letter to V. P. Botkin, 2–6 December 1847, 12:445.
26. See Hegel, Ästhetik, 1:77–79.
27. Cf. 2:488; 3:180, 481; 4:165; 11:275.

According to Belinskij's own acknowledged principle, the ideal and the real aspects of a work of art are complementary, and this is how Belinskij usually sees things from the beginning to the end of his career.[28] But this conception is often disturbed, undermined, or actually nullified by other usages of the terms "ideal" and "real."

There is, first of all, the "historicized" conception, according to which the art and poetry of certain ages gravitate either toward the "ideal" or toward the "real." Ancient Greek poetry was real, medieval poetry was ideal, and contemporary poetry is returning to the real. This is substantially Hegel's scheme, and it is consistent with the basic principle of the concreteness of the work of art, so long as one keeps in mind that *any* work of art (ideal or real, Greek, medieval, or modern) represents a fusion of idea and form, the idea being "ideal" and the form "real."

But then, time and again, Belinskij uses the word "ideal" in the colloquial sense of "idealized, idealizing, imaginary, fanciful," meaning by "ideal art" any art which ignores the ordinary, the lowly, the everyday aspect of life and deals only with life's loftier sides. "Real art" then means any art which has its feet planted firmly on the ground of "real life." Here, Belinskij often inexcusably confuses poetic with empirical reality and, similarly, the poetic with the empirical ideal.[29] As a consequence—a very serious one—Belinskij took Gogol' for the founder of Russian *realism,* because his works were set on a lower plane socially and in many details of form represented a "lowering of genre" (thus being closer to Belinskij's empirical reality). This mistake was eventually corrected by the course which Russian literature took after Gogol' 's and Belinskij's death. The Russian *realistic* tradition followed Puškin rather than Gogol', as Symbolist critics were first to recognize.

As early as in his essay "On the Russian Short Story and the Short Stories of Mr. Gogol' " (1835), Belinskij distinguishes "ideal" from "real" poetry in the sense that the former transforms life (*peresozdaet žizn'*) according to its peculiar "ideal," while the "real" presents life as it is, "in its whole naked truth" (1:262). Belinskij, so perceptive otherwise, forgets that all art—according to his own often-repeated principle—"transforms life," a fact which he almost immediately proceeds to emphasize: only a few pages farther he compares "real poetry" to a "convex mirror which reflects, under a certain point of view, the varied phenomena of life, selecting those among them which are needed for a full, vivid, and complete picture" (1:267). Also, it is Belinskij himself who

28. See 1:34; 2:442; 3:355; 5:480, 549, 583; 7:181.
29. Cf. Billig, *Der Zusammenbruch*, p. 16. Ambrogio tries to defend Belinskij on the grounds that his realist aesthetics is primarily a work program (*un programma di lavoro*), applicable to and devised for a concrete historical situation—the poetics of the "new" literature (the Natural School)—rather than anything that would claim universal validity (Ambrogio, *Belinskij*, pp. 223-24).

time and again defends Gogol', the champion of "real poetry," against the charge of crude naturalism and points out the ideas which animate his seemingly naturalistic stories—much as Hegel had defended Flemish genre painting by insisting that it was animated by *ideas,* no less than the noblest historical paintings.

On the side of the "real," Belinskij sins against his own aesthetic principles by offering praise to works of literature merely on account of their author's willingness to depict Russian everyday life in all its drabness, sordidness, and cruelty: a virtue which he could also have easily found—as Černyševskij would point out—in police reports and assorted statistical tables (regarding crime, disease, alcoholism, prostitution, and pauperism) regularly published by the Ministry of the Interior. Belinskij acted as the advocate of the Natural School even when its members engaged in the crudest "physiologism" or "ethnographism," with the "ideal" totally absent from their depictions of Russian life.

Such aberration from the principle of the complementarity of the "ideal" and the "real" could be rationalized on various grounds. Obviously Belinskij felt, sometimes at least, that these bleak statements of plain material facts did in fact exhaust Russian reality—there was no "ideal" aspect. Then, too, the "ideal" could still be latent in the very inhumanity, degradation, and soullessness of an Akakij Akak'evič's life, and even surface on occasion—as it did in the famous "humanitarian passage" of *The Overcoat.* Finally, there was the important extrinsic consideration—probably decisive—that in times such as Belinskij experienced under the reign of Nicholas I, anything in print that was a form of protest against the existing order had great merit, no matter what the artistic qualities of the piece in question. In other words, it was a situation similar to that in the Soviet Union where, as Evtušenko once put it, simple civic courage might be a poet's highest virtue.

But Belinskij is also guilty of sinning on the side of the "ideal." Occasionally he will praise a work with which he agrees ideologically, even if it lacks reality. In his article "Russian Literature in 1841," Belinskij discusses Elena Andreevna Hahn (1814–1843), a woman writer in the manner of the early George Sand. He observes that she "lacks the touch of reality, the skill to grasp and to describe with tangible precision and definiteness even the most ordinary phenomena of everyday life" (5:583). However, Belinskij continues, this failing is compensated by "an inner content, the presence of vivid social interests, and an ideal view of the dignity of life, of Man in general, and a woman's in particular" (ibid.). Belinskij forgets, at least for a moment, that art ought to be a synthesis of the "ideal" and the "real," and issues praise to a writer who "lacks the touch of reality"—only because her ideals are noble. Belinskij's extravagant praise of George Sand is to be explained in the same terms.[30]

30. At the height of his enthusiasm for French utopian socialism, Belinskij writes to

The later Belinskij will tolerate the excesses of the "ideal" if they meet with his sympathy, but will challenge them if they do not. While he greets the blatantly idealistic—not to say mystic and fantastic—theories of the French utopian socialists with enthusiasm, he has nothing but sarcasm for the idealist mysticism of his former idol Schelling, who was making a strong comeback in the 1840s and had, in fact, "infected" some of Belinskij's close friends, such as Katkov.

Nevertheless, Belinskij believes to the end that a true work of art is a fusion of the "ideal" and the "real." To be sure, he insists that the ideal aspect of a work of art be immanent in historical reality, that it be, if ever possible, contemporary and relevant to Russian society rather than transcendent, esoteric, or mystical (Belinskij in the 1840s is a militant atheist). Still, he insists that it be there. This requirement has been maintained by much of Russian literature and literary criticism to this day. The demand for *idejnost'* in Socialist Realist aesthetics follows this tradition.

Content and Form

Another version of the polarity inherent in Belinskij's conception of the work of art involves "content" and "form." Belinskij's initial view is that of German objective-idealist aesthetics, in which the relation between "form" and "content" is that of the objective, phenomenal aspect of the Spirit to the absolute Spirit, or, to put it metaphorically, that of "body" and "soul." Belinskij himself uses this metaphor. For example, in an early polemic article, "On the Criticism and Literary Opinions of *The Moscow Observer*" (1836), Belinskij says that in the works of Victor Hugo ideas will appear "which are not connected with their form as a soul is connected to its body, but for which a form has been arbitrarily selected by the author" (2:152).

Much as with the "ideal" and the "real," Belinskij will sometimes forget that in a true work of art "content" and "form" ought to be inseparable, so that a flaw in either will inevitably destroy the whole. But by and large he stays with a strong organic conception of the *content : form* relationship,[31] as in the following example from his essay on A. V. Kol'cov (1846): "Whenever form is

---

N. A. Bakunin, 24 August 1843: "I have read *Le Compagnon du Tour de France*—a divine work!" (12:171) This is decidedly one of George Sand's weaker novels—but Belinskij obviously finds it "divine" on account of its socialist message. In a letter to the same correspondent, 7 November 1842, Belinskij asks the latter if he has read George Sand's novel *Horace*, which had recently appeared in *La Revue indépendente* and in a badly mutilated Russian translation in the *National Annals*, then goes on to exclaim: "This woman is decidedly the Joan of Arc of our time, a lode star of salvation, and the prophetess of a great future" (12:115). For more details, see Nečaeva, *Belinskij*, 4:39–41.

31. See 3:261, 419; 5:504–5, 545; 7:144–45; 9:535; 10:253–54.

the expression of content, it is so tightly connected with it that to separate it from the content means to destroy the content itself, and vice versa: to separate the content from its form means to destroy the form also" (9:535).

Belinskij's usage of the term "content" (*soderžanie*) corresponds to that of German *Gehalt,* as used by Hegel. Specifically, Belinskij draws a clear line between "content" and *sujet* (*sjužet*).[32] Nor is "content" simply a particular representation of the objective world. Rather, it is "something higher, something from which all beliefs, convictions, and principles flow," it is "the poet's personal experience of his own existence in this world and the presence of the world in the inner sanctum of his spirit" ("1841," 5:552). In other words, it is—at this still strongly Hegelian stage in Belinskij's development—the absolute and objective Spirit as it manifests itself through the poet's consciousness. At a later stage, it will be a representation of reality, governed and illuminated by a rational idea.

Content, in Belinskij's criticism, is subject to all the vicissitudes of the historical process. This explains why "as far as form is concerned, Puškin is the equal of any poet in the world, while in his content he cannot stand comparison with any of the poets of world stature" (ibid., 5:558). The same point is made on other occasions.[33] Belinskij's opinion, also stated more than once, that Lermontov was inferior to Puškin in artistry and virtuosity, but was ahead of him in the content of his poetry, falls in line with this historicist notion.[34] Belinskij's bland assertion that "form belongs to the poet, while content belongs to history and to the reality of the poet's nation" ("1841," 5:558) is, incidentally, a convenient loophole allowing one to explain the imperishability of great art in the face of historical progress. It had been advanced by A. W. Schlegel. Today it still plays a prominent role in the aesthetics of Socialist Realism.

Another corollary of such "historization" of the *content : form* category appears in Belinskij's attitude toward literary borrowing. If content and form are organically linked, it would seem to be a violation of the organic principle to graft the "form" of the art of one nation or period to the "content" of another. Following the lead of his German predecessors (beginning, in this case, with the classicist critic Lessing), Belinskij charges that the French classicists, "having failed to understand that every age and every nation has its own ideas and consequently its own forms, which are in accord with these ideas, created an art after the fashion of the Ancients and . . . slavishly and without understanding its essence copied its form and its external traits" (essay on the general

32. See 6:219, 240; 7:297. *Sjužet* is "a sequence of events, artistically arranged" in a work of literature. See B. Tomaševskij, *Teorija literatury,* 4th ed. (Moscow and Leningrad, 1928), p. 136.

33. See, e.g., 7:431–32; 9:441.

34. See, e.g., 12:84–85.

meaning of the word "literature," 5:628). Similarly, Belinskij asserts that the epics of Vergil, Tasso, Milton, and others, in spite of some excellent details, had to be failures as "artistic wholes," simply because they failed to give "a contemporary form to a contemporary content" and, instead, chose to borrow an ancient form ("Explanation to an Explanation," 6:414).

This obviously erroneous conception is explained by Belinskij's careless semantics. He fails to keep in mind that, if *sujet* is not "content," "form" does not amount to specific details of versification, such as the use of a classical meter, to the selection of specific poetic devices, or the introduction of certain mythological figures, but is rather the integrated sum of all these details. Of course, the *chefs d'oeuvre* of French classicism have both a "content" and a "form" which are distinctly their own. Nor was Vergil a slavish imitator of Homer: his "content" as well as his "form" was quite different from that of the Homeric epos, even though he adopted the principles of Greek versification, many of Homer's devices (such as the "Homeric simile"), and used many of his motifs.

This ambiguity of the meaning of "form" leads to some other contradictions and equivocations in Belinskij's thinking. In discussing Russian folk poetry in "The Russian Folk Tale" (1841), Belinskij at first states routinely that "the form of the folk epos is in complete accord with its content: that same Gargantuan power—and that same poverty, that same vagueness, and that same monotony in expression and imagery" (5:427). But then, as he delves deeper into his subject, Belinskij observes that the form of the Russian folk epos is highly complex and sophisticated in its details, among which he very perceptively notes "semantic rhyme" (*rifma smysla*). What has obviously happened here is that Belinskij's keen perception and critical sense have simply prevailed over his preconceived dialectic scheme. His further analysis of the Russian folk song brings him very close to a realization that "form" (that is, rhythm, play with language, imagery) is really the "content"—what is aesthetically important—about the Russian folk song.

Belinskij initiates a long-lasting trend in Russian literary criticism by approaching the work of art from the side of "content" rather than "form," even while insisting on their unity. When he expresses the notion (later stated so categorically by Tolstoj in *Anna Karenina*, and so often and so emphatically by Benedetto Croce) that only a poet who has actually expressed himself is worth talking about, and that it is quite useless to discuss poets who were "potentially great," he builds his formulation around "content" rather than "form." Belinskij compares the notion of a poet who "could have been great" with that of a "potential military genius" who, having discovered a certain fearfulness in his nature, chose a career in the civil service. A poet who got bogged down in the flashy trivialities of form and never got around to expressing anything worthy of serious attention, even though he may have carried it in his soul, is not even

potentially a great poet. Jazykov is the example here ("The Poetry of Poležaev," 6:123).

In the course of his polemic with K. S. Aksakov in 1842, Belinskij raises the
question whether the perfect image of a flower or the imperfect but credit-
ably drawn image of a great and noble man is of greater value (the occasion being, of course, Aksakov's comparison of Gogol' with Homer and Shakespeare).
Belinskij says emphatically that even a mere sketch of the ideal of a great man
is greater than the most perfect representation of a beautiful flower. He also
rejects Aksakov's evaluation of Gogol''s greatness as extravagant, on the grounds
that Gogol''s work lacks a "great idea" or "content" (6:257–58). In the same
sense, Belinskij continues, Goethe is a giant in comparison with Heine, though
as an artist Heine could stand comparison with the great man. Belinskij does
not realize, in the heat of the dispute, that he is contradicting his own principle, so jealously guarded most of the time, the principle of the organic unity
of "content" and "form." If Gogol''s art is artistically perfect, it can still be
assigned a smaller value than Shakespeare's (nor would his opponent object to
that), because it is smaller in range and in volume. But it is not inferior to
Shakespeare's art, or Homer's.

With his usual sure critical instinct, Belinskij in the end arrives at the correct
position quite inadvertently when he says he is willing to grant his opponent
that Gogol' and Homer have one thing in common: they are both great poets.
The corollary of this is that an artist who paints a perfect picture of a flower
and one who paints a perfect portrait of a great and noble man are both
great painters, while the artist who paints an imperfect portrait of the same
"great and noble man" is inferior as a painter, even though his work may have
greater social value. Belinskij here, as so often, is caught in a *quid pro quo* of
aesthetic value, an absolute, and social value, which is relative.

In a review of 1845 ("The Physiology of Petersburg") Belinskij produces a
striking example of this kind of equivocal thinking when he says that "one of
Krylov's better fables is better than all of Ozerov's tragedies taken together"
(here, the criterion of excellence is "form"), while even the best of Krylov's
fables could not possibly be compared with Puškin's *Evgenij Onegin* (here, it is
"content") (9:220). Such pitfalls are easily avoided by refusing to separate
content from form. The moment one begins to evaluate not the work of art,
but either its form or its content alone, one is no longer speaking of that work
of art. Belinskij knew this most of the time, but sometimes he would forget
it. His successors, especially those of the Left, converted Belinskij's occasional
lapses into a system.

The Universal and the Particular

Belinskij's dualistic conception of the work of art also appears in the polarity of the "universal" or "general" (*obščee*) and the "particular" (*osobnoe* or *čast-noe*). In a lengthy discussion of the "general" and the "particular" in one of his essays on the Russian folk tale (1841, 5:310–19), Belinskij explicitly identifies his term (*obščee*) with German *Allgemeinheit*. This particular polarity overlaps in part with some of the dichotomies discussed above, especially with that of the "individual" versus the "national" (or "national" versus "universally human"), as well as with one described below—"individual" versus "type."

To Belinskij, art is a fusion of the "universal" and the "particular" as much as it is of the "ideal" and the "real."[35] In fact, quite often the universal is identified with the ideal, and the particular with the real.[36]

While Belinskij always stresses that the "universal" manifests itself in the "particular,"[37] meaning that a fusion of both is what one expects of a work of art, he values the universal more highly than the particular. It must be stressed that Belinskij's position is by no means a self-evident one: an aesthetics that places great value precisely on the artist's ability to grasp the concrete particular, the individual trait, the accidental detail, and the fragments, no matter how indistinct, of an elusive transcendence had been in vogue among the romantics and was to return in "modernism."

But Belinskij had learned from Hegel that "the universal is higher than the particular, the absolute higher than the individual, reason higher than the particular person" (Fifth essay on Puškin, 1844, 7:307); he went on to place the label of "universality" on what he assumed to be of high value. Of course, one can hardly argue with Belinskij when he credits Puškin with "all-encompassing and many-sided universality" ("1841," 5:557), while assigning Kol'cov to "that group of artists whose creations cannot pretend to be an all-embracing and many-sided expression of life, but who, having selected *one* side of life, exhaust it deeply and powerfully" (ibid., 5:579). But the hollowness of Belinskij's use of this particular aesthetic category is bared when he asserts, in his polemic with K. S. Aksakov (which, altogether, is not one of the highlights of Belinskij's career), that the works of Sir Walter Scott embrace "the content of *universal life*," while in those of Gogol' (here, *Dead Souls*) " 'universal life' appears as a mere hint, as an *arrière-pensée*, elicited by the *total absence* of the universally human in the life described by him" (6:417). Even Puškin, Belinskij feels obliged to admit in another article of the same exchange, "cannot rise above his epoch or his country" (6:258–59). But James Fenimore Cooper is

35. See 1:290; 4:88, 197, 492, 531; 5:305–6, 316, 404–5; 6:35, 257; 7:310.
36. "It is precisely that living, organic fusion of the universal (the idea) with the particular (age, country, individual personages) which represents the essence and the merit of Walter Scott's novels" (6:35).
37. "The universal will manifest itself only in the particular and he who does not belong to his country will never belong to humanity either" (4:88). Cf. 6:35; 10:250.

listed among those writers whose works have "universal historical significance" (6:421).

Belinskij has better success with another, more concret version of the same
polarity, namely, that of "type" versus "individual." In Belinskij's aesthetics,
as in that of German objective idealism, the creation of types (*tipizacija*)
amounts to the artist's discovery of the "universal" or "ideal" in the "particular" fact. The quality of being typical (*tipizm*) amounts to a perfect fusion of
the universal and the particular, or more specifically, to the creation of characters (or situations, or relationships) which, while they express the essence of
many people (situations, relationships), are at the same time real individuals
(real situations) in the full sense of that word. This quality is achieved not by
schematic abstraction but only by intuitive incarnation (*voploščenie*). Belinskij defines "type" as follows:

> Type (archetype [*pervoobraz*]) in art is the same as *genus* (*rod*) and *species*
> (*vid*) in nature, and *hero* in history. In type, we observe a triumph of the or-
> ganic fusion of two extremes—the *universal* and the *particular*. A typical per-
> sonage is the representative of a whole genus of persons, the generic name of
> many objects, yet expressed by its own proper name. ("The Russian Folk
> Tale," 1841, 5:318–19)

Belinskij's logic is not quite sound here. A historical "hero," who stands for
a whole epoch (Napoleon, for example), and even a literary "type" standing
for a certain kind of man (Belinskij gives Othello and Xlestakov as examples)
have something which is absent in a specimen of a zoological species: an individuality which distinguishes them from all the other individuals for whom
they stand. Othello is not just any passionately jealous husband. He is also an
old soldier, a noble and generous man, and black. But Belinskij knows this,
and it is quite clear what he means here.

Belinskij's conception of "type" evolves from a "universally human" to a
more specific, national or historical, and finally, to a social definition. In the
early essay "On the Russian Short Story and the Short Stories of Mr. Gogol' "
(1835), we find this definition:

> To complete my characterization of what I call *real* poetry (*real'naja poèzija*)
> I shall add that the eternal hero (*večnyj geroj*) and the perpetual subject of
> its inspiration is man, an independent being, acting freely, an individual (*su-
> ščestvo individual'noe*), a symbol (*simvol*) of the world whose finite manifes-
> tation he is, a curious riddle to himself, the ultimate question of his own
> reason, the last riddle of his own striving for knowledge. . . . The solution
> of this riddle, the answer to this question, and the solution of this problem
> must be full *consciousness*, which is the mystery, the goal, and the cause of
> his existence. (1:267)[38]

38. Cf. 1:281, 295–96, 322; 3:52; 4:220.

The position taken here is one of Schellingian objective idealism, "anthropological" rather than "historicized" (as in Hegel). Like Schelling, Belinskij stresses that the literary "type" ought to be a "living image" (*živoj obraz*) (essay on *Hamlet,* 1838, 2:290). He finds that Gogol' 's utterly prosaic Pirogov (in "Nevskij Prospect") is a marvellous "type," precisely because, while universal, he is also perfectly real and ordinary ("On the Russian Short Story and the Short Stories of Mr. Gogol'," 1835, 1:296–97). And, much as Puškin and the romantic critics of the preceding generation, Belinskij stresses, again and again, that Shakespeare's types are so much superior to those of the French classicist drama because, while "ideal," they are also individuals "taken as a whole" and as though "from everyday reality" rather than artificial compounds of abstract traits (essay on *Hamlet,* 2:290).[39]

During his Hegelian period, Belinskij begins to visualize "type" as an entity which is defined both historically and nationally, in addition to its universal human significance. Reviewing Kvitka-Osnov'janenko's *Marusja* (1839), Belinskij observes—not before having delivered another lengthy diatribe on the essence of "type"—that the characters of this tale, while exemplifying all the specific traits of the Ukrainian nation, lack the artistic quality of true types because they are not also individuals ("*one* person, whole, individual") (3:53). Again, Shakespeare and Gogol' are mentioned as creators of genuine types.

In his important essay "Woe from Wit" (1840), Belinskij calls Gogol' 's Taras Bul'ba "a hero, the representative of the life of a whole nation, of a whole political society during a certain epoch of its life" (3:439). Similarly, Puškin's Onegin and Lermontov's Pečorin are seen as symbols of their respective ages, while also being full-fledged individuals.

In the 1840s, Belinskij's analyses of fictional characters become more and more socially oriented. In some instances, as in his discussion of Herzen's *Whose Fault?* and Gončarov's *The Same Old Story* ("1847," 10:319–44), Belinskij approaches a Dobroljubovian sociologism as the border line between literary criticism and social critique begins to disappear. Certainly Belinskij created the precedent for Dobroljubov's practice of using works of contemporary fiction as texts for sermons on assorted social problems.[40] Belinskij's "sermons" deal with morality, human dignity, the Russian "superfluous man" (Belinskij, however, did not coin this expression), romanticism and the Russian romantic, and a variety of other topics.

39. Cf. 3:21, 53, 463–64; 5:203, 317.
40. See, e.g., his discussion of love and marriage in his Ninth essay on Puškin, devoted largely to Tat'jana (7:473–504); his interpretation of Dostoevskij's *Poor Folk* (9:554); his discussion of Bel'tov in Herzen's *Whose Fault?* (10:321–22) where he deals with the problem of the educated, progressive Russian nobleman who cannot find a way to apply his talents to any worthwhile cause; and his comments on the younger Aduev, hero of Gončarov's *The Same Old Story* (10:327–44).

Belinskij's aversion to allegory and schematism continues just as strong in his later writings. In his last major article, "A Survey of Russian Literature in 1847," he heaps sarcasm on those writers who create "not characters but rhetorical personifications of abstract virtues and vices" (10:295). But the later Belinskij is inclined to be lenient toward schematism and allegory when they are combined with the "right" ideology. This is true, for instance, in the cases of Grigorovič's *Anton Goremyka* and *The Village,* as well as Herzen's *Whose Fault?* But Belinskij does not conceal the fact that he is not perfectly happy with his own acceptance of these works, and he feels obliged to make some reservations. Thus, he says of Herzen: "It was his thoughtfulness that saved the author: with his intellect, he correctly understood the positions of his heroes; yet he expressed them merely as a clever man would, having grasped the fact of the matter, and not as a poet" (ibid., 10:321).

THE WORK OF ART AS AN ORGANIC WHOLE

Belinskij sees different ways in which the inherent polarity of the work of art reveals itself as a unifying principle. To begin with, he regards the work of art as organically embedded in "life." A work of art is like a beautiful flower, a closed world in itself, yet intimately connected with all of nature ("A Hero of Our Time," 1840, 4:202). The human spirit, torn away from the absolute Spirit by its individuality, still senses its mysterious unity with life at large, and it is in the work of art that this unity finds its most eloquent expression ("The Poetry of M. Lermontov," 1841, 4:485). We meet similar observations in Belinskij's essay "The Poetry of Apollon Majkov" (1842, 6:13), in his review of Baratynskij's poetry (1842, 6:463), in his essays on Puškin (e.g., 7:272, 376), and in his many essays and reviews dealing with Gogol'.

When Belinskij encounters a remark by Nestor Kukol'nik, to the effect that Gogol', while a writer of talent, "describes things which do not exist in nature," he angrily rejects this statement as a *contradictio in adiecto:* either Gogol' has no talent and actually "describes what does not exist in nature," or he has talent, and what he expresses in his works must be the truth of life (review of *The Summits of St. Petersburg* by Ja. Butkov, 1845, 9:356).[41]

The bridge from an organic relationship between the work of art and the world at large to an organic conception of the work of art is established by Belinskij with the aid of the notion that artistic creation, namely, the transformation of "life" into "art," must be a "living," "organic," and conscious process. Belinskij is a firm believer in E. T. A. Hoffmann's Serapiontic Principle (*das serapiontische Prinzip*), according to which a work of art as a whole, and every single separate detail of it, must come to life in the artist's aesthetic consciousness. A passage from Belinskij's article "Russian Literature in 1841," stating

41. Cf. 10:194.

this principle, was conceivably written under Hoffmann's direct influence, for Belinskij was an admirer of *Die Serapionsbrüder*,[42] but more likely it is a corollary of Schelling's conception of artistic creation (which was also Hoffmann's source):

> Puškin's poetry is replete, it is wholly imbued with content, like a polished crystal hit by a ray of light: Puškin has not produced a single poem which did not emerge from life, nothing that might have been written on account of a vague desire to write something, hoping that perhaps it would come out all right. . . . It is this circumstance that sharply distinguishes Puškin from all the earlier poets. Puškin's artistic integrity is unparalleled in our literature before him: he sent out from the world of his soul only fully mature, fully ripe creations of his poetic imagination, which were themselves demanding to be released. (5:556)

Belinskij restates this principle many times, especially during the last years of his life. The following concise statement appears in a review of 1845: "The poet is a poet because he takes all of reality through his own 'I,' so that it emerges from him as pure gold from a crucible" (9:121–22; cf. 10:247, 303).

Belinskij likes to compare the metamorphosis of life into the microcosm of the work of art with the organic process of birth, where this metaphor suggests that the whole and living stream of life gives birth to an equally whole and living artistic creation.[43] The following passage states Belinskij's organicist position on the nature of the work of art and its genesis in unequivocal terms:

> The essence of every work of art consists of the organic process of its appearance (*javlenie*), from the possibility of being to the reality of being. Like an invisible seed, the idea (*mysl'*) falls into the artist's soul, and develops and grows from this abundant and fruitful seed into a distinct form, into images full of beauty and life, appearing in the end as a world which is entirely distinct, integral, and complete in itself (*osobym, cel'nym i zamknutym v samom sebe*), where all parts are commensurate with the whole, and each part, existing in and of itself, also exists at the same time for the sake of the whole, being its necessary part and contributing to the impression created by the whole. ("A Hero of Our Time," 1840, 4:200)

Belinskij has an acute sense for the wholeness of life and of its expression in art. He likes to use an anatomist's preparation of what was once a living organism—but no longer is—as a simile of mechanical and uninspired presentation of life (e.g., 10:158). This is one of the more popular clichés of organic aesthetics. We find it, for instance, in the *Schülerszene* in Goethe's *Faust*. Belinskij believes that there is, in the creation of a true work of art, a moment of "inner

---

42. Pypin suggested that the works of Hoffmann were a kind of "school of aesthetics" for Stankevič and his circle, and especially for Belinskij. See Pypin, *Belinskij*, pp. 89–90.
    43. E.g., 1:287–88, 295; 2:132, 439–40; 4:483–84, 596–98; 6:216, 412.

vision" (or whatever else one may want to call the aesthetic experience) which imparts a quality of life or, as Belinskij liked to say, the "living spirit" (*duša živa*) to the impressions composing it, thus transforming it into a "living whole" or "organism."

The first and principal question which the critic Belinskij tends to ask is whether or not a given work of art is, as such, a "living whole." Usually the answer is in the negative. For instance, Zagoskin's *Jurij Miloslavskij* (1829), though admittedly "the first good Russian novel," is at the same time lacking in "artistic fullness and wholeness" ("Literary Reveries," 1:95), and Belinskij would never consider it great art, or even art. The short stories of N. F. Pavlov contain many first-rate descriptions which make one observe that nature has indeed been captured very accurately by this author. However, this is invariably true of parts and details only, and never of the whole ("On the Russian Short Story and the Short Stories of Mr. Gogol'," 1:280). Belinskij would never consider calling Pavlov's works art. The same is true of A. F. Weltmann. His fantastic tales "bear the mark of a real and genuine talent which, however, never creates anything that is whole, full, or harmonious" (review of Weltmann's *Ancestors of Kalimeros,* 1836, 2:115).[44] And therefore, Belinskij will refuse to call Weltmann's novels "works of art" (*xudožestvennye proizvedenija*).

Even Puškin is not always exempt from this kind of criticism. Belinskij finds fault with his verse epic *Poltava* because "as an architectural structure, it does not create a general impression, nor does it contain any dominant element to which all the other elements would be harmoniously related" (Seventh essay on Puškin, 1844, 7:426). Much the same is said of *Boris Godunov* (Tenth essay on Puškin, 1845, 7:526).[45]

Whenever Belinskij issues more than perfunctory praise to a work, he will almost invariably stress its wholeness and completeness. In his essay on *Hamlet* (1838), he points out that this play and all of Shakespeare's great tragedies show a living interplay of all their characters—"just as the history of the epoch designated by Napoleon's name is not the history of one man but of a whole nation during a certain epoch" (2:296). In the same essay, Belinskij develops the following simile to illustrate the wholeness of a work of art:

Each of Shakespeare's plays is a whole separate world, which has its focus, its Sun, around which the planets and their satellites revolve. But Shakespeare is not contained in any one of his plays, just as the universe is not contained in any one of its planetary systems; but a whole series of plays does indeed embrace Shakespeare—a symbolic word (*slovo simvoličeskoe*), the meaning and content of which is as great and infinite as the universe. (2:288)

44. The same evaluation is repeated in 5:212.
45. Cf. 1:185; 2:238, 412; 4:196; 5:71, 560; 11:395.

Belinskij does not seem to see all the implications of this simile. If there are as many possible poetic worlds as there are planetary systems in the universe, or individual human destinies in "real life," then art loses much of its cognitive value, because, in that case, getting to know Hamlet would mean no more and no less than meeting any interesting individual in real life—on very intimate terms, to be sure. The problem here is that by postulating the organic completeness and uniqueness of a work of art, one also tends to accept the notion that it is "closed," or "windowless." Belinskij does just that, specifically in his famous interpretation of *The Inspector-General* ("Woe from Wit," 1840, 3:452-69),[46] where his notion of the "closed state" (*zamknutost'*) of Gogol''s comedy is of pivotal importance.

Belinskij's "organicism" reaches its height in his essays on Lermontov (1840-41). They show that Belinskij has a very clear conception of structure. His not infrequent likening of the poet to an architect ("The Poetry of M. Lermontov," 4:516) is a significant detail. Belinskij is most enthusiastic about Lermontov's "Song of the Merchant Kalašnikov," a romantic pastiche of the Russian folk epic, and considers it vastly superior to even the best examples of the folk epic. His reasoning runs as follows:

> No matter how attentively you will look at Lermontov's poem, you will not find in it a single superfluous or missing word, trait, verse, or image: not a single weakness, everything in it necessary, full, powerful! In this respect it cannot be compared with the popular legends known under the name of their collector, Kirša Danilov. Those legends are the babbling of a child, often poetic, but equally often prosaic, often picturesque, but even more often allegoric, shapeless as a whole, full of unnecessary repetitions of one and the same thing. . . . (ibid., 4:516)[47]

Belinskij's point here, as in his analysis of *A Hero of Our Time* (4:196-204) and of Lermontov's lyric poetry (e.g., 4:480), is that a genuine work of art has no "accidental" details: every detail is important.

Time and again, Belinskij expresses the notion that formal details ought to be seen primarily in their relationship to the whole, taking for granted that in a true work of art such a relationship will necessarily exist.[48] For instance, in analyzing Puškin's *Captive of the Caucasus*, Belinskij observes that the poet never introduces a description of the Caucasus as a mere incidental episode (which would be too "didactic," and therefore "prosaic"), but connects each

---

46. Cf. Wellek, *Modern Criticism,* 3:249.

47. Cf. 5:356, where Belinskij claims that the Russian fairy tale lacks an "organic" structure! This opinion accords with Belinskij's consistent lack of understanding of stylized art and stylized structures.

48. See, e.g., Fifth essay on Puškin, 1844, 7:302.

description organically with the action of the poem (Sixth essay on Puškin, 1844, 7:373).

When Belinskij wishes to offset his mild criticism of Dostoevskij's *The Double* with some strong words of praise, he says that, if he were given a free hand to eliminate from that work every passage which he felt was prolix and superfluous, he could not cut out a single passage (review of *A Petersburg Almanac*, 1846, 9:564). Belinskij had identified *The Double* as a work of high artistic quality, and to admit that it contained important weaknesses of detail would have been, to his thinking, a contradiction in terms. It is in the light of this insistence on the wholeness of the work of art that we must understand the reluctance and diffidence with which Belinskij challenges the patriotic effusions in *Dead Souls*. He quite frankly disliked them, especially if they were associated with a downgrading of other nations (as in the famous passage at the end of the fifth chapter), but then, how could a work of art, so obviously whole and genuine as *Dead Souls,* contain any imperfections?

When Belinskij recognizes that a work is less than perfect, his criterion will often be "a lack of unity," as in the following evaluation of Apollon Majkov's "Roman Sketches":

> Many excellent verses, but few poems in which everything is consistent, where everything is in accord with everything else, poems which by their wholeness, plenitude, and completeness (literally, "quality of being closed," *zamknutost'*) would give the reader an impression that is simple and unified, rather than complex, clear, yet full, powerful, and deep. . . . Bright sparks of true creativity are seen in specifics and in details rather than in the whole. (10:84)

Good idealist that he is, Belinskij always insists that the continuous presence in a work of art of a clear and consciously perceived idea is the surest guarantee against aesthetic imperfection. Details of form, if conscientiously checked against the main idea, will naturally assume the right proportions:

> If the idea of a poetic work is true, as such, and if the poet has a clear and definite conception of it, if his work is correctly conceived (*verno koncepirovano*) and has gone through a sufficient period of gestation in the poet's soul, then it cannot possibly contain misshapen details, nor weak passages, nor dark and unintelligible expressions, nor insufficiencies as regards external polish. The work will be, in that case, an organic whole (*organičeski celostno*): nothing is superfluous in it, nor is anything missing; it is well rounded; its beginning introduces the reader to its meaning; the last word concludes its whole content, so that the reader is fully satisfied and could not possibly ask: "And now what?" ("The Works of Deržavin," 1843, 6:592)

Belinskij stayed with his initial conception of the wholeness of the work of art until the end of his life. In his "Survey of Russian Literature in 1846," he says, as a matter of course, that "the creation of every great poet represents a completely distinct, original world" (9:28) and bases his assertion on the presence in each work of art of a "living individuality" (*živaja ličnost'*). Belinskij's organicism, as applied to the individual work of art, is a conscious, ever-present conception, fruitfully and consistently used in his practical criticism. It is decidedly idealistic and Hegelian in that it seeks, in theory as well as in practice, to explain details of style and structure as necessary "realizations" of a single generative idea which is the "soul" of the entire work.

POETRY AND NONPOETRY

Belinskij's value judgments must be viewed in the context of his organic conception of the work of art. There is, to begin with, the all-important distinction between "poetry" and "nonpoetry." The distinction between "art" and "nonart" partially overlaps with it, but moves, at least theoretically, on a different level. As far as Belinskij is concerned, a work can very well be "poetic" yet not "artistic."

"Poetry" in the broadest sense is to Belinskij the presence of "life": "All that comes from the heart (*iz duši*), with feeling, in short, from the plenitude of life, and is expressed with warmth and passion, contains poetry, because it has immediacy or the quality of an image (*neposredstvennost' ili obraznost'*) about it" (review of N. Polevoj's *Ugolino*, 1838, 2:441).[49] The antonyms of "poetry" are, for Belinskij, "rhetoric," "versification" (*versifikacija, stixi, stixotvorstvo, stixosloženie, razmerennye i zarifmennye stročki*), "literature" (*belletristika*), and "prose."[50] All of this is consistent with the romantic usage of the word "poetry." To the Schlegel brothers, "poetry" was not any particular human activity (or the faculty for it), but "an all-pervading primeval power" (*eine all-durchdringende Urkraft*), as Friedrich Schlegel put it in his *Gespräch über die Poesie* (1800).

In the context of artistic creation, "poetry" depends on the action of "creative imagination" (*tvorčeskaja fantazija*).[51] No work from which it is absent can be "poetic."[52] It is for this reason that imitators, no matter how skillful, are not poets, nor their works poetry, Vergil and his *Aeneid* being an example (5:35-36). "Descriptive poetry," which copies nature without letting its subject pass through the crucible of the imagination, is likewise nonpoetry (5:66-67). Again, this view was retained by Belinskij until the end of his life.

49. Cf. 1:368; 4:489; 6:125; 7:94, 321, 337.
50. For examples of "rhetoric," see 1:364; 5:349, 534; 7:319. For "versification," see 2:150; 4:27-28, 156, 479; 9:119-21. For "literature," see 5:67; 9:157-58. For "prose," see 7:319; 9:300.
51. Hegel and Hegelian aestheticians, such as Vischer, also use the word *Phantasie* (rather than *Einbildungskraft,* which occurs in Kant) in the sense of "creative imagination."
52. See 1:360, 369; 4:479-80.

The following passage from a review of Èduard Guber's verses (1845) is quite typical:

> We find, in these poems, good versification, much feeling and even more genuine sadness and melancholy, a fine mind, well educated. And yet we must admit that we see in them very little poetic talent, not to say none at all. Everywhere in these poems we meet a heart, everywhere, too, we meet a mind which thinks less than it reflects, that is, reflects upon the poet's own feelings and thoughts; but nowhere do we meet an imagination which creates! (9:121)

Belinskij knows that a man may very well be a poet in his heart, in his feelings, in his life, yet produce verses—or prose—which lack "poetry," because their author lacks creative imagination.[53] Creative imagination, in turn, is an ability "to turn ideas into images (*obrazy*), to think, to reason, and to feel in images" ("The Works of Deržavin," 1843, 6:592).

By and large, Belinskij is well able to distinguish "creative imagination" from "fantasy"—here one should not be confused by Belinskij's rather annoying indiscriminate use of *voobraženie* and *fantazija*, both appearing in a positive meaning as "creative imagination," and in a pejorative meaning as "idle fancy, daydreaming." The following passage from Belinskij's "Survey of Russian Literature in 1847" shows how well Belinskij knows the difference:

> Of all the faculties of the mind, they [the romantics] have developed most their imagination and fantasy (*voobraženie i fantazija*), but not that fantasy through which the poet creates, but rather that fantasy which makes a man enjoy his dreams of the good things in life more than the reality of the good things in life. (10:332)

A criterion closely related to that of the presence of "creative imagination" is that of "originality" (*original'nost'*). "Poetry" is "original" by definition. "Why is he original?" Belinskij asks, speaking of Gogol'. And he answers his own question: "Because he is a poet" ("The Russian Short Story and the Short Stories of Mr. Gogol'," 1:297). In his essays on Puškin, Lermontov, and Kol'cov, Belinskij frequently stresses the "originality" of these poets.[54] Needless to say, the criterion of originality is connected with the romantic notion of the uniqueness of the "creative individuality." It is one of Belinskij's criteria of artistic excellence which his followers of the Left will downgrade, and those of the Right will stress even more.

Two of the most important, and most ambiguous, terms in Belinskij's aesthetics—and in all Russian aesthetics—are *xudožestvennyj* and *xudožestvennost'*, literally, "artistic" and "artistic quality."

To begin with, *xudožestvennyj* is often used interchangeably with *poètičnyj*.

53. See 1:360, 369; 4:479–80.
54. See 4:445; 7:311, 441; 9:535.

A work which lacks "poetry" (which, in turn, equals "life") cannot be "artistic." Belinskij resolutely rejects any work that is merely elegant, amusing, or entertaining, without being an expression of true feeling or a reflection of real life. Specifically, Belinskij is opposed to the fashionable muse of the salons of high society (covered by the term *svetskost'*, from *svet* "(high) society," promoted by Ševyrev, Belinskij's lifelong opponent). He considers it a profanation of true art.[55]

Belinskij is unwilling to pursue the line of thought, started by Schiller and developed by the romantics, according to which art is a form of play. It is fully consistent with this attitude that Belinskij rejects stylized art on both the highest and lowest social levels: as has been pointed out above, Belinskij had no use for stylized folk art either. This has far-reaching consequences. Tying "art" to "life," and in particular to life in its social aspect, precludes the development of many tendencies which were to dominate Western art and literature in the twentieth century. The aesthetic conservatism of Belinskij's epigoni boils down to a stubborn defense of Belinskij's social organicism.

In Belinskij's aesthetics there simply is no provision for works which are "artistic" (*xudožestvennyj*) without being "poetic," full of life and feeling. However, more often than not, *xudožestvennost'* implies certain qualities in a work of art over and above *poètičnost'*, meaning that a work which is *xudožestvennyj* and *poètičnyj* is superior to one which is only *poètičnyj*. To give only a few examples, Polevoj's translation of *Hamlet* (2:426–27), Kvitka-Osnov'janenko's *Marusja* (3:52), Lermontov's *Hero of Our Time* (4:267), Deržavin's poetry (5:254; 7:431), Russian folk poetry in general (5:330), and much of Žukovskij's poetry (5:545–46) are all credited with being "poetic," yet are also said to be lacking in "artistic" quality. In other instances, Belinskij will concede that a work is excellent "literature" (*belletrističeskoe proizvedenie*), but insist, in the same breath, that it falls short of being "artistic." Such works are Herzen's *Whose Fault?* (10:318) or Puškin's *Captain's Daughter* (4:198; 11:508).

What is *xudožestvennost'*? Or rather, what does *xudožestvennost'* imply that is not already given in *poètičnost'*? On the surface there seems to be no difficulty. As early as 1838, Belinskij writes, in distinguishing "artistic" works from "pseudoartistic" (*mnimo xudožestvennye*) ones: "So then, in truly artistic works, which were created by the laws of [inner] necessity, there is nothing accidental, nothing superfluous, nothing insufficient, but everything about them is necessary" (review of N. Polevoj's *Ugolino*, 2:439).

In his essay on Kol'cov (1846), Belinskij still believes that "by *xudožestvennost'* one should understand wholeness, unity, plenitude, completeness, and consistency of thought and form" (9:535). Many similar statements, more or

55. See "On the Criticism and Literary Opinions of *The Moscow Observer* (1836), 2:172–73.

less to the same effect, can be found throughout Belinskij's writings.[56] Puškin's poetry is, of course, the epitome of *xudožestvennost'*:

> In Puškin nothing is ever superfluous, nor is anything lacking; but rather,
> everything fits, everything is in its proper place; the end is in harmony with
> the beginning. Having read a piece by Puškin, one feels that nothing could
> be taken away from it, nor could anything be added to it. In this, as in oth-
> er respects, Puškin is the artist par excellence. (Fifth essay on Puškin, 1844,
> 7:330)

Clearly, *xudožestvennost'* here is very close to what earlier critics had called
"beauty." The introduction of the concept of beauty inevitably plays havoc
with a realistic conception of art, such as Belinskij's, for it means that an extra dimension is added to what, without this criterion, is a question of more or
less successful expression of feeling, representation of life, or description of nature.

There are enough passages to show that Belinskij knew very well that "art"
is "life" *plus* an extra "something," more difficult to define in positive terms
than to point out as lacking in a given work. "I see in the face of the Medice-
an Venus, in her attitude, in her entire wholeness, a certain *something* which I
cannot name, which I cannot express," Belinskij writes in one of his reviews of
Benediktov's poetry (1838, 2:421). He goes on to say that every short poem
by Puškin has that little *something*—while Benediktov's poems lack it. This
certain "something" is variously hypostatized as the presence of a "living
soul" (*duša živa*), the quality of having been "born" rather than "made," being "visible" rather than "only imaginable"—all in good romantic style.[57] This
"something" is apparently more than the mere presence of life which produces
"poetry." It is, rather, the presence of life in a higher power of plenitude,
vigor, and harmony.

In Belinskij's critical arsenal, the term "beauty" (*prekrasnoe, krasota,
izjaščnoe*) does not play a significant role. The Neoplatonic conception of
Beauty as the embodiment of the divine Idea, or its shining through the veil of
phenomenal life, occurs occasionally in Belinskij's earlier writings.[58] In later
years, whenever Belinskij runs into the concept of Beauty in the writings of
others, he usually reacts with open hostility. In responding to Nikitenko's

---

56. In declaring that the works of Bestužev-Marlinskij are nonart, Belinskij bases such
judgment on their lack of naturalness, truthfulness, reality, and simplicity (4:35–38). In
reviewing the rather weak poetry of a young beginning poet, A. D. Verderevskij, Belinskij
suggests that "only a mature, true feeling will express itself in artistic form" (3:38). Another criterion of *xudožestvennost'* is concreteness: a truly artistic work is always national, substantial, and specific (see 5:317, 633). Cf. 9:292, 300.

57. Cf. 1:161, 406; 2:169–70, 212, 495; 4:112; 5:543; 7:268.

58. E.g., 3:404, 424.

"Discourse on Criticism" (1842), Belinskij devotes a lengthy diatribe to Beauty, seeking to dismantle his opponent's Neoplatonic conception. First of all, says Belinskij, the idea of "the plenitude and perfection of life" should not be confused with the idea of Beauty. And secondly, "beauty" (*izjaščestvo i krasota*) alone is not everything in art. At least today, says Belinskij, it is mostly "intellectual content" (*razumnoe soderžanie*) and "historical meaning" (*istoričeskij smysl*) that one demands of art. Beauty for the sake of beauty, and art for the sake of art, "are resolutely rejected by our age," Belinskij declares (6:276–77), conceding that perhaps in ancient Greece "pure art" was possible. What Belinskij does here—and very often subsequently—is to subsume "beauty" as a *sui generis* aesthetic dimension or quality, which can be divorced from the cognitive and moral value of a work of art. From this time on, Belinskij tends to identify "beauty" with ornamental, decorative, "pretty" art, and to disapprove of it as of something trivial and unworthy of true art.

But since Belinskij's intuitive judgment of literature told him that certain works were "true works of art," while others, equally or even more meritorious from a cognitive, social, and moral point of view, were not, he still needed a term to distinguish these works from the rest. Since the conventional terms "beautiful" and "beauty" seemed hardly appropriate for a work of the Natural School, Gogol''s *Overcoat*, for example, *xudožestvennost'* was summoned to fill the gap.

Looking at Belinskij's definitions of *xudožestvennost'* and the contexts in which he uses this term, one sees that it covers rather the same semantic area as "beauty" in classicist aesthetics and criticism: it is that certain plenitude, completeness, maturity, and harmony which one finds in nature, too, but which the artist of genius succeeds in imparting consistently to all of his works. Some works which Belinskij values highly are lacking in these qualities.[59] Other works possess them, yet do not earn Belinskij's approval. Goethe's idyllic verse epic *Hermann und Dorothea* and Gončarov's short novel *The Same Old Story* are examples to this effect.[60] And while *Evgenij Onegin* is a perfect work of art, Belinskij does not hesitate to find fault with the circumstance that it idealizes—so he feels, rightly or wrongly—the life of the Russian landowner.

By suggesting that *xudožestvennost'* was not the only virtue of a work of art

59. See 2:566; 3:311; 5:632–33; 9:362.

60. In a brief review of a Russian translation of *Hermann und Dorothea* (1842, 6:559), Belinskij calls Goethe's epic "an exceedingly sorry work in the pudgy-watery-sentimental style of the bucolic epopoeias of Gessner and Bitaubé" and insults it quite outrageously throughout. Belinskij (and Černyševskij later) was obviously irritated by Goethe's sympathy for bourgeois philistinism. Belinskij's review of Gončarov's first novel *The Same Old Story* ("1847," 10:326–44) grudgingly grants Gončarov that he has talent ("not first rate, but strong, remarkable"), but will grant him very little else: "In Mr. Gončarov's talent, poetry is the first and the sole agent. . ." (10:344).

and admitting that it might sometimes be less important than social relevance, political effectiveness, and educational value, Belinskij opened a Pandora's box. Half a generation later, Černyševskij would heap violent abuse on a work of perfect beauty such as *Hermann und Dorothea*, because he saw in its idyllic qualities nothing short of a betrayal of social progress. And Pisarev would denounce *Evgenij Onegin* as an expression of little else but the hedonistic pleasures of an idle, effete, and depraved aristocracy.

In one respect, Belinskij's treatment of *xudožestvennost'* marks a long step forward as opposed to the use of "beauty" by earlier critics: *xudožestvennost'* has nothing to do with the subject matter; it is entirely intrinsic to the work of art. Gogol' 's *Dead Souls*, certainly the way Belinskij read that work, presented a most unattractive, drab, dreary, and sordid world—but *Dead Souls* was also a work of superb artistry, plenitude, harmony, and completeness.

The Fantastic

Belinskij distinguishes "art" from "nonart" in specific ways. It is significant that the formal criteria of eighteenth-century sensualistic and psychologistic aesthetics (symmetry, "proper" size and proportions, "good taste," and the like) are notably absent from his discussions of art and literature.

Very consistently and really from the very beginning, Belinskij disapproves of the fantastic in art and poetry on the grounds that there is enough poetry in real life and that art is much too serious and responsible an undertaking to be wasted on chimeras. Belinskij, like Hegel, is an uncompromising advocate of realism in art. Wherever the fantastic (in the sense of anything "unreal, purely imaginary," "highly implausible," "quite exceptional," or "morbid") appears in poetry or fiction, Belinskij will roundly condemn it.[61] He has, of course, full understanding of the fantastic as a literary device for a poet who is, however, concerned with reality.[62] But he has nothing but disapproval for anyone who attempts to create a dream world of fairies and spirits merely to relieve the boredom of his prosaic public. "As though there were no poetry in real life, and as though truth and reality were not the most excellent poetry!" he exclaims, having made this point in his discussion of a novel by Edward Bulwer-Lytton (1835, 1:248). As early as in his first great essay on Gogol' (1835), Belinskij seeks to discourage that writer from pursuing fantastic subjects (1:303). And in 1838, he declares that "an insane person cannot be the subject of art" (essay on *Hamlet*, 2:312), an opinion he was going to reiterate frequently, as in his discussion of Dostoevskij's *Double*, which he criticized for its "fantastic tendency" (10:41).

61. See 1:248, 303; 2:312; 3:432; 4:46; 5:616; 8:231, 311–12; 10:23, 41, 351.
62. See 6:493; 8:314–15. This is applicable to E. T. A. Hoffmann in particular, e.g. 11:508.

On occasion, especially during the earlier period of his career, Belinskij would recognize the possibility that the fantastic might express "premonitions of life's secrets" or glimpse the hidden depths of the human soul.[63] But by and large he insists, like Hegel, not only on a rational, comprehensible relationship between art and objective reality but also on the basic rationality of the human psyche as well.

Belinskij's attitude toward the great master of the fantastic, E. T. A. Hoffmann, shows two things: that Belinskij could not escape the charm of the German storyteller whom he considers, of course, a genius,[64] and that he could not bring himself to accept wholeheartedly an art which seemed so pointedly anti-realistic and antirational. As a kind of compromise, then, Belinskij declared Hoffmann an "insane genius" (6:519).[65] This more or less agrees with Hegel's (and Goethe's) opinion of Hoffmann.

Belinskij's judgment of the works of Russia's leading romantic storyteller, V. F. Odoevskij, follows the same pattern. Belinskij has words of the highest praise for Odoevskij's more realistic tales (Hoffmann's stories, too, have strong realistic elements and some of them lack the fantastic element altogether), while he severely condemns the more fantastic ones. The following passage is characteristic:

> The first of these [stories], "Opere del Cavaliere Giambatista Piranesi," is—who would have thought of such a thing?—an apotheosis of insanity. . . . What else, if not a desire to create an apotheosis of insanity, could have induced the author to take upon himself the task of presenting an architect who has embraced the fixed idea to construct buildings from mountains? . . Such a condition is, in my opinion, no mark of genius at all but, on the contrary, evidence of a weak nervous system which cannot stand the strain of rational activity. (review of *Sočinenija knjazja V. F. Odoevskogo*, 1844, 8:311–12)

Belinskij was a strong and lifelong enemy of romantic escapism. He sensed that romanticism, especially its German version at its best, in spite of all its brilliant, universal culture, deep sensitivity, good-natured humor, and artistic virtuosity, ultimately amounted to "giving up" on life in society, on the common man, and on progress, and that it was bound to lead into the ivory tower of "pure art." As early as 9 December 1841, Belinskij wrote to N. A. Bakunin: "The world of daydreams (*mir mečtanij*) is a world of phantoms and mirages, and he who stubbornly refuses ever to leave it, will either become a narrow-minded person or he will perish terribly" (12:77).

As an advocate of realistic art, Belinskij is also in favor of rational art, mean-

63. See 3:75; 4:98; 11:508.
64. See 4:106, 318; 11:204, 507–8.
65. Cf. 8:231, 314–15.

ing that he believes a "normal" human being to be rational, so that "typical" and "real" human conflicts must also be rational. Belinskij's opinion of the French *école frénétique* and its Russian imitators was consistently and bitterly negative. He thoroughly disliked those of Gogol' 's stories which bore a trace of it, "A Terrible Vengeance," for example. Belinskij felt that "mentally ill people belonged in asylums, not in literature" (10:41), as he said in discussing Dostoevskij's novel *The Double*, whose hero goes insane. Belinskij disliked all manifestations of the sickly, the contradictory, and the complex in literature, as the following passage illustrates:

> Tat'jana lacks the morbid contradictions from which excessively complex natures tend to suffer. Tat'jana is made, as it were, of a single whole piece, without any additions or admixtures. Her whole life is permeated by that integrity (*celostnost'*), by that unity which in the world of art represents the highest merit of a work of art. (Ninth essay on Puškin, 1845, 7:482)

Again, Belinskij's attitude corresponds to that of Hegel and Hegel's immediate followers. Belinskij's rejection of the fantastic, the morbid, and the irrational in art conforms with his organicism. The sickly, the counteractive, the indeterminate are out of place in a biological organism. The same should be out of place in art, too.

Naturalism

Yet Belinskij also rather consistently rejects what would later be called "naturalism." He used the term *naturalizm*, but not pejoratively, since it referred to the Natural School, whose herald and patron he was. As early as 1836, Belinskij observed that a poet "should be a slave neither of history nor of real life, for in either case he would become a copyist rather than a creator" ("On the Criticism and Literary Opinions of *The Moscow Observer*, 2:132). This thesis is reiterated frequently.[66] A passage from one of Belinskij's essays on Russian folk poetry (1841) is particularly revealing:

> It is clear, then, that the organic, living plenitude of art consists of a reconciliation of two extremes: artificiality and naturalism (*estestvennost'*). Each of these extremes alone is a lie; but mutually interpenetrating one another, they together form truth. Artificiality, as a one-sided and extreme phenomenon, produced dead pseudoclassicism; naturalism, as a one-sided and extreme form, produced the literature of city squares, taverns, jails, slaughterhouses, and houses of ill repute. (5:301–2)

Whenever Belinskij defends the Russian "naturalists," such as Dal', Butkov, and Grigorovič, he usually takes care to draw a distinct line between the

---

66. See 2:342, 359; 3:415; 4:493; 5:567; 9:56; 10:42.

"physiological" genre and "true art."[67] In his "Survey of Russian Literature in 1847," he devotes a lengthy passage to a renewed rejection of naturalism (10:303–4).

The Poetry of Reality

Thus, Belinskij can be considered an apologist of what is called *xudožestven-nyj realizm*, "artistic realism," in Russia, meaning a representation, in art, of empirical contemporary reality (with emphasis on its social aspect), transfigured and elevated by the immanence in it of certain ideal entities—a fusion of the "real" and the "ideal," in other words. Actually, Belinskij does not use the term "realism," but the notion is there, expressed in such terms as "the poetry of reality" (3:434), "artistic representation of reality" (10:294), art as a "manifestation of life" (7:305), and the like.

Often enough a modern Western reader will be irked by Belinskij's loving attention and lavish praise for a work solely on the grounds, it would seem, that it "depicts people not as they ought to be, but as they are" (3:432), or that it describes "not what one has seen in a dream, but what exists in society, in reality" (5:568),[68] dealing with "the prose of life" (7:50).

It must be said, in Belinskij's defense, that his enthusiasm for "the poetry of reality" was burning in an atmosphere still saturated with the affected, lifeless, mechanical products of assorted romantic epigoni, Russian as well as foreign, and not totally free of vestiges of an even mustier classicism. And if Belinskij's notion of the poetry of reality is sometimes naïve, he must still be credited with a genuine grasp of what realistic art is all about. The following passage from "A Survey of Russian Literature in 1847" approaches a modern conception formulated by Erich Auerbach:

> A gypsy camp, with ragged tents amidst the wheels of carriages, with dancing bears and with naked children in baskets carried by donkeys, was unheard of as a setting for a bloody tragedy. But in *Evgenij Onegin* ideals gave way to reality even more, or at least they were merged to form something new, something in between these two, so much so that this work may justly be considered the beginning of our contemporary poetry. Here, naturalness (*natural'nost'*) appears not as satire, not as something comical, but as truthful representation of reality, with all of its good or evil, with all of its everyday trivia; next to two or three characters who are poeticized or slightly idealized there appear ordinary people, not to be made fun of, not monsters, or exceptions of the general rule, but individuals who comprise the majority of society. (10:291)

67. See, e.g., "1846," 10:42–43.
68. Cf. 6:496, 535.

In the same article, Belinskij develops the notion that the poetry of reality is not a temporary tendency, a new literary school, as it were, but the realization of a fundamental principle which has existed, even in Russian literature, since its beginnings. Kantemir, says Belinskij, was the initiator of this "striving for reality" (*stremlenie k dejstvitel'nosti*), and Lomonosov headed the opposite tendency, a "striving toward an ideal" (*stremlenie k idealu*). While Ozerov, Žukovskij, Batjuškov, and Dmitriev continued Lomonosov's idealizing tradition, Fonvizin, Deržavin (in part), and Krylov pursued the trend toward "naturalism" started by Kantemir. In Puškin, and especially in Gogol', this "striving for reality" has finally emerged victorious (ibid., 10:289). Belinskij did not realize that this particular conception was difficult to synchronize with the other historical schemes by which he sought to explain the "progress" of Russian literature. But it was fruitful as still another attempt at polarizing the essence and the movement of literature in terms of basic historical tendencies.

Belinskij's conception of "the poetry of reality" is clearly that of an art which, while it deals with the pragmatic social aspect of life, still does so "organically," seeking to capture the inner meaning and the historical movement of life. Mere "copying" of nature will not do, because the truth, the meaning, and the movement of life require a true artist's intuition to be revealed. The simple, unadorned truth of life is difficult enough to capture and to express. It will, therefore, strike the reader as true art, and as poetic creation.[69] Belinskij bolsters the aesthetic merits of Russian Naturalism by arguing for its affinity to the spirit of Russian life and for its verity (taking for granted that these works—which were, after all, works of fiction—indeed faithfully depict Russian reality). Belinskij angrily rejects any notion that the French *école frénétique* had any influence on Gogol' and the Natural School (10:254–57, 314), for he knows that his case for Russian Naturalism would collapse if it were proven that its essence was "literary" rather than inspired by life itself. Modern scholars have demonstrated that there was a great deal more in what the opponents of the Natural School said about its connection with certain trends in contemporary French literature than Belinskij was willing to admit.

Toward the end of his career, Belinskij lapses into hypostatizing "faithfulness to reality" (*vernost' dejstvitel'nosti*), meaning an author's willingness to present the seamy side of life in unadorned down-to-earth fashion, as an artistic virtue *per se*. To accommodate writers such as Butkov and Grigorovič who had "no talent for writing novels or tales" but satisfied the critic's demand for "faithfulness to reality," he establishes a special category of poetic talent and, in effect, a new poetic genre: "Grigorovič has not the slightest talent for the short story, but he has remarkable talent for those sketches of social life which are termed 'physiological' in today's literature" ("1846," 10:42). A lengthy passage on Butkov, much to the same effect, is quoted above.

69. See "1843," 8:89.

Intuition and Reflection

Belinskij follows the romantic tradition—and, in this case, the aesthetics of German idealism from Kant to Hegel—in drawing a distinct line between "intuition" (usually called "instinct" or "immediate knowledge")[70] and "intellect," and in explicitly rejecting "intellectualism" in art. The higher faculty of understanding (*razum*) can be achieved both through intuition and intelligence. Nor will Belinskij deny that the intellect may play an important and beneficial role in the creation of a work of art.[71] But this is true only provided intuition is also present. Any work of art created by the intellect (*rassudok*) alone is inevitably inferior from an aesthetic point of view.[72]

By today's standards Belinskij greatly overestimates the cognitive powers of intuition, assigning to it a capacity of taking shortcuts to an awareness of important social, psychological, and historical truths. Belinskij believes that "all an artist needs is a single fact, a single hint, in order to visualize the life of a nation during a given epoch" (review of two novels by I. I. Lažečnikov, 1839, 3:19), and that "*xudožestvennost'* is precisely that quality which allows an artist to present in a single trait, in a single word, vividly and fully, what could not be expressed in ten volumes without it" (review of vols. 11 and 12 [1838] of *The Contemporary,* 1839, 3:53). A striking corollary of his thought is that "in order to find out if an idea expressed by a poet is indeed true, one ought to determine, first of all, whether or not the work in question is artistic" (*xudožestvennyj*) ("Menzel, a Critic of Goethe," 1840, 3:397). Belinskij uses the same line of thought in one of his last articles, "A Rejoinder to *The Muscovite*" (1847, 10:257).

Belinskij's faith in intuition remains intact until the very end. In his Fifth essay on Puškin (1844), he makes the startling statement that "Puškin's lack of familiarity with the Greek language notwithstanding, his many-sided, profound artistic intuition (*xudožničeskij instinkt*) was a substitute for the study of classical antiquity" (7:323). And, in his Fourth essay on Puškin (1843), Belinskij gives rise to the myth, so popular later, that Puškin's genius allowed him to move freely from one sphere of life, or period of history, to another, so that "with a few tercets in the spirit of Dante's *Divine Comedy* he would do more to acquaint Russia with Dante than any number of translators possibly could" (7:289). Belinskij's extravagant notion that the historical intuitions of Sir Walter Scott are worth more than the laborious compilations of many scholarly historians has been mentioned above.

Generally speaking, Belinskij's faith in the powers of intuition is stronger in

70. A lengthy discourse on "immediate knowledge" is found in Belinskij's essay "The Idea of Art" (1841, 4:593–95).
71. See 1:284; 4:254, 520; 6:428, 472–73; 10:305.
72. See 2:160; 3:353, 413–14, 493–94; 4:143, 237–38; 6:13, 22, 107; 7:312.

the earlier part of his career, and the tendency is for him to give more and more weight to the powers of reflection. In a letter to V. P. Botkin, 24 February 1840, Belinskij still says: "Once more, it was our good fortune that Puškin's nature did not yield to reflection: this is why he was a great poet" (11:474). But a few months later, in another letter to Botkin, 16 May 1840, Belinskij writes: "Don't believe that I reject the need for, or the value of, reflective poetry: on the contrary, I now consider it, for our uncultured public, more important than the products of true creativity . . . for, to the crowd, reflection is more accessible than true art" (11:524).

In his great essay on Lermontov's *A Hero of Our Time* (1840), Belinskij sees reflection as "a transitional state of the spirit, in which the old has already been destroyed and the new is still only a possibility of something real in the future, yet only a complete illusion (*soveršennyj prizrak*) in the present" (4:253). Belinskij then proceeds to quote "Thus conscience does make cowards of us all," calling *Hamlet* "that apotheosis of reflection" (ibid.). A little farther in the same essay, Goethe's *Faust* is called "the apotheosis of reflection in our age" (4:254). Lermontov's Pečorin is seen as still another example of this transitional stage. However, here the "poetry of reflection" is no longer considered so definitely inferior to the "immediate poetry" of intuition, particularly since Belinskij is now beginning to call his own age "an age of reflection" ("The Poetry of M. Lermontov," 1841, 4:518-19).

By 1842, the presence of "reflection" is listed as one of the principal assets of *Dead Souls* (6:428). In his last years, Belinskij allows conscious reason a progressively larger role in art. He seeks to justify this by pointing out that Shakespeare possessed equal "wealth of creative imagination" and "wealth of all-encompassing intellect" (10:305): Shakespeare is still the absolute measure of all art, and the whole science of aesthetics is, in a way, a description of Shakespeare's art (as Tolstoj would charge later). All in all, it is always evident that Belinskij knows very well that reflection, reasoning, or intellect alone, without intuition, cannot produce a genuine work of art.

CONCESSIONS TO UTILITARIANISM

There is an aspect of Belinskij's aesthetic theory and critical practice which seems to jeopardize his generally consistent organicism: his concessions to the role of extrinsic factors in shaping a work of art, that is, concessions to moralism, didacticism, rhetoric, in short, to a utilitarian conception of art.

Rhetoric

In his earlier years, Belinskij will reject out of hand everything that suggests rhetoric, teaching, or preaching, along with any work of literature which has been "made" to serve an extrinsic purpose rather than "created" for its own sake.[73] Around 1842, he begins to be more tolerant. He will now apply the still-pejorative label of "rhetoric, rhetorical" mostly to works which he considers "unnatural," "affected," or "unreal," even if they were clearly created without any ulterior motive. Classicistic tragedy (French as well as Russian), Karamzin's prose, and a large part of all romantic poetry (including Žukovskij's) are thus labeled "rhetorical."[74] At the same time, Belinskij will not only tolerate, in the literature of his own age, works which are obviously "rhetorical" in the sense that they were created to serve an extrinsic sociopolitical purpose rather than "pure art," but will actually encourage their authors. Nor will he apply the label of "rhetoric" to these utilitarian works. What saves these works from being classified as "rhetoric," along with didactic, patriotic, religious, moralizing, and other such works of the past (which Belinskij often admits were "useful" in their own day), is obviously the fact that Belinskij considers them relevant to "reality" and to the spirit of his age.

Belinskij's thinking runs along these lines: In the eighteenth century, and even in the age of Puškin, Russian literature had not yet reached that mature level at which it would have been fit to assume an active part in the nation's life and thus become an agent of Russian history. It was enough for a poet to be a master of his craft and for a critic to have an understanding of the artistic merits of a poet's work. In fact, the creation of a language and of a literature which would be at least formally on the level of the languages and literatures of the great "historical nations" was in itself an important task, and its full achievement in the works of Puškin was a truly epoch-making event. But in Belinskij's own age, an extra dimension had been added to Russian literature: its direct relevance to the now-awakened social life of the nation. Therefore, the critic's task became a different one:

> Purely artistic criticism, which disregards the historical view, is no longer worthwhile, being one-sided, prejudiced, and thankless. Artistic quality (*xudožestvennost'*) is even today of great importance in a work of literature; however, if it lacks *that* quality which is characteristic of the spirit of our epoch, it will not be able to exert a strong appeal upon us. Therefore, today a work of art which is only "average" from an artistic point of view, but which affects our social consciousness, a work which raises questions, or solves them, is much more important than the most artistic work which contributes nothing to our consciousness outside the sphere of art. Altogether then, our age is an age of reflection, thought, bothersome questions, and not of art. Let us go even farther: our age is hostile to pure art, and pure art is impossible in it. As in all critical epochs, epochs with a disintegration of life, with a denial of the old, and with a premonition of the new, art is now not a

73. See 1:63, 123; 4:8, 41.
74. A lengthy diatribe against "rhetoric" in general is found in Belinskij's review of N. Košanskij's *Obščaja retorika* (9th ed., 1844), 8:503–13. Cf. 7:109, 186, 327–28.

master but a slave: it serves ends which are extraneous to it. (review of *Tarantas* by Count V. A. Sollogub, 1844, 9:77)

This statement, which obviously shows the influence of French utopian socialist thought (note the peculiar use of the term "critical epoch"), seems to imply that there are epochs in the history of nations when social problems and their solution become more important than the niceties of "pure art." Puškin, Belinskij reasons, still belonged to a relatively stable age, and so it was right for him to be "mainly an artist." But now things were different. And thus, Belinskij comes up, a little farther in the same review, with the monstrous expression "a work of art in the contemporary sense of that word" (9:78). Sollogub's *Tarantas,* a satirical journey from Moscow to Kazan', is anything but a work of art, and even its satire is superficial and uninspired. It is, however, directed against the Slavophiles and romantic dreamers in general, and is therefore "contemporary." We have here one of the many examples of the critic's tolerant attitude toward literary works of inferior quality, on the grounds that they were socially useful.

Belinskij was entirely conscious of the fact that the new tendency, which he was helping to promote, was sacrificing art to ideological expediency. In his famous "Letter to Gogol'" (1847), he summed it all up very bluntly: "This is why in Russia any author with a so-called liberal tendency is accorded general notice, even if he is poor in talent, and why the popularity of great poets quickly declines once they have taken to serving Orthodoxy, autocracy, and *narodnost'*, whether it be sincerely or insincerely" (10:217).

It appears that Belinskij did not see, or did not want to see, the whole depth of the aesthetic problem which he faced here. He saw the matter concretely, rather in the following way: Puškin's *Ruslan and Ljudmila* was without any doubt artistically excellent, and delightful reading; but it was also socially irrelevant and therefore uninteresting. Herzen's *Whose Fault?* on the other hand, was evidently not a great work of art (if it was art at all, which was doubtful), but it was extremely relevant and very interesting. Being a lover and connoisseur of literature, Belinskij never ceased to welcome works which, while socially relevant, were also artistic. One may note his delight at the appearance of Dostoevskij's *Poor Folk.* In fact, Belinskij was ready to welcome artistic excellence even when it was not linked with any social relevance, as evidenced in his warm and knowledgeable reception to the "anthological" lyrics of Apollon Majkov, Fet, and others. But there is no question that, from 1842 on, social relevance definitely came first.

What Belinskij seems to have failed to do was to give some thought to the problem of the relationship between artistic excellence and social relevance, or better, social usefulness (that is, social relevance with the "correct" political tendency). To consider these two things separately, as Belinskij always did, was to avoid the issue. Belinskij's successors were more resolute on this point. A Grigor'ev or a Dostoevskij (who, like Belinskij, were strong believers in the social role of art) would quite categorically say that an "unartistic" novel or play could not possibly express a living truth, and that an artist who was the bearer of a great truth would necessarily create "artistic" works. A Černyševskij or a Dobroljubov would ask only if a work was "true to life" and socially relevant, whether it displayed the correct political and ideological attitude, and whether it was a useful contribution to the cause of progress. If so, they asked no more.

Belinskij's readiness to separate "social content" from "artistic form" was decidedly a violation of the organic principle which he otherwise adhered to and defended. Belinskij may have been right in his pragmatic recognition of a plurality of purposes in literature, more right for all practical purposes than those who, like Grigor'ev, would always adhere to a strict organicist viewpoint. But what must be held against Belinskij is that certain untidiness with which he alternately defended an organic conception of art, then again abandoned it in favor of a utilitarian approach.

Moralism

Belinskij's attitude toward moralism in literature furnishes an illustration of the unsolved problems and contradictions in his aesthetic thought. A condemnation of moralism, that is, of the presence of a preconceived moral message in a work of art, was one of the basic tenets of romantic aesthetics—in antithesis, of course, to classicist emphasis on the moral message. The early Belinskij thus believes that any work of art which expresses the objective truth in artistic fashion must be necessarily "moral" as well. In other words, so long as artistic integrity prevails, there can be no danger to morality in art.[75]

In his essay on *A Hero of Our Time*, Belinskij points out that, while Pečorin is no paragon of virtue, Lermontov's novel is by no means an immoral work. By honestly describing Pečorin's vices, prejudices, and errors, all of which are characteristic of the man and his age, Lermontov, far from approving of them, points toward the positive potentialities dormant in this character (4:263–64). The implication of this is that a positive moral message will emerge from a work of art only if it is true to social reality and if it faces in the right direction, that is, brings out the positive trends already latent in society.

Belinskij finds a strong and explicit message in Gogol''s *Inspector-General*, *Dead Souls*, and Petersburg stories, in Herzen's *Whose Fault?*, in Grigorovič's *Anton Goremyka*, and in Dostoevskij's *Poor Folk*. In fact, he values these and

75. Cf. 1:299; 2:247–48, 419; 3:406, 411; 4:237; 5:168–69, 218–20, 519; 6:16, 211; 7:253, 345, 452, 644.

many other works largely on account of the moral message which he believed to have found in them and which he hoped they would communicate to the Russian literate public. And so we find in Belinskij's writings of the later period a rather explicit endorsement of what is, in effect, "moralism," provided the moral is to Belinskij's liking.

Didacticism

In "Thoughts and Notes on Russian Literature" (1846), Belinskij says outright that Russian literature has been, and continues to be, "a living fountain, even of practical moral ideas for our society" (9:434). He then goes on to claim that "the comedies of Fonvizin had even greater merit for Russian society than they did for Russian literature" (ibid.)—a statement which would have delighted any classicist critic. (In his "Literary Reveries" of 1834 and other early writings, Belinskij had dismissed Fonvizin's moralizing as a wooden, unnatural, and ineffective gesture, a mere formal concession to the canon of classicist poetics.[76]) Then, shifting to the contemporary scene, Belinskij goes on to express a serious belief that Gogol' 's humor would have a great and a beneficial influence on the further progress of the mores of Russian society.[77] The didacticism implied here is so obvious that one wonders how Belinskij failed to realize that he was contradicting his own many statements against didacticism in art.[78]

Belinskij's move toward the conception that would consider literature as an active factor in contemporary affairs had its justification in a Hegelian historicist synthesis of the "ideal" and the "real" in art: what was, in effect, "didacticism" (or moralism, or intellectualism, or simply "tendentiousness") was desirable, and "artistic," whenever its message coincided with the "living historical process."

As Ambrogio has pointed out, Belinskij (no less than Hegel) was guilty of the logical error (pointed out by Marx, among others) of operating with identities between the ideal and the empirical planes, with only a totally arbitrary formula for establishing these identities.[79] The abstract formula that true art is always in step with the progress of history, whether correct or not, does not warrant the empirical inference that the message of a given contemporary work is also the message of history. Belinskij's error has been and continues to be repeated in Russian literary criticism within the framework of many different philosophies of history.

76. See 1:50–51.
77. For some of Belinskij's many statements on the educational and civilizing role of art, see 1:16; 2:47; 3:417; 4:85–86, 237; 7:35, 223, 342–43.
78. See 1:299; 3:291; 5:63–64; 6:32, 318, 603.
79. Ambrogio, *Belinskij,* pp. 105–6.

Psychologically, the situation is simple: "Moralism," "didacticism," and "tendentiousness" are generally perceived only when the subject (reader, critic, historian) does *not* share the moral, political, or ideological bias in question. If he does, the "ideal" coincides with the "real" (as far as the subject is concerned), and "true art" is, subjectively, the result.

Thus, Belinskij could see the didacticism and moralism in the works of F. V. Bulgarin, but not the didacticism and moralism in the "progressive" literature of his day. The question did not occur to Belinskij directly whether that vaunted Kantian "disinterestedness" of the aesthetic idea was merely an optical illusion or a rare and precious property of truly great art. In his later writings, he certainly said many times that there was no such thing as "pure," that is, totally disinterested, art.[80] This notion became a dogma to Černyševskij and Dobroljubov, and was later vigorously driven home by Marxist critics. It caused the Marxist critics to search for concealed private and class interests even in the most innocuous, stylized, and purely nonrepresentational art.

In his dependence on the various ideologies which he embraced during his lifetime, Belinskij can be likened to a bird which has flown into a large cage full of attractive food. The door is still open, and the bird might still fly away to freedom. Belinskij felt that he was a free man, doing and saying what he thought was right. He was unaware of the great danger of becoming the captive of some narrow ideology. The door snapped shut on most of those who followed him. In this particular context, the fact that Belinskij changed his ideology readily and repeatedly speaks very much in his favor.

THE TAXONOMY OF POETRY

Genre

An important segment of organic aesthetics concerns the theory of genre. Belinskij devoted to it a whole major essay, "The Division of Poetry into Kinds and Genres," and frequently commented on it elsewhere throughout his writings. The essay is purely Hegelian, and we know that Belinskij used Katkov's conspectus of Hegel's lectures on aesthetics in composing it. Every major point about Belinskij's theory of genre can be traced to the aesthetics of German idealism, Hegel, Rötscher, and Jean Paul being the principal sources.

Belinskij's firm belief, never seriously questioned, in the unity of all art forms is characteristic of German idealist aesthetics. The organization of this unity into a historicized hierarchy is particularly characteristic of Schelling and Hegel. The placement of poetry at the top of the pyramid, with architecture at its bottom, is specifically Hegelian.

The breakdown of the unity of poetry into three, and only three, genres—the

80. See "1847," 10:304.

epic, the lyric, and the dramatic—is, of course, a part of the classical heritage. In Belinskij, it is identified with certain fundamental attitudes of the human spirit and is historicized in terms of Hegel's dialectic pattern of history (ibid., 5:10).[81] As a result, Belinskij—much like Hegel and the German romantics— operates with the adjectives "epic," "lyric," and "dramatic" more than he does with the nouns "epos," "lyric poem," and "drama." He also freely speaks of "epic traits" in a drama, the "dramatic qualities" of an epic work, and so forth.[82]

Belinskij's dialectic scheme of the three genres is that of Hegel rather than that of Schelling, whose scheme is also dialectic but not historicized,[83] or that of Jean Paul, who lets lyric poetry precede the epos in time.

In the epos, "poetry realizes the meaning of the idea in the external and organizes the spiritual world in very definite, plastic images" (ibid., 5:9). The poet himself is not in evidence: epic poetry is objective. Like Hegel,[84] Belinskij insists that the epos presents a closed and integral view of the world, the totality of a national spirit and of a nation's life (ibid., 5:37–39).[85] For this reason, the *Igor' Tale*, being episodic, is not a true heroic epos ("The Russian Folk Tale," 1841, 5:347). Also like Hegel, Belinskij sees the epos as the first genre of poetry, created by a nation when it is still young. Attempts by poets of more advanced ages to create epic poetry must inevitably fail.

Following Hegel's lead, Belinskij believes that the novel is "the epos of our time" (6:254).[86] Here, Belinskij—along with some of the Young-Hegelians, such as Vischer—goes a little further than Hegel, who had seen in the novel a new and rather modest beginning, while Belinskij (perhaps under the direct influence of Friedrich Schlegel) sees in it the ultimate genre of verbal art, "the broadest, all-encompassing genre of poetry, in which a talent feels infinitely free, in which all the other genres of poetry are united" ("1847," 10:315).[87] On the same occasion, Belinskij correctly points out that the novel incorporates in itself a variety of nonfictional forms, transforming them into art (ibid.). Here, Belinskij anticipates Georg Lukács's conception of the novel as *Kunst im Werden*. As B. I. Bursov has pointed out, Belinskij saw one flaw in the novels of Walter Scott and J. F. Cooper (both of whom he greatly admired otherwise):

81. Cf. 3:434.

82. See 3:449–51; 5:22–23, 30–31.

83. According to Schelling, lyric poetry is the infusion of the infinite into the finite (*Einbildung des Unendlichen ins Endliche*, where *Einbildung* could also be translated as "the grafting upon" or "the molding into"), epos is the representation of the finite in the infinite, while drama is the synthesis of the universal and the particular, or the infinite and the finite (Schelling, *Philosophie der Kunst*, 3:391).

84. Hegel, *Ästhetik*, 2:406, 438.

85. Cf. 2:241; 7:403.

86. See, e.g., Hegel, *Ästhetik*, 2:452. Cf. 5:25, 39; 6:414.

87. Cf. 1:271; 5:39–42; 6:91, 414; 10:106–7.

their excessively "epic" quality and the absence in them of a subjective component. Belinskij felt that the modern novel was reflecting a changing, tension-ridden world in which epic calm and stability were out of place.[88]

Belinskij's view of lyric poetry is precisely that of Hegel: it is an expression of "the realm of subjectivity, of the inner world, of the world of inceptions, which remains inside the Self and fails to penetrate outside it" ("The Division of Poetry into Kinds and Genres," 1841, 5:9). Belinskij often stresses the close relationship between lyric poetry and music (ibid., 5:9, 15, 49). He also points out the vague, indistinct, alogical nature of lyric poetry which, "without any particular meaning, though not lacking a common meaning, will still express its spontaneously significant meaning through the sheer musicality of its verses" (ibid., 5:10). Desdemona's willow song is quoted as an example. Certainly, these are romantic clichés, yet Belinskij has absorbed them intelligently and is capable of imparting to them a genuine literary significance. Thus, he points out that "many Russian folk songs are ingrained in the memory of the people not through their content (for they have hardly any content at all), not through the meaning of their words (for these word combinations lack almost any meaning, and while they may have a grammatical significance, they have almost no logical meaning), but rather through the musicality of their sounds, formed by certain word combinations, the rhythm of their verse structure, and their melody" (ibid., 5:10).

The drama is to Belinskij, as it is to Hegel (and to Schelling before him),[89] the logical and historical synthesis of the other two genres and the "highest" genre of poetry (ibid., 5:10). In the drama, says Belinskij, "the inner Self ceases being restricted to the Self and steps outside it, manifesting itself in actions: the inner, ideal (subjective) becomes external, real (objective)" (ibid., 5:9).

Belinskij's theoretical remarks on the distinction between tragedy and comedy also follow Hegel (or the Hegelian Rötscher). Belinskij is opposed to a separation of the tragic and the comic. Nor does he see the comic as mere relief from, or effective contrast to, the tragic (a view which appears in French romanticism). Rather, Belinskij sees the tragic and the comic as two sides of the same coin, the human condition in its two basic manifestations. As early as 1834 in "Literary Reveries," comedy is viewed as "a drama in exactly the same sense as what is ordinarily called tragedy." Its subject is "the representation of life in contradiction to the idea of life," says Belinskij (1:81). This anticipates his later, Hegelian formulations.[90]

In "The Division of Poetry into Kinds and Genres," Belinskij views comedy

---

88. B. I. Bursov, *Tolstoj i russkij roman* (Moscow and Leningrad, 1963), p. 14.

89. Hegel, *Ästhetik*, 2:518; Schelling, *Philosophie der Kunst*, 3:391.

90. Schelling's conception does not seem to have influenced Belinskij. According to it, the dramatic struggle between freedom and necessity appears in tragedy as a clash between

as a more modern type of dramatic poetry—in typically Hegelian fashion, even the dichotomy *tragedy : comedy* is historicized. While the tragic hero is driven by the substantial forces of human nature and clashes with rational necessity, the world of comedy is one of chance occurrences, of illusions and appearances, which have no existence in reality. The characters which populate the world of comedy have rejected the substantial basis of their spiritual nature. The essence of comedy is thus the contradiction between the phenomenal aspect of life and its spiritual and essential purpose. In a sense, then, the world of comedy is a picture of life in the negative (5:60).

In his great essay "Woe from Wit" (1840), which deals with Gogol''s *Inspector-General* as much as it does with Griboedov's comedy, Belinskij brilliantly applies to Gogol''s play the Hegelian conception of comedy as the negation, by the subject, of the substantial forces of life, and so of "reality" itself:[91] the Skvoznik-Dmuxanovskijs live in a phantom world; the great "idea" of Gogol''s comedy lies in his recognition that Russian life is "life in the negative"; all the feverish activity in the play is illusory; it is a "negative reality" that emerges from the struggle of the irrational, chaotic element of life against a higher, rational reality. Belinskij's explanations of various details of Gogol''s play as realizations of the same basic "idea" are convincing and contribute toward a creative and powerful stage interpretation of *The Inspector-General.*

In the same essay, Belinskij insists that the world of Gogol''s comedy presents a totality (*celost'*, which translates, as Belinskij himself suggests, Hegel's *Totalität*), a closed and complete world which "resembles the reality of life more than the reality of life resembles itself" (3:460). Since the reality of life also contains the true, substantial forces of life, as well as the positive ideal, the ideal is immanently present in Gogol''s play: life is shown "as it is, so as to lead us to a clear conception of life as it should be" ("The Division of Poetry into Kinds and Genres," 5:61).

Belinskij's opinion of didactic classicistic comedy is a very low one. Since the characters and the whole microcosm of a work of art should be "real," characters manufactured to depict preconceived moral notions must remain lifeless, Belinskij never tires of reiterating.[92] He does not even exempt Molière from such negative judgment. Belinskij consistently excludes satire from the realm of art, precisely because it lacks the organic quality, the concreteness, the wholeness, and the totality of true art. It is not that satire is denied a respected and important position in literature, or a useful social role.[93] It is not

---

the hero's free will and a determinate world (Fate), and in comedy as the spectacle of fixed characters in an unpredictable, ironic world.

91. Hegel, *Ästhetik,* 2:572.
92. E.g., 3:455; 5:61; 6:369–70.
93. Hegel, too, excludes satire from the domain of art. See, e.g., *Ästhetik*, 2:552.

art.[94] It is for this reason that Belinskij indignantly rejects the notion that *Dead Souls* might be a satire (6:220).

In the aesthetics of Socialist Realism, satire is given the status of a "fourth genre." This is one of the very few instances in which the aesthetics of Socialist Realism clashes with Belinskij's.

Belinskij's theory of tragedy is also conventionally Hegelian, meaning that he conceives tragedy as the representation of a collision between two important principles personified by characters of heroic stature ("The Division of Poetry into Kinds and Genres," 5:54).[95] The foundation of tragedy is the presence in life of substantial forces vying for supremacy. Time and again, Belinskij explains the scarcity of the Russian tragic muse ("Russian tragedy was born and died with Puškin," he said [ibid., 5:58–59]) from the facts of Russian history:

> In Russian history there never took place any inner struggle of these [political] elements, and therefore its character is epic rather than dramatic. A variety of passions, the clash of internal interests, and the differentiation of society—these are the conditions without which there can be no drama; and nothing of the kind ever existed in Russia. Puškin's *Boris Godunov* had no success precisely because it was a profoundly national creation. For the same reason, *Boris Godunov* is no drama at all, but at most an epic poem in dramatic form. ("The Russian Theater in Petersburg," 1841, 5:497)

Belinskij goes on to say that Russian dramatists, beginning with Sumarokov and ending with Belinskij's contemporary, Kukol'nik, have been doing the exact opposite of the French tragic poets: while the French tragedians had presented Frenchmen in the garb of classical heroes (figuratively speaking, of course), the Russians had always put on stage Frenchmen or Germans dressed up as Russians and mouthing an occasional Russian phrase. By this, Belinskij wants to say that the "conflicts" in these plays are not *Russian* conflicts at all.

Belinskij's theory depends on the soundness of his conception of Russian history. That conception was false: Russia, no less than other nations, knew class struggle, ideological struggle, and political tensions. The clash between Ivan IV and Prince Andrej Kurbskij, for example, was not an isolated episode, but represented a deep-rooted political and ideological antagonism—which, moreover, was still a fact of Russian life in Belinskij's day. That the facts of Russian history were less "substantial" than those of, say, German history, can hardly be defended on any grounds. On the other hand, Belinskij is apparently correct in his low estimation of Russian tragedy. The reasons for its relative insignificance must be sought elsewhere, though. Polevoj, for instance, suggested that the relative ineffectiveness of Puškin's *Boris Godunov* was simply due to the fact that Puškin's talent was not of the "dramatic type."

94. See, e.g., 8:89.
95. Cf. 6:18; 7:507.

Belinskij's Hegelian view of tragedy reappears, in a modified version, in the symbolist interpretation of Dostoevskij's "novel-tragedies" (*roman-tragedija*, a term used by Vjačeslav Ivanov) as visions of the great historical cataclysm of the Russian revolution. It has been retained, without any modifications, in the aesthetics of Socialist Realism. Its stereotyped revolutionary hero, whose death at the hands of the counter-revolution is vindicated by the ultimate victory of the revolution, is a properly historicized version of the tragic hero of classical tragedy.

Language and Style

Belinskij's conception of language and style is equally dominated by his organicist ideas. His theory of language is consistent with his organic aesthetics. In his review of Glinka's "Sketches of the Battle of Borodino" (1839, one of his "reactionary" pieces, but there is no reason to assume that Belinskij ever changed his philosophy of language), Belinskij explicitly rejects the mechanistic language theory of the eighteenth-century *philosophes*, including their conception of "universal language," and develops his own, or rather, a Hegelian theory of language, according to which language came to man not as an invention but as a revelation. If man is a rational being, says Belinskij, this implies that he possesses language, "for the spoken word is reason in action" (*potomu čto slovo est' razum v javlenii*). Speech, Belinskij believes, precedes man's awareness that he possesses the power of speech. "Reality, as reason apparent and incarnate, always precedes consciousness, because in order to be conscious one needs to have an object to be conscious of" (3:326–27). Therefore, Belinskij sees human speech as an end in itself, not a mirror of reality, but itself reality, something that "originates and develops of itself, without having a cause outside of itself, and the birth of which is, therefore, a mystery" (3:327). This is the conception of language generally accepted by the German romantics and by German objective idealism.[96]

From such a theory of language, it follows quite naturally that "style" is not a technical ability or skill, not the habit to write smoothly and elegantly, or according to the rules of grammar and rhetoric, but "the immediate, innate ability of a writer to use words in their true meaning, to say much in a few words . . . to effect a tight fusion of idea and form, and imprint upon everything the original, native seal of one's personality, of one's spirit" (review of the 2d edition

96. "Language," says Schelling, "is from one point of view the immediate expression of something *ideal* (*eines Idealen*)—of knowledge, thought, feeling, willing, and so on—in something *real*, insofar as it is itself a work of art. On the other hand, it is quite as certainly a work of nature, insofar as it is the one necessary form of Art which cannot have been invented, or even be conceived as having been invented, by Art. It is thus a natural work of art, much as everything produced by nature" (Schelling, *Philosophie der Kunst*, 3:502).

of *A Hero of Our Time*, 1841, 5:454). In other words, style is the art of effective expression. To have style, a writer must have something to express, to begin with, and then the ability to express it.

In his article "Russian Literature in 1843," Belinskij explicitly draws a line between "style" (*slog*) and "language" (*jazyk*), meaning by language a formal mastery of the rhetorical skills and the resultant virtues of clarity, good taste, balance, and harmony. "Style, on the other hand," Belinskij continues, "is talent itself, is thought itself; style is the plasticity, the tangibility of thought; in style you have the whole man; style is always original, like a personality, like a character." And then, this forceful conclusion: "You cannot divide style into three levels—high, middle, and low; style is divided into as many kinds as there are great, or at least talented, writers in the world" (8:79).

Belinskij's insistence that style is an integral part of the work of art, organically linked with its content, is characteristic of his practical criticism. He never tires of pointing out how in the truly great works of a Puškin, a Gogol', or a Lermontov, "style," that is, the choice of particular words, phrases, and sentence structure, on the one side, and meaning, on the other, form an inseparable whole. This is one of Belinskij's doctrines which his disciples—in this case, mostly those of the Left—tended to take lightly. In Černyševskij, in Dobroljubov, in Gor'kij, not to speak of the critics of Socialist Realism, one finds only too often statements to the effect that the moral and ideological merits of a given work allow one to overlook its stylistic deficiencies. The socialist realist *chef d'oeuvre How the Steel Was Tempered* by Nikolaj Ostrovskij is a famous case in point. Rather than seek to demonstrate that its admittedly semiliterate style was precisely the right form for its proletarian message (which Belinskij, or any other good organic critic would have done in such a case), its official critics have apologetically minimized the importance of style in a work of such great moral and ideological value.

It is regrettable that Belinskij, who had an acute sense of style, never took the time to subject any of the Russian classics of his age to a reading close enough to allow him to identify the peculiarities of their individual styles. What we get from Belinskij are mainly commonplaces, which are a credit to Belinskij's judgment but will not help a reader to understand the literary and artistic "personality" of Gogol', Lermontov, or the young Dostoevskij.

Humor and Pathos

One can observe an evolution in Belinskij's conception of "humor." Originally, he keeps "humor" and "satire" scrupulously apart, humor being the sign of rare artistic talent, satire "nonart" by definition. In his earlier writings on Gogol', for example, Belinskij credits Gogol' 's humor with its absence of any anger, hatred, or negativism ("On the Russian Short Story and the Short Stories of Mr.

Gogol'," 1835, 1:298). This conforms with the romantic notion, also found in Gogol' 's own writings, according to which humor is but an inverted striving for the ideal, which Jean Paul likened to the bee-eater, a bird which legendari-ly flies heavenward, tail first.

But then, as Belinskij begins to apply a Hegelian historicist scheme to litera-ture, he discovers that "humor" is the negative aspect of "pathos," or more concretely, "that most powerful tool of the spirit of negation which destroys the old and breaks ground for the new" (essay on the general meaning of the word "literature," 5:645). Such is, for instance, Belinskij's interpretation of "The Tale of How Ivan Ivanovič Quarreled with Ivan Nikiforovič" ("1841," 5:566–67). Eventually, this leads to giving "humor" (as opposed to čistyj komizm, "the purely, or simply, comic") a certain "social purposefulness," as Lavreckij puts it.[97] Belinskij's interpretation of *Dead Souls* suggests that he understood Gogol' 's humor in that work as having an entirely negative effect, with all those uproariously funny details being really very sad, often outrageous, and sometimes outright terrible. Here, Belinskij's interpretation clashes head on with that of K. S. Aksakov, who saw much more of a positive, epic, constructive quality even in Gogol' 's humor.

In a warm and eloquent passage of "Russian Literature in 1843," Belinskij re-news his definition of "humor" as "negative pathos," and describes the humor-ist (he has Gogol' in mind) as a poet who "evokes a vision of the exalted and the beautiful, and a longing for the ideal, by depicting the lowly and the trivial aspect of life" (8:90). In this context, Belinskij observes that comedy is "the flower of civilization, the fruit of a well-developed social structure" (ibid.), and notes that only a sophisticated audience will appreciate the more profound, philosophic content of great comedy. Belinskij fails to see the problem of rela-tive historical chronology hidden here. Elsewhere, he had observed that Russia was not ready for great epic or tragic themes and that the Russian ideal could be stated only in negative terms—as Gogol' had done. But Aristophanes (whom Belinskij mentions to illustrate his point) was the *last* of the great poets of the Attic stage, while Gogol' was, according to Belinskij, the *beginning* of a truly original national literature in Russia.

In his last articles, Belinskij more and more identifies humor with the truthful

---

97. *Obščestvennaja celeustremlennost'* (Lavreckij, *Èstetika Belinskogo*, p. 205). Hegel saw the implication of "social protest" in the comic genre. He points out that the prevalence of low-class characters in comedy is motivated by the fact that comedy is inherently an assault on the existing order of things to which such characters are op-posed: "For in the comic genre individuals have the right to rebel [against the existing order], as best they will or may" (Hegel, *Ästhetik*, 1:191). Of course, Hegel's empha-sis and sympathy are diametrically opposed to Belinskij's. Vischer, much more "lib-eral" than his master, also observes, but approvingly, that "everything that belongs to the comic genre is democratic in the broadest sense" (Vischer, *Aesthetik*, 1:470).

exposure of social ills (though he still refuses to call this "satire"). Time and again, we see Belinskij equating "humor" with "social truth."[98] The difference between satire and humor is seen in the circumstance that satire exposes abstract or nonexistent ills, while humor attacks the real social ills of contemporary life. This does not seem to agree with Belinskij's observation, often made virtually in the same breath, that "humor is almost as rare as genius" (9:482).

The best explanation for this contradiction seems to be that Belinskij is using "Aesopian language." He is thinking of a real challenge to the ruling regime, following the wrecking job done by social critique in literature. "Satire," of course, was the obvious label for this kind of literature. But the term "satire" had an inferior, classicist ring (the influence of romantic aesthetics) and so "humor" becomes a term signifying the exposure of the absurdity, injustice, and hopeless stagnation of the existing order. This may have had something to do with the fact that Gogol', the principal exponent of the "new" literature, was a "humorist," as was his British counterpart, Dickens. Somehow, humor became associated in Belinskij's mind with the "new" literature and its socially and morally desirable qualities. Belinskij was willing to accept the notion that contemporary Russian reality was utterly ridiculous and absurd—which made Gogol' a humorist and a realist at the same time—but he was unwilling to go further and say this of life at large. This resulted in his narrow, "historicized" interpretation of Gogol'.

In the process, Belinskij overlooked a simple question: Why was Gogol' a great humorist, while other writers who were as poignantly critical of Russian social reality, say, Herzen, were not humorists at all? And all together, whatever Belinskij has to say about humor is disappointing. In this connection, his German contemporaries, especially Arnold Ruge and Vischer, devoted a great deal of thought and loving attention to the aesthetics of humor, and considered humor the highest manifestation of poetic genius.[99] Belinskij also could have found many interesting and a few profound thoughts about humor in the writings of Jean Paul and E. T. A. Hoffmann, with both of whom he was familiar.

98. See 9:388, 459, 615, 619–20.
99. See, e.g., Vischer, *Aesthetik*, 1:453.

6

The Artist

Belinskij often uses the term "artist" (*xudožnik*) in lieu of "poet," "writer," "dramatist," implying by such usage that the author in question produces genuine works of art. At the same time, the term "poet" (*poèt*) often appears with reference to a prose writer of genius, Gogol', for example.[1] This means that Belinskij uses *poèt* in the sense that the Germans use *Dichter*, that is, as an antonym of *sočinitel', literator* ("littérateur"), German *Schriftsteller*. Russian *literator* is not pejorative: Merežkovskij once said that Tolstoj was a great writer (*velikij pisatel'*) but not a great littérateur (*literator*), while Dostoevskij was both. But by applying the word *poèt* to Gogol', a writer of prose, Belinskij wants to emphasize that Gogol' is an artist exactly in the same sense as the poet Puškin.

Belinskij is aware of the difference between "man" and "artist," and will often point it out quite explicitly. For instance, in "A Survey of Russian Literature in 1847," after Belinskij's break with Gogol', the critic says that "he has always praised Gogol' 's works, and not Gogol', praised them on their own merits, not on account of their author" (10:357).[2]

Belinskij holds that one is born a poet and that one cannot become one through diligent study, hard work, or long experience.[3] This does not mean that erudition, hard work, or experience are not among a poet's assets.

QUALITIES OF THE ARTIST

Inspiration

Of the qualities that distinguish a poet from a mere versifier or littérateur, "inspiration" (*vdoxnovenie*) is foremost: Belinskij decidedly believes in that certain irrational quality about the creative process (*process tvorčestva*) which

1. Belinskij refers to Gogol' as a "poet-storyteller" (*poèt-povestvovatel'*) (1:284).
2. Cf. 1:57; 3:397; 8:73.
3. See 2:80; 4:495; 6:463; 7:308, 605; 8:51; 11:153.

179

resists any rational analysis, which the creative individual himself cannot control, and which is given only to a few exceptional individuals.[4] In fact, from a certain point of view, it is a deviation from the normal. "Inspiration," says Belinskij in his article "On the Russian Short Story and the Short Stories of Mr. Gogol'" (1835), "means suffering and is, one might say, a morbid condition of the soul" (1:273).[5] There is no reason to assume that Belinskij ever abandoned his belief in inspiration as a *conditio sine qua non* of creation.

Creative Imagination

What "inspiration" is to the creative subject, creative imagination (*tvorčeskaja fantazija, tvorčeskoe voobraženie*) is to creation in general. It, too, is an irrational phenomenon.[6] The inspired artist who freely follows his creative imagination may and will reveal great moral and historical truths—even contrary to his own conscious, rational intentions as a man of his age and a member of his society. Cervantes and his *Don Quixote* are often mentioned as a case in point.[7] In a way, then, the creative imagination transcends the life of which it was born.

Gogol' is another example. So long as he followed "the powerful urgings of his genius intuitively, unconsciously," he was a leader of men and a teacher of his nation. But the moment he abandoned his intuition and turned to reason, the result was shallow philosophizing which put him in the rear of the movement of Russian society ("1847," 10:306).[8]

While Belinskij never abandoned this mystic conception of the creative process, a certain shift toward a more sober and rational view is evident in his writing after 1841. Specifically, the early Belinskij rejects the role of reason in the creative process in art, considering that process "sudden, unexpected, and entirely independent of the will"; at this time, he also attributes great importance to the "unconscious" element in the creative process, although the role of the conscious, rational element is not altogether ignored.[9] Later, Belinskij's emphasis

4. See 3:399; 4:500; 6:626; 7:311; 11:169.

5. In the same article, Belinskij writes: "And so the principal, distinctive trait of creativity lies in a certain mysterious clairvoyance, in a certain poetic somnambulism. The artist's creation is still a secret to all, he still has not so much as lifted his pen—and yet already he can see them clearly, already he can count the folds of their dresses, the wrinkles on their brow, furrowed by passion and grief, already he knows them better than you know your father, brother, friend, your mother, sister, the woman you love . . ." (1:286). Cf. 1:48, 84, 322–23; 2:421; 3:272–73; 4:118, 201; 6:474; 7:308, 377.

6. See 1:156; 2:133; 4:93, 386–88; 5:505; 6:163, 591–92; 7:386, 604; 8:89; 10:332.

7. See review of *Kuz'ma Petrovič Mirošev* by M. N. Zagoskin (1842), 6:33.

8. The same is said in Belinskij's famous "Letter to Gogol'" (10:213).

9. "On the Russian Short Story and the Short Stories of Mr. Gogol'," 1:286. See also 1:99, 288, 320, 400; 2:209.

shifts to the opposite. Here, it must be kept in mind that even the most mystically inclined among the German romantics, such as Novalis, always insisted that true poetry required the rational, conscious work (*Besonnenheit*) of the craftsman no less than the poet's inspired intuition.

Belinskij is constantly aware of the distinction between works that were "created" (or "born") and works that were only "made" (*sozdannye* versus *sdelannye*).[10] Several times he suggests that dream consciousness is a good analogue of the creative act,[11] thus indicating the intuitive nature of the creative process. That "genuine, artistic, creative poetry" is always associated with intuition ("immediate creation") Belinskij took for granted.

In a review of a volume of poems by Èduard Guber (1845), Belinskij seeks to define that peculiar trait of all great poetry, which permeates Puškin's poetry "like a ray of light penetrates a crystal," but is absent in the poems under review. "This trait" (*èlement*), says Belinskij, "is the product of an ability to conceive impressions immediately and, through the action of the imagination, reproduce them in poetic images—an ability which is the same as creative talent" (9:120–21).

The early Belinskij insists that artistic creation is not necessarily, is in fact only rarely, linked with passion: "True inspiration is always quietly contemplative," he writes in a review of A. A. Bestužev-Marlinskij's works (1840, 4:46), and immediately adds: "True inspiration has full command of its subject, never letting the subject take possession of it, although it sees and feels it." Furthermore, the act of creation does not simply reproduce, much less "imitate," passion—or any other fact of reality—but re-creates its subject, transcending it in depth, intensity, and vigor.[12]

All this gives the creative process a mystic quality. In fact, in Belinskij's early writings the act of artistic creation is repeatedly called "sacred": "The ability to create is a great gift of nature; the act of creation which takes place in a creative soul is a great mystery; the minute of creation is a great sacrament" ("On the Russian Short Story and the Short Stories of Mr. Gogol'," 1:285).

Moreover, "creation" is an absolute, even in presence of the fact of historical evolution: "The laws of creation are eternal, as are those of reason, and Homer wrote his *Iliad* following the same laws as Shakespeare writing his plays, or Goethe when he wrote his *Faust*" (review of *Jurij Miloslavskij* by M. N. Zagoskin, 1838, 2:565). It did not seem to have bothered Belinskij that the acceptance of this tenet—it seems to be empirically irrefutable—creates the greatest theoretical difficulties for an evolutionist and progressist view of the history of art and poetry.

10. See 3:92; 7:312.
11. 1:288; 6:286.
12. See 5:237–38; 10:318–19.

In the latter half of his career, though never abandoning these organicist positions, Belinskij puts increasingly more stress on the role of the conscious and rational elements of the creative process, as well as on the importance of external, and especially social, stimuli.

In his discussion of Nikitenko's "Discourse on Criticism" (1842), Belinskij says quite explicitly that "conscious creation is of necessity superior to unconscious creation" (6:275). A year later, in his article "Russian Literature in 1843," he goes even further: "Imagination is only one of the main gifts which make one a poet; but it alone does not make one a poet; what a poet also needs is a deep intellect (*glubokij um*) which discovers the idea in the fact, the general meaning in a particular phenomenon" (8:89). And in a review of the poetry of A. A. Grigor'ev and Ja. P. Polonskij (1846), Belinskij explicitly rejects the view which to some extent had once been his own, namely, that a poet needs only talent and inspiration, but no knowledge, since "his imagination is said to be a source of revelation of all the secrets of Being" (9:591). Belinskij identifies this view, not quite justly, with "romanticism, bless its soul." But in the same breath Belinskij also dissociates himself from what he calls "the other extreme," namely, "the opinion, now popular, that a man could become a poet even without talent, provided he had familiarized himself with some facts and had acquired the right ideas about certain things" (ibid.).

One must agree with Mordovčenko when he suggests that "it is incorrect to reproach Belinskij for having, to the very end, 'failed to overcome his underestimation of the conscious creative process.' "[13] In his "Survey of Russian Literature in 1847," Belinskij, after having once more asserted that "life is one and whole," goes on to defend the presence of conscious reason in the creative process, in these explicit terms:

> It is said that in learning one needs reason and intellect (*um i rassudok*), and for [artistic] creation, imagination (*fantazija*); and the people who say so think that this settles the matter very neatly, once and for all. But is it true that a scholar can get by without imagination? No, it is not true! The truth is that, in art, imagination plays the most active and the foremost role, while in learning reason and intellect do. Of course, there are some works of poetry in which one sees nothing but a powerful, brilliant imagination, but this is not at all the general rule for works of art. In the works of Shakespeare one does not know what to admire more, the wealth of his creative imagination or the wealth of his all-encompassing mind (*um*). (10:305)

Belinskij's appreciation of conscious reason, in artistic creation in general as well as in Shakespeare in particular, is nothing that would run against the grain of German idealist aesthetics, even though Belinskij himself seems to have

13. Mordovčenko is refuting the view of A. Lavreckij. See A. Lavreckij, *Belinskij, Černyševskij i Dobroljubov v bor'be za realizm* (Moscow, 1941), pp. 70–71.

thought otherwise. Schelling, no less than Hegel, makes a point of emphasizing that philosophy (intellectual creation) and art (imaginative creation) pursue the same goal and ultimately express the same truths.[14] As regards Shakespeare, A. W. Schlegel often said that he was a profound thinker with a "superb cultivation of mental powers, a practiced art, and worthy as well as maturely considered intentions." A combination of great powers of the intellect and a high degree of imagination was something with which the German romantic idealists were well familiar. Some of them—Novalis, Schelling himself—were poets as well as philosophers. Goethe and Schiller were, of course, great examples of poet-philosophers.

Nevertheless, since imagination is beyond the artist's conscious control—it cannot be conjured at will, or altered, or manipulated—Belinskij, by postulating its existence, excludes the possibility of any true artistic creation which is controlled solely by the artist's intellectual consciousness, or of true works of art with no other ingredients but the artist's rational ideas (original or borrowed) and his technical skill.[15] In this sense, Belinskij is solidly aligned with the Neoplatonic tradition of aesthetic thought. It is with this aspect of Belinskij's thought that a positivist, like Pisarev, or a formalist, such as Šklovskij, will disagree.

Inner Vision

Belinskij's belief in the artist's inner vision leads to a whole series of irrational corollaries. Most important of these is the belief that, somehow, the artist's inner vision is true not only "poetically" (in that it leads to the creation of great art) but also morally (in that it presents a shortcut to the knowledge of important moral truths).[16] Belinskij tended to hold the opinion—almost certainly fallacious—that the power with which a "truth" is expressed is proportional to its objective historical validity and moral value. He failed to acknowledge that, in Russian literature as elsewhere, many incontestably great writers

14. "Art is the real, the objective, while philosophy is the ideal, the subjective. The task of a philosophy of art might be predefined as representing the real, which appears in art, in the ideal" (*das Reale, welches in der Kunst ist, im Idealen darzustellen*) (*Philosophie der Kunst*, 3:384). Schelling points out that it is unlikely for an artist to have any truly profound understanding of his own creations: "Only through philosophy may we hope to attain a truly scientific view of art" (ibid., 3:381). Finally, Schelling formulates the relationship of art and philosophy as equivalent to that of native intuition and intelligence (*In der idealen Welt verhält sich die Philosophie ebenso zur Kunst, wie in der realen die Vernunft zum Organismus*) (ibid., 3:403). A historicized version of this conception appears in Vico, and later in Hamann, Herder, and romantic thought in general.

15. See 1:211, 232; 4:500.

16. See 1:287; 2:154, 209; 3:25; 4:463; 7:49, 376; 8:89.

and poets were, if seen in a historical perspective, on the side of what from his own viewpoint had to be "reaction."

Belinskij was not, however, unaware of this issue. In fact, in his essay on the poetry of Baratynskij (1842), who was by then expressing clearly "reactionary" views, Belinskij meets the issue head on. To Baratynskij's contention that the poet is, as it were, the passive catalyst of a higher form of being, who produces "fleeting visions which appeared to him in an illuminated minute of divine revelation," Belinskij responds that, while this is true in a general sense, it is also possible for a poet to become the organ of a wrong direction of thought. In that case, says the critic, the poet will inevitably lose his power and experience a decline of his talent (6:476). In other words, Belinskij equates "poetic truth" and "historical truth." Belinskij applied this standard to his own contemporaries and had, of course, a striking example in Gogol', who apparently had lost his creative powers when he ceased being a "progressive" writer.

As far as Russian literature was concerned, Belinskij never faced the dilemma of having to account for a truly great writer, such as Dostoevskij, creating works of genius in the service of political and social "reaction." However, he could have easily gathered from other literatures that being in step with the times politically and ideologically is not a necessary virtue in a great poet. Belinskij's young opponent V. N. Majkov expressed the view that great poets tend to form the rear rather than the vanguard of the movement of ideas, giving an artistic form to ideas which were developed earlier by thinkers, scientists, and statesmen.

Power

The notion of the poet's inner vision leads to the conception of the poet's "power," the notion that human experience and the reflection of the world in it are somehow raised to a higher power in the poet's consciousness:

> Who, then, is the poet with regard to other people? He is a receptive, excitable, always active organism (*organizacija*) which at the slightest contact gives off sparks of electricity, which suffers more painfully, enjoys more vividly, loves more ardently, hates more strongly than other people; in short, one that feels more deeply; a nature in which both aspects of the spirit, the passive as well as the active, are developed to a higher power. ("The Poetry of M. Lermontov," 1841, 4:495)[17]

In seeking to refute K. S. Aksakov's thesis that Gogol' 's *Dead Souls* is an epopoeia in the sense of the Homeric epos, Belinskij observes that there exists a certain similarity "not only between Homer and the French songster Béranger but also between Shakespeare and the Russian fabulist Krylov." Their

17. Cf. 1:33, 287, 386; 2:462; 6:463; 7:339; 8:51, 462; 9:123; 10:127; 11:61.

common ground is "creativity" (*tvorčestvo*—italicized by Belinskij).[18] There exists, then, a mysterious power, shared by poets of all ages, different nationalities, and diverse talents, which seems to transcend the laws of history and of society. Belinskij, certainly during the latter part of his career, realizes this with a wistful sigh: he would have wished Russia's greatest genius to have been more than "only a great artist."[19] The critic is obviously unhappy with Puškin's conception of the poet as someone who stands above the crowd in one particular, perhaps rather narrow, "something," but who otherwise may be "perhaps the lowliest of men."[20]

We have here another contradiction in Belinskij's thought, a contradiction of which he does not seem to have been aware, at least not often. On the one hand, the poet's power is seen as something *sui generis*, as something incommensurate with any other human phenomenon, as an absolute which stands above the laws of history, as that "something" which Homer and Gogol', Shakespeare and Krylov have in common. But on the other hand, a constant effort is made to integrate this power with the movement of history and the process of social progress.

Poetic Temperament

From this antinomy there arises Belinskij's attempt to establish two different types of poets. There is, Belinskij suggests, the poet who is "all artist" (*poèt-xudožnik*), whose "greatest delight is to be, in his capacity for creation, forever the rival of nature" and to "capture a given subject in its whole truth, to breathe life into it." And there is the poet who, as he describes life, is interested in his creative task only insofar as it will reveal, to him and to his audience, the deeper meaning of the phenomena described ("1847," 10:318-19).[21]

Often—though not in this particular passage—this dichotomy is historicized, meaning that certain historical periods will produce poets of the first, and other poets of the second type. Poets such as Shakespeare and Puškin are satisfied to present the world as it is, theirs being a relatively happy period of national and social stability. Other poets, such as Byron and Lermontov, are dissatisfied with the present. They subject the world to an incisive analysis and seek an ideal which lies outside it.[22] It is the dissatisfied type of poet who can become a leader of his nation, for he is "ahead of his time." As Belinskij pointed out,

18. "Explanation to an Explanation," 6:416. Cf. 10:28 for a repetition of this statement.

19. See 2:9; 7:34–35, 36, 318, 569.

20. Puškin's poem "The Poet" (1827). Cf. Erlich's discussion of Puškin's image of the poet in his *Double Image*.

21. Cf. chap. 3, n. 35.

22. See "1843," 8:76–77.

directly in his "Letter to Gogol' " and obliquely in many of his writings meant for publication, Russian society, on the verge of a great forward move, certainly saw in its writers and poets heralds of a better future and potential leaders.

Without doubt, Belinskij's dichotomy is ultimately a reflection of Schiller's essay "On Naïve and Sentimental Poetry." Its historicized version may have been taken from Hegel, or even from French utopian socialist thought. By the 1840s it had become a cliché. Belinskij's relative evaluation of these two types of poets undergoes an evolution which is consistent with the development of his other views. The early Belinskij much prefers the "naïve" and "objective" poet. After 1842, it is the "critical" and "subjective" poet. Belinskij's relative evaluation of Goethe and Schiller, with Goethe standing for the "poet-artist" and Schiller for the "poet-philosopher" (where "philosopher" is Aesopian language for "social and political critic"), is symptomatic of Belinskij's ideological development.

The actual value of this dichotomy for literary theory and a critical judgment of literature is another matter. It would seem that it did Belinskij's literary criticism more harm than good. Belinskij used the type of the "poet-philosopher" to include such authors as Herzen in his general definition of "artistic literature" (*xudožestvennaja literatura*), and Belinskij's epigoni to this day use the same conception to treat ideologically desirable but artistically weak works on a par with works of unquestioned artistic value.

Freedom

One of the principles to which Belinskij adheres from beginning to end is that of the freedom of the artist. In his early essay on *Hamlet* (1838), we read: "The essence of all art lies in its freedom; without freedom, art is a trade, for which one need not be born, but which one can learn" (2:305). In "A Survey of Russian Literature in 1847," we find this position still intact:

> As regards the choice of the subject of his work, a writer cannot be guided either by someone else's will or even by his own arbitrary judgment, for art has its own laws, and without respecting them it is impossible to write well. Art demands, first and foremost, that the writer be true to his own nature, to his talent, and to his imagination. (10:300)[23]

Historical optimist that he is, Belinskij makes light of the possibility of a serious conflict between an artist's freedom and the iron necessity of history. (The factor of external, naked force, very much a reality in Russia, could not be introduced into the argument; but this hardly matters philosophically, for no one ever seriously defended the legitimacy of the gendarme's power over the poet.)

23. Cf. 3:407; 6:275, 603; 11:147.

Though Belinskij was aware of the existence of social classes and of their role in the progress of history, he tended to see the development of Russian literature in his own day as an integrated, single-minded, progressive movement. There were, of course, literary reactionaries, the Bulgarins, the Grečs, the Senkovskijs. But they seemed no more than minor irritations, certainly not anything like an independent historical force. At most, they could fight hopeless delaying actions. Besides, they were really uninspired scribblers. At any rate, the problem of "progressive" versus "reactionary" art does not exist for Belinskij. It is precisely on this score that conscientious Marxist critics have denied Belinskij the title of "socialist" and "precursor of Marxism," and quite correctly so from their point of view.[24] Belinskij's naïve historical optimism, which takes for granted that "true" art will also inevitably be "progressive," has been accepted in one form or another by most of his successors and persists in much of Russian literary criticism to this day.

It was also Belinskij who established the practice of projecting his own optimistic philosophy of history into works of literature, such as *Dead Souls* or *A Hero of Our Time*, the attitude (*pafos*) of which was certainly quite contrary to such a world view. However, the dialectic "handle" used by most of Belinskij's epigoni to integrate more or less "reactionary" works of literature into a deterministic and "progressive" scheme of historical evolution was different from his. Belinskij naïvely believed that an artist of genius had to be basically well intentioned and humane, like himself, and therefore assumed that a "negative ideal" was present in *Dead Souls* or *A Hero of Our Time*. Marxist critics have "rescued" *Crime and Punishment* and *Anna Karenina* by asserting that the "historical truth" (progressive, of course) emerges from these seemingly reactionary works *in spite* of their authors' political and religious beliefs, on account of a mystique inherent in artistic creation which will not allow a true artist to tell a historical falsehood.

Leadership

Another corollary of Belinskij's belief in the poet's "power" is a tendency toward what we call élitism today. Contrary to his generally democratic attitude, Belinskij sometimes feels forced to admit that true art is inaccessible to the masses and attainable only to a select few.[25] Also, Belinskij is willing to concede that great art can, and often does, flourish among the highest classes of society.[26] The following passage is significant, since it dates from Belinskij's last years:

24. This is the main theme of Ščukin's book *Belinskij i socializm*.
25. See 1:57; 4:35, 166, 481–82, 494–95; 5:565; 9:159–60, 455, 523.
26. See Eighth essay on Puškin, 7:448.

Prompted by the voice of those few to whom it is given actually to understand the exalted in life (*vysokoe žizni*), the crowd may be ready to see a great genius even in Byron, in whom they, the crowd, could not understand half a thought or half a line. However, the crowd is truly enthralled and attracted only by a theatrical and melodramatic parody of the exalted side of life, as we find it in the tales of Marlinskij, or by that which is true and actually beautiful, yet at the same time not too great, somewhat immature and childish, for the crowd itself is nothing but a perennial adolescent, something resembling an aged child or an old man in his dotage. ("Thoughts and Notes on Russian Literature," 1846, 9:545–46)

This remarkably perceptive observation conforms with Dostoevskij's appraisal of the popular taste: what the people like best, said Dostoevskij, is a "sentimental 'high style.'" Also, the artistically unsophisticated tend to have the same taste, regardless of their educational and social level. As a literary critic of genius and a connoisseur of poetry, Belinskij could not help noticing that there was a rift between his own understanding of literature and the tastes and preferences of much of his audience.

There is another side to this realization. Belinskij is interested in literature not only for its aesthetic but also for its educational, that is, "propaganda," value. If "true art" is incomprehensible to the masses, a somewhat lower level of art should serve as an intermediary between the masses and "true art." It is for this reason that Belinskij shows great tolerance for what he calls *belletristika*, popular literature which is not on the level of true art, though it may aspire to such status.[27] Belinskij is willing to grant the practitioners of *belletristika* that they meet a legitimate need. His attacks against the prose of Bestužev-Marlinskij or the poetry of Benediktov are designed to separate *belletristika* from "true poetry," never questioning their right to a place in Russian literature.

There are, however, passages in Belinskij's later writings in which this descent to the level of the "masses" is seen not as a matter of social expediency but as an absolute historical tendency. Thus, in his article "Russian Literature in 1845," Belinskij writes:

If we were asked what the principal merit of the new school in our literature was, we would answer: precisely that for which it is being attacked by short-sighted mediocrity or base envy, namely, a turn from the higher ideals of human nature and of life to the so-called crowd, a choice of no one but it to be its hero, studying it with deep attention and making it acquainted with itself. (9:388)

Belinskij goes on to say that this tendency toward a preoccupation with the ordinary life of common people is the true road toward a Russian national

27. See 9:160–63, 310–11; 10:114.

literature. Accordingly, Belinskij hails Gogol' as the trailblazer of a purely national, native Russian literature.[28] Belinskij sees a historical movement toward an ascendancy of the common people, and promptly concludes that a shift to their point of view, their interests, and their values is a mark of forward-looking, independent, and original art. It is difficult to escape the conclusion that this line of thought amounts to a "socialization" of aesthetic values.

It appears that Belinskij never recognized a problem here. The way he saw the situation was this: Without any doubt, Gogol' was as great an artist as Puškin, though his art was very different from Puškin's. At the same time, Gogol''s art was clearly more democratic, closer to contemporary Russian reality as Belinskij knew it, and it engaged a broader spectrum of Russian society. Therefore, with these added virtues, Gogol''s art meant "progress." Belinskij never asked the next question: What about those writers of the Natural School who were lesser artists than both Puškin and many of the poets of Puškin's "galaxy"? What decided their absolute and relative importance—their inferior craftsmanship or their progressive (that is, more "realistic") aesthetics and their more "social" (really, more "democratic") thematics? If no Gogol' had appeared, but only an assortment of Butkovs and Grigorovičs, would the Natural School still have been a "step forward" from the poetry of a Baratynskij, a Tjutčev, or a Jazykov? Belinskij's successors very boldly asked this question. Those of the Left, headed by Černyševskij, said that social values, such as the enlightenment of the public and the promotion of correct socioeconomic ideas, had to take absolute precedence over any putative aesthetic values. Those of the Right, notably Dostoevskij, declared that "art is a basic need of man, just as food and drink" and that "a striving for beauty and for the creativity which incarnates it is inseparable from man, so that without it man would perhaps not even want to be alive."[29]

There is one fact on the debit side of Belinskij's critical achievement. Today, in retrospect, it would seem that Gogol''s greatness had very little, if anything, to do with his alleged "realism." In fact, in the heat of his polemic with the enemies of Gogol' and the Natural School, even Belinskij pointed out that Bulgarin and Senkovskij, in their novels, were often guilty of the same violations of *bon ton*, descriptions of prosaic trivia, coarse language—a general "lowering of genre"—which they were finding so offensive in Gogol''s writings.[30] In his praise of Gogol', Belinskij leans heavily on the criterion of realism ("complete truthfulness to life" [*soveršennaja istina žizni*] he calls it as early as 1835).[31]

28. Cf. 6:425–27; 8:80; 12:461.
29. F. M. Dostoevskij, *A Writer's Diary* (1873), in *Sobranie sočinenij*, 13 vols. (Moscow and Leningrad, 1929–30), 11:139.
30. See, e.g., 6:361–64.
31. "On the Russian Short Story and the Short Stories of Mr. Gogol'," 1:292–93.

Since there is no indication that he means by this anything but ordinary truth-fulness to common everyday reality and naturalness (*estestvennost'*) of expres-sion, it is difficult to escape the conclusion that Belinskij appreciated Gogol' for the wrong reasons.

Belinskij's appreciation of Puškin is also tainted. He could see clearly enough that socially and historically Puškin stood for the ideals of the Russian gentry, that in the 1840s these ideals were no longer "progressive," that in some ways Puškin's art was "getting old," and that it was no longer interesting as a result. But Belinskij also had a clear enough intuitive understanding that, relevant or irrelevant, Puškin's poetry was still beautiful. He made valiant, though often rather awkward, efforts to justify his love and admiration for it in terms of an idealistic "aesthetics of content" (*Gehaltsästhetik*),[32] seeking to show how Puškin's creations were "true," and therefore "good," as well as beautiful. This interpretation was properly debunked by Pisarev in the 1860s, but is taught to this day, more or less unchanged, in Russian schools.

GENIUS AND TALENT

Much like German romantic critics, Belinskij consistently draws a distinction between "genius" and "talent,"[33] yet at the same time acknowledges the con-tinuity of the scale of poetic power from average poetic ability to talent and from talent to genius. On one occasion Belinskij compares mankind to an army: among thousands and millions of soldiers, there is only one field marshal, and to every few hundred or thousand men, there is an officer (review of *A New Year's Gift: Two Fairy Tales* by Hoffmann, 1840, 4:81).[34]

A "genius," then, is a man who possesses certain abilities given to all men, but in an extraordinary degree of power and concentration. There are several ways in which this power manifests itself. A genius does not depend on favor-able conditions for the development of his gifts, since his powers are such that he is able to impose his will on his environment and conquer adversity to which a mere "talent" would succumb.[35] A genius is always profoundly "original."[36] He creates new forms. He develops new aspects of the spirit of his nation and of mankind.[37] He often pursues tasks which ordinary human wisdom regards as irrational (7:522). In a genius, the individual, even the personal and private, becomes universal, as he is *personally* the bearer of Nature's will and drive, a manifestation of the power of the human spirit.[38] The genius *is* History. Thus,

32. Orsini suggests "contentualism.' See Orsini, "Organic Concepts," p. 25.
33. See 1:217-18, 223; 7:559; 8:58-59, 419; 9:454-56, 528-31, 592.
34. Cf. 1:288, 386; 6:119-20; 8:569; 9:528-29; 11:131.
35. See 1:385-87; 2:186; 6:95; 7:522.
36. See 5:318, 452; 9:535.
37. See 1:31-32, 70, 106, 156, 223; 3:503; 5:297; 7:516; 8:186; 9:527; 10:31-32.
38. See 1:386; 2:185; 4:175, 520-21; 5:318; 9:530.

paradoxically, by being more strictly "himself" than ordinary people, a genius is more universal as well.

With mere talent, says Belinskij, the man and his individuality may well be separated from his creative efforts, but not so with genius: "The power of genius is based on a living, inseparable unity of *the man* and *the poet*. Here, the spectacularness of *talent* emerges from the spectacularness of *the man* as a *personality*, as a *character*" ("On the Life and Works of Kol'cov," 1846, 9:530). Belinskij suspects that the secret of genius lies not so much in an artist's intellectual powers, not in any particular ability, not even in a great heart, but rather "in some kind of spontaneous, creative capacity for inspiration, resembling revelation, which also contains in itself the secret of the human individuality" (ibid.). In other words, the poetic genius is an extraordinarily efficient catalyst of the Spirit. The passage just quoted dates from 1846, showing that Belinskij retained his organic and mystic conception of genius to the end of his life.

A genius is born—he cannot be made.[39] For some reason, Belinskij believes, women are sometimes given the spark of talent, but never that of genius (1:225). Genius can be recognized intuitively: "Like Čičikov's servant Petruška, he carries his own peculiar odor along with him at all times." Belinskij uses this image to suggest to his correspondent Botkin that Auguste Comte is not a genius: "He does not smell of genius" (letter to V. P. Botkin, 17 February 1847, 12:332). Another letter from that year (to K. D. Kavelin, 7 December 1847) shows that Belinskij, even this late in his career, was inclined to believe that a genius acted more or less unconsciously, intuitively, and naïvely, as an organ of some higher agency, whereas a person with mere talent would pursue his rational goals more or less consciously (12:461–62). Among Belinskij's epigoni, even the radical materialist Dobroljubov retains this irrational conception of genius, as does the aesthetic theory of Socialist Realism.

Finally, genius transcends time. In his review of Nekrasov's *Petersburg Almanac* (1846), Belinskij eloquently develops the idea that, with history moving forward in ever-widening spirals, future centuries will look back with wonder at the barbaric nineteenth century. But Shakespeare will still be Shakespeare, and future centuries will also find Byron and George Sand in the same nineteenth century (9:576–77).

Belinskij has somewhat less specific notions regarding the essence of "talent." It lacks the universality and independence of genius, being restricted to a narrower sphere (1:156), yet within this relatively narrow sphere a talent possesses "originality" (*original'nost*').[40] Although talent, like genius, is acquired at birth, it requires cultivation and can be greatly enhanced through hard work.[41] In a

39. See 1:31, 107, 141–42, 223–24, 386; 4:81; 6:121; 7:559.
40. See 1:95–96, 157; 9:563.
41. See 1:223, 362; 2:527; 3:261; 4:52.

lengthy discussion concerning the difference between talent and genius in his article "Thoughts and Notes on Russian Literature" (1846, 9:454–56), Belinskij comes to the conclusion that "talent" is a rather narrow and specific "ability to make, to produce," an ability related rather to the form of art, and is potentially independent of the possessor's general mental, emotional, and moral qualities. A "genius," on the other hand, possesses great human qualities of the mind as well as of the heart, in addition to his exceptional artistic ability.[42] While talent could be used to any end, good or evil, genius is necessarily morally good—a notion made popular in Russia by Puškin's *Mozart and Salieri.* Talent, then, depends on the social and historical circumstances. A "talent" follows the trend of the times or moves along with the masses; a "genius" is always a leader ("On the Life and Works of Kol'cov," 1846, 9:527–28).

Nothing is more ruinous to talent, Belinskij believes, than a misguided attempt to impersonate genius, that is, any claim to a degree of creative independence and originality which could be found only in a genius. Kukol'nik is cited as an example of such a "talent," Bestužev-Marlinskij is another.[43] M. N. Zagoskin's famous historical novel *Roslavlev* is discussed in the same terms. Had Zagoskin kept to what the limitations of his talent indicated, that is, reported what he had himself seen as an eyewitness of the campaign of 1812 and stayed within a framework of the private life of those classes of society which he knew so well, his novel would have had some merit; but he decided to capture the whole historic significance of the grandiose events of 1812, a task for a writer of genius, and failed ("1843," 8:55). Curiously, much the same criticism was leveled at Tolstoj's *War and Peace* by none other than I. S. Turgenev.

Furthermore, Belinskij believes that, while genius is always "right" (historically, that is), a person with mere talent, possessing a certain amount of technical skill, expressive ability, and even imagination, but no genuine vision, may well create works and whole trends of literature which are in effect aberrations, deviations from the straight path of historical progress. They may be temporarily successful, but are soon recognized for what they really are: perversions of taste and sensibility. Benediktov and Bestužev-Marlinskij are often cited as examples to this effect.[44]

Nonetheless, throughout his writings, Belinskij emphasizes the importance of ordinary talents, honest journeymen of their trade, alert and diligent littérateurs. The body of literature, consisting of works of very different value,

---

42. A. W. Schlegel emphasized that genius embraced fancy, understanding, imagination, as well as reason. Cf. Wellek, *Modern Criticism,* 2:46. Belinskij's conception of genius fully coincides with Vischer's (*Aesthetik*, 2:394–96).

43. See "1843," 8:58–59; review of the 2d edition of Bestužev-Marlinskij's *Collected Works* (1847), 10:361.

44. See 1:83, 273; 4:40–42; 8:62.

intensity, and diverse intellectual and aesthetic levels, requires "field marshals" and "officers" as well as plain "soldiers," to use Belinskij's own simile.

Belinskij's conception of talent and genius wholly coincides with that of German objective idealism. The distinction between talent as a relatively narrow, specific ability, and genius as universal greatness is made by Hegel.[45] The notion that a genius achieves supreme universality merely by being himself is one of the pivotal thoughts in Hegel's *Philosophy of History*. It is a corollary of the idea that the "free" genius is, in effect, the willing instrument of a higher, irrational power, and every work of genius, in effect, "an affirmation of the Divine."[46] Talent, meanwhile, operates consciously, and on a merely "human" level.[47]

REFLECTIVE AND EMOTIVE ARTISTS

Belinskij distinguishes between cognition by reasoning and cognition by intuition, but tends to consider only intuitive knowledge truly "poetic."[48] Similarly, Belinskij is generally aware of the distinction between "feeling" and "aesthetic intuition." However, he follows Hegel in refusing to accept Kant's compartmentalization of the human mind, with the "aesthetic idea" separated from "feeling" on the one side, and from the "intellectual idea" on the other. Rather, he sees intuitive, poetic cognition as leaning either more toward "feeling" (*čuvstvo*) or somewhat toward "reflection" (*refleksija*).[49] Of contemporary poetry, Belinskij demands both feeling (poetry without feeling is "cold ratiocination" [*rezonerstvo*]) and power of reflection. Feeling as such, Belinskij asserts, does not constitute poetry (meaning modern contemporary poetry); it ought to be "feeling born of thought" ("The Poetry of E. A. Baratynskij," 1842, 6:466). The ideal work of modern literature presents a felicitous union of feeling and thought (ibid., 6:472-73).[50] It is for this reason that Belinskij welcomes the increased role of "reflection" in Gogol''s works, specifically *Dead Souls* (6:428-29).

In Belinskij's famous eulogy of *Dead Souls* (6:209-22), the critic probably

45. Hegel, *Ästhetik,* 1:37.
46. Schelling, *Philosophie der Kunst,* 3:480. Cf. also Schelling, *System des transzendentalen Idealismus,* in *Werke,* 2:616.
47. Schelling, *Philosophie der Kunst,* 3:480. The dichotomy goes back to Plato. One of its more widespread forms is the distinction, found in the writings of the Church Fathers, between "divine images" and "artificial images." In the divine, the relation between image and archetype is one of unity. In the artificial, it is one of likeness. It will take genius, "divine inspiration" to create a "divine image," but only talent to make an "artificial image." Cf. Close, "Philosophical Theories," pp. 182-83.
48. See 1:365; 3:327; 6:13; 11:524.
49. See 4:89, 254, 518-19; 6:428-29.
50. Cf. 7:321; 10:305.

means to welcome Gogol' 's epopoeia as a work which expresses rational and progressive ideas with genuine feeling, with the synthesis of both producing its inimitable *pafos*. Belinskij does not realize that this kind of reasoning leads to a disintegration of his earlier, organic conception of the creative process. In effect, both aesthetic "intellectualism" and aesthetic "emotionalism" are thus admitted through the back door, as it were.

In his discussion of Herzen's *Whose Fault?* the critic asserts that the writer's "main strength lies not in his creativity, not in any artistic quality of his work, but in thought, deeply felt, made fully conscious, and well developed." A talent of this kind, Belinskij proceeds, is just as natural as purely artistic talent: "The activities of these talents form a special sphere of art, where imagination appears in second place, and reason in first" ("1847," 10:318). Clearly this stands in violation of the principles of organic aesthetics: reflection is accepted as a substitute for intuition. Herzen's novel, incidentally, is artistically mediocre at best.[51]

In his earliest, romantic writings, Belinskij expressed the notion that true feeling, if sincere and pure, would guide the poet to the truth, even without the aid of reflection.[52] During his Hegelian period, he rid himself of every vestige of aesthetic emotionalism: "Even our own feelings are only then the subject of our enjoyment when we free ourselves of their tiresome heaviness and their quavering excitement, which take away our breath and make us lose our consciousness, and relive them in our memory" ("The Poetry of M. Lermontov," 1841, 4:490). Belinskij's practical criticism of that period bears out this notion of poetry as "emotion recollected in tranquillity." For instance, the critic finds Žukovskij too emotional to be truly "artistic."

But after 1842, aesthetic emotionalism, too, enters Belinskij's criticism through a back door, as the critic begins to approve, more and more, of a certain kind of "humane subjectivity" in literature. In a review of Apollon Grigor'ev's poetry (1846), Belinskij seems to be torn between his earlier, "aesthetic" conception and his new, "social" approach. With his critical intuition, he senses that Grigor'ev, toward whom he has developed a lively, sympathetic interest, "is not a poet, not a poet at all." His verses show "flashes of poetry, but poetry of intellect, of indignation" (*probleski poèzii, no poèzii uma, negodovanija*, 9:593). But then, the critic discovers a poem, "The City," the message of which cannot but have appealed to him: it is an indictment of what later became known as "Dostoevskij's Petersburg." And so Belinskij

51. Herzen is not the only beneficiary of this conception. For instance, Belinskij says of Grigor'ev that "he became a poet not because of an abundance of talent, but because of an abundance of intellect (*um*)" (9:393). This sympathetic statement (Belinskij is well disposed toward Grigor'ev) does credit to Belinskij's critical acumen: Grigor'ev appears in the history of Russian literature as a minor poet, but a great critic.

52. See 1:365; 2:77–78.

promptly credits Grigor'ev with "deep feeling and deep understanding—which sometimes make him a poet" (9:594).

When Dostoevskij appears on the scene, Belinskij, on the basis of what today would seem to have been a rather shallow interpretation of *Poor Folk* and *The Double*, applauds him precisely for what Apollon Grigor'ev would soon castigate as "sentimental humanitarianism." In short, Belinskij will accept "reflection" on the one hand, as well as "emotionality" on the other, provided their tendency is right.

When the emotion in question is not of the kind Belinskij is apt to share, that is, when he uses his unbiased critical judgment, he will continue to reject aesthetic emotionalism, as in the following pronouncement occasioned by the poetry of Èduard Guber (1845): "*Feeling* is one of the prime movers of a poetic nature; without feeling there can be no poet and no poetry; and yet one can possess feeling, even write passable verses which are permeated by feeling through and through—and still not be a poet" (9:118).

Psychologically, the difference between the early, romantic Belinskij and the later, *socialisant* Belinskij is this: The earlier critic had absolute, naïve trust in poetic genius and felt that truth, morality, and the social role of art would be served best if the poet was left alone and the aesthetic act of disinterested and dispassionate expression of a warmly and sincerely felt experience allowed to run its course; the later Belinskij, obsessed with social change, progress, and ideology, is impatient with the poet. He would like to see more poets work harder for the ideals which are so much on his own mind. What will help them in this endeavor? Ideology (which Belinskij calls "reflection," "thought," "ideas"), of course, on the one hand, and a powerful feeling of indignation, compassion, and protest, on the other. Let the poet think more and harder, let him become indoctrinated with the right ideas, and, without sacrificing any of his "feeling," sincerity, or immediacy, he will be a better worker for the cause of progress. Belinskij just will not admit the possibility that the interests of "progress," as he conceived it, and of art, as he knew it intuitively, might clash.

Meanwhile, Belinskij trusts that the artist of *true* talent will naturally pursue a course which will be in concert with the better interests and with the progress of society. He should be encouraged by the critic to follow his genius freely. It is in this spirit that Belinskij eventually makes his peace with Goethe's "indifferentism." In one of his last essays, "Notes on the Contemporary Scene" (1847), Belinskij points out that the biographical fact of Goethe's private indifference toward the social and political movements of his age does not imply that the poet's works are irrelevant to the life and progress of his nation, and of Europe. "As an artist, as a poet," says Belinskij, "Goethe was wholly a son of his country and of his age, and expressed many, if not all, of the most essential aspects of contemporary reality" (10:93–94). The implication is that

Goethe, a man of genius, could not possibly have failed to be in step with historic progress—even if Goethe the private individual and philistine was uninterested in or actually opposed to progress.

In an eloquent passage in a minor review of 1845 (9:40–41), Belinskij deals with the phenomenon of the minor poet who is not totally lacking in talent and who writes poetry to express his commonplace personal feelings, to flaunt his unoriginal discoveries, and to satisfy the petty whims of his fantasy. Belinskij says that such poets must be exposed for what they are and chastised severely, for while the totally untalented poet is harmless, the self-centered, egotistic, sentimental semitalent can do a great deal of damage: by his example, he may divert his youthful readers from study and useful work, induce them to imitate his pursuit of a petty and cheaply acquired fame. The pitfalls inherent in Belinskij's position are obvious: Who is to decide that Goethe (or Lermontov) is a poet of true talent, to be left alone by the critic, while Benediktov is not and should be pointed in the right direction by the same critic?

SUBJECTIVE AND OBJECTIVE ARTISTS

Much the same pattern of a disintegrating organic conception can be observed in Belinskij's statements regarding the "objective" and the "subjective" artist. To the early Belinskij, the successful self-expression of an artist of genius produces the most perfect objectivity.[53] What renders a work of art "subjective" is that residue of thought or feeling which the artist has failed to objectify and which therefore remains extraneous to the work. The philosophic foundation of this conception lies in the Neoplatonic notion that the heightened consciousness of the poet is a catalyst, an outlet, or an organ of the Absolute, and so of "truth." It is for this reason that the great poetic genius is always "objective." Shakespeare is, to the early Belinskij, the "objective" poet par excellence, who had an uncanny ability to separate himself from his own person and to live the lives of his characters. In an interesting passage in his essay on *Hamlet*, Belinskij conceives an actor of genius as being a particularly revealing example of the creative artist in general. An actor of genius, says Belinskij, is guided by inspiration no less than any other artist, and he creates his interpretation of a role freely; yet he also expresses the dramatist's will and is bound by it: "Having assumed a role, he is no longer himself, he no longer lives his own life, but rather the life of the character whom he represents. . ." (2:306). This is precisely the simile that Schelling had used to explain his conception of artistic creation as a synthesis of "freedom" and "necessity."[54]

53. See 1:268, 419–20.
54. "A poem is beautiful if in it the greatest freedom is contained by necessity. Art is then an absolute synthesis or fusion of freedom and necessity" (Schelling, *Philosophie der Kunst,* 3:403).

Belinskij brings up the early Schiller as an example of a subjective artist who in his plays "depicted people not as they were, but as he wanted them to be" ("A Journal Note," 1838, 2:465). Belinskij's own contemporary, Bulgarin, who prides himself on the "truthfulness" of his novels, is equally a subjective writer, says the critic, because his assorted "scoundrels" and "monsters" are mere allegoric constructs, manufactured by their maker solely for the purpose of exposing a given vice—where the construct is an abstract concept of the author's mind rather than a concrete phenomenon of life (ibid.).

Every character created by a genuine artist, Belinskij writes in a review of two novels by I. I. Lažečnikov (1839), "should be for him an object completely external to him" (3:11). It should be an objective entity into which the author has introduced none of his own concepts or feelings (ibid.). The power of poetic genius, Belinskij says, lies precisely in his ability to transcend his own subjectivity, for "subjectivity is the death of poetry" (ibid., 3:25).[55]

Belinskij's cult of objectivity reaches its height in the "reactionary" essay "Menzel, a Critic of Goethe" (1840). Here, objectivity is defended on both aesthetic and moral grounds:

> The sufferings of the subjective spirit can be the subject of art, and therefore need not be offensive to morality, provided they are presented objectively, illuminated by thought, testifying to the rational necessity of these sufferings. But if these are the wails of the poet himself, they cannot be artistic, for he who wails in suffering is not above his suffering—therefore, he cannot see its rational necessity, but rather, he sees it as an accident, and any accident offends the spirit, causing it to feud with itself; consequently, it cannot be the subject of art. (3:417–18)

Goethe's *Werther* is given as an example of such an offensive work: "It is not a work of art, but a harsh, creaky dissonance of the spirit" (ibid.).[56] These thoughts are Hegelian in letter as well as in spirit. Belinskij's "reconciliation to reality" (*primirenie s dejstvitel'nost'ju*, translating Hegel's *Versöhnung mit der Wirklichkeit*) as well as his endorsement of Hegel's famous dictum "What is rational, is real; and what is real, is rational"[57] are in full accord with the thoughts that Hegel had so eloquently expressed in his preface to *The Philosophy of Law*. Hegel's point, fully grasped by the perceptive Belinskij, is that it is the philosopher's—and, by implication, the artist's—job to understand and to express the rational (today we would say "structured") aspect of that which is, rather than to set up imaginary "ideals" bearing no particular relation to

55. Cf. 3:241.

56. Cf. Hegel, *Ästhetik*, 1:202, 237. Belinskij's view that Werther was "the ancestor (*rodonačal'nik*) of a series of weak, sickly characters, in which transitional epochs so abound" (10:108) may well derive directly from Hegel.

57. Hegel, *Philosophie des Rechts*, p. 14.

reality.[58] Incidentally, this position is not inherently reactionary, or even conservative, since Hegel's conception of what is "rational" is a dynamic one (in today's language: he deals with dynamic rather than with static "structures"). If Belinskij was guilty of any misinterpretation of Hegel, it had to do with ignoring, at least momentarily, the dynamic, dialectic nature of the rational in Hegel's philosophy. Ščukin has correctly observed that Hegel's insistence on a living connection between ideas and reality was one of the philosopher's principles which Belinskij permanently retained, with only temporary deviations. Specifically, Ščukin suggests, Belinskij's eventual coolness toward French utopian socialism (after a period of uncritical infatuation in 1842–43) is to be explained by the fact that Belinskij saw only too well that utopian socialism was, as far as Russia was concerned, a purely "literary" phenomenon, without any basis in social and political reality. While Belinskij was groping for an ideal, he felt that utopian socialism was not what he was really seeking.[59]

Besides, though Hegel's justification of objectivity in art sounds unctuous and labored, there is a great deal to be said for it on empirical grounds: it accurately describes the known attitude of many, if not all, great artists. This Belinskij knew. In the same essay on Menzel, he emphasizes the fact that the creative evolution of Schiller (the best known example of a great subjective artist) represented a successful struggle away from subjectivity and ever closer to a Goethean objectivity.

However, Belinskij soon transferred the argument to a different plane—a moral and political rather than aesthetic one. As early as in a letter to V. P. Botkin, 30 December 1840, he castigates Goethe for his political "indifferentism," says that he is "beginning to hate him," and is tempted to come around to Menzel's view (12:7). But at this point Belinskij obviously still finds no way to deny that Goethe was a great poet and that the only way for him to be such a great poet was by being the objective artist he was.

In his analysis of Lermontov's *Hero of Our Time* (1840), Belinskij combines a recognition of the virtues of objectivity with a warm acceptance of the subjective quality of that work. Lermontov's novel is short of artistic perfection, says Belinskij, because the character whom he has depicted is "so close to himself that he was unable to separate himself from it and objectify it" (*ob'ektivirovat' ego*) (4:267). Lermontov's novel has a marvelous completeness (*zamknutost'*) about it, "but not that higher, artistic completeness which a work of art receives from the unity of its poetic idea, but rather a completeness derived from a unity of poetic feeling" (ibid.). Belinskij goes on to observe that all works which express a social movement, a ferment of ideas, have this particular quality about them, and he mentions Goethe's *Werther* as an example. What such works lack in artistic perfection they make up in the immediate

58. Ibid.
59. Ščukin, *Belinskij i socializm*, p. 144.

cathartic effect which they have upon the contemporary mind: they help to express, to formulate, and to recognize its problems, and are thus a step toward their solution. The corollary of this analysis is quite obvious (though Belinskij does not make it explicit): a changing society requires subjective art.

So far so good. Lermontov, a great soul and a poetic genius, in expressing his anguish as well as his striving and hope, became the mouthpiece of a whole generation. And clearly, as far as Belinskij was concerned, Lermontov's striving and hope were aimed entirely in the right direction. But soon or later, Belinskij was bound to meet a poet whose "subjectivity" did not coincide with what he, the critic, believed to be the "right" direction of history, of public sentiment, of Russian literature as he saw it.

In an essay (1842) on the young post-romantic poet A. N. Majkov (1821–1897), Belinskij rejects Majkov's notion, expressed in the poet's poem "Doubt" ("Somnenie"), that a poet's fantastic world of beauty, while objectively untrue, may still represent a subjective aesthetic value. If the poet himself no longer believes in dryads, Helios, or Thetis, he should abandon these images, says Belinskij, and seek new, no less poetic representations of nature, which would, however, be compatible with a modern world view based on experience and science (6:11–12). This is a most revealing passage, characteristic of Belinskij as well as of the whole organic trend in Russian literary criticism. It means a resolute rejection of subjective idealism and of any aesthetic theory—or art—based on it. Belinskij senses that Majkov is tempted to withdraw into a romantic Atlantis, to use a metaphor from E. T. A. Hoffmann's story *The Golden Pot*, that is, to establish a subjective poetic world independent of life at large. Belinskij, who was well familiar with the narcotic effect of romantic poetry and fiction (Hoffmann's tales had been likened to an opiate by many), will not tolerate this: poetry must remain organically linked with all of life. The question whether the subjective world created by the poet has aesthetic (or perhaps even moral?) value, quite aside from its hedonistic appeal, is never seriously considered. Belinskij simply will not consider the notion of splitting life into "subjective" (individual and private) and "objective" (historical and social) sectors.

In a brief review of a Russian edition of Goethe's works (1842, 6:181–83), Belinskij completes his turnabout regarding objective and subjective poetry. Goethe is now said to have been "the king of the inner world of the soul, largely a subjective and lyrical poet" who was quite alien to any historical movement or interest, and "an adept in spiritual comfort to the point of insensitivity to everything that would disturb his tranquility" (6:182). While still an admirer of the tranquil and serene art of a Puškin or a Goethe, Belinskij is now impatient with their relative conservatism. He cannot help wishing that Goethe and Puškin should have been not only great poets but also "progressive" political thinkers and social rebels.

In his famous passage on Gogol' 's subjectivity in *Dead Souls* quoted earlier,

Belinskij all but says explicitly that "subjectivity" means, in effect, as much as "progressive social tendency." The meaning of the passage is clearly that a poet should express his outrage at social injustice, his anger at government and private inefficiency, his indignation at corruption and hypocrisy everywhere. "Objectivity" thus amounts to an acceptance of the social and political *status quo*, while "subjectivity" means an active opposition to it.

This change in Belinskij's aesthetic thought makes more sense than would appear at first glance. The point is that Belinskij—contrary to his earlier views —assumes that art, and thus the creative process, must change along with the historical changes in social life. An objective artist who accepts life as it is will not be out of place in a stable age and a flourishing, content society. But in a "critical" age, which destroys the old and builds the new, the artist must become a fighter, must stand for the new, and march in the forefront of progress. He will have to be "subjective." In his discussion of Nikitenko's "Discourse on Criticism," Belinskij advances a full-fledged program of what could be rightly called *critical* realism:

> What is art itself in our time?—Judgment, analysis of society, and, consequently, criticism. The reflective element (*myslitel'nyj èlement*) has now been actually fused with the artistic—and to our age a work of art is dead when it describes life merely in order to describe life, without any potent subjective stimulus rooted in the prevailing ideas of the epoch, if it is not a wail of suffering or a dithyramb of delight, if it is not a question, or an answer to a question. (6:271)

This theoretical conception is carried over into Belinskij's practical criticism. For example, in a discussion of Count Sollogub's short stories, Belinskij praises the author for his truthful depictions of reality, but then finds him "indifferent to his depictions," which, in the critic's opinion, "is injurious to the full success of his works, depriving them of sensitivity and deep feeling, the marks of ardent convictions and profound beliefs" ("1842," 6:536).[60]

Certainly this whole tendency, so persistently expressed in Belinskij's writings after 1842, contradicted his earlier beliefs. It also contradicted Belinskij's empirical experience as an intuitive critic who knew all too well that the great poets and artists of the past as well as of the present tended to be of the "objective" and "dispassionate" type.[61] In fact, it contradicted Belinskij's own observations, made during the last years of his life, on those numerous occasions

60. Cf. 7:50; 12:446.

61. In a letter to V. P. Botkin, 4 March 1847, Belinskij embarks upon a comparison of Gončarov, a writer of strong talent who is "only an artist," and P. N. Kudrjavcev, a writer-publicist with whose views Belinskij sympathizes. Belinskij's frank opinion of Gončarov as a person is negative ("He is a trivial and nasty little man"), but as an artist he is an "adult" and his art gives one profound enjoyment. Kudrjavcev, on the other hand, is "spiritually a minor" and "without being in the least subjective, has an inimitable talent to produce works which haven't the tiniest bit of objectivity, and vice versa" (12:347–48).

when he would point out the artistic inferiority of subjective creations by his literary opponents. Thus, in discussing a play by Nestor Kukol'nik (review of *Dva Ivana, dva Stepanyča, dva Kostyl'kova,* 1847, 10:128-29), Belinskij dwells upon the merits of artistic objectivity, saying that the artist "must not justify, defend, or accuse," but must be wholly dispassionate, "never yielding to the moral point of view, nor to the accepted ideas of his age."

No wonder we see the critic trying to convince himself that the subjective artist is not inherently inferior to the objective. No wonder he tries to suggest—obviously as much to himself as to his reader—that even "Shakespeare's personality shines through his works, even though it may appear that he is indifferent to the world described by him, as Fate is when it saves or destroys his heroes" ("1847," 10:305).

In his effort to save the aesthetic value of art while placing it in the service of social progress, Belinskij largely overlooks the historicist loophole which would allow him to have his cake and eat it, too, and which he knew very well theoretically, as the passage just quoted (6:271) suggests. This loophole amounts to historicizing the creative process, or rather, the types of creative artists: "objective" and "dispassionate" artists would be the natural product of stable ages of flowering and maturity, while "subjective" and "involved" artists would come to the fore in critical periods of history. In that case, the subjective, *socialisant* art which Belinskij was defending would not have to stand for art as such, but merely for art during certain very special periods, one of which happened to be his own. Meanwhile, Homer, Shakespeare, Goethe, and Puškin would remain undisturbed in their glory of "objective" artists and manifestations of their respective historical epochs. At times, Belinskij is very close to taking precisely such a view, especially as regards Puškin, but he never applies it systematically.

A little further in the same essay, Belinskij ascribes the rapid decline of the popularity of Victor Hugo, Balzac, Dumas, Janin, Sue, and de Vigny to the fact that these writers never sincerely shared the interests of their society, which responded by taking them for mere entertainers (*potešniki i zabavniki*) and eventually grew tired of them. And still these were writers of great talent. Belinskij then goes on to point to that "woman of genius" (*genial'naja ženščina*), George Sand, as an example to the contrary effect: her poetic powers as well as her popularity are steadily growing, because she has strong and sincere convictions which link her inseparably with the vital interests of her nation.

At this point, Belinskij forgets that he had begun his passage with the words "The spirit of our time," implying that what he was going to say was valid only for his age (a "critical age"). He now launches into an impassioned indictment, directed not just against the poets of his own age, but against all poets who, "anointed at birth with the oil of inspiration," act as though they were "birds," floating "above mankind, above their suffering brethren" and call their "poeticized egoism" life (6:279). Clearly, none other than Goethe, who said "I sing as the bird sings," is the principal target of this passage. And thus the conditions of a "critical" age are generalized and the loophole closed. Belinskij's epigoni, and Černyševskij in particular, were to compound Belinskij's error.

CLASSICAL, ROMANTIC, AND REALIST ARTISTS

One of the more popular dichotomies applied to the artist in the age just preceding Belinskij's was that of the "classical" and the "romantic" artist. Belinskij himself will occasionally use these terms generically rather than historically. Thus, he will speak of Batjuškov the classical poet as opposed to Žukovskij the romantic poet (Third essay on Puškin, 1843, 7:224), even though these two poets were in every sense contemporaries.

Belinskij knows—at least whenever he cares to give the matter some thought—that the word "romanticism" is used in different meanings. In his late essay on Polevoj (1846), he attempts once more to define it and observes, in the process, that in France it is first and foremost a reaction against "revolutionary rationalism" and against the normative aesthetics of French classicism; in Germany, mostly a reaction against rationalist Protestantism, and also against French classicism; in England, on the other hand, it is largely a progressive movement (9:684–86). Elsewhere, Belinskij sees it essentially as a universal, "human" rather than a historical phenomenon.[62]

In his Second essay on Puškin and elsewhere, Belinskij fails to bring out the deeper aspects of the romantic revolution of morality, philosophy, and aesthetic thought: its historicism, organicism, and individualism. Similarly, Belinskij overlooks the more subtle ideological traits of classicism: its universalism, its mechanistic rationalism, and, specifically in aesthetic thought, its formalism. "Classicism" is to Belinskij, by and large, "mere rhetoric," scholasticism, pedantry, external effects, affection, the graceful and noble pose, declamation.[63] Except in his earliest writings, Belinskij tends to see "romanticism" as an excess of subjectivism, mysticism, and emotionality. He consistently sees Bestužev-Marlinskij's prose as the "true expression of the romantic trend in Russian literature" (9:384). Puškin was a romantic only insofar as he refused to be affected and stilted, and as he insisted on creating his own forms and ideas.[64] Romanticism, to the later Belinskij, had merit only as an effective reaction against the affectation and hollow rhetoric of classicism.[65]

62. See, e.g., his Second essay on Puškin (1843), where there is a lengthy discussion of romanticism in general. Cf. 5:548; 7:159, 173–74.

63. See 1:69, 186; 2:136; 5:295–96, 543; 6:367, 370; 7:109, 302. Belinskij is rarely concerned with or inspired by the art and poetry of classical antiquity. However, under the direct influence of Hegel, he defines classical art as "the harmoniously balanced fusion of idea and form" (this is Hegel's definition), as opposed to romantic art, in which the idea gains precedence over form (3:423–28; cf. 10:309). French classicism, in this context, is seen as mere formalist imitation of the ancients (3:428–29).

64. See 1:69; 5:557.

65. See 5:296; 6:518–19; 7:144–56, 179.

The romantic period is seen as a transitional period which in Russia lasted from the early 1820s to the mid-1830s. Thereafter, as far as Belinskij is concerned, it essentially has only reactionary vestiges.[66] After 1838, Belinskij never tires of stressing that his own age has overcome romanticism, its mysticism, fantastic dreams, otherworldliness, and emotionality; for him, the romantic is a negative, reactionary type.[67] In his discussion of Puškin's Lenskij, the critic declares almost vehemently that "people such as Lenskij turn into perfect philistines, or, if they retain their original character, become antiquated mystics and dreamers who more than anyone else are the enemies of all progress, more so than ordinary, trivial people without pretensions" (Eighth essay on Puškin, 1844, 7:472). In discussing Gončarov's Aleksandr Aduev from *The Same Old Story*, Belinskij takes the occasion to expose once more the type of the Russian romantic and devotes a lengthy sermon to it ("1847," 10:331–42).

In Russia no less than in Germany and Austria, many men who had written romantic poetry in their youth were, by the 1830s and 1840s, pillars of the reactionary governments of these countries. The philosopher Schelling, in particular, was on Belinskij's mind when he spoke of "antiquated mystics and dreamers." Belinskij was well aware of the political meaning of Schelling's appointment to the university chair once held by Hegel. Prince P. A. Vjazemskij (1792–1878), Puškin's friend, a leader in the Russian romantic movement, and very nearly a "rebel" in the 1820s, already had the reputation of a reactionary in Belinskij's time. Even Count S. S. Uvarov (1786–1855), Minister of Education and President of the Academy of Sciences under Nicholas I, had written romantic verse in his youth (in German). At any rate, Belinskij's somewhat vehement and aggressive opposition to romanticism in literature was in part politically motivated. Belinskij failed to identify with "romanticism" such features of his own philosophy and aesthetic theory as idealism, historicism, organicism, a belief in artistic intuition, "inner vision," and the cognitive as well as prophetic powers of the artist.

Juxtaposed to the romantic poet and writer, there appears, virtually from the very beginning of Belinskij's activity as a critic, "the poet of reality" (*poèt dejstvitel'nosti*).[68] Belinskij's conception of both is simplistic: everything else being equal, the poet or writer who sticks to "reality" will produce more worthwhile work, and even without much talent he may produce work that is socially useful. But at least much of the time, Belinskij makes no distinction between poetic truth and empirical truth. The notion that Bestužev-Marlinskij may have been a second-rate writer, not because he wrote in the romantic manner but because he was a second rate romantic writer, does not occur to Belinskij.

66. See 6:521; 8:441–47; 9:384–88, 685; 10:23, 132, 334. Cf. Lebedev-Poljanskij, *Belinskij*, p. 135.
67. See 3:431–33; 7:472; 9:380–82.
68. See 1:81; 2:134, 482; 3:300, 434; 5:205, 301–2, 495, 534; 6:535; 7:50.

Belinskij seriously believes that to deal with "simple everyday reality" (*prostaja ežednevnaja dejstvitel'nost'*), if not a guarantee of artistic success, is certainly a step in the right direction. In discussing a story by P. N. Kudrjavcev, Belinskij writes: "In his previous stories, he described both characters and situations which seemed somehow exceptional and unusual; in his last story, he boldly penetrated into the depths of simple everyday reality and succeeded in finding—in its banality and prose—passion, and therefore, poetry, too" ("1844," 8:484).[69]

It is in this context that Belinskij's defense of the Natural School should be viewed. The critic sees essentially two types of opposition to what he considers an honest depiction of contemporary Russian life and its many shortcomings. There is the "rhetorical school" (Belinskij's own term) of the Bulgarins and Grečs, which attacks the Natural School because it competes with them on their own grounds. Bulgarin prided himself on being a writer who exposed and chastised the moral shortcomings of his contemporaries, and on addressing himself to the "people"—who were allegedly also the subject of his narratives. The Natural School, Belinskij felt, had exposed Bulgarin's "reality" as being mere allegory, his *narodnost'* a manufactured pseudo-*narodnost'*, and his moralizing as hypocritical exercises in rhetoric. Therefore, it was quite understandable that Bulgarin and his cohorts would strike back at the competition, claiming that the world depicted by the Natural School was fanciful, farcical, and sordid.

The other detractors of the Natural School were the Slavophiles. Their opposition to a realistic description of Russian life, Belinskij said, was motivated by false pride and a romantic view of life. Russian life looked bleak, soulless, and incredibly banal in the stories, plays, and sketches of the Natural School. The Slavophiles were claiming that such presentation was a libel against the Russian people in that the positive phenomena of their lives were not brought out in these works.[70] Belinskij's trump card in his defense of the Natural School is the precedent of Flemish genre painting (he mentions Teniers specifically), which depicts the trivia of life, yet is acknowledged to be great art.

Hegel had already made this point.[71] But it is precisely Hegel's argumentation which seems to prove the Slavophiles right and Belinskij wrong—though only in theory: as a practical critic, Belinskij was, of course, right in considering some of the works of the Natural School (Gogol', Turgenev, Dostoevskij) first-rate art. Hegel had said that the presence of art in the *form* of the Flemish paintings and the presence of the lively and highly positive spirit of popular life in their *content* made them both enjoyable and important as a manifestation

69. Cf. 6:496; 7:195–96; 8:89.
70. See "A Rejoinder to *The Muscovite*" (1847), 10:240–60.
71. Hegel, *Ästhetik*, 1:164.

of a substantial idea (essentially that of a bourgeois democracy). The charge raised against the Russian naturalists was obviously well founded: they were presenting the extreme banality of Russian life without a breath of the positive spirit of that life, without its vitality, its resilience, its sound moral foundation in religion. The same Slavophile critics, however, had warm praise for Turgenev's *Sportsman's Sketches*, in which the positive qualities of Russian popular life were certainly apparent.

Belinskij's position in this dispute was somewhat awkward, since he could not say precisely what *he* would have liked to see in these stories in addition to a correct presentation of the unpleasant truth about Russian life: its poverty, social injustice, and moral perversion. He could not say, in so many words, that he wanted Russian literature to be imbued with a spirit of vigorous protest, of active opposition to the existing order. In fact, he could not very well point it out even when it was present in a given work. As a result of this awkward position, Belinskij emerges as a defender of naturalism for the sake of its "honesty" alone. This would mean a defense of art without an ideal—something which is against Belinskij's whole aesthetic philosophy. And thus, toward the end of his career, Belinskij becomes at least *de facto* a proponent of the aesthetic naturalism which he abhorred all his life.

However, Belinskij's readers knew how to read between the lines. Černyševskij and Dobroljubov were perfectly justified in claiming that the critic's later writings were in substantial accord with their own views regarding the social role of Russian literature.

7

Belinskij's Heritage

THE LEGACY OF AN AESTHETIC PHILOSOPHY

Many of Belinskij's principal ideas became a permanent part of Russian aesthetic thought after his death. Virtually all of them have retained their vitality to this day. Belinskij's is an organic world view which is structured both synchronically and diachronically. Except for isolated and rare moments of doubt,[1] Belinskij all his life believed in a teleological structure of man's world. However, he changed his conception of the nature of this teleology several times. In the end he was left with a belief that the spirit of mankind in general, and the spirit of the Russian people in particular, was inherently so structured as to strive toward more and deeper knowledge, a better and more just society, and loftier moral and aesthetic values. Belinskij knew that this striving sometimes expressed itself in negation of existing knowledge, beliefs, and values. Belinskij's epigoni of the Right replaced the critic's rather vague humanism and mild nationalism with a strong religious and nationalist mystique, while those of the Left eventually made socioeconomic relationships (and specifically "class struggle") the motor of the entire structure.

Art is seen as a *sui generis* human activity which is, however, integrated with life at large. The artist of genius expresses the spirit of his age, his nation, and ultimately mankind. The work of art is a microcosm symbolic of life. A national literature is an organic entity and acts as the nation's consciousness and conscience. Along with nations and humanity, national literatures undergo an evolution which is in step with historical evolution at large. This evolution is

---

1. There are moments when Belinskij sounds strangely unlike his usual optimistic, enthusiastic, sanguine self. In a letter of 13 April 1842, written under the impact of the recent death of the wife of his employer, A. A. Kraevskij, Belinskij muses about death, in particular about the untimely death of his beloved friend Stankevič two years earlier, and produces an eloquent passage, entirely in the spirit of Turgenev at his most pessimistic, about "dead and unconsciously rational Nature, which like a mother watches over her kinds and species, in her politicoeconomical calculations, yet treats individuals worse than a wicked stepmother" (12:97). The passage shows Belinskij's momentary deep pessimism about mankind, history, and progress.

marked by objective progress, which is historically determinate. Belinskij always insisted on pointing out the progress which Russian literature had made since the days of Peter the Great, and was firmly convinced that it had by no means reached its highest level in either Puškin or Gogol'. He paid little attention to the empirical antinomy inherent in this position, namely, the problem presented by a great artist with blatantly reactionary political views, or a great artist living in an age of general stagnation and decay. He disposed of the one serious case of this kind with which he had to deal (Gogol') by avoiding a head-on clash with the problem. Belinskij's successors of the Left have generally followed his example as regards Gogol', whose "reactionary" writings and thoughts were declared artistically as well as intellectually "inferior." All of Belinskij's successors had to struggle with this problem in connection with some other great writers.

Since Belinskij sees history as a process in which the human spirit is realized in a multitude of national spirits, rather than directly, his conception of art, and especially of literature, has strong nationalist overtones. Russian history and Russian literature are given a sharply individualized *Gestalt*. Belinskij, a Westernizer and admirer of Peter the Great, views pre-Petrine Russia—and thus its civilization and literature—as "ahistorical" in the special Hegelian sense of that term, meaning that pre-Petrine Russia had no true national identity and made no contribution to the development of world civilization. Eighteenth-century Russia and her literature were only beginning to develop a national identity, which found its first full-fledged manifestation in the poetic genius of Puškin. Russian literature, Belinskij felt, played a key role in developing this identity, that is, creating a society possessing common interests, occupied by the same ideas, and having common goals.

Belinskij sees Puškin as a synthesis (in the Hegelian sense) of the whole preceding movement of Russian civilization and Russian literature: he made the Western examples which his predecessors had imitated fully his own and created poetry which was both European and Russian. Belinskij sees Puškin's universality, his alleged ability to express in Russian verse the spirit of all Western nations, as a trait characteristic of the Russian national spirit. He also sees Russian civilization as heir apparent to West European civilization. But unlike his Slavophile opponents, he sees this Russian civilization of the future as a creative synthesis of West European national civilizations rather than as a homegrown Slavo-Byzantine product. In this, Belinskij anticipates Herzen and the *počvenniki*.

Gogol' is seen as an antithesis of Puškin: a purely Russian artist who dealt with Russia's own problems and who, while lacking Puškin's universality and serene beauty, was by far the poet's superior in social importance and originality. Belinskij's view of Gogol' as a "social poet," a "realist," and founder of the Natural School projects upon this great writer—quite perversely, of course—

the traits characteristic of the "progressive" and "democratic" movement in
Russian literature which Belinskij helped to inaugurate.

Belinskij's vision of Russian literature as the vanguard of social and political
progress was realized by succeeding generations, though in a manner that would
have disappointed the critic had he lived to see it. He would have been elated
by the tremendous power wielded by literature in his nation's public life, but
would have been saddened by the fact (quite obvious by the 1860s) that many
of Russia's poets and writers of genius were not on the side which he thought
stood for justice and progress.

Russian literary criticism inherited from Belinskij a Hegelian tendency to
think of literature as an organic whole rather than as an aggregate of individual works. Conversely, the individual work would be seen largely in terms of its
synchronic and diachronic relationships with Russian social and national life at
large rather than in terms of its own structure and aesthetic merits. This tendency, started by Belinskij, would be a blessing, but also a curse. It would give
Russian literature, and art in general, more secular power than it had in any
society of the Western world; it would make the writer a public figure and literature a matter of public concern. This would be a marvelous thing so long
as literature and art would be free. As Georg Lukács has said so eloquently,
nineteenth- and early twentieth-century Russian literature impresses the Western reader with the breadth of its concerns, with the confidence and boldness
with which it attacks the greatest problems and the deepest questions, with its
justified sense of its own importance and worth, and with its great moral seriousness. But the moment literature would cease being free and the "organic"
ties between society and literature become maintained by ideological control,
the blessing would turn into a curse. A ruling ideology which considered the
arts and literature politically irrelevant—"mere entertainment," for instance—
would have left them alone. A political movement or regime whose ideology
necessitated a "social organicist" view of art would inevitably have to turn to
the monstrous practice of "positive" censorship. The systematic regimentation
of the arts instituted by those who considered themselves heirs to Belinskij's
ideas proved the critic's conception of "social organicism" correct, though in a
way they could hardly appreciate. Those innumerable works which were to
demonstrate the organic unity between the dominant ideology and the "creative visions" of "inspired artists" turned out to be, almost without exception,
vapid allegories at best, ugly monsters at worst: either there had been no "vision," and the works in question were simply abortions, outright "nonart,"
manufactured by uninspired, insincere hacks; or the macrocosm, of which
these works were an "organic" representation, was what they were—incredibly,
perversely banal, masochistically drab, and frequently quite absurd.

Belinskij's logical error, inherited from Hegel and passed on to his successors,
lay not in his conception of social, national, and historic organicism as such,

but rather in an unwarranted extension of an ideal position to an empirical plane. The abstract notion that true art is sensitive to the *Zeitgeist* and may, in fact, recognize its drift, that it is an organ of social life and a herald of its new tendencies—all this does not warrant the empirical assumption that, at a given moment in history, one tendency or school of literature—say, the Natural School (or *počva*, or Symbolism, or Socialist Realism)—can be pointed out as representing "progress" or "Russia's bright future," while other schools or tendencies are to be rejected as reactionary and undesirable.

Belinskij's most dangerous gift to succeeding generations was a Pandora's box containing the various social functions of art. Belinskij rightly held that the application of art to a variety of social tasks ("didacticism," "moralism," political propaganda, and so forth) did not per se destroy or even harm art. He also believed that making utilitarian considerations the prime concern in art most certainly destroyed it. But Belinskij felt that in a "critical age" such as his own it was well worth the risk to welcome some unartistic but well-intentioned and socially useful works to Russian literature. Art, Belinskij felt, though an autonomous and important enough phenomenon in its own right, would have to yield to the overwhelming social problems of the day as a prime object of the critic's concern. Many of Belinskij's successors lacked his ability to distinguish between social and aesthetic values, and gave free and absolute rein to the utilitarian criteria which Belinskij had admitted discriminatingly and with certain reservations. Belinskij never advocated any "abolition of aesthetics." He merely suggested that aesthetic criteria were not the only ones by which the value of a work of art ought to be judged, and that these other criteria could be, at times, more important.

Similar pitfalls are connected with the national mystique in art. While there undoubtedly exists a connection between nationhood and literature, it does not follow that certain literary tendencies—say, a preoccupation with folk poetry—are more "national" than others. Belinskij's position on this particular score was a sensible one—more so than that of the Slavophiles or of many of his successors. Likewise, Belinskij was relatively immune to the populist mystique to which many of his successors succumbed. He saw very clearly that a love for the Russian people and a desire to help them by no means entailed an obligation to write edifying tales about idealized Russian peasants. Still, Belinskij was largely responsible for this tendency, as it was he who established the precedent of critical praise for "correct" choice of genre and subject matter, as well as for correctly placed social sympathy. While ridiculing Ševyrev, who asked for more "elegant" works dealing with the refined life of high society, Belinskij was himself a victim of the same fallacy when he praised mediocre works of the Natural School for their "honest" treatment of "ordinary" life among the lower classes of society, and lauded their compassionate attitude toward the poor and the downtrodden. Eventually, this tendency led to a "classicistic canon" in reverse, in which plots and characters were determined entirely by social labels. The groundwork for the Socialist Realist canon of fiction was laid very early, in Belinskij's and Dobroljubov's essays and reviews.

Belinskij had a sincere aversion against romantic escapism, against any art or literature that would give up on real life, the people, and Russia and withdraw to a fantasy world of "pure art." Obviously, to do just that was an alluring proposition in a country where life was harsh, drab, and change discouragingly slow. The German romantics, whom Belinskij knew well, had made this escape with brilliant virtuosity. It is to a considerable extent to Belinskij's credit—or fault—that this tendency never acquired respectability in Russia. This is no mean accomplishment considering the fact that the image and example of Puš-kin had to be neutralized in the process.

Belinskij's conception of the work of art is thoroughly "organic," and succeeding generations left it largely unchallenged. Only the Formalists of the 1920s dared to raise the question whether a novel, if successful, was necessarily an "organic whole," or perhaps rather an aggregate of more or less skillfully connected separate motifs. The organic model of the work of art, as reflected in Belinskij's critical method, is dualistic: the work of art is seen as the realization of an idea, or a fusion of the "ideal" and the "real." The poetic idea, or "content," does not exist independently of its artistic "form." This conception leads to an energetic rejection of aesthetic intellectualism, schematism, and allegory on the one hand, and to an equally resolute rejection of aesthetic naturalism and formalism on the other. The idea immanent in a work of art should be concrete, not abstract. It should be totally fused with the form in which it is realized. Specifically, a character meant to represent a given idea should also be a complete and unique individual: Pečorin, who stands for the inner conflict of a whole generation, is still an individual, as well as an expression of his creator's personality.

Belinskij's aesthetics, much like Hegel's, is decidedly an aesthetics of *content* (*Gehaltsästhetik*), and his practical criticism is concerned largely with the poetic idea (always seen in "substantial," social, moral, and historical terms), and only secondarily, often marginally, with its adequate poetic expression. Quite alien to Belinskij is the formalist aesthetics which sees the creative process as the more or less successful solution of problems of artistic technique, as the more or less felicitous application of novel artistic devices to a material not previously treated in this fashion, or as the generation of structures in space, time, or some other medium. Certainly Belinskij, more than anyone else, is responsible for the contentualism which dominates Russian critical and aesthetic thought to this day. It is no accident that the Russian Formalists had little love for Belinskij.[2]

2. Boris Eichenbaum once said of Belinskij's Puškin criticism: "We used to speak about

The artistic realization of the poetic idea is conceived as an organic micro-cosm called *xudožestvennyj obraz* ("artistic image," "artistic form," or "artistic symbol"). It generates a "pathos" (*pafos*) through which the work of art exerts an influence upon the macrocosm of life. We thus get a circular chain reaction: *life → poetic idea → xudožestvennyj obraz* ("artistic image") → *pafos* → *life*. It is this particular model and these particular terms which Socialist Realist critics use even today in explaining the feedback between art and life at large.

The "artistic image" often appears in the form of a "type" (*tip*) which symbolizes a nation's, a society's, or a generation's ideal of life, either in positive or in negative terms. Belinskij believed that Russia was not yet ready, in his day, to produce a positive ideal. The succeeding generation, headed by Černyševskij, thought that this time had come when it created the "type" of the heroic revolutionary.

Belinskij's conception of the creative individual and of the creative process is idealistic, mystic, and romantic. The gift of creativity is seen as an innate power which is given to different individuals in quite different degrees: as an ordinary gift, as a talent, or as genius. Only to a genius is it given to create new values. A person of talent gives aesthetically adequate expression to the ideas and values of his age, his nation, and his society.

The belief in genius has been accepted by all of Belinskij's successors, although those of the Left have been cautious in applying this label to any particular poet or artist. Belinskij's historicized conception of "genius" opened the door to a confusion between the historical success of an artist's political attitude and his artistic achievement. Maksim Gor'kij is the principal example. He was the only Russian writer of any stature who, during the period preceding the Revolution, identified with the Bolshevik movement. He was eventually declared a genius, if for no other reason than to enhance the historical legitimacy of the cause. It is true, however, that Gor'kij anticipated, even before the Revolution, both the principal ideas and the basic mood of what was to be called Socialist Realism in the 1930s. He was, in this sense, ahead of his time. If being ahead of one's time is a criterion of genius, Gor'kij deserves to be called one. But the conception of "genius" found in Socialist Realist criticism is every bit as mystic as Belinskij's. For example, in discussing Gor'kij's genius, A. Metčenko, a contemporary Soviet critic, produces this formulation: "A great artist is always unique (*nepovtorim*), but in his creations and in his personality there are expressed the deep tendencies (*glubinnye tendencii*) of the historical

---

him [Puškin] in a scholastic, dead language, repeating a thousand times over those hasty and vague words of Belinskij" (*Puškin-Dostoevskij* [Petrograd, 1921], p. 76). The Gogoliana of such Formalist critics as Eichenbaum, Vinogradov, and Tynjanov amount to a refutation of Belinskij's image of Gogol''s art.

process."[3] This is Belinskij's conception in a slightly modernized phrasing.

Belinskij firmly believes in the cognitive powers of artistic intuition. Creative imagination, he believes, pursues and often reveals important truths no less than scientific study does, and is sometimes successful where science fails. Belinskij is not interested in delving into the psychological or anthropological background of intuitive cognition, but takes it for granted in terms of the familiar Plotinian "inner vision." On the whole, he accepts the *sui generis* nature of the creative imagination as distinct from intellectual cognition on the one side, and emotional or sense impulse on the other. Belinskij's famous definition of art as "the *immediate* contemplation of truth, or thinking in *images*" brings out the cognitive power of art, its distinction from abstract thought, and the immediate and "whole" nature of intuitive cognition.

This implies, to Belinskij, that it is impossible to create a true work of art by an analytic process. The whole is, in the case of a genuine work of art, more than the sum of its parts. In this sense, a work of art is born, not made. Psychologically, inspiration (*vdoxnovenie*), a mental state occurring in individuals of talent or genius, is a *condition sine qua non* in the creation of a true work of art. It is essential that each and every detail and aspect of the work of art pass through the crucible of inspiration. Belinskij is not interested in the psychological details of inspiration, but conceives of it as of a state of aesthetic alertness and receptivity which far exceeds man's ordinary mental faculties.

Belinskij's concern with the sociopolitical sphere of life directly affected his conception of the creative process. Since some of his most cherished ideas originated from philosophers, historians, economists, and natural scientists, rather than from poets and writers, he felt tempted to concede that rational, analytic thought also had a legitimate place in literature, provided that it was combined with creative imagination. Many of Belinskij's successors tended to forget about this condition. In any case, Belinskij cannot be held responsible for the practice of many Russian novelists to insert into their fiction lengthy treatises on anything from the immortality of the soul to soil conservation. This practice, also encountered in French and English novels, has to do more with the hybrid nature of the novel, a genre which combines elements of fiction and nonfiction, than with any concessions made by Belinskij or other critics to the social and ideological function of literature.

After some initial vacillation, Belinskij took the position that the artist should be morally engaged in the affairs of this world and express at all times his righteous feelings and convictions. He took for granted that the true artist would be guided entirely by positive, humane, and progressive impulses. This

3. A. Metčenko, *Zaveščano Gor'kim: Rol' A. M. Gor'kogo v razvitii socialističeskogo realizma* (Moscow, 1969), p. 16.

position opened a back door to aesthetic emotionalism, which Belinskij otherwise explicitly rejected. Once the "correct" emotional attitude of a work was recognized as one of its virtues—granted it also had aesthetic merit—the door was half open to the admission of emotionally appealing nonart. In Dobroljubov's criticism the door was already wide open.

All in all, we have in Belinskij a critic and thinker who, whenever he so chooses, can distinguish art from nonart. His conception of "artistic quality" (*xudožestvennost'*) never changes. Though Belinskij does not like to use the word "beauty," his definition of "artistic quality" clearly coincides with the traditional conception of beauty: a work which possesses this quality is "alive," it is a "whole," and it presents a perfect fusion of the "ideal" and the "real."

However, as Belinskij became involved in the movement of political thought which was then getting under way in Russia, he tended to pay more and more attention to aspects of literature which were, as he well knew, aesthetically irrelevant, and less and less attention to the aesthetic merits of a given work. Belinskij was saved from flagrant misjudgment of any work of Russian literature by his natural aesthetic sense and his genuine love of art. Berdjaev is right when he observes that Belinskij's *socialisant* criticism shows "that narrowing of consciousness and that displacement of many values which strikes us so painfully in the revolutionary intelligentsia of the 1860s and 1870s."[4] Belinskij was often quite wrong on foreign authors, but this was excusable in view of his insufficient command of foreign languages. Besides, Belinskij's contemporaries in the West were guilty of the same errors (overestimating J. F. Cooper and George Sand, underestimating Victor Hugo, and so forth). Still, as a matter of principle, Belinskij to the very end protected the integrity and autonomy of art, if not actively, at least by not violating it in any important way.

And thus, Belinskij had his cake and ate it, too. He succeeded in integrating Russian literature into the historical development of the Russian nation as he saw it, and in presenting the major works of Russian literature as organic products of the Russian national spirit as well as of the *Zeitgeist*. Even more important, he was instrumental in creating a relationship of regular and conscious mutual feedback between Russian literature and Russian sociopolitical thought. Yet he was able to do critical justice to most of the Russian works which he discussed and to appreciate them as works of art.

Belinskij's comments on the aesthetic merits of the works which he so eloquently discussed from a moral and sociohistorical viewpoint were usually competent but not very incisive. His "contentualism" prevented him from concentrating on the artistry of any particular work, not excluding even Puškin's lyric poetry, which he discussed at length. But his evaluations were probably the most consistently correct, in the judgment of history, of any major critic of his

4. Berdjaev, *Russkaja ideja*, p. 61.

age, Russian or Western. But at times Belinskij was remarkably fortunate in his judgments. More than once he praised the right author, but for the wrong reason (Dostoevskij being an example, and Gogol', at least to some extent, another).

In the hands of critics who lacked Belinskij's aesthetic sense and lucky touch, the master's method broke down. On the one hand, the much greater wealth and complexity of Russian literature in the second half of the nineteenth and in the twentieth centuries made a successful integration of literature into a rational pattern of sociohistorical development quite impossible: either there was no rational pattern of sociohistorical development, or for some reason literature did not fit it. And on the other hand, it soon became clear that aesthetic and sociopolitical criteria of value could clash very violently. Belinskij's example led to the malpractice of clinging to the notion that there could be no such clash. The result had to be either a falsification of a recalcitrant author's sociopolitical image or the downgrading of his stature as an artist. Of course, neither of these tendencies is new or limited to Russia.

THE BELINSKIAN RIGHT

As early as the 1850s, there was a discernible "left" and "right" trend among those Russian critics who considered themselves Belinskij's heirs. The Left emphasized Belinskij's democratic, utilitarian, materialistic, and *socialisant* tendencies, while the Right concentrated on his idealistic and organicist aesthetics.

Grigor'ev

A. A. Grigor'ev (1822–1864) is considered by some to have been Russia's greatest critic. He had a marked influence on Dostoevskij and Straxov. Grigor'ev was eventually rediscovered and greatly appreciated by the Symbolists. He has been neglected in the Soviet Union and could hardly be called a "living influence" today.

Grigor'ev considered himself a disciple of Belinskij's,[5] and he frequently referred to Belinskij's writings. Grigor'ev divided Belinskij's career into four periods: the "pre-Hegelian" period (about 1834–36) of his association with *The Telescope*, the period Grigor'ev approves most; a Hegelian period (about 1837–40), beginning with Belinskij's association with *The Moscow Observer* and characterized by a fixation on objectivity, "reconciliation with reality," and "artistic quality" (*xudožestvennost'*); a period which Grigor'ev describes as being dominated by the concept of *pafos* (about 1840–44); and a final period, during which Belinskij fell into a cult of "reality" (*dejstvitel'nost'*) and

---

5. On this point, see Leonid Grossman, *Tri sovremennika: Tjutčev, Dostoevskij, Apollon Grigor'ev* (Moscow, 1922), p. 56.

positivism.[6] Grigor'ev totally disapproves of only the last period, or rather, he disapproves of it to the extent to which Belinskij, in his writings of that period, went against his former views.

Grigor'ev's principal criticism of Belinskij was that Belinskij's excessive historicism tended to stifle any appreciation of the absolute in life and in art. "The fault," Grigor'ev once said, "was not Belinskij's, but was that of Hegelianism, one aspect of which Belinskij interpreted more potently than anyone else in Russia, namely, *a faith in progress to the exclusion of everything else, a faith in the supreme truth of the last minute*, a faith in that all-devouring *Gott im Werden* who peels off shell after shell. . ." ("Famous European Writers before the Tribunal of Our Criticism").[7]

The distinction between Grigor'ev's "organic criticism" (his term) and Belinskij's "historical criticism" (also Grigor'ev's term) can be illustrated by the following metaphor: With both viewing the train of history as an intricate pattern of waves, Belinskij mainly sees its movement, and Grigor'ev mainly the structure of its segments.

Grigor'ev was in some respects the Russian counterpart of Carlyle, with whose writings he was well familiar and whom he greatly admired. Even Grigor'ev's style may have been to some extent influenced by Carlyle's. However, Grigor'ev, a man of profound academic erudition, was also familiar with the German philosophy from which Carlyle had derived his ideas, and he rethought them independently in Russian terms.

The most distinctive trait of Grigor'ev's philosophy is a Schellingian vitalism,[8] a constant emphasis on the notion that social life as well as art must be understood as a "live," organic process rather than as a logical scheme.[9] Grigor'ev himself admitted that this vitalism was a veritable fixation with him. In this attitude Grigor'ev does not contradict Belinskij, though his emphasis is somewhat different.

Grigor'ev's irrational organicism becomes more meaningful if seen in antithesis to the mechanistic positivism of his contemporaries Černyševskij and Pisarev. Certainly Černyševskij, too, was in a sense a "vitalist," at least in his aesthetics. He, too, thought that Beauty was "life that had fully realized its potential." But to Černyševskij, the positivist, this potential equaled the "normal" biological and social functions of life as known to positive science. To Grigor'ev, the

6. See Apollon Grigor'ev, "Zamečanija ob otnošenii sovremennoj kritiki k iskusstvu" (1855), *Sočinenija* (Villanova, Pa., 1970), pp. 88–89. Also, "Paradoksy organičeskoj kritiki" (1864), *Sočinenija* (St. Petersburg, 1876), pp. 620–21.

7. "Znamenitye evropejskie pisateli pered sudom našej kritiki," *Vremja* 1861, no. 3: 47; quoted by Straxov, *Bor'ba s zapadom,* 3:292.

8. Cf. Grossman, *Tri sovremennika*, p. 51.

9. Cf. A. P. Marčik, " 'Organičeskaja kritika' Apollona Grigor'eva," *Izvestija Akademii Nauk SSSR* 25 (1966): 517.

mystic, this potential was much higher. He felt that in art, in religion, in mystic experience, life attained a much higher intensity, power, and beauty than could be accounted for by any rational naturalistic or sociological conception.

Belinskij, too, had put art above "ordinary life," but not so much because of its absolute value as for its being the bearer of humanitarian ideals, prophetic visions, and noble passions. In Grigor'ev, we meet a mystic who places art in the immediate vicinity of religion.[10] Unlike the atheist humanist Belinskij, Grigor'ev was an Orthodox Christian believer. His ideal of art had much the same religious overtones as appeared somewhat later in Dostoevskij, Vladimir Solov'ev, and eventually in Russian Symbolism. Thus, Grigor'ev saw Gogol' first and foremost as the bearer of a Christian illumination (ozarenie), something which he missed in the other exponents of the Natural School.[11] Grigor'ev's reaction to Gogol' 's Selected Passages was therefore a highly positive one.

Grigor'ev, no less than Belinskij, resisted the attraction of aestheticism and was a staunch adversary of l'art pour l'art. He also explicitly warned against the romantic tendency to succumb to the "grandioseness and fascination of Evil, which saturates the atmosphere surrounding such characters as, if not Konrad or Manfred, certainly Pečorin and Lovelace."[12] But the temptation was there. Grigor'ev's anthropology lacks Belinskij's optimistic egalitarianism. He was the first in Russia to divide all men into "meek" and "predatory" (smirnye and xiščnye)[13] and considered as wasted efforts of what he called "sentimental humanitarianism" to arouse compassion for meek underdogs such as Akakij Akak'evič Bašmačkin and Makar Alekseevič Devuškin. Rather, Grigor'ev felt, the "predatory" should be perfected and humanized through religious and aesthetic education.

Grigor'ev's conception of the cognitive function of art was more frankly mystical than Belinskij's: "Criticism must have a deep understanding of the fact that it hears the living voices of life in art's responses [to life], that great mysteries (velikie tajny) of the world of the human soul and of the national organisms (narodnyx organizmov) are revealed in works of art" ("A Critical Survey of the Foundations, Importance, and Devices of Contemporary Art Criticism").[14]

10. A passage from Grigor'ev's late essay "Paradoksy organičeskoj kritiki" is characteristic: "To me, 'life' is truly something mysterious, that is, it is mysterious because it is something inexhaustible, 'an abyss, which swallows all finite reason,' to use an expression from an old mystic book, a boundless space in which the logical conclusion of the cleverest head will often get lost, like a wave in the ocean, even something ironic, but at the same time full of love, in spite of this deep irony. . ." (Sočinenija, 1876 ed., p. 618)
    11. Cf. Mordovčenko, Belinskij, pp. 228–29.
    12. Apollon Grigor'ev, "Russkaja izjaščnaja literatura v 1852 godu," Polnoe sobranie sočinenij i pisem, ed. Vasilij Spiridonov, (Petrograd, 1918), pp. 142. Konrad is the hero of Mickiewicz's verse epic Konrad Wallenrod.
    13. Grossman, Tri sovremennika, p. 60.
    14. "Kritičeskij vzgljad na osnovy, značenie i priemy sovremennoj kritiki iskusstva" (1858), Sočinenija, 1876 ed., p. 228.
    Cf. the following passage from Grigor'ev's article "Neskol'ko slov o zakonax i terminax

Consistent with his belief that art represents a higher order of reality than "ordinary life," Grigor'ev took the position that "ordinary life," what Belinskij used to call "social life" (obščestvennost'), should find in art its deepest wisdom, its purest ideals, and its prophecies of a better future.[15] Art, on the other hand, should trust only itself and refuse to be influenced by extrinsic considerations, no matter how reasonable, moral, or necessary they might seem. On this point, Grigor'ev was explicitly opposed to Belinskij's attitude during Belinskij's last period of activity.

Grigor'ev's view of art was also "historical," in that he believed art to be the "organic" product of an age and of a people, a living echo of their concepts, beliefs, and moral convictions.[16] Furthermore, Grigor'ev at all times emphasized the living continuity of historical development in art.[17] And finally, like Belinskij, he believed in historical "movement" (though he disliked the term "progress"), specifically in the context of Russian history. In fact, he was willing to consider certain epochs and personages as mere trailblazers and harbingers of later, fuller, and more perfect realizations of certain ideas. English playwrights before Shakespeare, religious reformers before Luther would be in this category.[18]

Grigor'ev's historicism had more of a mystical bent than Belinskij's. A favorite conception of his was that of "historical sense" (istoričeskoe čuvstvo), which he defined as an intuitive appreciation of the organic unity and continuity of mankind and its history, the recognition of eternal, absolute ideals, and the ability to perceive these ideals in the drift (vejanie, dyxanie) of a historical epoch. In other words, "historical sense" is an ability to recognize the meaning of history: "Without it, there is no history, but only senseless glimpses of a galanty show."[19]

But there is a more fundamental distinction between Grigor'ev's historicism and Belinskij's. Belinskij was always looking for change, for anything that seemed new and promised progress. Phenomena of the past, and even of the present, interested him only insofar as they bore within themselves the seeds of the future. Grigor'ev, on the contrary, liked to dwell on the maturity and

---

organičeskoj kritiki" (1859): "And thus there developed logically the general meaning of this [organic] criticism: a view of art as a synthetic, integral, immediate and, perhaps, intuitive understanding of life as distinct from *knowledge*, i.e., analytic, step-by-step, cumulative understanding, verified by factual data. With equal logic, there followed from this the meaning of art itself as a focused or concentrated reflection of life in that eternal, wise, and beautiful form which is concealed beneath its accidental phenomena" (*Sočinenija*, 1876 ed., p. 334).

15. See, e.g., "Kritičeskij vzgljad," *Sočinenija*, 1876 ed., pp. 226–27.

16. See ibid., pp. 219–20, or "Russkaja literatura v 1851 godu," *Polnoe sobranie sočinenij*, pp. 99–102.

17. Ibid. Cf. also "Paradoksy organičeskoj kritiki," *Sočinenija*, 1876 ed., p. 619.

18. See "Neskol'ko slov o zakonax i terminax organičeskoj kritiki," *Sočinenija*, 1876 ed., pp. 336–37.

19. "Kritičeskij vzgljad," *Sočinenija*, 1876 ed., p. 223.

beauty with which an epoch, in its own inimitable way, had captured "the eternal truth of the human soul."[20] He disliked Hegel's conception of nations, cultures, societies as mere fleeting, phantomlike forms of an abstract idea, and emphasized the immutable and absolute qualities of each national spirit, its "individuality," as it were. One of Grigor'ev's favorite ideas was that every modern Russian writer of any consequence would, in his maturity, show ever more clearly those traits of Russian style, ethos, and pathos which were already characteristic of Kievan and Muscovite literature.[21]

Wellek sees a contradiction between Grigor'ev's belief in the absolute, immutable ideal of the human soul and the national spirit, on the one side, and his vision of Russian literature as a succession of "types" as well as his evolutionism, which he shared with the radicals, on the other.[22] Obviously, Grigor'ev's aesthetic absolutes (values which hold regardless of the "march of progress") depend on Grigor'ev's "historical sense," which will allow a man to partake of the spirit of different ages—past, present, and even future.

Grigor'ev's nationalism is more emphatic than Belinskij's, though there is no basic disagreement between them. Like Belinskij, Grigor'ev believed that literature should express the spirit, the concerns, and the interests of the whole nation rather than those of any social class. He rejected *la littérature populaire* as a phenomenon "pertaining not to art, but to education."[23]

Grigor'ev steadfastly refused to define *narodnost'*,[24] but his conception of a nation as an individual, integral, organic entity suggests that he understood it as some irrational, mystic quality which was essential to anything "living" in art and literature. Grigor'ev rejected socialism and cosmopolitanism precisely because they lacked that quality and were therefore "dead." Like Belinskij, Grigor'ev believed that only a national literature could produce "living" works.

That literature was an organic part of social life was for Grigor'ev as much of an axiom as it had been for Belinskij. Also like Belinskij, he was aware of the fact that literature was playing a very special role in Russia. He observes, tongue in cheek, that while West Europeans know how to keep their ideas separate from their practical life, Russians, "a crude and primitive people," have not as yet learned to separate ideas from life.[25] Of course, Grigor'ev is in sympathy with those "crude" Russians. Since literature, especially in Russia,

20. Ibid., p. 210.

21. See, e.g., "O komedijax Ostrovskogo i ix značenii v literature i na scene" (1855), *Polnoe sobranie sočinenij*, pp. 216–25.

22. Wellek, *Modern Criticism*, 4:268.

23. "Posle *Grozy* Ostrovskogo," *Literaturnaja kritika*, ed. B. F. Egorov (Moscow, 1967), p. 400.

24. "Definitio periculosa est," he stated flatly in an essay of 1855. See "Zamečanija ob otnošenii sovremennoj kritiki k iskusstvu," *Sočinenija*, 1970 ed., p. 81.

25. "Russkaja literatura v 1851 godu," *Polnoe sobranie sočinenij*, pp. 66–67.

seemed to be organically connected with social life at large, Grigor'ev had no argument with Dobroljubov's practice—which he admitted to be his own also —"to write criticism not about works of literature, but apropos (*po povodu*) of works of literature, and to treat relatively unimportant works as catalysts of deeply important, crucial social phenomena."[26]

But on the other hand, Grigor'ev was more categoric than Belinskij about keeping art free of any extraneous elements, whether they were political, social, or moral. He had the fullest confidence, that, if only left alone, art would fulfill its political, social, and moral role splendidly. In practical terms this meant that Grigor'ev did not expect literature to engage in any conscious and organized propaganda, a notion to which Belinskij was not immune.

The difference between Belinskij, Grigor'ev, and Dobroljubov is, very roughly, the following. Belinskij is willing to make a compromise. He believes in the autonomy of art as well as in its cognitive and prophetic powers, but he sees no harm in using it as a medium for the dissemination of ideas not derived by artistic intuition or even fully assimilated by it. To Belinskij, art may be an end in itself, but also a tool in the service of social progress. It may be self-sufficient, but it may also use help from "ideology." It may be all-important and sacred, but then there are times when other things (such as freeing the peasants) are much more important. Grigor'ev and Dobroljubov do not compromise. Grigor'ev believes—really against all empirical evidence—not only that autonomous and disinterested art will serve social progress best, but also that society would be well advised to heed its poets and artists rather than vice versa. Dobroljubov is interested in art solely as a tool of social progress.

Grigor'ev's conception of the work of art again largely coincides with Belinskij's, but once more the emphasis is a different one. Much like Belinskij, Grigor'ev viewed the work of art as the expression of an idea in terms of "real life," or a fusion of the "ideal" and the "real."[27] With Grigor'ev the emphasis was on the ideal all along. If art was reality condensed into a "pearl of creation" (Grigor'ev liked to quote Gogol' 's dictum), Grigor'ev's interest lay with the pearl rather than with the reality from which it was formed. With Belinskij it had been the other way round. Grigor'ev's "realism" is "realism in a higher sense" (*istinnyj realizm*, "true realism," as opposed to *golyj realizm*, "naked realism"). To Grigor'ev, art is primarily the bearer of the ideal in life, which he saw as something "organic" and specific: "Everything ideal is nothing but the fragrance and flower of the real. But of course not all that is real is

26. "Kritičeskij vzgljad," *Sočinenija*, 1876 ed., pp. 192–95.
27. "The activity of any true artist is composed of two elements: the subjective, or the striving for an ideal, and the objective, or the capacity to reproduce the phenomena of the external world in typical images (*obrazy*). Only when these two elements are fused do they produce creativity" ("Russkaja izjaščnaja literatura v 1852 godu," *Polnoe sobranie sočinenij*, p. 153).

ideal, and this is where the difference between an idealist and a pantheist view lies" ("A Critical Survey," p. 202).

While Belinskij's "ideal" was that of progress toward humanity, brotherhood, and democracy, Grigor'ev saw his in more specifically "Russian" traits, such as a true evangelical love of one's fellowman, Christian humility, tranquil, restrained moral strength nurtured by faith and often expressed in a deep, good-natured and optimistic sense of humor. He saw this ideal expressed best in Ostrovskij's plays.

While Grigor'ev believed that "the ideal of the human soul is always and everywhere the same," he also knew that it never presents itself in pure and universal form: only "colored truth" (*cvetnaja istina*), rather than pure "white truth" (*belaja istina*) is accessible to man.[28] Art, then, being an expression of such colored truth, is real as well as ideal. Grigor'ev, no less than Belinskij, excluded "daydreams and reveries" from the domain of true art. He did not, however, hypostatize the presentation of "ordinary reality" as an end in itself, the way Belinskij had done. As Wellek has pointed out, realism was to Grigor'ev merely a necessary stage in the development of Russian literature, a technical invention (like the discovery of perspective in painting), and not an end in itself.[29]

Grigor'ev, like Belinskij, distinguished between epochs during which the tension between the "ideal" and the "real" was heavy and painful, and others, when the ideal and the real were in a state of relative harmony. He saw his own age as one in which "a pure, absolute immediacy of the artist's relationship to reality was something quite impossible," because there existed too great a rift between the ideal as it might arise in a poet's soul and the reality in terms of which he would have to express it.[30]

Grigor'ev, like Belinskij, took for granted that the true work of art is an organic whole. Characteristically, this quality of wholeness was derived, so he thought, from the artist's "inner vision" rather than from his technical skill:

> The so-called technical blunders of an artist (I am taking for granted that we are dealing with a serious artist) derive from some moral source, from an attitude toward the problem in question which is not perfectly straight and clear. In these blunders there are reflected either an incomplete view of life, or a vacillating of this view, or a vague but stubborn presentiment of a different solution of the psychological or social problem in question, a solution which is unlike the customary one. ("A Critical Survey," p. 204)

28. Grigor'ev puts great stock in this metaphor. The purity of the white diamond stands for the absolute idea, the beauty of color for the relative truths made manifest in nature and in art. See "Neskol'ko slov o zakonax i terminax organičeskoj kritiki," *Sočinenija*, 1970 ed., p. 212.

29. Wellek, *Modern Criticism*, 4:269.

30. "Russkaja izjaščnaja literatura v 1852 godu," *Polnoe sobranie sočinenij*, p. 153.

In a discussion of Turgenev's novel *A Nest of Gentlefolk*, Grigor'ev very aptly compares this work to a huge canvas which is only partially covered with
the fragments of a large panoramic picture. Technically speaking, it is a most
imperfect work. But even though it has remained "unfinished" and sketchy,
it is not a manufactured, but a living, live-born work (Grigor'ev puns: *xotja i
nedodelannoe . . . no zato nedelannoe*), because it is based on genuine "vision."[31]

Grigor'ev's understanding of the creative process and his image of the poet
followed the well-known lines of romantic aesthetics. This, of course, had
been true of Belinskij as well. Creativity is conceived as a "power" which is
given to the artist from above. It transcends human reason, being subject to a
"higher law."[32] "Genius" is the highest concentration of power met in a human being. To a genius it is given to see and to express those eternal truths
with which all art is ultimately concerned. Like Belinskij, Grigor'ev believed
that it was given to a genius, such as Gogol', to reveal universals of great social
import by merely expressing the inner life of his own soul. Grigor'ev wholeheartedly welcomed Gogol' 's own comment to the effect that "all his latest
works had been the history of his own soul" and suggested that this made
them ever so much more precious.[33] Like Belinskij, Grigor'ev saw the poetic
genius as a bearer of "a new word." However, he also stressed that in the creations of a genius not only the future emerged with prophetic power and plasticity, but also life's living ties with the past and the true potential of the present were rendered clear and tangible.[34]

Grigor'ev was a staunch defender of intuitivism in art, a believer in creative
inspiration and the "inner vision" produced by it: "When the supply of all
these things [he is speaking of experience, conscious observation, and gathering of material] has reached a certain required state, then some kind of light-
ning illuminates the artist's spiritual world and his attitude toward life—and
creation begins" ("A Critical Survey," p. 203).[35] During his entire critical
career, Grigor'ev attacked the "theoreticians" of the radical camp (*teoretiki*, a
pejorative label used both by Grigor'ev and Dostoevskij), seeking to demonstrate the fallaciousness of their rational, mechanistic, and analytic conception
of art. "Art," Grigor'ev wrote, "being synthesis and inspiration, grasps life
much more broadly than any theory can, so that theory will always fall short

31. "Ivan S. Turgenev i ego dejatel'nost," *Literaturnaja kritika*, p. 272.
32. "He [the artist] has his own, personal nature and his own personal life. But he also
has the power which is given to him, or to put it better, he is himself a great creative power,
which acts according to a higher law" ("Kritičeskij vzgljad," *Sočinenija*, 1876 ed., p. 203).
33. "Russkaja literatura v 1851 godu," *Polnoe sobranie sočinenij*, pp. 108–10.
34. "Kritičeskij vzgljad," *Sočinenija*, 1876 ed., pp. 217–18.
35. Cf. "Russkaja literatura v 1851 godu," *Polnoe sobranie sočinenij*, p. 107, where Grigor'ev refers back to Gogol' 's "Portrait."

of art."[36] The case in point here is Ostrovskij's play *The Thunderstorm* which, Grigor'ev claimed, said a great deal more—besides being more right about what it said—than Dobroljubov's brilliant analytic treatise "A Kingdom of Darkness."

While he believes that an artist of genius may express a great deal of profound truth without being aware of it, Grigor'ev stresses that the creative process as such is largely a conscious one, and the greater the artist the more so it becomes.[37] Along with the romantics and Belinskij, he sees creation as a fusion of inspiration and conscious craftsmanship.

Grigor'ev's conception of his own craft, literary criticism (he was, and considered himself, only a minor poet), is particularly revealing of his organicist aesthetics. His critical method was one of intuition, checked and verified by careful pragmatic study and logical reasoning.[38] Grigor'ev defined "organic criticism" as "viewing art as something synthetic, integral, immediate (*sinteti-českoe, cel'noe, neposredstvennoe*), and as what might be called an intuitive understanding (*intuitivnoe razumenie*) of life as distinct from 'knowledge,' i.e., analytic understanding which is gradual, aggregative, and verifiable by data" (*počastnyj, sobiratel'nyj, poverjaemyj dannymi*).[39] It is quite obvious that Grigor'ev's conception of criticism is close to that of Benedetto Croce.

Dostoevskij

Very little has to be changed, added, or taken away from the above account of Grigor'ev's aesthetic views to produce a description of Dostoevskij's aesthetics.

After a romantic period in his adolescence, Dostoevskij received much of his education in aesthetic theory either directly from Belinskij or through the literary ambiance in which Belinskij was the dominant figure.[40] Like Belinskij, he was for a time under the spell of French utopian socialism. In the 1860s, Grigor'ev, his collaborator on the staff of *Time* and *Epoch*, was his principal guide on matters of aesthetic theory.[41] Unlike Belinskij and Grigor'ev, Dostoevskij apparently had no direct contact with the philosophy of German objective idealism.[42]

Like Grigor'ev, Dostoevskij was aware of the apparent conflict between "pure

36. "Posle *Grozy* Ostrovskogo," *Literaturnaja kritika*, p. 372.
37. Cf. Marčik, " 'Organičeskaja kritika,' " p. 518.
38. Cf. Grossman, *Tri sovremennika*, p. 40.
39. Marčik, " 'Organičeskaja kritika,' " p. 516.
40. Cf. V. Ja. Kirpotin, *Dostoevskij i Belinskij* (Moscow, 1960).
41. Details on the mutual influence between Grigor'ev, Straxov, and Dostoevskij can be found in Linda Gerstein's book *Nikolai Strakhov* (Cambridge, Mass., 1971).
42. Jones, "Echoes of Hegel," pp. 500–520.

art" and the social, national, and historical mission of art, yet believed to the end of his life that this conflict was by no means an irresoluble one. In his brilliant essay "Mr. —bov and the Question of Art" (1861), Dostoevskij dramatizes the conflict in a little parable. Let us imagine, he says to his reader, that the great Lisbon earthquake has just destroyed that flourishing city, killed thousands, and made many more thousands homeless. What if, on the morning after this terrible calamity, a Lisbon newspaper had printed, prominently and on its first page, Fet's virtuosic anthological poem "A Whisper, Subdued Breathing, a Nightingale's Trills. . ."? Would not the good people of Lisbon have seized the poet and hanged him to the nearest lantern post for his callous disregard of the public weal? Having conceded to his imaginary opponent that the indignation of the good people of Lisbon was indeed well placed, Dostoevskij turns the argument around and points out that neither anthological poetry as such nor Fet's exquisitely beautiful love poem had been at fault: only the poet's timing in publishing his poem had been infelicitous. No doubt, Dostoevskij concludes, fifty years later the good people of Lisbon would have erected a monument to that same poet, remembering him only as the creator of those beautiful lines: "A whisper, subdued breathing. . . ." Dostoevskij's message is clear: the aesthetic value of art is absolute, its social (and moral, political, and other) value is relative and incidental.

All his life, Dostoevskij was convinced that free and independent art, serving its own aesthetic ends before anything else, would also be more useful socially than any work created *ad hoc* with the intention of achieving a given social, political, or didactic end. Clearly, his was also a case of wanting to have one's cake and eat it, too. Dostoevskij charged that his opponents, Dobroljubov in particular, were essentially practical men who were not interested in art, yet produced and used art to their political ends.[43] Dostoevskij's opponents could easily have reversed the argument, claiming that Dostoevskij was essentially an artist, to whom art was an absolute value, but who insisted nevertheless that his art-oriented works carried as much weight socially as the opposition's sober, politically oriented writings.

Much like Grigor'ev, Dostoevskij placed the value of art very high: "Art is a need of man, just as food and drink are. The need for beauty, and for creation which incarnates it, is inseparable from man, and without it man perhaps would not even want to live in this world" ("A Contemporary Misconception," *A Writer's Diary*, 1873).[44] Thus, Dostoevskij, on the one hand, asserted the autonomy and absolute value of art. But on the other hand, Dostoevskij claimed

43. "G. —bov i vopros ob iskusstve," *Sobranie sočinenij*, 23 vols. (St. Petersburg, n.d.), 19:67.
44. *Sobranie sočinenij*, 13 vols. (Moscow and Leningrad, 1929–30), 11:139. Cf. "G. —bov i vopros ob iskusstve," *Sobranie sočinenij*, 19:77.

that art, even while remaining true to its freedom, was still organically linked to every other aspect of human life. He was just as strong a proponent of social, national, and historic organicism as Belinskij or Grigor'ev.

A number of antinomies are inherent in this position. One of them became apparent to Dostoevskij in connection with his own work. His personal ideal of absolute beauty bore the features of "classical" serenity, calm, and harmony. Claude Lorrain's Arcadian landscapes, suffused with a warm and tender light which would seem to emanate from an unearthly source, were his favorites. Yet his own works rarely expressed this ideal, for they tended to disclose the dark, disfigured, morbid, and contradictory nature of modern man, while barely succeeding even to intimate a striving for the ideal.[45]

What was even more serious, Dostoevskij knew and often described that perverse union of inhumanity and a keen aesthetic sense which is so often found in modern man. He also knew that "the beauty of Sodom" and "the beauty of the Madonna" could very well coexist in the mind of the same person. Not without some justification, Dostoevskij himself earned the name of a "cruel talent."[46] How could the identity of moral and aesthetic values be defended under these circumstances?

Dostoevskij refused to solve this dilemma by taking advantage of the Hegelian concept of the "negative ideal," which both Belinskij and Grigor'ev had applied to Gogol', apparently to their own satisfaction. Rather, he insisted on an active presence of the positive ideal, which he identified with the moral ideal suggested to him by his evangelical faith. Moral beauty, being of a higher, spiritual order, was to fill the vacuum created by the absence of classical aesthetic beauty. The sensuous, amoral, pagan "beauty of Sodom" was declared to be a sham, a ruse of the Devil.

So far so good. The religious ideal could quite rightfully supersede the aesthetic ideal, and moral beauty could legitimately replace aesthetic beauty. In religious art, the weak, the sickly, the malformed had been traditionally associated with spiritual beauty. But Dostoevskij insisted that the achievement of spiritual beauty should bring with it a transfiguration of the ugly, misshapen, sordid world of contemporary Russian life into the aesthetically beautiful, luminous, and serene atmosphere of "Cana of Galilee." He categorically insisted on the oneness of moral and aesthetic beauty, and consistently sought to introduce the motif of their fusion in connection with his own positive characters. (By the same token his negative characters are often revealed as having aesthetically repulsive traits, in spite of apparent good looks and brilliant minds.)

45. Cf. Robert Louis Jackson, *Dostoevsky's Quest for Form: A Study of His Philosophy of Art* (New Haven, 1966), p. 3.
46. N. K. Mixajlovskij, "Žestokij talant," first printed in *Otečestvennye zapiski*, 1882, nos. 9–10.

Furthermore, Dostoevskij also insisted on the objective historical truthfulness of his visions: his "beautiful" characters (Prince Myškin, Makar Ivanovič Dolgorukij, Father Zosima, Aleša Karamazov) are all understood to be representative of actual trends in contemporary Russian life. A historical optimist much like his radical opponents, Dostoevskij sincerely believed that the moral and aesthetic ideal which he was seeking to synthesize in his works was also prophetic of actual social trends, the first signs of which he believed to have observed in contemporary Russian life. Dostoevskij believed in an incipient "religious revolution" much as his opponents of the Left believed in an imminent social revolution.

Dostoevskij's belief in the cognitive powers of intuition was as firm as Grigor'ev's, and so was his contempt for what he, along with Grigor'ev, called "theoretical" thought applied to matters of morality, nationality, and art. Dostoevskij's—and Grigor'ev's—rationale for rejecting the services of scientific and logical thought in solving important "human" problems was grounded in metaphysics. Dostoevskij literally and consciously believed in the existence of transcendent realms of light and absolute darkness, both of which would make incursions into the twilight zone of "ordinary human life." Obviously, this transcendence was what really mattered in human life. Rational scientific thought could grasp only "ordinary life." But to the artist it was given, more than to other humans, to see the transcendent shine through the world of ordinary appearances. In expressing his visions of seemingly exceptional or even fantastic phenomena, the artist becomes what Dostoevskij calls "a realist in a higher sense":

> I have my own peculiar view of reality in art, and that which the majority calls almost fantastic and exceptional is sometimes for me the very essence of reality. The commonplaceness of events and a standard view of them is, in my opinion, not realism at all, but actually its opposite. . . . In every newspaper you run across accounts of the most real and most elaborate facts. To our writers they seem fantastic, and they do not even bother with them. Yet they are reality, because they are facts.[47]

Time and again, Dostoevskij charged that his opponents and critics were mistaking the irrelevant trivia of everyday life or the sterile abstractions of their own minds for "reality," claiming that they had grasped the objective essence of things in general, and of Russian life in particular. Actually, these men were sad victims of stillborn delusions. True reality could only reveal itself in the form of living inner visions.

Dostoevskij's image of the artist and the poet was naturally an exalted one. Puškin's "Prophet" was his favorite poem. He was willing to grant a great

47. Letter to N. N. Straxov, 26 February – 10 March 1869, *Pis'ma*, ed. A. S. Dolinin, 4 vols. (Moscow and Leningrad, 1928–59), 2:169–70.

poet—Shakespeare in particular, as well as Puškin—the title of "prophet" in the most literal sense of that word. However, Dostoevskij's view of the creative process and the genesis of a work of art was circumspect and sober—much as it had been with such romantic mystics as Novalis. Dostoevskij distinguishes three stages in the creative process. The first, a preparatory stage, is that of rational, alert, empirical observation of the world. Like his predecessors Belinskij and Grigor'ev, Dostoevskij believed that the artist should always be in active touch with public life. Like them, he was himself a successful journalist and an active participant in political, legal, and ideological discussions. The second and decisive stage belongs to "the poet." It is a period of intense inner work, partly subconscious, in the course of which the "inner vision" of the work emerges. During this stage the artist has no control over his work: it is a matter of inspiration. The third stage belongs to "the artist." It is marked by careful, attentive, painstaking labor, during which the whole work, part by part, image by image, detail by detail, passes through the artist's consciousness as a confrontation with his ideal "inner vision."

Dostoevskij, like Belinskij and Grigor'ev before him, was a believer in the "Serapiontic principle." It was of great consequence for his own creative practice. He ridiculed "notebook" writers who believed that they could capture reality by reproducing faithfully and "scientifically" the various details of their subjects' speech, customs and habits, and their social and economic condition. This method, Dostoevskij asserted, led to stillborn works. He himself sought to capture the "spirit" and the quintessence of Russian life by taking it through the crucible of his creative imagination, by reliving himself every detail of his narrative. This practice led to a charge by many critics (among whom we find Belinskij and Tolstoj) that all of Dostoevskij's characters "talked alike," namely, like their creator, Dostoevskij. Posterity, however, has sided with Dostoevskij. His many minor violations of factual and linguistic authenticity are no longer noticed, and the individual voices of his characters emerge as sharply individualized entities.

The Symbolists

Dostoevskij's aesthetics, along with the rest of his philosophy, had a profound influence on Russia's greatest philosopher, Vladimir Solov'ev (1853-1900); directly as well as through Solov'ev, it also influenced V. V. Rozanov (1856-1919), D. S. Merežkovskij (1865-1941), and ultimately Russian Symbolism. But in the case of these writers, one can hardly implicate Belinskij's heritage, since they all also went back to Belinskij's and Grigor'ev's sources: Plato, Neoplatonism, German idealism, Carlyle, and romantic thought in general, not to mention the influence of Western neoromantic thought. Nevertheless, the aesthetic theory of Russian Symbolism largely retains the principal tenets of Belinskij's aesthetics, frequently in outright opposition to Western Symbolism.

For one thing, Russian Symbolism, in spite of its renewed ties with the art, the philosophy, and the poetry of the West, continues to pursue the nationalist mystique which had been so strong in Belinskij, Grigor'ev, and Dostoevskij. The poetic hypostatization of *Rus'* ("Russia") is one of the most frequent recurring motifs in Russian symbolist poetry.

Secondly, Russian Symbolism, at least in many of its leading representatives, such as Merežkovskij, Zinaida Hippius, Belyj, Blok, and Vjačeslav Ivanov, was also socially *engagé*. Many of the symbolists seriously believed in the social and national mission of the movement and saw themselves as prophets, leaders, and reorganizers of Russian life. In addition, of course, there was the religious ("theurgic") conception of art, which was strong in Solov'ev and which emerged at various times in the poetry and criticism of Belyj, Blok, Vjačeslav Ivanov, and other symbolists.

Finally, Russian Symbolists were eminently conscious of the movement of history. To capture the secret rhythm of time, to prophesy Russia's future, to be heralds of the Russian religious revolution were some of the main concerns and poetic ambitions of many of them, Belyj, Blok, and Zinaida Hippius in particular.

To the relationship between art and reality Russian Symbolism brought nothing new, unless a return to a Neoplatonic mysticism can be called "new." Rather, the aesthetic pronouncements of the symbolists tended to repeat the clichés of organic aesthetics which we know so well from Belinskij and his immediate followers: "Symbols must emanate, naturally and spontaneously, from the depth of reality. But if the author invents them artificially (*iskusstvenno vydumyvaet*) in order to express some kind of an idea, they turn into dead allegories."[48] Belinskij himself could have written this:

> How could one define symbolist poetry more exactly? It is a poetry in which two contents are fused (*slivajutsja*) organically rather than forcibly: a hidden abstractness (*otvlečennost'*) and a visible beauty are fused just as easily and naturally as the waters of a river are harmoniously fused with the sunlight on a summer morning. However, in spite of the concealed meaning of one or the other symbolic work, its immediate, concrete content is always complete in itself, and has, in symbolist poetry, an independent existence rich in nuances.[49]

Here we are dealing with the familiar concept of a fusion of the ideal and the real. Even the phraseology has remained the same: "organically," "naturally,"

---

48. D. S. Merežkovskij, "On the Causes of the Decline of and on New Trends in Contemporary Russian Literature" (St. Petersburg, 1893); quoted from *Literaturnye manifesty ot simvolizma k Oktjabrju* (Slavische Propyläen reprint, Munich, 1969), p. 15.

49. Konstantin Bal'mont, *Gornye veršiny*, 1 (Moscow, 1904); quoted from *Literaturnye manifesty*, p. 26.

"harmoniously," "immediate, concrete content," "complete in itself"—all are expressions previously found in Belinskij.

The symbolists believed in the cognitive powers of art and in intuitive cognition in general. Vjačeslav Ivanov defined art as "cognition through genius" ("iskusstvo est' genial'noe poznanie") and Brjusov said that the highest and really the only purpose of art was "cognition of the world outside rational forms (*vne rassudočnyx form*), outside causal thinking."[50] Many similar pronouncements can be found in both the prose and poetry of all the Russian symbolists. Their formulations rarely differ much from Belinskij's and, as a rule, completely coincide with Grigor'ev's. Like Dostoevskij, the symbolists saw themselves as "realists in a higher sense," seers, expounders and prophets of a deeper metaphysical reality which was, however, immanent in the ordinary reality of contemporary Russian life:

> But you, artist, must firmly believe
> In beginnings and ends. You must know
> Where Hell and Paradise await us.
> To you it is given to measure
> All that you see with a dispassionate yardstick.
> May your eye be firm and clear.
> Wipe away all accidental traits—
> And you shall see: the world is beautiful.
>   Aleksandr Blok, "The Vindication," prologue)

The image used here is the same as Tolstoj's *snjatie pokrovov* ("removing the covers") in *Anna Karenina*, and ultimately Plotinus's sculptor, who liberates his inner vision of divine Beauty from the unformed marble block.

What is new about the aesthetics of Russian Symbolism, compared with that of Belinskij and his immediate followers, even of the Right, is a much stronger emphasis on "art" (Plotinus's $\tau\acute{\epsilon}\chi\nu\eta$) in the work of art, combined with the notion that it is precisely this aspect of the work of art that is most revealing of a deeper, transcendent reality. Poetic estrangement, often to the point of outright obscurity, is seen as a road to the light of metaphysical truth.[51] Andrej Belyj once formulated this notion in the following way: "Only *music* reveals to us that appearances are a cover (*pokrov*) thrown over an abyss. Poetry contemplates appearances musically, seeing them as a cover over the unspoken mystery of the soil. Such contemplation is musical contemplation. Music is the skeleton of poetry."[52]

50. Vjačeslav Ivanov, "Simvolizm, kak miroponimanie," *Trudy i dni* (Moscow, 1912); quoted from *Literaturnye manifesty,* p. 31. Valerij Brjusov, "Ključi tajn," *Vesy,* 1904, no. 1; quoted from *Literaturnye manifesty,* p. 29.

51. On this point, there is a recent study by James L. Kugel, *The Technique of Strangeness in Symbolist Poetry* (New Haven and London, 1971).

52. Andrej Belyj, "The Principle of Form," in *Simvolizm: Kniga statej* (Moscow, 1910), p. 179.

The word "music" is to be understood metaphorically: it stands for "art" in the work of art and is a synonym of "form." It is characteristic of a symbolist, such as Blok, to associate purely formal features of poetry, such as meter and sound patterns, with distinct phenomena of the world at large, for example, with the spirit of a certain historical epoch.

The symbolists' emphasis on what the layman calls "form," but which to the artist is really the "content" of his work (what *he* put into it), is the bridge between Neoplatonic objective idealism and a neo-Kantian subjective idealism. The moment the artist loses his faith in the objective existence of the transcendence revealed in his work and prefers to call it simply *his own* subjective creation, we arrive in the realm of "modernism," an aesthetic ambiance which is profoundly alien to the Belinskian tradition.

Blok's last public lecture, "On the Poet's Calling" (1921), delivered a short time before the poet's death, in which he once more presented his view of the poet and his work, was an open confrontation not only with the Soviet regime but also with Belinskij. Basing his observations entirely on Puškin and his cycle "on the poet," Blok distinguishes three stages in the poet's work. During the first, the poet "lifts the external covers and opens up the depths of his vision." This is the stage best described as "the voice of inspiration." Nobody can control it. During the second stage, "these sounds, raised from the depths, and alien to the external world," are cast into the solid mold of the spoken word. This is the stage of "craftsmanship" (*masterstvo*); it can be interfered with by various external influences, says Blok, and he immediately charges that Belinskij and his followers, through their insistence on the social and historical responsibility of art, were guilty of tampering with the poet's creative freedom and did irreparable damage to Russian poetry. Finally, during the third stage, the poet must introduce his creation to the world. At this point, there takes place Puškin's famous clash between "the poet" and "the crowd." Here, and only here, Count Benckendorff, chief of gendarmes and Puškin's censor, enters the picture. Thus—Blok makes it quite explicit—Belinskij was a much greater and more dangerous enemy of poetry than Count Benckendorff. Benckendorff could temporarily suspend the appearance of a poem. Belinskij could destroy the poem itself by diverting or perverting the poet's free inspiration.[53]

Was Blok fair to Belinskij? I think that he was unfair to Belinskij the critic and aesthetician, but accurately assessed the overwhelming influence of Belinskij the historical figure. Belinskij never dreamed of destroying aesthetics. But his zeal to engage Russian literature in the cause of social progress opened the door to those who would.

53. Aleksandr Blok, "O naznačenii poèta," *Stixotvorenija* (Leningrad, 1936), pp. 483–86.

THE AESTHETES

The nucleus of what was eventually to be considered the anti-Belinskian, "aestheticizing" tendency in Russian literature and literary criticism was headed by men who had been personally close to Belinskij and who thought that they were carrying on the traditions which the critic had started. In the decades after Belinskij's death, the politically liberal and westernizing "center" of Russian literature was headed by such men as V. P. Botkin (1811–1869), P. V. Annenkov (1812–1887), I. S. Turgenev (1818–1883), and I. A. Gončarov (1812–1891), to mention the most prominent, all of whom had been personal friends of Belinskij and often stated their allegiance to his intellectual heritage after his death. A. V. Družinin (1824–1864) did not belong to the circle of Belinskij's friends, but his debut with the short novel *Polin'ka Saks* (1847) took place under the auspices of the critic's warm approval.

Botkin, Annenkov, and Družinin

In the 1850s, Annenkov and Botkin worked for *The Contemporary* alongside Černyševskij and Dobroljubov. Sharp differences arose between the two groups headed by these men. The interpretation of the "social" novels of Turgenev and Pisemskij was a typical issue.[54] Botkin, Annenkov, and Družinin were defending the objective realism of these writers, while Černyševskij and Dobroljubov demanded that literature take a more decisive ideological and critical stand on the social and political issues of the day, and that it assume an active role as an organ of political enlightenment and social progress. Specifically, Černyševskij and Dobroljubov wanted literature to create heroes (*svetlye ličnosti*), "integral characters" (*cel'nye xaraktery*), and positive, future-oriented "types" instead of the antiheroes met in the novels and short stories of Turgenev and Pisemskij. For example, in his famous review of Turgenev's masterful short story *Asja*, "A Russian at a Rendezvous" (1858), Černyševskij reproached Turgenev for having, again, failed to produce a positive hero. Annenkov, in a rebuttal entitled "The Literary Type of the Weak Man" (1858), pointed out that the type created by Turgenev was both true and really positive in that it contained the seed of progress and creativity, most creative men being precisely such "weak characters." Both parties claimed that the authority of Belinskij was on their side.[55] When their differences ultimately led to the

54. For another example, Družinin greeted Pisemskij's *Sketches from Peasant Life* (1856) with enthusiasm, finding them objective, free of any ideological tendency, yet life-affirming and positive. Černyševskij responded by attacking Družinin (though he did not name him) and pointing out that precisely the things which Družinin had praised so highly were, in effect, serious failings: a lack of critical understanding of Russian life and a lack of desire to cure its ills.

55. See, e.g., K. Polonskaja, "Spor o Belinskom (Bor'ba vokrug nasledija Belinskogo v

departure of Botkin, Annenkov, and Družinin from *The Contemporary,* their
group was labeled "the aesthetes," their opponents "the publicists."

In actuality—if one discounts Černyševskij's theoretical statements in *Aesthetic Relations of Art to Reality,* to which even Černyševskij himself did not always adhere in his practical criticism—the views of both groups reflected the inner contradictions already found in Belinskij. Their differences were largely differences of emphasis. Dobroljubov's utilitarianism was combined with and tempered by his retention, implicit as well as explicit, of virtually all of the principles of organicist aesthetics. To a somewhat lesser extent, this is also true of Černyševskij's practical criticism.

The energetic insistence on the autonomy of art by Botkin, Annenkov, and Družinin was combined with an adherence to a Belinskian social and historical organicism. They called their criticism "artistic criticism" (*xudožestvennaja kritika*). Annenkov's favorite thought was that the "truth of life" (*istina žizni*) and the "truth of literature" (*literaturnaja istina*) were subject to different laws. Družinin kept reiterating that true art is "an end in itself." Botkin developed an interesting theory (which later reappeared in Symbolism), according to which "poetry acts not so much through word or image, concept and emotion, as through that elusive musical perspective, into which our feeling plunges pensively and joyfully, losing itself in its inward infinity."[56] And Botkin consistently emphasized the importance of the subconscious aspect of artistic creation—which his opponents downgraded.

If Černyševskij and his cohorts saw the future of Russian literature to lie in its "Gogolian trend" (by which they meant socially committed realist art, dealing mostly with the "low life" of Russia), the aesthetes believed that Puškin (and not Gogol' and the Natural School) should be the lodestar of Russian literature.[57]

60-e gody XIX veka)," *VLit* 12, no. 6 (1968): 118–37.

The following passage from a letter written by Černyševskij to Turgenev (whom he was seeking to "keep in line"—in vain, as it soon developed) in 1857 is significant: "You, in your kindness, listen with too much condescendence to all of these Botkins and their cohorts. They were all right so long as Belinskij kept them in line with an iron hand, and they were wise so long as he would stuff their heads with his ideas. . . . They are fine people, but in matters of art or anything of the kind they understand not a penny's worth. . . . Whatever Botkin and Družinin write is either a banal truism or senseless plagiarism" (N. G. Černyševskij, *Polnoe sobranie sočinenij,* 16 vols. [Moscow, 1939–53], 14:332). Needless to say, Černyševskij wholly misrepresents the relationship between Belinskij and Botkin.

56. Botkin developed this conception in a highly laudatory essay devoted to the poetry of A. A. Fet, an epigone of Romanticism and precursor of Symbolism. See V. P. Botkin, "Stixotvorenija A. A. Feta," *Sovremennik,* 1857, no. 1, pp. 1–42.

57. Družinin's article "A. S. Puškin i poslednee izdanie ego sočinenij" (1855, the edition being Annenkov's) developed the notion of Puškin the Olympian, the objective artist, who transcended his time, its struggles and its prejudices.

But notwithstanding all this, the "aesthetes" rarely departed from a Belin-skian organicism. They praised Fet and the other "anthological" poets (Belin-skij had praised them, too), but they also valued Turgenev and especially Tol-stoj, in whose work they saw their aesthetic ideal of "objective art" realized to perfection. Like Belinskij, they supported honest, down-to-earth realism and encouraged artists to deal with contemporary life. Thus, Družinin wrote: "A poet is not born for fantasies and utopias, but for hard work . . . and he must study the milieu which he depicts, he must live and work in the milieu, be linked to it with all its imperfections, and perhaps be imperfect himself."[58]

Likewise, the aesthetes emphasized the educational and civilizing role of art, though they rejected outright didacticism, moralism, and allegory—but so did Belinskij, and as a matter of principle, Černyševskij and Dobroljubov, too. "A great poet is always a great enlightener and his poetry is the Sun of our spiritu-al world which, though it might appear that it does not perform any good deeds and though nobody gets a penny out of it, still casts its light upon the whole world"—so wrote Družinin in his review of Gončarov's *Oblomov*.[59]

Družinin's discussion of *Oblomov* really follows the same social-organicist pattern as Dobroljubov's famous essay "What Is Oblomovitis?" Družinin, too, saw in Oblomov a marvelously perceptive and deeply truthful realization of a Russian "type." He, too, believed that Gončarov's novel would help Russians to understand themselves better. But while Dobroljubov perceived Oblomov as a thoroughly negative type and concentrated on his slothfulness, his apathy, his sybaritism, and his irresponsibility as traits characteristic of the dying class and the dying social order for which he stood, Družinin saw mainly Oblomov's gentleness and goodness, his loving, sensitive nature—and perceived him as a positive type.[60]

Turgenev

The aesthetic views of I. S. Turgenev, better known than those of his good friends Botkin and Annenkov (Turgenev did not get along well with Družinin), are fairly characteristic of the "center" of Russian literature from Belinskij's death to the Revolution.

Turgenev basically accepted all of the conceptions of organicist aesthetics: the autonomy of art, the organic unity of the work of art, the fusion of the ideal and the real, inner vision and inspiration, genius and talent, the spontan-

---

58. Review of Tolstoj's "Military Tales" and Saltykov-Ščedrin's "Provincial Sketches," in A. V. Družinin, *Sobranie sočinenij*, 8 vols. (St. Petersburg, 1865–67), 7:25.

59. Družinin, *Sobranie sočinenij*, 7:581.

60. This interpretation has been recently revived by Yvette Louria and Morton I. Seiden in an essay, "Ivan Goncharov's Oblomov: The Anti-Faust as Christian Hero," *Canadian Slavic Studies* 3 (1969): 39–68.

eous analogy between art and life (in its social as well as historical dimensions).[61] He also rejected, on principle, all those tendencies in art as well as in literary criticism which go against these conceptions: naturalism, emotionalism, didacticism and moralism, allegory, aestheticism, and all art not solidly anchored in "real life."

But in practice—and occasionally in theory—he made many concessions to the tendencies of which he disapproved in principle. He defended Zola (and his Russian counterparts such as Rešetnikov) and wrote some stories which he himself admitted were "naturalistic." Both leftist radicals such as Saltykov-Ščedrin and rightists such as Dostoevskij wholeheartedly condemned Zola.

Nor was Turgenev averse to using his art as an outlet for his own emotions. He could be subjective to the extent of appearing almost indiscreet. (This is what Dostoevskij attacked in his parody of Turgenev's lyric prose piece "Enough!" in *The Possessed* and why he was so incensed about Turgenev's description of Traupmann's execution.)[62] Turgenev's French critics noted the quality of "compassion" about his work (a quality they found absent in the works of Turgenev's French friends, Flaubert in particular). Jules Lemaître recognized in this trait a return to the sentimental humanitarianism of the French *roman-feuilleton* of the 1830s. More directly, it can be linked to Belinskij's doctrine regarding permissible and even desirable "subjectivism" in fiction—provided that this subjectivism was "that profound, all-embracing and humane subjectivity which reveals in an artist a human being possessed of an ardent heart, a sympathetic soul, and a spiritual and personal individuality" (Belinskij, 6:217–18).

In fact, Turgenev, many of whose works were by his own admission "tendentious,"[63] justified himself with Belinskij's arguments, even using Belinskij's phrasing. "There are," Turgenev said, "epochs when literature cannot remain *merely* art, when there are interests higher than poetic interests. The moment of self-realization and self-criticism is just as important in the development of national life as it is in the life of an individual. . . . "[64] And thus the writer would become an enlightener, a public figure, an intellectual leader, whose literary work would be immediately "useful." Turgenev sincerely believed that all of his major works "had been of some use." For instance, he said of *Fathers and Sons:*

61. Victor Terras, "Turgenev's Aesthetic and Western Realism," *Comparative Literature* 22 (1970): 19–35.

62. Letter to N. N. Straxov, 23 June 1870, *Pis'ma,* 2:274. Turgenev's account of the execution of the notorious mass murderer often dwells on the witness's reactions to the spectacle.

63. In a letter to V. P. Botkin, 1 March 1857, Turgenev actually calls himself "a writer with a tendency" (I. S. Turgenev, *Pis'ma,* 13 vols. [Moscow and Leningrad, 1961–67], 3:91). *Smoke* and *Virgin Soil* are novels with a strong and obvious political tendency, bordering on invective when it comes to baiting conservatives.

64. Letter to V. P. Botkin, 29 June 1855, *Pis'ma,* 2:282.

This novel appeared exactly at the right moment in our [that is, Russian] life. . . . I actually make bold to believe that I accomplished something useful there. . . . All this will become clear in time, and even if my reputation should perish, the cause itself will be victorious, and this is certainly what matters, the rest being mere trifles.[65]

Turgenev considered himself, and was considered by others, a "social novelist." In "A Preface to My Novels," he said that he had "tried, as best [he] could, to depict and to embody, conscientiously and dispassionately, in appropriate 'types,' what Shakespeare called 'the body and pressure of time.' "[66] By so doing, he felt he had done Russian society a useful service, and many critics agreed with him: Dobroljubov, Pisarev, Mixajlovskij, to name but a few, all said that Turgenev was, or had been, "useful." Such, then, were Turgenev's —very Belinskian—concessions to utilitarianism.

On the other side, there was Turgenev the aesthete, to whom art—and perhaps erotic love—were the only things which would allow a civilized, thinking man to recapture, temporarily, a blessed state of integrity and spontaneity. There was also Turgenev the author of a surprisingly large number of "fantastic" tales, the freethinker who regretted that he had no religious faith.

Turgenev's aesthetic views present, as it were, an organicist core, around which a number of eclectic notions, which contradict it, are grouped. This description is generally valid for other well-educated writers and critics of the liberal "center," who were not committed either to the aggressively utilitarian Left or to the equally doctrinaire "pure art" Right.[67] Turgenev's correspondence with A. A. Fet, a political conservative and a persistent proponent of "pure art," suggests that Turgenev was opposed to pure art no less than to the radical utilitarianism of Dobroljubov. It is significant that Turgenev dedicated his finest novel, *Fathers and Sons,* to the memory of Belinskij—after having broken with *The Contemporary.* Clearly, he felt that Dobroljubov and Černyševskij did not stand for the principles which he believed to have been Belinskij's.

THE BELINSKIAN LEFT

Černyševskij

Among Belinskij's epigoni of the Left, N. G. Černyševskij (1828–1889) did more than anyone else to make Belinskij the authority he is to this day, but his

65. Letter to P. V. Annenkov, 20 June 1862, *Pis'ma,* 5:11–12.
66. I. S. Turgenev, "Predislovie k romanam" (1879), *Polnoe sobranie sočinenij,* 12:303.
67. The aesthetic views of I. A. Gončarov were remarkably close to those of Turgenev. Cf. Milton Ehre, "Ivan Goncharov on Art, Literature, and the Novel," *Slavic Review* 29 (1970): 203–18.

own aesthetic thought anticipates virtually every positivist, materialist, and intellectualist deviation from Belinskian organicism that one may meet in Russian critical literature from Černyševskij's to our own days. Černyševskij openly declared himself Belinskij's successor. In his *Sketches of the Gogolian Period of Russian Literature* (1855–56), he quoted verbatim dozens of passages (up to several pages long) from Belinskij's works, justifying this as follows: "To this day, his [Belinskij's] criticism is to be viewed not only as a remarkable historical phenomenon, but also as a guiding example" (*rukovoditel'nyj primer*).[68]

Černyševskij, like Grigor'ev, noted the evolution in Belinskij's thought and naturally saw it as a movement toward ever closer contact between literature and social life.

Černyševskij was well read in aesthetic theory. He knew Plato, Aristotle, and Plotinus. He was also familiar with German aesthetic literature from Baumgarten and Lessing to Feuerbach and Vischer,[69] and viewed it with a sharp critical eye. In a review of a Russian version of Aristotle's *Poetics* (1854), he points out with some justification that the doctrine of the ideal basis of art (*učenie ob ideal'nom načale iskusstva*) is not Platonic, but Neoplatonic, and then proceeds to announce very casually—but again correctly—that he will refrain from expounding the ideas of Plotinus on the essence of Beauty, "because to expound them would mean practically the same as to expound the aesthetic principles now in vogue."[70] Both Plotinus and his modern followers are to Černyševskij mere dreamers, if not charlatans. He views all idealist aesthetics with supercilious irony. Yet at the same time, Černyševskij also rejected the aesthetic sensualism of eighteenty-century writers such as Burke, declaring it to be a naïve oversimplification of the facts.

Černyševskij easily recognized Belinskij's dependence on Hegel and analyzed it in some detail in his *Sketches of the Gogolian Period of Russian Literature.* Černyševskij explained the fact that Belinskij, from a devoted disciple of Hegel's, became an outspoken opponent of his philosophy because of the "dual nature" of that philosophy. Hegel's principles, Černyševskij said, were extremely potent and broad, but the conclusions which he drew from them were

68. N. G. Černyševskij, *Očerki gogolevskogo perioda russkoj literatury*, in *Polnoe sobranie sočinenij*, 3:298.

69. Evidence his essay "Kritičeskij vzgljad na sovremennye èstetičeskie ponjatija" (1854), published by P. E. Ščegolev as late as 1924 in *Zvezda*, no. 5, pp. 202–31. See also *Polnoe sobranie sočinenij*, 2:127–58. Likewise, Černyševskij's essay "Lessing, ego vremja, ego žizn' i dejatel'nost' " (1856–57), published in *The Contemporary*, 1856, nos. 10–12, and 1857, nos. 1, 3–4, 6, is a compilation from basic secondary sources (given by Wellek, *Modern Criticism*, 4:563), but it shows a respectable erudition. See also *Polnoe sobranie sočinenij*, 4:5–221. That Černyševskij was well read in Russian critical and aesthetic thought is demonstrated, of course, by his *Očerki gogolevskogo perioda russkoj literatury*.

70. *Polnoe sobranie sočinenij*, 2:280.

narrow and insignificant. Therefore, as soon as Belinskij had reached a stage at which he needed to apply his ideas to life and to the relationship between life and art, he inevitably had to turn away from Hegel. In so doing, Černyševskij proceeds, Belinskij became Russia's first independent and original critic. As for Russian critics after Belinskij, Černyševskij thought that whatever was of any value in their writings was a repetition of what Belinskij had said before them. In this, Černyševskij is not at all wrong: it is largely true in Grigor'ev's case.

Černyševskij's own aesthetics was, as he himself pointed out in a preface to the third edition of *The Aesthetic Relations of Art to Reality* (1888), an application of Feuerbach's materialistic philosophy to aesthetic theory.[71]

Černyševskij had little inclination and no talent for literary criticism. His interests lay in the areas of political science, sociology, and economics. He became a part-time literary critic and one of Russia's most influential writers on aesthetic theory, mainly because he realized that in Russia literature constituted virtually the entire intellectual life of the nation. In his *Sketches of the Gogolian Period of Russian Literature,* Černyševskij observed quite correctly that in Russia fiction served as a medium for many ideas which in the West would have been discussed in works of nonfiction, by economists, jurists, publicists, and philosophers. This, Černyševskij adds with a measure of pride, accounts for the originality of Russian literature.[72]

With all his revolutionary fervor and idealistic devotion to the cause of "the people," Černyševskij was a consistent materialist and determinist. He believed that so-called mental processes were physical processes not yet fully understood, but entirely determinate. Religion was the same as superstition. Scientific and technological progress, if rationally manipulated, would eventually take man out of history, time, and suffering.

Černyševskij also argued, in positivist terms, against any kind of aesthetic transcendence, rejecting the concepts of inner vision, inspiration, and genius as self-delusions of artists and poets overly convinced of their own importance:

> One cannot imagine a face that is more beautiful than those faces which one has happened to see in real life. Yet, on the other hand, one can *say* [italics

71. V. G. Astaxov, in his work *G. V. Plexanov i N. G. Černyševskij* (Stalinabad, 1961), points out that in spite of Plexanov's and even Lenin's explicit observations to this effect, some Soviet authors have chosen to ignore the influence of Feuerbach's philosophy on Černyševskij's aesthetic theory (p. 153). Georg Lukács sees Černyševskij's famous "anthropological principle," which he borrowed from Feuerbach, as the principal weakness of the Russian critic's aesthetics. It prevented him from taking a concrete historical and dialectical view of aesthetic phenomena, Lukács explains. See Georg Lukács, "Einführung in die Ästhetik Tschernyschewskijs," *Beiträge zur Geschichte der Ästhetik* (Berlin, 1956), pp. 147–49.

72. *Očerki gogolevskogo perioda,* in *Polnoe sobranie sočinenij,* 3:137–38.

added] all one wants to say. One can say: "iron gold," "warm ice," "sugary bitterness," and so forth. To be sure, our imagination cannot imagine "warm ice" . . . which is why these phrases remain completely empty for us, giving no meaning whatsoever to our imagination. Yet, having mixed some empty words with representations that are accessible to the imagination, one may delude oneself into believing that the dreams of fantasy are much richer, fuller, more luxurious than reality. (*The Aesthetic Relations of Art to Reality*)[73]

Černyševskij's argument is that of a man who is not only uninterested in art, but who actually has never bothered to find out what art is. It is the argument of a man unfamiliar with aesthetic experience.[74] Plexanov was quite right in calling Černyševskij an "enlightener" (*prosvetitel'*). In his aesthetic views, Černyševskij returned to pre-Kantian eighteenth-century ideas, seeking to account for aesthetic phenomena entirely in terms of either rational intelligence or simple sense experience. Much like eighteenth-century enlighteners, Černyševskij considered excessive passion, excitability, and fantasy to be nothing but pathological conditions to be treated by medical therapists. His ideal was that of a "normal" and "rational" development of man's "natural" faculties. Černyševskij's anthropology, much as that of the eighteenth-century Enlightenment, was optimistic: man, though naturally an egoist, was a rational being, well capable of pursuing his self-interest intelligently in accordance with the laws of nature, and with some enlightened consideration for other human beings; he was therefore perfectly capable of progress, that is, of creating ever-improving conditions of life for himself and his fellowmen.

The key notion of Černyševskij's aesthetics proper is a total rejection of the Kantian doctrine of the autonomous and specific nature of the aesthetic fact. Černyševskij did everything to destroy all the barriers separating art from science, from politics, from publicism, and from ordinary practical activity. He made a point of showing that so-called aesthetic concepts were by no means applicable to art and poetry alone. In a way, this "abolition of aesthetics" (as Pisarev later called it) amounted to organicism in reverse: art and life were still one, though in a quite different sense than had been the case in idealist organic aesthetics.

Astaxov points out that Černyševskij's unqualified identification of art with its nonaesthetic social functions failed to take into account the concrete historical fact of art's autonomous power. As a result, Astaxov thinks, Černyševskij lost his grip on the power of art, which he would have liked to control for the benefit of society.[75] Actually, Černyševskij's position was much more consistent

73. *Èstetičeskie otnošenija iskusstva k dejstvitel'nosti* (1855), in *Polnoe sobranie sočinenij*, 2:99.
74. I am paraphrasing A. M. Skabičevskij, *Istorija novejšej russkoj literatury* (St. Petersburg, 1891), p. 64.
75. Astaxov, *Plexanov i Černyševskij*, p. 243.

and logical than that of Belinskij, Plexanov, or their contemporary Soviet followers, all of whom (as mentioned earlier) want to have their cake and eat it, too. Černyševskij's combination of a frank and thorough utilitarianism with a low evaluation of the value of art makes a great deal of sense—provided, of course, one is not interested in art as such. If art is viewed exclusively as an educational, propaganda, and information medium (rather than as an end in itself), much is to be said for Černyševskij's aesthetics.[76]

As just suggested, Černyševskij arrived at an organicist position of sorts, though it was organicism with an inverse relationship. In idealist organicism, "ordinary" life is aestheticized. In Černyševskij's materialist aesthetics, art is subjected to the norms of ordinary life. Belinskij had tried to let art grow autonomously, hoping that it would proceed in step with—or even a step ahead of—social life. Černyševskij integrated art into social life by simply letting art meet the practical demands of society.

To begin with, Černyševskij flatly rejected the doctrine which had been the pivot of all post-Kantian aesthetics, namely, the notion of the disinterestedness of true art. "The foremost and the universal purpose of all works of art," said Černyševskij, "is the reproduction of those phenomena of real life which are of interest to man" (*vosproizvedenie interesnyx dlja čeloveka javlenij dejstvitel'-noj žizni*).[77] Art, Černyševskij believed, was a kind of running commentary on life, designed largely for an audience not well enough educated to comprehend a serious and factual scientific commentary on the same subjects. Černyševskij saw no basic difference between poetry and history, though he followed Aristotle in asserting that "a learned work tells you what precisely was or is, while a work of fiction tells you how things always, or usually, lean in this world."[78]

Furthermore, Černyševskij's aesthetics is characterized by an uncompromising naturalism—again, a trait which links him to eighteenth-century thought. "An apology of reality against fantasy, an effort to prove that works of art definitely cannot stand comparison with living reality—that is the essence of this treatise," he says of his dissertation.[79] To illustrate this thesis, Černyševskij points out that any French or English crime gazette contains many more interesting and far more intricate real-life stories than any writer of fiction could possibly conceive. The most beautiful landscape painting could not possibly serve as a substitute for a real landscape. And as for human portraits, "painting at its present level of technical proficiency cannot express well either the

76. Černyševskij's famous putdown of Art: "Let Art be satisfied with its exalted and beautiful calling: to serve, in the absence of reality, as a substitute of the same, and to be for man a textbook of life" (*Èstetičeskie otnošenija*, in *Polnoe sobranie sočinenij*, 2:90).

77. Ibid., 2:86.

78. Review of *Aleksandr Sergeevič Puškin, ego žizn' i sočinenija* (1856), *Polnoe sobranie sočinenij*, 3:627.

79. *Polnoe sobranie sočinenij*, 2:89.

color of the human body in general, or the human face in particular: its colors, as compared to the natural hue of a human face and body are nothing but
a crude, wretched imitation—instead of a delicate body, the painting shows
something greenish or reddish. . . ."[80] Černyševskij's naturalism reaches a
non plus ultra when he asserts that instrumental music, being in effect a feeble
imitation of vocal music, is much inferior to the vocal. Vocal music, in turn,
is naturally a direct expression of human emotions.[81] Both of these notions
were also widely popular in the eighteenth century.

At any rate, with astounding casualness Černyševskij reduces art to a surrogate of reality and rejects the fantastic in art, *l'art pour l'art,* romantic art—in
short, everything that does not fit his naturalist conception.

Černyševskij anticipated Tolstoj's rejection of Shakespeare, and on much the
same grounds. He even anticipated Tolstoj's observation that romantic aesthetics was created *ad hoc* to fit Shakespeare's art. Consistent with his uncompromising naturalism, Černyševskij systematically debunked all "aesthetic categories" (the Beautiful, the Sublime, the Tragic), reducing them to nonaesthetic
terms. Again, he arrived at a kind of organicism in reverse, as he defined Beauty as follows: "Beauty is life; beautiful is that being in which we see life as it
ought to be according to our concepts; beautiful is that object which is expressive of life or reminiscent of life."[82] This definition almost coincides with Belinskij's, or Hegel's, for that matter. In its practical application, however, Černyševskij's definition was an absurd reversal of Hegel's conception. Honest
materialist and positivist that he was, he developed his aesthetic theory from
his empirical observations of the pleasures and satisfactions of "ordinary" and
"natural" life rather than from any observation, ideal or empirical, of either
art, concrete works of art, or the creative process as conceived by artists or
critics: "For people who have not reached your dispassionate heights, a young
housewife who, like a child, rejoices at having neatly furnished her modest
apartment, consisting of three or four rooms, is more poetic than any Venus
of either Medici or Louvre could possibly be" ("A Critical View of Contemporary Aesthetic Concepts").[83]

Černyševskij decreed that only the honest representation of the simple good
life and of things that were a part of it was truly beautiful, and he arrived at a
model of "true art" (where "beauty" equals "life") by excluding from art everything that did not satisfy his demand for "naturalness," simplicity, whole-
someness, and rational, robust realism. Like Tolstoj in *What Is Art?* Černyševskij felt obliged to reject as "nonart" or "inferior art" much of what most

80. Ibid., p. 57–58.
81. Ibid., p. 63.
82. *Èstetičeskie otnošenija,* in *Polnoe sobranie sočinenij,* 2:107.
83. "Kritičeskij vzgljad na sovremennye èstetičeskie ponjatija" (1854), *Polnoe sobranie
sočinenij,* 2:155.

educated men would consider truly great art. Without being aware of it, Černyševskij had lapsed into eighteenth-century classicist thinking, for what he postulated in lieu of the romantic conception of Beauty as the perfect fusion of
the ideal and the real in effect coincided with Batteux's "imitation of beautiful nature."

Černyševskij's objectivism led to some outright absurd positions. Seeking
to demonstrate that the artist depended entirely on objective reality and could
not depart from it with impunity, he asserted, for example, that no painter
would ever paint a tree "without atmosphere, without a piece of land on which
it grows, without a landscape a part of which it represents, without an animal
or a human figure."[84] This is an amazing factual blunder in view of Černyševskij's otherwise impressive scholarship.

In refuting the Hegelian notion that "that object is beautiful in which an idea
finds its full expression," Černyševskij brings up Gogol''s description of a mudhole in "The Tale of How Ivan Ivanovič Quarreled with Ivan Nikiforovič,"
pointing out that the idea of a mudhole has found its fullest expression in that
passage—"yet you will agree with me that it was still a foul sight to see, and
smelled even fouler."[85] Here Černyševskij completely ignores what Aristotle
and Plutarch had already taken care to point out, namely, that in art it is not
the "what" that matters, but the "how." In effect, Černyševskij's example
proves Hegel right. Hegel himself, in defending Flemish genre painting, had
said precisely that a low and ungainly subject could be elevated by the *idea* imparted to it by art. Černyševskij had completely forgotten that Gogol''s story
had an *idea,* too.

Černyševskij similarly reduced the other "aesthetic categories" to ordinary
sense experience. He defined the Sublime as simply "that which is much larger
than anything near it or similar to it," and the Tragic as something strikingly
sad or terrible. Likewise, Černyševskij rejected the whole theory of genres, seeing no inherent difference between them, except in the external circumstances
of the presentation of a work—a matter of convenience and economy, no more.

Černyševskij's naïve objectivism led him into many difficulties. He knew, of
course, that some works of art which did not at all correspond to his notion of
what true art was supposed to be like gave some people a great deal of pleasure.
Černyševskij's explanation of this fact was the one later given by Tolstoj, by
Marxist aestheticians (Plexanov, in particular), and by Soviet critics of "modernism" today. In these instances, Černyševskij believed, we are dealing with
the decadent art of an idle and parasitic upper class:

> An artificially educated man has many artificial needs, distorted to the

84. Ibid., p. 138.
85. Ibid., p. 151.

point of complete falseness and fantastic dimensions, needs which can never be completely satisfied because they are really not natural needs, but mere daydreams of a corrupt imagination; to satisfy a man's whims does not mean to meet his needs. (*Aesthetic Relations*)[86]

Without noticing it, Černyševskij has fallen from extreme objectivism into extreme subjectivism: the quality of art is now determined by a moral evaluation of its consumer.

Černyševskij's naïve view which made him assume that objective reality was both rational and relatively simple to grasp led him to the extraordinary opinion that a clever and well-educated man, possessed of the right ideas and a sufficient number of correct empirical observations could very well create worthwhile works of art. This was possible because Černyševskij, in a way which was diametrically opposed to the organicist tradition, considered "form" merely an assemblage of mechanical details of execution and a decidedly secondary criterion of artistic merit. Such separation of "content" and "form," or complete subordination of "form" to "content," had to lead to a crude didacticism and moralism in Černyševskij's practical criticism. As a corollary, it also had to lead to an equally crude formalism, whenever "form" would come up in his discussions.

Černyševskij visualized the ideal poet as a man who, being himself possessed of rational, enlightened, and noble ideas, induces other people to share his humanitarian and progressive attitudes. He found the Governor-General's concluding speech in the second part of *Dead Souls* (an unctuous moral tirade) the best part of that work. Of course, he was guided by his attitude when he wrote his own fiction. On the other hand, Černyševskij observed that "for a single [formal] virtue of some kind, people are willing to forgive a work hundreds of faults," giving Horace and Vergil as examples of poets whose total lack of any other value is forgiven on account of their "elegant language."[87] In this way, Černyševskij unwittingly reverted to a pre-Belinskian "critique of details" and outright "formalism."

However, as regards formalism, Černyševskij was inconsistent. More often than not he would stick to the Belinskian organicist position, asserting that even the most elegant form could not possibly save a work which was ideologically and factually false from being anything but shapeless and ugly. Like Belinskij—and Hegel, of course—he tended to believe that an immoral idea would destroy itself by its own falseness and, in the process, also destroy the form in which it was expressed.[88] In fact, Černyševskij often denounced eclectic

86. *Èstetičeskie otnošenija,* in *Polnoe sobranie sočinenij,* 2:73.
87. Ibid., p. 37.
88. "Zametki o žurnalax: Ijun' 1856 goda," *Polnoe sobranie sočinenij,* 3:663.

art and eclectic criticism, using the familiar organicist arguments in so
doing:

> A human body is a whole; one cannot tear it into parts and say: this part
> is beautiful, while this is ugly. Here, too, as in so many other instances,
> selectivity, a mosaic structure, eclecticism result in incongruities: either ac-
> cept all, or accept nothing—only then will you be right, at least from your
> particular point of view. (*Aesthetic Relations*)[89]

The one corollary of this organic conception which Černyševskij failed to see
was that a poor or inadequate form could very well destroy the soundest idea
—a point on which Dostoevskij insisted with great vehemence. Černyševskij
carried Belinskij's "contentualism" to its extreme consequences, namely, the
notion that a sound "content" would somehow take care of its own expression,
making "form," the proper domain of the artist, a mere luxury.

In spite of his low evaluation of art, Černyševskij was as eager as Belinskij—
or Dostoevskij, for that matter—to integrate art, and especially literature, into
the country's social life and to make it into a vehicle of progress. However,
the role which Černyševskij assigned to literature was modest, as compared
with Belinskij's confident and enthusiastic vision of Russian men of letters
leading the country toward a better future. Černyševskij, who had a good
knowledge of history and the history of world literature, assessed the social
role of art and literature more soberly than Belinskij. In his essay on Lessing,
Černyševskij stated quite explicitly that, while literature always played a certain role in the historical process, this role was nevertheless invariably a secondary one.[90] As far as Černyševskij was concerned, literature merely "filled or-
ders" which it received from society,[91] for the public's judgment was far superior to that of most literary men (poets, critics, editors). Literature, said
Černyševskij, responds to the public needs of the day. So long as it refuses to
do that, pursuing its own intrinsic goals, it will remain not only ineffectual but
also insignificant in its own terms.[92]

Černyševskij's evaluation of Russian literature before Gogol' was even lower
than Belinskij's. He assigned to Puškin the largely "historical" role of Russia's
first genuine poet, who educated the Russian public to appreciate fine poetry.

89. *Èstetičeskie otnošenija,* in *Polnoe sobranie sočinenij,* 2:57.
90. "Lessing, ego vremja, ego žizn' i dejatel'nost'," *Polnoe sobranie sočinenij,* 4:6.
91. *Očerki gogolevskogo perioda,* in *Polnoe sobranie sočinenij,* 3:306-7.
92. "Indeed, all those authors who are the pride of recent European literature are
without an exception inspired by those strivings which move the life of the epoch.
The works of Béranger, George Sand, Heine, Dickens, Thackeray are inspired by ideas
of humanity and betterment of the human lot. Meanwhile, those talents whose activity is not permeated by these strivings have either remained unknown or have acquired
a fame which is not all favorable to them, having created nothing deserving of fame"
(ibid., 3:302). Belinskij had said much the same thing.

(Belinskij had said much the same thing.) But inasmuch as most of Puškin's works had "little live connection with society, they remained fruitless for society as well as for literature."[93] One of the works so characterized in Černyševskij's Fourth essay on Puškin is "The Stone Guest," considered by many one of Puškin's finest works.

Černyševskij's notion of how literature could contribute to social progress was simple. In order to remedy the unsatisfactory condition of Russian society, one had to recognize the ills which plagued it. "The initiative for change will not come from the peasants," Černyševskij wrote in an essay, "The Beginning of Change, Perhaps?" (1861), "but still, one must know their character in order to know what stimuli must be applied to make our initiative have an effect on them."[94] In the same essay, Černyševskij demanded a straightforward and unsentimental treatment of "the people" and their problems, instead of the sentimental humanism of Gogol' 's Overcoat or Grigorovič's Village. Russian muzhiks, he said, were simply people. They should not be either idealized or vilified, but educated and helped. Černyševskij's program for Russian literature was, accordingly, one of competent, positivistic "case studies." Therefore, he approved of Nikolaj Uspenskij's bleak, naturalistic stories, defending them against attacks by počvenniki and Slavophiles (who felt that Uspenskij had failed to bring out the godly side of the Russian peasant) as well as by liberals (who found fault with Uspenskij's stark, "unaesthetic" naturalism).

Thus, Černyševskij accepted the cognitive function of art, but on entirely different terms than had been the case in Belinskij's organic conception. The writer's intuition is replaced by fact-finding, inspiration by information, and creation by reportage. In a way, Černyševskij realized Balzac's metaphoric boast that a modern writer was a doctor of the social sciences.

What Belinskij had called the "ideal" in literature (incidentally, Černyševskij often used Belinskij's terms, such as "the ideal," pafos, and "type," and in the same sense), Černyševskij would rather see made explicit than presented in quintessential symbols: "The quintessence of a thing does not usually resemble the thing itself: theine is not tea, alcohol is not wine," he wrote in The Aesthetic Relations of Art to Reality.[95] Černyševskij was frankly in favor of literature which made a point of "serving a distinct tendency of moral strivings" (služenie opredelennomu napravleniju nravstvennyx stremlenij).[96] Gogol' was, in his opinion, the first Russian writer to have done this consciously and

93. "Sočinenija Puškina: Stat'ja 4-aja," Polnoe sobranie sočinenij, 2:515.
94. "Ne načalo li peremeny?" The Contemporary, 1861, no. 11. This essay (a review of N. V. Uspenskij's Rasskazy [1861]) contains the positive program of the revolutionary trend in Russian literature. See also Polnoe sobranie sočinenij, 7:863.
95. Èstetičeskie otnošenija, in Polnoe sobranie sočinenij, 2:65.
96. Očerki gogolevskogo perioda, in Polnoe sobranie sočinenij, 3:19–22, 136–38.

consistently. He was, in Černyševskij's opinion, the father not only of Russian prose, but also of the "critical tendency" (*kritičeskoe napravlenie*) in Russian literature.[97] To Černyševskij, as to Belinskij, Gogol' was Russia's "social poet" par excellence:

> No other Russian writer has expressed an awareness of his patriotic signifi-
> cance (*soznanie svoego patriotičeskogo značenija*) as vividly and clearly as Go-
> gol'. He straightforwardly considered himself a man called upon to serve not
> art, but his country, thinking of himself: "I am not a poet, I am a citizen!"[98]

Černyševskij approved of Gogol' even more wholeheartedly than did Belin-skij. He had words of the highest praise for the extant sections of the second part of *Dead Souls*. As Andrej Belyj once put it: "Belinskij had chastised Go-gol', Černyševskij rehabilitated him."[99] In fact, Černyševskij quite unreserved-ly placed Gogol' above Puškin.

The discussion thus far shows that Černyševskij carried Belinskij's cautious deviations from a Hegelian organicist aesthetics to bold extremes. This pattern emerges most clearly in Černyševskij's version of historicism. Since Černyševskij believes in absolute historical progress and that the value of the work of art de-pends solely on its relevance to contemporary interests and to progress, this value is inevitably bound to decrease with the passage of time. The greatest po-ets of the past are "of historical importance only" (one of Černyševskij's favorite phrases).

Černyševskij was convinced that the literature and criticism of the future would far outstrip those of his own age, that a period would come, presumably soon, "when everything that has existed or exists now in Russian literature, even including Belinskij's criticism, will appear unsatisfactory."[100] Often Čer-nyševskij voices judgments which give evidence of a thoroughgoing aesthetic relativism. For example, he will call Gogol''s "Hans Küchelgarten" a poem which was "very weak even for that age." The poem appeared in 1829, when Russian poetry was at a peak it was never to reach again. Or he will compare the critic Polevoj (with whose ideas he disagreed) to a doctor who has not been following the progress of medicine and keeps prescribing pills in the efficacy of which no one believes any more.[101]

To summarize, Černyševskij's aesthetics constituted, by and large, a relapse into some of the shallowest notions prevalent in the eighteenth century, the most fateful of which was probably his failure to distinguish "art" from "pleasure," on the one hand, and from "enlightenment," on the other. As a

97. Ibid., p. 19.
98. Ibid., p. 137.
99. Belyj, *Masterstvo Gogolja*, p. 37.
100. *Očerki gogolevskogo perioda*, in *Polnoe sobranie sočinenij*, 3:277.
101. Ibid., pp. 41–42.

result of this notion, artists, critics, and all those who enjoyed art become either epicureans, hypocrites, and idlers (fiddling while Rome burned, hiding their selfish interests behind allegedly "disinterested" art, and wasting their time amusing themselves), or enlighteners, moralists, and socially "concerned" altruists. There could be nothing in between. Likewise, Černyševskij conceived of works of contemporary literature as either useful analytic descriptions of objective reality, or useless, even harmful, exercises in frivolity, nebulous mysticism, and idle daydreams. Again, there was nothing in between.

Černyševskij's aesthetics involves an honest, straightforward, and eloquent treatment of art by an otherwise educated man who completely lacks aesthetic sense. Černyševskij was acquainted with a considerable volume of Russian and world literature. He correctly observed many important things about it— except the "art" in it. His judgments of some of the world's great poets, artists, and composers are veritable examples of Tolstoian *ostranenie* ("making it strange" by viewing an object naïvely, through the eyes of a man who lacks the conventional frame of reference for it): Homer is incoherent, offends by his cynicism, and lacks all moral feeling, Beethoven is incomprehensible and wild, Mozart's *Don Giovanni* is boring. Quite inevitably, Černyševskij's aesthetics is attractive to critics who share his handicap, critics who, like Černyševskij, deal with literature professionally, but lack the gift to either appreciate or understand it as "art." There have been many such critics in Russia, and there still are.

The attitude of Marxist critics toward Černyševskij's aesthetics has been ambivalent, both in and outside Russia. On the one hand, the democratism and materialism of Černyševskij's aesthetic theory is seen as a step forward. But on the other, his failure to develop any further, or even to retain, the elements of a historicist and dialectic approach found in Belinskij are recognized as a step backward.[102] Also, Černyševskij's crude naturalism is criticized, usually with a reference to Lenin's dictum that "human consciousness not only reflects reality, but is also capable of going beyond its limits."[103]

Dobroljubov

N. A. Dobroljubov (1836–1861) is next in importance to Pisarev as the most talented and influential practicing critic who applied Černyševskij's principles to the Russian literature of his age. Dobroljubov's aesthetics ostensibly coincided with Černyševskij's. However, he was a genuine critic, not without some poetic talent and with more aesthetic sense than he would himself admit. Whenever he made aesthetic comments on the works under discussion in his articles,

102. For a detailed critique of Černyševskij from a Marxist point of view, see Lukács, "Ästhetik Tschernyschewskijs," *Geschichte der Ästhetik,* pp. 135–90.
103. Cf. P. L. Ivanov, *O suščnosti krasoty,* p. 197.

they were often sound and perceptive. Dobroljubov's literary essays (really "sermons," for which works of Russian literature served as texts, as D. S. Mirsky put it) bear a strong resemblance to Belinskij's. Needless to say, Dobroljubov's love and admiration for Belinskij were great. Ordinarily austere and reserved in his judgment, he becomes unreservedly enthusiastic and unabashedly lyrical when he greets the appearance of *The Works of V. Belinskij* (1859).

Dobroljubov shared Černyševskij's optimistic anthropology. If anything, his faith in the rational and altruistic qualities of "natural man," unspoiled by society, was even stronger than Černyševskij's. The many ills of Russian life he saw entirely in terms of the "abnormal relations" (*nenormal'nye otnošenija*) established by a perverted social order, as, for example, Dobroljubov's famous statement about crime:

> He committed his crimes without any difficult or extended struggle with himself, but simply "so," accidentally, without being himself quite aware of what he was doing. . . . Whence comes such a phenomenon? It comes from the fact that every crime, rather than being a consequence of human nature (*sledstvie natury čeloveka*), is in fact a consequence of those abnormal conditions into which he has been placed with regard to society. And, the stronger this abnormality, the more often crimes will be committed, even by naturally decent individuals. ("A Kingdom of Darkness")[104]

It is this statement that Razumixin combats in Chapter 5 of Part 3 of *Crime and Punishment* (the scene at Porfirij Petrovič's flat).

Dobroljubov was as much of a fanatic of "enlightenment" as Černyševskij. Černyševskij had blamed Gogol''s ultimate failure to complete his life's work on the fact that Gogol', like all "half-educated" men, had no conscious conception of the world around him and could only go as far as his sound instincts took him. Dobroljubov used the same approach to Puškin (toward whom he was more disrespectful than Černyševskij, although not quite as disrespectful as Pisarev): "The direction taken by Puškin during his last years did not at all develop from the natural urgings of his soul, but was merely a consequence of his weakness of character, which lacked the inner support of serious convictions, independently developed."[105]

To Dubroljubov, the fact (doubted by no one by then) that Puškin had been a great poet was insignificant compared with the fact that he had done little to promote the causes of social and scientific progress in Russia. Time and again, Dobroljubov stressed that the aesthetic aspect of contemporary literature was

---

104. N. A. Dobroljubov, "Temnoe carstvo" (1859), *Sobranie sočinenij,* 9 vols. (Moscow and Leningrad, 1961–64), 5:46–47.

105. Review of *Sočinenija Puškina* (1857), *Sobranie sočinenij,* 2:174.

of secondary importance and that what really mattered was its social mission: "Aesthetic criticism has now become the domain of sentimental young ladies," he remarked in the introductory paragraph of his famous review of Turgenev's novel *On the Eve,* "When Will There Really Be Day?" (1860).

Like Černyševskij, Dobroljubov is often guilty of flagrant aesthetic intellectualism, as he assumes that a knowledge of the "correct facts" and possession of the "right ideas" can seriously help an artist:

> The free transformation of the highest intellections into living symbols . . . is an ideal which would mean the complete fusion of science and poetry and which no one has as yet attained. But an artist who, in his general concepts, is guided by the right principles still has an advantage over an uneducated or falsely educated writer, in that he can follow more freely the urgings of his artistic nature. His immediate feeling will always point out things to him correctly. But if the writer's general concepts are false, an inner struggle, doubts, and indecision will inevitably occur in his mind, and even if his work will not prove to be completely false as a result of this, it will still be weak, colorless, and misshapen.[106]

And, quite concretely, Dobroljubov will give preference to a work which is "true to reality," though aesthetically imperfect, over a work which is aesthetically perfect, yet distorts life and the meaning of life ("The Stories and Short Stories of S. T. Slavutinskij").[107] Dobroljubov is quite unaware of the "formalism" which is implied in this assumption.

Dobroljubov's conception of "correct ideas" and "right convictions" as the fruits of a "sound education" involves materialism, positivism, and scientism unchecked by any traditionalist, teleological, or idealist "superstitions." His view of the heritage of Byzantine and Muscovite Russia is aggressively negative. He explicitly rejects all teleological thinking, making fun of people who think that the eye was miraculously made by God so that man could see, or that the Volga flowed toward the Caspian Sea because it had a striving for it. And he exclaims: "The time has come to free life from the oppressive tutelage imposed on it by the ideologues!" ("On the Degree of *narodnost'* in Russian Literature").[108]

Dobroljubov's version of social organicism is simple and straightforward: Literature is to serve society and specifically social progress (by which he means "the revolution," although he cannot say it, of course). Also, he believes—and here he inadvertently lapses into teleological thinking—that Russian literature, as a body, will devote itself freely and enthusiastically to this cause, "considering

---

106. "Temnoe carstvo," *Sobranie sočinenij,* 5:24.
107. "Povesti i rasskazy S. T. Slavutinskogo" (1860), *Sobranie sočinenij,* 6:63.
108. "O stepeni učastija narodnosti v razvitii russkoj literatury" (1858), technically a review of A. Miljukov's *Očerk istorii russkoj poèzii* (1858), *Sobranie sočinenij,* 2:222.

service to the cause of social improvement its most sacred calling."[109] Nevertheless, Dobroljubov has a more thoughtful view of what literature can do for society than Černyševskij and most of the other Nihilists. To be sure, exposing social ills and extolling all that is good and noble are still literature's main tasks, he thinks. And accordingly, he believes that it is the principal task of literary criticism "to explain those phenomena of reality which have called forth certain works of art" ("When Will There Really Be Day?").[110] In other words, he wants the literary critic to discuss social problems as reflected in works of art—which is what he practices himself.

In so doing, Dobroljubov is not ignoring his opponents' charge that he is not discussing works of literature; he is merely using these works as occasions for his extra-literary observations. He counters it by pointing out that the authors whose works he discusses—Turgenev, in particular—actually invite this kind of criticism, for they are obviously intent upon making their works true mirrors of Russian life and expressing definite views on its problems and its progress.

To be sure, Dobroljubov, like Černyševskij, favors an uncompromising naturalism in art: "Is it not a fact that man is incapable of inventing as much as a grain of sand which was not already in existence in this world? Good or bad— all is equally taken from nature and from the reality of life."[111]

But then, Dobroljubov places a higher evaluation on the artist's contribution than Černyševskij did, and he gives it a much more specific content. To begin with, he observes that the artist can choose important and interesting subjects, rather than trivial and boring ones, like the proverbial roses and nightingales. Moreover, the artist can also see the reality of life truthfully, clearly, and broadly—or less so, or not at all. Here, Dobroljubov reverts to a Belinskian position, granting the artist a measure of cognitive power: Art can grasp intuitively what science learns analytically. Having made the shrewd observation that outside literature there is little opportunity to see people and society as they really are, since in virtually all of our contacts we meet people only in their "official" functions, Dobroljubov goes on to say:

> An artist-writer, even if he does not care about making any general conclusions regarding the conditions of public opinion and morality, always knows how to capture their essential traits, how to illuminate them brightly, and how to place them directly before the eyes of thinking people. . . . Here, then, a writer's talent will be measured by how broad a grasp he has of life, and by how solid and inclusive the symbols (*obrazy*) are which he has created.[112]

109. Review of Saltykov-Ščedrin's *Gubernskie očerki* (1857), *Sobranie sočinenij*, 2:124.
110. "Kogda že pridet nastojaščij den'?" (1860), *Sobranie sočinenij*, 6:99.
111. Review of *Gubernskie očerki*, in *Sobranie sočinenij*, 2:142.
112. "Kogda že pridet nastojaščij den'?" *Sobranie sočinenij*, 6:98.

The principal power of a talented writer lies, then, in his ability to create "types" which help an intelligent reader to recognize important facts of social life and of social change: "Sometimes these very symbols will lead a thinking man to the formulation of a correct conception regarding certain phenomena of real life."[113] Gončarov's Oblomov is precisely such a "type." The story of Oblomov's sorry failure in life is a trivial one as such, says Dobroljubov, but it is a perfect reflection of an important aspect of Russian life which, Dobroljubov adds prophetically, will henceforth be called "oblomovitis" (*oblomovščina*). The word, in turn, will serve as a key to the understanding of many phenomena of Russian life. And so, the appearance of Gončarov's novel is an event of social import.

Eventually, Dobroljubov develops a conception of the social role of literature which can be called "dialectic." In an essay, "Loyalty and Activity" (1860), which deals with the contemporary Russian short story, he formulates a theory which is far more specific than anything that Belinskij had had to say about *social'nost'* and which comes close to the ideal of Soviet literature in Socialist Realist aesthetics. He points out that works of fiction can play a useful role in accelerating and intensifying society's conscious work at effecting certain necessary social changes. The more artistic plenitude and power is found in a work, the more effective it will be as a catalyst of such change.[114]

Černyševskij had assigned an ancillary (*služebnyj*) historical role to literature, though he, too, had believed in its partial effectiveness as an instrument of social change, specifically in Russia. Dobroljubov does not accede to this without a reservation. There have been, he says, in the history of world literature, some geniuses, such as Shakespeare, whose gifts were so great that they could intuitively grasp and vividly express great truths which philosophers could merely guess at in their theories. Such geniuses were able "to rise above the ancillary role of literature and join the ranks of active historical personages who helped mankind to grasp more clearly its own living powers and natural strivings" ("A Ray of Light in the Kingdom of Darkness").[115] This is a return to a Belinskian, that is, Hegelian, position.

When it came to evaluating concrete examples of socially active literature in his own time, Dobroljubov did badly. The populist mystique of his age had a much stronger hold on him than on Belinskij. Also, his emotional involvement in the cause of the revolution, which by this time was beginning to shape up as a political reality, made him susceptible to overestimating works which he found ideologically congenial. Thus, unlike Belinskij, who almost always

113. "Temnoe carstvo," *Sobranie sočinenij*, 5:23.
114. A. I. Herzen, in his essay "Ešče raz Bazarov" (1868), develops the notion of the dialectic interaction of literary types and trends in "real life" quite consciously and in some detail. Bazarov is his example; Goethe's Werther is another.
115. "Luč sveta v temnom carstve" (1860), *Sobranie sočinenij*, 6:309.

retained his critical sense, Dobroljubov spent a good deal of time pointing out the merits of some third-rate works. For example, he wholeheartedly defended Marko Vovčok's[116] populist peasant stories, and specifically one of her characters, a freedom-loving peasant woman named Maša, against the anticipated charge (Dobroljubov had enough aesthetic sense to realize that something was wrong with these stories: the charges were actually raised by Dostoevskij and Družinin) that these peasants, and especially Maša, were idealized, abstract, manufactured, and completely untrue to life. Dobroljubov admitted that the form which Maša's love of freedom and resentment of serfdom took in Marko Vovčok's story might indeed be exceptional, but not the basic idea, or content, he felt. Dobroljubov was strongly convinced that what was obviously the projection of a Russian intellectual's (and thus, his own) feelings upon idealized peasant characters was, in fact, an objective reflection of Russian reality. In the end, he asserts that Marko Vovčok's tales "are true to Russian reality, touch upon extremely important aspects of popular life," and that in them "one meets, in spite of their easy touch, traits which reveal the hand of a skillful master as well as profound, serious study of the subject matter."[117] Of course, Dobroljubov was wrong, and Dostoevskij, who exposed Marko Vovčok's stories as the sentimental fabrications which they were, was right—as a literary critic. However, Dobroljubov was right in another sense: the sentiments expressed by Marko Vovčok and innumerable other populist writers of that period ultimately seeped through to the people, and literature—inferior literature, for the most part—had a hand in it. *Uncle Tom's Cabin* was not a good novel, but as a historical and social event it outweighed some great novels. The same happened in Russia.

A characteristic antinomy vitiated Dobroljubov's thinking regarding "the people." On the one hand, he agreed with Belinskij that the life of the plain Russian people was "ahistorical" in the sense that it was governed not by any rational ideas, but rather by the merest accidents of trivial everyday living. But on the other hand, Dobroljubov approved of a literature which was ideologically oriented and expressed "the natural strivings of the people" (*estestvennye stremlenija naroda*).[118] In fact, his essay "On the Degree of *narodnost'* in Russian Literature" (1858) presents a sketch of the history of all Russian literature from the organicist and historicist viewpoint of its growing identification with the "actual" interests of the Russian people as a whole rather than with those of a small segment of it. Thus, the teleological principle enters Dobroljubov's aesthetic theory through a back door, as it were, clothed in the assumption that, somehow, the literature of every age will meet the needs of its epoch:

116. Pseudonym of Mar'ja Aleksandrovna Markovič (1834–1907).
117. "Čerty dlja xarakteristiki russkogo prostonarod'ja," *Sobranie sočinenij,* 6:240–41.
118. Ibid., pp. 286–87.

In their own day, not only Puškin and Lermontov but even Karamzin and Deržavin were useful to our society. If a poet with that very same content as Puškin were to appear today, we would not pay any attention to him; Lermontov—but even he is not what we need now. . . . But so long as no poet of comparable talent has appeared, we pay careful attention to everything which reveals a healthy living content, even though it be without particular power or talent. ("The Poetry of Ivan Nikitin")[119]

The inner contradictions which had first developed in Belinskij's critical thought are thus dramatically enhanced in Dobroljubov's criticism. The conflict is between Dobroljubov the positivist and Dobroljubov the populist and revolutionary optimist. The positivist prevails when Dobroljubov discusses the objective—largely negative—phenomena of Russian life, the optimist when his mystic faith in the Russian people and Russia's bright future comes to the fore. Though Dobroljubov's revolutionary ideal is ostensibly a rational and presumably a realizable one, it is no less an abstract ideal than Dostoevskij's "spiritual regeneration." And if Dobroljubov believes that this ideal ("the natural strivings of the Russian people") is and ought to be expressed by Russian literature, he is, in effect, postulating a "realism in a higher sense" no less than his idealist predecessors and opponents. Thus, after all, Dobroljubov ends with an art which is a fusion of the "ideal" and the "real."

Dobroljubov's real differences with the *počvenniki* are political and ideological, not aesthetic or literary. Dobroljubov believes in creative intuition. Like Belinskij, he often speaks of "artistic instinct." His conception of the creative process clearly coincides with Belinskij's, being essentially that of an "inner vision" transforming the impressions of objective reality into an organic whole:

[The artist must] create an artistic whole . . . give solid, typical life to the personages whom he presents. . . . To accomplish this, he needs a great deal more than only knowledge and a sure eye as well as narrative talent: He needs not only to know, but to have himself deeply and strongly refelt, relived that life; he needs to feel a strong living bond with these people; he needs to have thought with their heads, to have wished with their will; he must slip into their skin and into their soul. To do all this, a man who has not himself actually emerged from this milieu must possess a very substantial gift—a gift which belongs to artistic natures, a gift which cannot be replaced by any kind of knowledge. ("The Stories of Slavutinskij")[120]

Dobroljubov believes that "artistic instinct" (or "artistic sense") will guard even an ideologically biased author against presenting an untruth. For example,

119. "Stixotvorenija Ivana Nikitina" (1860), *Sobranie sočinenij*, 6:168.
120. "Povesti Slavutinskogo," *Sobranie sočinenij*, 6:55.

Dobroljubov points out, Ostrovskij certainly sympathizes with all the beautiful ideas expressed by Žadov, a character in his play *A Profitable Job* (*Doxodnoe mesto*). Yet his artistic instinct tells him that to make Žadov *do* these things (rather than just *say* them) would mean to distort actual Russian reality; "Here the demands of artistic truth stopped Ostrovskij from being carried away by an extraneous tendency and helped him to avoid the path taken by Messrs. Sollogub and L'vov."[121] By the same token, Dobroljubov is inclined to dismiss as "artistically untrue" a work such as Pisemskij's famous novel *One Thousand Souls* (1858) by stating that "the whole social aspect of that novel was forcibly hitched to a preconceived idea."[122]

Very definitely, too, Dobroljubov is a believer in the reality and importance of the creative imagination and its product, the poetic image. He uses the terms *obraz* ("image," "form," "symbol") and *izobraženie* ("image," "representation") in exactly the same meaning as Belinskij or Grigor'ev:

> If a man knows how to foster in his soul the image (*obraz*) of an object and eventually to present it vividly and fully, this means that he possesses both alert impressionability and depth of feeling. . . . He can, so it would seem, stop life in its tracks and crystallize, stand permanently before us even its most fleeting moment, so that we might look at it forever and ever, learning from it and enjoying it. ("What Is Oblomovitis?")[123]

Furthermore, Dobroljubov draws a strict line between impression and expression: "What is important for us is not so much what the author *wanted* to say, as what *was actually said* by him, even though this may have happened unintentionally, simply as a result of a truthful reproduction of the facts of life."[124] We met this particular conception in Belinskij. It is also met frequently in contemporary Soviet criticism. Balzac, the *légitimiste*, who, his political conservatism notwithstanding, exposed the ills of French post-Restoration society, is often cited as an example. Such understanding is tantamount to a recognition of "unconscious" creation and an admission of the notion, so important in romantic thought, that the work of art can outgrow and overwhelm its creator. Certainly, a positivist such as Dobroljubov will simply say that the truth of life surmounted the author's personal bias, while a mystic will assert that the "inner vision" of an inspired artist, being God-given, could not possibly be false. But the substance of the conception is the same in both instances, namely, that an organic bond, which is to some extent independent of the artist's conscious control, exists between "objective truth" and "poetic truth."

121. "Temnoe carstvo," *Sobranie sočinenij*, 5:26.
122. "Kogda že pridet nastojaščij den'?" *Sobranie sočinenij*, 6:98.
123. "Čto takoe oblomovščina?" (1859), *Sobranie sočinenij*, 4:313.
124. "Kogda že pridet nastojaščij den'?" *Sobranie sočinenij*, 6:97.

Dobroljubov believes in "talent" and "genius," using both terms in exactly
the same sense as Belinskij or Grigor'ev. "Talent" is essentially "power":

Talent is a property of human nature, and for this reason it undoubtedly
guarantees the presence of a certain power (*sila*) and breadth of natural strivings in the individual whom we recognize as having talent. Consequently,
his creations, too, must be created under the influence of these natural, regular needs of nature; his consciousness must be clear and vivid, his ideal simple and rational, nor will he ever consent to serve an untruth or nonsense—
not because he would not want to do it, but simply because he could not do
it, even if he would decide to do violence to his talent. ("A Ray of Light")[125]

Thus, Dobroljubov fully shares Belinskij's—and Grigor'ev's as well as Dostoevskij's—belief in artistic "talent" (not to speak of "genius") as a reliable safeguard against the creation of "false" works and a sure guide to the "truth of
life." Yet with a virtually identical aesthetic theory, Dobroljubov, on the one
side, and Dostoevskij, on the other, arrive at diametrically opposed evaluations
of "objective reality" and its representations in contemporary works of art.
When Dobroljubov says that "poetry has to do with life, with living human activity, with man's eternal struggle and eternal striving for harmony with himself and with nature,"[126] he repeats what Belinskij and Grigor'ev had said before him. But when it comes to pointing out the nature and the cause of the
dissonance which poetry expresses and seeks to resolve, Dobroljubov completely disagrees with his idealist opponents: while they see it in "the dualistic organization of the human creature" (*v dualističeskom ustrojstve čelovečeskogo
suščestva*),[127] Dobroljubov presupposes that the roots of this eternal conflict
and alienation are social and economic.

With the same confidence with which Dostoevskij proclaims that true art will
inevitably lead man to a metaphysical view of life, Dobroljubov asserts the contrary. Dobroljubov, like Belinskij before him and his opponent Dostoevskij,
rejects the notion that the artist be a mere copyist of nature. As he upbraids
Dostoevskij for having let the pure, noble, and strong-willed Nataša fall in love
with the weak and worthless Aleša Valkovskij (in *The Insulted and Injured*),
he uses precisely the same organicist arguments as found in Grigor'ev's or
Dostoevskij's attacks on populist fiction:

But we know, of course, that the artist is not a photographic plate which
reflects only the present moment: if it were otherwise, there would be neither
life nor sense in works of art. With his own artistic sense, the artist supple-
ments the fragmentariness of a moment captured; in his soul, he generalizes
particular phenomena; from uncoordinated traits he creates an organized whole;

125. "Luč sveta v temnom carstve," *Sobranie sočinenij,* 6:313.
126. "Stixotvorenija Ivana Nikitina," *Sobranie sočinenij,* 6:176.
127. Ibid.

he finds a living tie and consistency between seemingly disconnected phenomena; the varied and contradictory aspects of living reality he fuses and transforms into the universals of his world view. Therefore, a true artist, as he creates his work, carries it in his soul, whole and complete, from beginning to end, with all its hidden springs and concealed corollaries, which are often incomprehensible to logical reasoning, yet reveal themselves to the artist's inspired gaze. ("Downtrodden People")[128]

Dobroljubov's point is clear: while the romance between Nataša Ixmenev and young Valkovskij could very well happen in real life, as an isolated case, it is not "typical," not revealing of the universal truth of life. Dostoevskij strongly believed that the contrary was the case, for he insisted on presenting essentially the same "mismatch" over and over again. The argument between Dobroljubov and Dostoevskij obviously has to do with philosophical anthropology, not with aesthetic theory. To Dobroljubov, man is essentially a rational being with a natural striving toward the Good, the True, and the Beautiful. Dostoevskij's image of man is dualistic: man is inherently rational and irrational, good and evil, he "naturally" strives toward the True and the Beautiful, but equally so toward the Lie and toward the Perverse. But both Dobroljubov and Dostoevskij believe that "true art" is necessarily a faithful reflection of the human condition as they conceive of it.

Dobroljubov's real enemies, as far as aesthetic theory and literary criticism are concerned, are Kant, subjective idealism, and formalism. In essence, he has no real argument with Grigor'ev or Dostoevskij—not as far as aesthetic theory is concerned. Of course, neither he nor Dostoevskij realized this, as they both projected their political differences into the aesthetic sphere. In summary, Dobroljubov's criticism is largely organicist, though with exceedingly strong emphasis on "social organicism."

Pisarev

Among the Nihilist critics, D. I. Pisarev (1840–1868) was by far the most talented. His theoretical position is one of singular clarity and consistency. Pisarev saw the antinomies in the aesthetic theories of his predecessors and sought to resolve them. In the process, he arrived at an explicit rejection of the organic tradition started by Belinskij. In his polemic essays on "Puškin and Belinskij," he cleverly debunked Belinskij's efforts "to see something organic and necessary in every versified prank of a Batjuškov, Žukovskij, or Puškin," and to give a deep historical meaning to sundry trivialities of life simply because they had been correctly captured in literature.

Even though he destroyed Belinskij's most cherished positions, Pisarev insisted

128. "Zabitye ljudi" (1861), *Sobranie sočinenij*, 7:233–34.

that he did so "not to mock the sacred memory of our great teacher Belinskij, but to show to the reader how very dangerous and fatal an involvement with things aesthetic can become even to the strongest and most remarkable minds."[129]

In his brilliant essay "The Abolition of Aesthetics," Pisarev drew some correct conclusions from Černyševskij's *Aesthetic Relations of Art to Reality:* the science of aesthetics, he said, had a *raison d'être* only if the concept of Beauty had any meaning at all that was independent of the infinite variety of individual tastes.[130] Černyševskij had proved to Pisarev's satisfaction that this was not the case. Therefore, the whole science of aesthetics had been rendered superfluous.

Pisarev raised the question of the priority of values in connection with art and literature (a question raised in our own day by I. A. Richards, among others) and, puritan that he was, decided that moral and intellectual values were to be placed high above aesthetic values. The right to pass ultimate judgment on any serious work of literature should belong not to those who were inclined—and competent—to judge its form, but to "thinking men who would judge its content, that is, judge it by [its relationship to] the phenomena of life."[131] Pisarev then decided that much of Russian literature, past and present, has aesthetic value only. He gladly ceded these works to his opponents of the so-called school of "pure art" which was then upholding the Puškinian tradition in Russian literature. They were, of course, hopeless and contemptible sensualists, as far as Pisarev was concerned.

Not surprisingly, Pisarev had a low opinion of Puškin—essentially on the same moral grounds that Tolstoj would later have in *What Is Art?* Pisarev also demonstrated, very deftly, how Belinskij, having implicitly condemned Puškin's aestheticism, had still avoided drawing the logical conclusion from Puškin's cycle "on the poet": that most, if not all, of Puškin's poetry was purely "imaginary," that it had none but aesthetic value, and that its relevance to the reality of Russian life was negligible.

Somewhat more surprisingly, Pisarev found Dobroljubov guilty of the same error which, in his opinion, had vitiated much of Belinskij's criticism: in Pisarev's opinion, Dobroljubov, too, construes "organic" ties between works of Russian literature and Russian life where there simply are none objectively. For example, in his essay "A Ray of Light in the Kingdom of Darkness," Dobroljubov had asserted that the rebellion of Katerina, heroine of Ostrovskij's drama *The Thunderstorm,* was symbolic of the imminent breakup of "the kingdom of darkness" of Russian backwardness, barbarity, and superstition. Pisarev

129. D. I. Pisarev, "Puškin i Belinskij," *Sočinenija,* 4 vols. (Moscow, 1955–56), 3:400.
130. "Razrušenie èstetiki" (1865), *Sočinenija,* 3:432.
131. Ibid., p. 434.

disagrees with his optimistic interpretation. He finds Katerina quite "untypical" in the first place. That this adulteress and suicide be a positive character, as Dobroljubov had asserted, he finds questionable. And besides, her "rebellion" is purely personal and has nothing to do with any breakup of "the kingdom of darkness." And all together, Pisarev refuses to see any "ray of light" in it.[132]

Still more surprisingly, Pisarev found that even the satirical works of Saltykov-Ščedrin were of rather dubious extra-aesthetic value. In an article devoted to Saltykov-Ščedrin, "Flowers of Innocent Humor" (1864), Pisarev exclaims:

> Yes, Ščedrin, the leader of our exposé literature (*obličitel'naja literatura*) can be called quite justifiably a perfectly pure exponent of our latest version of pure art. Ščedrin does not subject his writings either to a cherished idea or to the voice of wrought-up emotion; nor does he ask, as he seizes his pen, whom his accusing arrow will hit—friend or foe, "titular councilor or nihilist." . . . Ščedrin's pointless and aimless laughter, as such, is as useless to our social consciousness as Fet's pointless and aimless cooing. ("Flowers of Innocent Humor")[133]

Pisarev, like Černyševskij before him, took an uncompromisingly utilitarian view of art. His position was sounder than Černyševskij's, however. Unlike Černyševskij, Pisarev was a man of brilliant literary talent and keen aesthetic sense. He knew very well that a work of art could have aesthetic value quite regardless of its merits before society. In fact, he arrived at the conclusion that most works of art that he knew were of aesthetic value only. Like Černyševskij, Pisarev was more interested in economics, education, and politics than in art. Accordingly, he held aesthetic values in low esteem and considered it a waste of time to discuss aesthetic problems. Therefore, he was perfectly willing to leave the "aesthetes" alone and let them indulge in their childish games. In his essay "The Realists" (1864), Pisarev thus defined his position:

> It is precisely the presence of a higher guiding idea in the mind of a consistent realist and the absence of such an idea in the aesthete's mind that make up the difference between these two groups of people. What is this idea? It is the idea of the common weal or of universal human solidarity. Like all people . . . both aesthetes and realists are perfect egoists. But the egoism of an aesthete resembles the senseless egoism of a child who is ready any

132. "Motivy russkoj dramy" (1864), *Sočinenija*, 2:366–71.
133. "Cvety nevinnogo jumora" (1864), *Sočinenija*, 2:340. I. I. Ivanov suggests that Saltykov-Ščedrin as late as the 1860s was still looking for an ideology, without having settled on any one tendency in particular, and therefore attacked left, right, and center quite indiscriminately. See I. I. Ivanov, *Istorija russkoj kritiki*, 4 vols. (St. Petersburg, 1898–1900), 4:668–69. Dostoevskij made the same point in his polemic sketch "Otryvok is romana *Ščedrodarov*" (1864).

moment to stuff himself with the cheapest candy or honey cake. Meanwhile, a realist's egoism is the conscious . . . egoism of a mature person who provides himself with a supply of ever-fresh delight for his whole life.[134]

Pisarev thus wholly rejected Belinskij's aesthetic organicism. His utilitarian view of art left the door wide open to sensualist or Kantian subjective-idealist "aesthetic criticism," untrammeled by any sociohistorical or moral determinism. By relinquishing much of art and literature as "socially irrelevant," Pisarev really invited the aesthetes to claim it as their sole possession. No wonder, then, that Pisarev found more implacable enemies in the left-wing followers of a Hegelian "organic" aesthetics, such as Plexanov, than in right-wing believers in the autonomy of art. Dostoevskij rather liked Pisarev, in spite of Pisarev's radical "nihilism." With his unerring intuition, Dostoevskij must have sensed that Pisarev was really a friend of Art in disguise. Needless to say, "official" Soviet opinion of Pisarev has been consistently negative.

Saltykov-Ščedrin

Among all of Belinskij's followers in nineteenth-century Russian literature, M. E. Saltykov-Ščedrin (1826–1889) was probably the one whose conception of literature and its relationship to society came closest to an orthodox Socialist Realist position—so much so that M. S. Gorjačkina, a contemporary Soviet scholar, is actually apologetic about his "didactic tendencies" (*prosvetitel'skie tendencii*).[135] It is no accident that Saltykov-Ščedrin, himself a great satirist, agrees with Socialist-Realist critics regarding the position of satire: he does not for a moment consider excluding it from the domain of art. Belinskij, it must be remembered, had refused satire a place in "art."

Saltykov-Ščedrin liked to quote Fet's famous lines, "I am not even aware that I shall soon begin to sing, yet already my song is maturing within me" (*I ne znaju ja, čto budu / Pet', no tol'ko pesnja zreet*) as an example of what art should *not* be like. He asked for conscious, rational, goal-directed, utilitarian, social art. He strongly emphasized the importance of a correct ideology.

In a review of a volume of verse by Ja. P. Polonskij (*Snopy,* 1871), Saltykov-Ščedrin wrote: "We assert that the lack of a clear world view (*nejasnost' mirosozercanija*) is so important a fault that it will reduce to naught an artist's entire creative activity."[136] Saltykov-Ščedrin preferred frankly tendentious works, considering ambiguity, "objectivity," and indistinctness to be dangerous, because these traits would cloud the issues, confuse the uninitiated, and distract

134. "Realisty" (1864), *Sočinenija,* 3:63.
135. M. S. Gorjačkina, "Saltykov-Ščedrin–kritik," in Gorodeckij et al., eds., *Istorija russkoj kritiki,* 2:149.
136. N. Ščedrin (M. E. Saltykov), *Polnoe sobranie sočinenij,* 20 vols. (Moscow and Leningrad, 1933–41), 8:423.

people from the straight and narrow path of progress. He lumped the views of his various opponents under the label "street philosophy" (*uličnaja filosofija*). In an article of that title (1869), he counts Gončarov, Pisemskij, Leskov, and Dostoevskij among the many writers whose genuine talent was ruined by a faulty or confused ideology.[137]

Saltykov-Ščedrin also resolutely rejected Zola's naturalism, mainly on the grounds that its ostensible objectivity left it without any ideological basis or direction. Very much an "organicist" in this respect, Saltykov-Ščedrin insisted that only a clearly and consciously conceived idea could give a work of art organic unity and a "life-giving spirit" (*životvorjaščij dux*). As for the "idea," he did not mind at all if it was called a "preconceived tendency" by those who were opposed to it, so long as it was "the right idea." Saltykov-Ščedrin all but actually uses Lenin's term *partijnost'* when he writes: "Literature and propaganda are one and the same thing. Though this is an old truth, it has to this day entered the consciousness of literature so little that it is not at all superfluous to repeat it here."[138]

Of course, Saltykov-Ščedrin takes for granted that the "propaganda" which he identifies with "art" is based on a "correct" ideology. To put it bluntly, propaganda serving the radical cause—which Saltykov-Ščedrin naturally sees as the cause of "humane strivings," liberty, and progress—may very well be "art," while propaganda serving the opposition, vitiated by "incorrect" ideas, inevitably becomes nonart or inferior art. Incidentally, Saltykov-Ščedrin felt this way not only with regard to outright "reactionaries," but also with regard to populist writers such as Gleb Uspenskij, whose faith in the "native socialism" of the Russian peasantry he considered to be "a Utopia" and positively harmful, politically as well as artistically.

As for *l'art pour l'art,* or any other kind of allegedly "objective" art, Saltykov-Ščedrin saw it as a mere diversionary maneuver on the part of reactionaries who were seeking to throttle the efforts of honest artists to join the struggle for progress.[139] Saltykov-Ščedrin's criticism of and polemic with A. A. Fet features a conscious and systematic social and political interpretation of their differences. Saltykov-Ščedrin sees Fet's aestheticism, melancholy, and alienation as a perfectly natural complement of the poet's aggressively reactionary political views. Fet's reactionary publicism and aestheticizing poetry were, in Saltykov-Ščedrin's opinion, different aspects of the ideology of a dying class: the class of the Russian landed gentry, to which Fet belonged.

With all this emphasis on ideology and rational thought, Saltykov-Ščedrin,

137. See "Uličnaja filosofija" (1869), *Polnoe sobranie sočinenij,* 8:115–47.
138. Ibid., pp. 116–17. Cf. Gorjačkina, "Saltykov-Ščedrin–kritik," p. 155; Lavreckij, *Èstetika Belinskogo,* p. 191.
139. See, e.g., Saltykov-Ščedrin's review of Kljušnikov's novel *The Gypsies* (1871), *Polnoe sobranie sočinenij,* 8:452–53.

himself an artist of great talent, had considerable faith in the cognitive and active political powers of art. He believed that literature, if only given a free hand and allowed to express itself fully, would not at all "exaggerate or distort reality, but would merely reveal that *other* reality which likes to hide behind the facts of everyday life and is accessible only to an extremely attentive observer."[140] This is, in effect, once again the old metaphor of "removing the covers."

Saltykov-Ščedrin was a great believer in and defender of the typical (*tipič- nost'*) in literature: ". . . every phenomenon must be viewed primarily in its typical traits rather than in details or in deviations from the norm. The latter should naturally not be left out of sight; however, they certainly have no right to obscure the basic nature (*glavnyj xarakter*) of the phenomenon."[141] He conceived of literary "types" as being aesthetic universals of great cognitive value. In particular, he believed in a future-oriented literature and invited writers to express the *potential* of social types and typical situations as much as their actuality. The following statement, appearing in many variations, is characteristic of his thinking:

> Literature foresees (*providit*) the laws of the future, it creates the image of future man. It is not afraid of utopianism, for utopianism can frighten and stymie only the Street (*ulicu*). Types which were created by literature always reach farther than those whom one meets in the marketplace. This is why they impress their seal even upon a society which appears to be wholly under the sway of empirical cares and worries. Under the influence of these new types, contemporary man, unbeknownst to himself, acquires new habits, assimilates new views, gets a new slant on things; in short, he gradually works up toward becoming a new man. ("A Summing Up")[142]

Saltykov-Ščedrin's historicism and nationalism follow the familiar Hegelian patterns introduced into Russian literary criticism by Belinskij. Like Belinskij, he sees the "living organism" of the Russian people, with its peculiar traits, as the necessary result of its historical development, and Russian literature as an integral element of that development. And he is convinced that the Russian people and Russian literature will have to realize their ideal in national, "Russian" terms.[143]

In particular, Saltykov-Ščedrin, too, uses the conception of the "negative ideal," which Belinskij and Grigor'ev had already applied to Gogol''s art, to account for the specific nature of Russian literature:

140. *Pompadury i pompadurši* (1863–73), in *Polnoe sobranie sočinenij*, 9:203–4.
141. "Naša obščestvennaja žizn'" (1864), *Polnoe sobranie sočinenij*, 6:322.
142. "Itogi" (1871), *Polnoe sobranie sočinenij*, 7:455. Cf. "Naša obščestvennaja žizn'" or "Peterburgskie teatry," *Polnoe sobranie sočinenij*, 6:208–9; 5:174.
143. "Aleksej Vasil'evič Kol'cov" (1856), *Polnoe sobranie sočinenij*, 5:25, 35.

The intrusion of new life into our literature, in particular . . . has tended
to take the form of satire, [an art form] which escorts everything that is ob-
solete to the kingdom of shadows. . . . This makes sense, too, for our new
life is still in the process of taking shape; it could not possibly express itself
other than in negative terms, in the form of satire, or in the form of premo-
nition or prevision.[144]

This passage—and there are many like it in Saltykov-Ščedrin's writings—suggests that he thinks entirely in Belinskian (that is, Hegelian) terms.

RUSSIAN MARXISTS

Plexanov

If Saltykov-Ščedrin is distinctly a forerunner of the socially and politically
oriented "orthodox" ("partisan") wing of Socialist Realism, G. V. Plexanov
(1856–1918), the father of Russian Marxism, is the principal authority of those
Soviet critics who wish to emphasize the creative autonomy of art.[145] Plexanov's interpretation and critique of the writings of Belinskij, Černyševskij, Dobroljubov, Pisarev, and other "revolutionary democrats" (he wrote a great deal
on all of them, but especially on Belinskij and Černyševskij) still serve as an important catalyst of a "liberal" aesthetics in the Soviet Union. To orthodox Socialist-Realist critics, Plexanov exemplifies the ideological pitfalls of excessive
reliance on the artist's intuition and insufficient attention to correctness of
ideology and conscious, vigilant control of the artist's creative inspiration.
Lebedev-Poljanskij provides a typical evaluation:

Plexanov's position, from which he magnanimously allowed art to serve
society *passively*, getting angry when art made pretensions to fulfill its function of serving society *actively*—which happens to be Belinskij's position—
can be explained from a historical point of view.[146]

"Plexanov's position," which Lebedev-Poljanskij views with such venomous
hostility, can be defined as an advanced version of Belinskian aesthetics, with
its organicist principles intact and carefully guarded against any tendency to
let sociopolitical expediency dictate its terms to art.

The central feature of Plexanov's aesthetic theory is the notion that art, while

144. Review of *Novye stixotvorenija* by A. N. Majkov (1864), *Polnoe sobranie sočinenij*, 5:372.
145. See P. A. Nikolaev, *Vozniknovenie marksistskogo literaturovedenija v Rossii* (Moscow, 1970), and his *Èstetika i literaturnye teorii G. V. Plexanova* (Moscow, 1968). Also,
N. Gej and V. Piskunov, "U istokov marksistskoj literaturnoj kritiki," *VLit* 11, no. 8
(1967): 131–52. A good Western treatment of Plexanov is found in Peter Demetz, *Marx,
Engels, and the Poets: Origins of Marxist Literary Criticism* (Chicago, 1967).
146. Lebedev-Poljanskij, *Belinskij*, p. 326.

it is, of course, a function of social life and is determined by the socioeconomic conditions of the society which gave birth to it, is also an autonomous, *sui generis* activity of the human spirit. Plexanov accepts the conception of an autonomous "aesthetic sense," though rejecting, of course, the idealist notion of its "divine" nature. He finds Schiller's idea of art as a form of "play" to be a most sensible one.[147] Furthermore, while Plexanov does not believe that there exists an absolute criterion of beauty in art, he is inclined to feel that artistic success or failure can very well be evaluated objectively. His criterion is purely Hegelian (or Belinskian): "The more the form of a work of art corresponds to its idea, the more successful it is—there you have an objective yardstick!"[148]

As Plexanov's opponents (Lunačarskij, for example) were quick to point out, his aesthetics as a whole, and specifically his concept of Beauty in art, had a decidedly neo-Kantian flavor. While the straightforward, materialist Černyševskij had refused to single out the aesthetic fact from among the rest of human experience, Plexanov was willing to accept Kant's notion of a specifically *human* aesthetic sense, the action of which "humanizes" (*očelovečivaet*) the objective world surrounding man. Plexanov also concluded from the autonomy of the aesthetic sense that art is happiest if free of utilitarian considerations (which are the domain of the intellect). His critics point out that this attitude led him into such an "error" as a failure to appreciate properly Nekrasov's populist verse, Černyševskij's novel *What Is to Be Done?* and Gor'kij's novel *The Mother*.[149]

Peter Demetz, who shows that Plexanov was well aware of the conflict between Marxist utilitarianism and the Kantian notion of "disinterested pleasure" associated with the creation and reception of art, thinks that Plexanov was never able to resolve this conflict.[150] But Plexanov himself (like Belinskij before him) thought that he had a solution: Tendentious art, he suggests, is not per se nonart. Yet much of it is bad art, because its tendency is reactionary, antihumanitarian, and immoral. Therefore, whenever true artists insist on the autonomy of their art (here Plexanov quotes Flaubert's "L'Art c'est la recherche de l'inutile"), what they are really asking for is freedom from having to protect entrenched regimes, vested interests, and antihumanitarian ideologies.[151] True art, whether its creator be aware of it or not, is "utilitarian," but it serves noble, humanitarian, and progressive ends. It is "disinterested" in the sense that the artist is not pursuing any selfish personal ends in creating it. Plexanov, like Belinskij, is a great optimist. He takes for granted the basic goodness, truthfulness, and progressiveness of men in general, and of great artists in particular: "Whenever

147. Plexanov, "Literaturnye vzgljady N. G. Černyševskogo," *Sočinenija*, 5:316–17.
148. "Iskusstvo i obščestvennaja žizn'" (1912), *Sočinenija*, 14:180.
149. See, e.g., Astaxov, *Plexanov i Černyševskij*, pp. 290–91.
150. Demetz, *Marx, Engels, and the Poets*, pp. 258–59.
151. "Iskusstvo i obščestvennaja žizn'," *Sočinenija*, 14:175.

an artist of talent is inspired by a false idea, he will spoil his own work. And an artist of our age cannot possibly be inspired by a correct idea if he wants to support the bourgeoisie in its struggle against the proletariat."[152]

Yet at the same time Plexanov emphasizes that, while "an artist of any talent at all will greatly enhance his creative powers by becoming imbued with the great libertarian ideas of our age," it is also necessary that "these ideas become a part of his flesh and blood, that he express them exactly as an artist should."[153]

Plexanov's "social organicism" is more specific than Belinskij's, since Plexanov, a Marxist, operates with the notion that social structure, class interests, and class struggle are necessarily reflected in art. Thus, in an essay, "French Dramatic Literature and Painting of the Eighteenth Century from a Sociological Point of View,"[154] Plexanov seeks to demonstrate the aristocratic basis of these art forms and the gradual emergence and eventual ascendancy in them of a bourgeois world view.

Plexanov's most interesting application of this notion relates to his diagnosis of twentieth-century alienated "modernist" art. He liked to quote Leconte de Lisle's dictum which says that poetry gives an ideal life to those who no longer have a real life. The modern bourgeois artist's alienation from society and his efforts to create a "dehumanized art" Plexanov sees as the reaction of a desperate man who has lost all hope and desire to live a meaningful life.

Mysticism—in which Plexanov sees mere superstition—is likewise a sign of bourgeois decadence: foreseeing the imminent demise of its way of life, the bourgeoisie escapes into religious mysticism, theosophy, and occultism. As for "formalism," it is just another symptom of sociopolitical "indifferentism" on the part of men who know that they have had their say in "real life" and in history.

Plexanov's principal argument with Belinskij, and even more so with Černyševskij, was that these men had failed to take into account the concrete, objective facts of history and historical change (interpreted correctly only by Marx), but had veered into ahistorical idealist fantasies, such as utopian socialism, idealization of the "natural life" of the Russian peasant, and the like. Specifically, Plexanov chastises these predecessors of his (whom he consistently calls "enlighteners," a pejorative term) for having refused to treat Puškin, Lermontov, Gogol', and other Russian poets and writers, in terms of these writers' age, the social class to which they belonged, and the sociohistorical tendencies of the period. In particular, Plexanov stresses that it was completely wrong on

152. Ibid., p. 160.
153. Ibid., p. 179.
154. "Francuzskaja dramatičeskaja literatura i francuzskaja živopis' XVIII veka s točki zrenija sociologii" (1905), Sočinenija, 14:95–119.

the part of Černyševskij (not to speak of Pisarev) to dismiss Puškin, or even the Russian school of "pure art," as irrelevant to Russian life. All art is a significant expression of social relationships, Plexanov asserts, although sometimes— as in the case of so-called pure art—the social ties of art are subtle and hidden. But precisely such difficult, complex, and opaque phenomena ought to challenge the perceptive critic.

Plexanov justly observes that Belinskij was closer to a "correct" (that is, Marxist) approach to literature than any of his epigoni. He also observes that Belinskij, while he ostensibly rejected Hegel on account of Hegel's objectivism and reactionary political views, remained a Hegelian to the end of his life, certainly as far as his aesthetic theory was concerned.[155] In Plexanov's mind, this was a strong point in Belinskij's favor—and a point against his successors, Černyševskij, Dobroljubov, and Pisarev. It meant, Plexanov felt, that Belinskij never abandoned either the notion that the work of art is an organic, living whole (rather than a mechanical construct) or the assumption that the relationship between art and reality is "organic" and dialectic rather than one of simple mechanical projection. It also meant that Belinskij had been inclined to conceive of history as a dynamic, yet determinate process, and had retained, by and large, a "historical" view of literature, while his successors had reverted to eighteenth-century "anthropologism." Finally, it meant that Belinskij (as opposed to many of Hegel's German followers who had yielded to neo-Kantian tendencies) had clung to the Hegelian thesis, according to which it was a logical historical necessity that in modern art "content" should outweigh "form."

On the other side, Plexanov also pointed out, quite correctly, that while Belinskij had never developed a positivist, mechanistic, and utilitarian aesthetics of the type found in Černyševskij, he made, during the last few years of his life, many isolated statements pointing in that direction, and thus in a fashion paved the way for Černyševskij's and Pisarev's crude utilitarianism.

Plexanov is much more severe in his criticism of Černyševskij's aesthetics, even though he finds that it was based on a sound idea (inherited from Belinskij), namely, that the sphere of Art was considerably broader than the sphere of Beauty.[156] But Černyševskij's basically sound approach, says Plexanov, was vitiated by an entirely simplistic underestimation of the complexity of the problems which he had to face. Černyševskij's principal mistakes were, according to Plexanov, his failure to take into account the all-important factor of historical movement, and his naïve schematization of the relationship between art and reality:

In actuality, the historical movement of mankind is a process in which the successes of some of its aspects do not imply proportional successes in all of

155. "Belinskij i razumnaja dejstvitel'nost' " (1897), *Sočinenija*, 10:238-39.
156. "Èstetičeskaja teorija N. G. Černyševskogo" (1897), *Sočinenija*, 6:250.

its other aspects, and sometimes directly make for backwardness—or even decline—of some of them. ("The Literary Views of N. G. Černyševskij")[157]

Černyševskij, unaware of this circumstance (easily verified by an empirical survey of history), had extended the sociopolitical norms of the situation in Russia at the time of the great reforms—which he diagnosed correctly—to the historical past of Russia and other countries. As a result, he had arrived at the totally false position from which he had to judge, say, French classicism by the standards of Russian midnineteenth-century "critical realism." Belinskij obviously had been less guilty of this particular error, because, good Hegelian that he was, he had generally taken for granted that a Puškin had to be judged and appreciated in the absolute terms of all great art, and as a product of his country, his social class, and his age rather than in terms of the new "Gogolian" age which he did not live to see.

Plexanov noted, quite correctly of course, that Černyševskij's aesthetic theory and the arguments with which he defended it bore a strong resemblance to Tolstoj's view of art as expounded in *What Is Art?*[158] He did not investigate the causes of this curious coincidence. They were fairly obvious, however: both Černyševskij and Tolstoj chose to ignore history; both postulated a universal anthropology (for which the Russian peasant—idealized, of course—served as a model), in total disregard of the empirical data available on historical cultures; both assigned to art a more or less ancillary role; the *summum bonum* of both was conceived in terms of a subsistence farmer's simple needs. No wonder then, that Černyševskij and Tolstoj arrived at virtually the same negative evaluation of the world's great art, music, and poetry.

Vorovskij, Lunačarskij, and Trockij

Plexanov represented a "rightist deviation" from the Dobroljubov-Černyševskian tradition and, in many ways, a return to Belinskian organicism. Other Marxists, with some of whom Plexanov polemicized sharply, stayed closer to Dobroljubov and Černyševskij. The critical articles of V. V. Vorovskij (1871–1923), in particular, represent a conscious return to Dobroljubov. Thus, Vorovskij published a critical essay on two controversial plays, J. Najdenov's *Vanjušin's Children* and M. Gor'kij's *The Burghers,* under the title "A Schism in 'the Kingdom of Darkness'" (1902–3) and treated his subject matter entirely in Dobroljubov's style. He followed the same procedure in many other instances. His emphasis was very much on establishing social "types" and assigning them a place in the historical dynamics of his age. At the same time, Vorovskij, A. V. Lunačarskij (1873–1933), and the other Marxists often referred back to Belinskij,

---

157. "Literaturnye vzgljady N. G. Černyševskogo," *Sočinenija,* 5:325.
158. "Èstetičeskaja teorija N. G. Černyševskogo," *Sočinenija,* 6:250n.

always with fondness and respect. Their references to Pisarev, on the other hand, tended to be quite negative.

Plexanov had scornfully brushed aside A. A. Bogdanov's theory of a new "proletarian art," as well as any art that was politically "partisan" in an even narrower sense. Most of the other Marxists, such as Vorovskij, Lunačarskij, Maksim Gor'kij, and Lev Trockij, on the contrary, were outspoken adherents of partisan art, though they differed among themselves on the question of the historical role of proletarian art, even as to its right to exist. The principles of what eventually became known as Socialist Realism were laid down by these Russian Marxists in the 1910s and 1920s.[159]

Lunačarskij very simply explained the rationale for the partisan quality of the new art (he constantly used the term *partijnost'* long before the Revolution):

> The Social-Democrat movement is not simply a party, but a great cultural movement. Even the greatest of all that have been in existence so far. Only powerful religious movements can be, to some extent, likened to it. And no one laughs if one speaks of "Christian art." ("The Tasks of a Social-Democrat Art")[160]

Lunačarskij, Vorovskij, and the other Marxists joined Plexanov in seeing the various trends of contemporary art and literature entirely in sociohistorical and ideological terms. They insisted that there was no such thing as "art without a tendency," and that "pure art" was either an illusion or conscious camouflage. They equated literary "decadence" with the decay of the bourgeoisie.[161] They interpreted "naturalism" as the pessimistic outlook of a diffident and alienated *petit bourgeois*,[162] and saw Futurism (and other, related movements of the avant-garde) as an expression of the *Weltgefühl* of an at least potentially progressive *déclassée* intelligentsia.[163]

159. See, e.g., B. A. Bjalik, "M. Gor'kij—kritik," in Gorodeckij et al., eds., *Istorija russkoj kritiki,* 2:665–720; Metčenko, *Zaveščano Gor'kim;* K. D. Muratova, *Vozniknovenie socialističeskogo realizma v russkoj literature* (Moscow and Leningrad, 1966); O. V. Semenovskij, *Marksistskaja kritika o Gor'kom: Iz istorii obščestvenno-literaturnoj bor'by predoktjabr'skogo perioda* (Kishinev, 1969). Cf. also the works listed n. 145 above. The literature on this subject is very large.

160. A. V. Lunačarskij, "Zadači social-demokratičeskogo xudožestvennogo tvorčestva," *Kritičeskie ètjudy: Russkaja literatura* (Leningrad, 1925), p. 6. Cf. Metčenko's comments on Gor'kij's *partijnost'* in *Zaveščano Gor'kim,* p. 44.

161. Cf. Lunačarskij, *Kritičeskie ètjudy,* p. 37. Also V. V. Vorovskij, "O. M. Gor'kom" (1910), *Literaturno-kritičeskie stat'i* (Moscow, 1956), p. 57; Metčenko, *Zaveščano Gor'kim,* p. 109.

162. See, e.g., Vorovskij, "Leonid Andreev" (1910), *Literaturno-kritičeskie stat'i,* pp. 296–97, where Andreev is given as a typical example of this phenomenon. Cf. Metčenko, *Zaveščano Gor'kim,* p.59, for a paraphrase of Gor'kij's opinion to the same effect.

163. See, e.g., A. V. Lunačarskij, *Sud'by russkoj literatury* (Leningrad, 1925), pp.

The principle of "social organicism" is firmly entrenched in the thinking of the Russian Marxist critics. They see art as a *sui generis* and to some extent autonomous human activity which is, however, naturally an organic part of human life. They return to Belinskij's dialectic conception of the relationship between art and social life, as opposed to Černyševskij's mechanistic model. Trockij put it as follows:

> To a materialist, religion, law, morals, and art represent separate aspects of one and the same process of social development. Though they become differentiated from their industrial basis, become complex, strengthen and develop their special characteristics in detail, politics, religion, law, ethics, and aesthetics remain, nonetheless, functions of social man and obey the laws of his social organization. The idealist, on the other hand, does not see a unified process of historical development which evolves the necessary organs and functions from within itself, but a crossing or combining and interacting of certain independent principles—the religious, political, juridical, aesthetic, and ethical substances, which find their origin and explanation in themselves.[164]

This tirade is directed not only against the Russian Formalists (and other neo-Kantian trends in literary theory) but also against the Černyševskian tradition which would deny the status of "separate aspects" of life to Art and other elements of the "superstructure." Elsewhere, Trockij explicitly asserts that "a work of art should, in the first place, be judged by its own law, that is, by the law of art."[165]

The new art which the Russian Marxists approved of and encouraged was assumed to be necessarily *realistic*, the rationale for this being that the art of a young and vigorous class must not be afraid of the truth, but can afford to be brutally frank and will certainly welcome a bold and penetrating analysis of social life. Maksim Gor'kij's alleged "cruelty" was therefore applauded by Marxist critics.[166]

Yet at the same time, the Marxists insisted that the new art should be the bearer of the progressive ideals of the Revolution and of the emerging new society, an active and a positive ideal.[167] As Lunačarskij once put it, the new art

---

47–51; Vorovskij, "O buržuaznosti modernistov" (1908), *Literaturno-kritičeskie stat'i,* pp. 175–83; Leon Trotsky, *Literature and Revolution* (New York, 1957), pp. 130, 141–42.

164. Trotsky, *Literature and Revolution,* p. 182.

165. Ibid., p. 178.

166. Lunačarskij, "Dačniki," *Kritičeskie ètjudy,* pp. 293, 320, and *passim.* Lunačarskij also quotes Gor'kij's dictum, "Truth is the God of free men!" and then goes into a long tirade on reliance on truth as the natural basis of the new literature (pp. 296–97).

167. The new literature is also to create new types, such as Gor'kij's *čelovek-tovarišč* and *čelovek-vrag* (see Metčenko, *Zaveščano Gor'kim,* p. 64). Certainly it must create a "positive hero" (ibid., pp. 66–68). Cf. Lunačarskij, "O česti," *Kritičeskie ètjudy,* p. 273

amounted to "realism plus enthusiasm, realism plus a fighting spirit."[168] The Marxists also felt that it should not be difficult for a writer of a progressive bent of mind to incorporate this ideal into his works, for "in young and healthy classes, personal interest coincides with class interest, and even with the interest of all mankind."[169]

We have, then, in the aesthetic theory of the Russian Marxists, yet another form of the Belinskian fusion of the real and the ideal. However, the historical force which is assumed to produce it is defined more precisely. Belinskij had assumed implicitly, and Dobroljubov explicitly, that all artists of sound mind, healthy moral character, and real talent would necessarily be aware of the movement of history, attune themselves to it, and express it in their works. The Marxists limit this assumption to those artists who represent the most progressive social class of the moment, and concretely, to those who fight for the proletarian revolution and their fellow travelers. Vorovskij, in an article "On the Bourgeois Nature of the Modernists," very skillfully blends an organicist and historicist view of art with a rationale for a measure of tendentiousness in art:

> In his work, an artist transforms a piece of real or imagined life. His individual "I," acting as a canvas of his work, gives it that subjective coloration which indicates the author's "tendency." In some works this tendency is social, in others it is antisocial. In some it is progressive, in others it is reactionary. But if a work is not simply manufactured, then this tendency acts as a hidden nonmaterial force.
>
> But it may happen that an artist, even a very talented artist, is carried away by the tendency which has taken possession of him and rushes to pronounce the new ideas which he has conceived. As a result, he will bring into the world undigested images (*obrazy*), untried in life—artificial, unartistic products of hurried thought. In that case, to be sure, the tendency will be coarse, loud, obtrusive. It will come to the fore, concealing the sparks of true talent behind it.[170]

Vorovskij, like Plexanov, was rather critical of Gor'kij's *Mother,* though he stressed the fact that it was extremely useful as "propaganda." But whom Vorovskij mainly had in mind when he wrote the above statement was Leonid Andreev.

The Marxists' social and historical organicism, then, largely follows in Belinskij's footsteps. Their historical optimism is not quite as boundless as Belinskij's

---

(where the author quotes Guyau on the necessity of a "living ideal" in literature) and Vorovskij, "Leonid Andreev," *Literaturno-kritičeskie stat'i,* p. 289.

168. Metčenko, *Zaveščano Gor'kim,* p. 104.

169. Lunačarskij, *Kritičeskie ètjudy,* p. 262.

170. "O buržuaznosti modernistov," *Literaturno-kritičeskie stat'i,* pp. 182–83.

in that they take cognizance of the presence of reactionary and inimical art, which competes with their own "progressive" art. But they have no doubts as to the outcome of this struggle. In the 1920s, Marxist critics freely admitted that a censorship of literature existed in the Soviet Union. But the understanding was that such censorship was a temporary measure directed entirely against outright counterrevolutionary propaganda, and not against outspoken dissenters who had sincerely accepted the humanitarian goals of the Revolution.[171] The requirement that a positive humanitarian ideal be present in a work of art (*idejnost'*) was, theoretically at least, more important than a strict adherence to the letter of the Party line. Lunačarskij went as far as quoting Vladimir Solov'ev—and agreeing with him, too—when it came to asserting the importance of *idejnost'* in art:

> It would be a good thing to make our high-flown aesthetes of pure art and our "superpure" artists think about the aesthetic teaching of Vladimir Solov'ev. . . . According to Vladimir Solov'ev: "The purpose of art is to incarnate in sense images (*v oščutitel'nyx obrazax*) that higher meaning of life which the philosopher expresses in concepts, which is preached by the moralist, and realized by the historical personage."[172]

Lunačarskij summarizes his conclusions by saying: "So, then, the true work of art is a philosophy in images" (*filosofija v obrazax*). This coincides with Belinskij's famous definition of art both literally and conceptually.

The Marxists' ideal of truly progressive contemporary art was generally stated in terms with which not only Belinskij and Dobroljubov would have agreed, but also Dostoevskij and Grigor'ev. Thus, Lunačarskij, like Belinskij and Černyševskij before him, explicitly equates "art" with "life," but unlike the latter—and like Belinskij, of course—is willing to accept the romantic Neoplatonic notion that art is a quintessence of life: "And so, it is the artist's task to condense life (*koncentrirovat' žizn'*), to intensify it, to let us experience as much as possible—however, without overstraining our nerves, that is, [it is the artist's task] to give, per unit of receptive energy, a much higher dose of sensations than one would receive from ordinary life."[173] Lunačarskij goes on to point out that the "infection" (the Tolstoian *zaraženie*) effected by art must not necessarily be limited to morally "good" emotions. Rather, it ought to induce a heightened interest, *élan,* and love of life in general. What Lunačarskij finds dangerous are representations of weakness, disease, narrowness, of everything that is

171. See, e.g., Trotsky, *Literature and Revolution,* p. 140, where it is explicitly stated that "the actual development of art and its struggle for new forms are not part of the Party's tasks, nor any of its concerns." Cf. Lunačarskij, *Sud'by russkoj literatury,* pp. 52–53.

172. *Kritičeskie ètjudy,* p. 178.

173. Ibid., p. 31.

wretched, colorless, and drab. He roundly condemns "decadent" as well as "naturalist" art.

All together, then, the Russian Marxists shared Belinskij's confidence that all genuine art would inevitably promote the cause of progress. The literary and censorship policies of the Soviet regime in the 1920s bear out this optimistic, self-confident view. The regime tolerated a great deal of genuine realism in literature, obviously assuming that in the long run the facts would speak in its favor.

The Belinskian conception of the cognitive powers of art is also retained by the Russian Marxists. The following passage from Lunačarskij is characteristic and represents, more or less, even the current "official" view:

What a talented biographer can give us only in the most essential traits, and with the interest of his treatment concentrated in the intellectual activities of a historical personage, an artist can give us in an incomparably more refined, delicate, multicolored, and warm form through his creation of a typical character or of a typical phenomenon of social life. Between the economic condition of society and the deeply concealed, highly complex, and exceedingly subtle movements of the human soul there lies an intricate, entangled, zigzagging path which can be discovered only by a writer who combines a sociologist's scholarly method with an incisive analytic intellect, a sympathetic ability to feel the movements of another man's soul, and that extraordinary intuition which makes the true artist stand out from among a crowd of hack writers. He will then guide the masses of his readers with him along this path.[174]

This is essentially the conception that had caused Belinskij to claim that a historical novel by Sir Walter Scott was often a better source of historical truth than the painstaking investigations of objective historical scholars.

Much like it was to Belinskij, Dobroljubov, and Plexanov—but also Grigor'ev, Dostoevskij, and the Symbolists—art is to Lunačarskij and the other Marxists a powerful catalyst of "the new man" ("Soviet man," after the Revolution). In his novel *The Mother* (1907), challenged by many critics, including some Marxists, as too "tendentious" and therefore "unrealistic," Maksim Gor'kij had, in his own opinion, anticipated the historical reality of the future, much as Černyševskij's Raxmetov had anticipated the Russian revolutionary of the future. In his play *Odd Fellows* (*Čudaki*), Gor'kij explicitly defended his heroine by letting the hero of that play, the writer Mastakov, exclaim: "Well, all right, my old woman is a lie, they'll say, I know it, they'll say it! 'There are no such women!'

174. "Social'naja psixologija i social'naja mistika," *Kritičeskie ètjudy,* pp. 64–65. On the prophetic role of literature, cf. Vorovskij, "A. P. Čexov," *Literaturno-kritičeskie stat'i,* pp. 252–53. Note that Gor'kij called literature *čelovekovedenie* ("anthropology"); cf. Metčenko, *Zaveščano Gor'kim,* p. 76.

they'll scream. Well, Lena, today there are no such women, but tomorrow
there will be some—do you believe me, Lena, that there will be such women?"
Whereupon the heroine, Lena, answers: "Yes, you help them to be, and
they'll be."

Here, then, the conception of art as a catalyst of social "types" is stated in
terms of a dialectic relationship, with art an equal partner: inspired by living
people and living social situations, art "helps" new social types to come into
being. The educational role of art is thus conceived in the widest possible
sense and given an all-important role in the building of a new society. The
wholesale mobilization and integration of writers and artists into the promotion of the first Five-Year Plan was born of a belief in the miraculous power
of art "to push time forward," as Majakovskij put it. Very much in the spirit
of Belinskij and Dobroljubov, many of the bolševik intellectuals of the pre-
Stalin era were confident that the creation of a "new man" and the "building
of socialism" would inspire writers and artists to create works of art such as
the world had never seen before.[175]

Like Belinskij toward the end of his life and his followers of the Left, the
Russian Marxist critics of the early twentieth century, while insisting on the
organic unity of "content" and "form,"[176] tended to make concessions to
"contentualism," believing that a positive, truthful, and progressive content
could hardly be spoiled by a somewhat awkward form, and that, provided the
right "content" was there, "form" was essentially the working out of "details."[177]

Nevertheless, the Russian Marxists of the early twentieth century were believers in creative intuition (which they placed somewhere between "emotion"
and "intellection"),[178] as well as talent and genius. They all operated with the
Belinskian concept of *xudožestvennyj obraz* ("artistic image"). Finally, the
Russian Marxists also believed in an innate striving for aesthetic creativity (or
simply Beauty) as a necessary part of being human.[179] And they all believed
that the aesthetic aspect of life would dominate in the society of the future.[180]

175. See, for instance, Lunačarskij, "Literaturnyj raspad i koncentracija intelligencii,"
Kritičeskie ètjudy, p. 107.

176. See, e.g., Trotsky, *Literature and Revolution*, pp. 171–73.

177. For a paraphrase of Gor'kij's opinion on this point, see B. A. Bjalik, "M. Gor'kij—
kritik," in Gorodeckij et al., eds., *Istorija russkoj kritiki*, 2:703–4. Cf. Lunačarskij, "K
zvezdam," *Kritičeskie ètjudy*, p. 238.

178. Trockij, the least "literary" of the Marxist critics, has this to say: "A purely
logical approach destroys the question of artistic form. One must judge this question
not with one's reason, which does not go beyond formal logic, but with one's whole
mind, which includes the irrational, insofar as it is alive and vital" (*Literature and Revolution*, p. 143).

179. See Metčenko, *Zaveščano Gor'kim*, p. 87, for a paraphrase of Gor'kij's opinion.

180. See also A. Ležnev, "Delo o trupe," *Sovremenniki: Literaturno-kritičeskie očerki*

THE COURSE OF BELINSKIJ'S AESTHETIC TRADITION IN THE 1920s

The 1920s brought the first serious threats to the Belinskian organicist tradition in Russian aesthetic thought. To be sure, there had been the utilitarian challenge to organicism, mounted by Černyševskij and his followers. But their position was so much in conflict with the empirical social and psychological facts of artistic creation that it failed to be accepted, or even taken seriously, by writers and poets of any talent at all. There had been, on the other side, occasional surges of a subjective idealist aesthetics, for which Puškin's cycle "on the poet" was an ever-present fountain of rejuvenation. Some of the Symbolists, specifically Brjusov, had at least temporarily abandoned the objective-idealist conception of an immanent and teleological analogy between art and life. But a full renunciation of Art's claim to immediate relevance to social life and of the artist's national leadership and prophethood had not often been made, and then not by very important poets or writers. Often, the very poets and writers who proclaimed the autonomy of art, either explicitly or by virtue of the content of their works, arrogated for themselves the status of teachers, prophets, and leaders. Critics such as A. L. Volynskij and Ju. A. Eichenwald deplored the integration of Russian literature into Russian political life started by Belinskij as a pernicious sellout of the integrity, freedom, and proper self-sufficiency of art, but their voices were generally ignored or misunderstood.[181]

The challenge to organic aesthetics became a serious one in the 1920s, when a new form of utilitarianism raised its head in the RAPP (proletarian writers) movement, while the Formalist school challenged every position of organic aesthetics, offering plausible alternatives to each of them.

The Formalists

Rather than insist on a necessary and complete analogy between "art" and "life," the Formalists preferred to leave open the question concerning the ultimate relationship between "art" and "life."

What used to be the cognitive role of art in organic aesthetics was perceived by the Formalists as a subjective process by which a thing was removed from its "normal" context in life. Viktor Šklovskij called this process *ostranenie,* "making it strange." The same term (*Fremdmachen*) had been used by Novalis to describe the creative process. Novalis, incidentally, used *Fremdmachen* as a synonym of *Poetisieren* ("to poeticize"). More specifically, Šklovskij defined

---

(Moscow, 1927), p. 31. Trockij says much the same thing (*Literature and Revolution,* pp. 136–37). Naturally, this is an old utopian-socialist idea.

181. A. L. Volynskij [Flekser], *Russkie kritiki* (St. Petersburg, 1896). For a concise statement of Eichenwald's position, see the Introduction to his *Siluèty russkix pisatelej,* 6th ed., 3 vols. (Berlin, 1929), 1:1–49.

art as "a way to experience the making of a thing, while what is made is not important."[182]

The concept of "aesthetic image" or "symbol" (xudožestvennyj obraz), focal to Belinskian aesthetics, was seriously challenged. Šklovskij explicitly rejected Belinskij's famous definition, "Art is thinking in images." He asserted that, for one thing, there was a large area of art forms which addressed themselves directly to the emotions without the aid of images or symbols. Secondly, if and whenever images (symbols) existed in art, they did not necessarily demonstrate its meaning or its dynamic principle. On the contrary, they tended to be constant and functionally neutral, while their rearrangement and reorganization made up the content and the dynamic principle in art.[183]

The unity of all art forms, defended by the organic tradition, had to collapse once the reality of "inner vision," "aesthetic idea," and "artistic image" (obraz) —allegedly common to all art forms—was put in doubt. Instead of a hierarchical unity of all arts, Formalism preferred to deal with autonomous art forms. What was seen as common to all of them was "creation," a conscious, active, organizing treatment of the material in question (words, colors, shapes, tones).

The Belinskian conception of the work of art as the realization of an idea was replaced by a radically different model. The organicist "body-and-soul" analogy was ignored and, instead, there appeared the conception of the "thingness" (veščnost') of the work of art. The mystic—and pretentious—concept of the generative idea which inspires the artist was replaced by the much humbler zadanie ("job," "plan," "task," "order"), the analogy now coming from the more narrow domain of the artisan or tradesman. Šklovskij expressed the strong suspicion that the celebrated unity of the work of art was a mere myth, and he supported his contention with the empirical observation that poets would often incorporate into their poems extraneous passages not originally meant for the poem in question. Puškin's Evgenij Onegin was a case in point.[184]

182. Viktor Šklovskij, O teorii prozy (Moscow, 1929), p. 13. For general information on Russian Formalism, see Victor Erlich, Russian Formalism: History – Doctrine, 2d ed. (The Hague, 1965). Also, Krystyna Pomorska, Russian Formalist Theory and Its Poetic Ambiance (The Hague, 1968).

183. See Šklovskij, O teorii prozy, p. 8. Boris Eichenbaum put it this way: "The conception of poetry as 'thinking in images' and the equation 'poetry = imagery' derived from it were blatantly out of keeping with the facts observed and in contradiction to the general principles the facts suggested" ("The Theory of the Formal Method" [1927], quoted from Readings in Russian Poetics: Formalist and Structuralist Views, L. Matejka and K. Pomorska, eds. [Cambridge, Mass., 1871], p. 11). Later, Šklovskij considerably qualified his stand as regards the role of obraz in poetry; in his recent work, Tetiva: O nesxodstve sxodnogo (Moscow, 1970), we actually find an apology of obraz in response to Roman Jakobson's structuralist conception of poetry (pp. 235–45).

184. Šklovskij, O teorii prozy, p. 215. Roman Jakobson, in his essay "The Dominant," points out that Šklovskij later retreated from this radical position, substituting for his

The Formalists challenged the organicists' "contentualism," or rather, reversed the *content : form* relationship established by the Belinskian tradition and put into practice Nietzsche's paradox which said that, to the artist, what the layman called "form" was really the "content" of his work, that is, what really mattered to him and for which he felt responsible.[185] Historical events and philosophic ideas, social tensions and upheavals, national triumphs and calamities, and, of course, the peripeties of the artist's personal life were seen as *material* for the artist's work, potential themes and motifs. The artist's philosophy, his *Weltanschauung,* and the organizing principle of his work were to be sought in the techniques of his craft. "To be precise, the ontology of his literary form determines the writer's consciousness," said Šklovskij, paraphrasing Marx and so suggesting that "literary form" (that is, "craftsmanship," "technique") was to art what socioeconomic facts were to human life at large.[186]

The practical criticism of the Formalists transformed these principles into action, and a radically new interpretation of the Russian classics emerged from their studies. Boris Eichenbaum's famous study *How Is Gogol''s "Overcoat" Made?* is an example of the Formalists' inversion of the traditional content : form relationship. Gogol''s art was seen by Eichenbaum in terms not of the expression of an idea but in the use of a large variety of verbal devices aimed at the creation of a certain grotesque effect.[187]

The Formalists' emphasis on form led to an outright rejection of organicist historicism, that is, the notion that the history of art and literature is an integral part of general history. Šklovskij pointed out that the history of literature does not run in a straight line, but rather in a zigzag: great writers often have no direct offspring, and are themselves descended from second-rate literature (like Dostoevskij from the so-called *roman-feuilleton*). Eichenbaum sarcastically observed that "literature as such played no role whatsoever" in the conventional "histories of Russian literature," from among which he singled out the work of A. N. Pypin, an ardent follower of Belinskij. "It has been totally

---

conception of the work of art as the mere sum of artistic devices "a conception of a poetic work as a structural system, a regularly ordered hierarchical set of artistic devices" (quoted from *Readings in Russian Poetics,* p. 85).

185. See, e.g., Eichenbaum, "The Theory of the Formal Method," in *Russian Poetics,* p. 13.

186. See Šklovskij, *O teorii prozy,* p. 205. One of the Formalist slogans was: "New form comes about not in order to express new content, but in order to replace old form" (Eichenbaum, "The Theory of the Formal Method," in *Russian Poetics,* p. 14).

187. E. A. Poe had expressed precisely this principle in his essay "The Philosophy of Composition" (1846). Following Baudelaire's lead, Vladimir Majakovskij duplicated Poe's effort in his essay "How to Make Verse" (1926) in which he relates, in great detail, the genesis of his famous poem "Sergeju Eseninu" (1926).

supplanted by material taken from the history of social movements, from biography, and so on," he said, with considerable justification. Eichenbaum then proceeds to call the historicism of Pypin and other exponents of the Belinskian tradition in Russian literary scholarship "primitive" and explains that the Formalists have replaced their "historicism" with "an understanding of literary evolution as the dialectic change of form."[188]

Left Art

The Formalist movement, whose principal exponents were primarily scholars, was allied with several groups of the avant-garde formed by creative writers, poets, directors, film makers, and journal critics, often lumped under the label "Left Art" (*levoe iskusstvo*). Their theory and practice likewise clashed sharply with the organicist tradition of the past—and soon enough with its guardians on the contemporary scene.[189]

The theory and practice of the Left-Art movement were directed toward a radical deaesthetization of poetry (and other art forms), meaning an elimination of the boundaries between art and nonart, fiction and nonfiction, literature and journalism, poetry and propaganda. In practice, this meant a strong penchant for applied art, for the utilization of modern mass media (film, radio, billboard advertising), and a resultant "democratization" of language and style.[190] In a bold grasp for a new and radical utilitarianism, the concept of art as an end in itself was replaced by a functional view. Art, and specifically poetry, was a medium of information, propaganda, and popular entertainment. The artist was no longer an inspired "seer," but a competent professional trying to produce a quality product and to sell it to a mass audience. That he was also loyal to the Soviet regime was a contingency no more and no less important in his case than in that of an engineer or an agronomist. Obviously, this broke the "organic" tie between art and morality, replacing it by a purely coincidental connection. The defenders of the old organic aesthetics promptly called this position "amoral."[191]

188. Eichenbaum, "The Theory of the Formal Method," in *Russian Poetics*, p. 33.

189. Cf. H. Borland, *Soviet Literary Theory and Practice during the First Five-Year Plan, 1928-1932* (New York, 1950); Edward J. Brown, *The Proletarian Episode in Russian Literature 1929-1932* (New York, 1953); Herman Ermolaev, *Soviet Literary Theories 1917-1934: The Genesis of Socialist Realism* (Berkeley and Los Angeles, 1963). D. G. B. Piper's recent work, *V. A. Kaverin: A Soviet Writer's Response to the Problem of Commitment* (Pittsburgh, 1970), contains an excellent chapter on the Left-Art movement (pp. 15-62).

190. Osip Brik asserted that the "old art" tended to "aestheticize" its subject matter and to remove it from the domain of everyday life. The old theater, music, painting, and poetry were by their very nature elitist, he said. The task of the new art was to break down the barriers between "art" and "life" (O. Brik, "Za legkij žanr," *Novyj Lef*, 1928, no. 2: 34–39).

191. A. Ležnev, a bitter opponent of the Left-Art movement, pointed out that by

Equally contrary to the old organic aesthetics was the tendency of Left Art to "dehumanize" art by removing its concrete aspects: psychology, "individualization," naturalistic detail, especially of everyday life (*byt*). Osip Brik, the principal theoretician of the Left-Art movement, insisted that the new art present *actions* (campaigns, mass movements, collective enterprises) rather than the fate of concrete human individuals. This move, realized in Majakovskij's poetry, meant a tendency toward allegoric and schematic art. It contradicted the main principle of organic aesthetics, namely, that the "ideal" be expressed through a fusion with the "real," the abstract idea through a concrete, living symbol or image, the "typical" through the "individual."

It is no accident that whenever Majakovskij met with the disapproval of conservative critics, it was almost invariably on account of his violations of the principles of organic aesthetics: his lack of concreteness,[192] his wanton rejection of "realism" in art,[193] his open mockery of "historicism" (with resultant distortions of social and historical "truth"),[194] and his "moralizing" and "rhetoricalness."[195]

There is a strange and disquieting paradox about the aesthetics of Futurism, *Lef,* and Constructivism. On the one hand, their proponents displayed a desire to remove the barriers between "art" and "ordinary life": a literature not of fiction but of fact ("factography") was a notion frequently discussed and actually realized; there was a vigorous and successful effort at a democratization of

pleading "professionalism" the artist renounced his responsibility and initiative as an idealogue and citizen. See "Delo o trupe," *Sovremenniki,* p. 8.

192. "Simplistically 'slogany' (*uproščenno-lozungovaja*), superficially propagandistic, abstractly odographic, it [Majakovskij's lengthy poem "Xorošo"] is based, contrary to the poet's own promise, not on facts, documents, live material, but on clichés and commonplaces. But if truth is concrete, artistic truth is doubly concrete. He who violates this law inevitably falls into falsehood" (A. Ležnev, "Lefovskaja odopis'," *Literaturnye budni* [Moscow, 1929], p. 232).

193. "But Futurism meant not only a rebellion against Symbolism but also a departure from realism into nonobjective art. . . . Literature—and art at large—took on an even more 'nonobjective' character. A struggle against realism ('naturalism,' 'trivialism' [*bytovizm*], 'descriptiveness,' etc.) becomes an article of its faith. It would seem as though realism were forever buried under the waves of this purposely 'difficult,' eccentric, 'torn-apart,' multileveled poetry" (Ležnev, "Xudožestvennaja literatura revoljucionnogo 10-letija," *Literaturnye budni,* p. 256).

194. Trockij actually found fault with Majakovskij's presenting President Woodrow Wilson as enormously fat, "while everybody knew that he was very thin." Ležnev claimed that Majakovskij's poetic puns about "shooting" (*rasstreljat'*) Rastrelli and Raphael were fully supported by serious statements, in prose, by Majakovskij himself and by the theoretician of *Lef,* Osip Brik (see A. Ležnev and D. Gorbov, *Literatura revoljucionnogo desjatiletija* [Kharkov, 1929], p. 22). For a strong assertion of Ležnev's belief in the historical continuity between the old and the new art, see his article "Delo o trupe," *Sovremenniki,* p. 15.

195. Ležnev called Majakovskij's later works (as opposed to the early, rebellious pieces, for which he had high praise) the works of a "cold rhetorician and raisonneur" (ibid., p. 10).

poetic language, a general "lowering" of genre to the level of popular consumption; an elimination of any "philosophy" that might be alien to the common man. But, on the other hand, there was that tendency toward an objectivization, not to say "dehumanization," of art, expressed in the slogan *veščnost'* ("thingism"). A. Z. Ležnev, one of the principal critics of the Left-Art movement, was obviously puzzled by this contradiction:

> The trouble with Constructivism is not that it has not succeeded in excluding the aesthetic moment, for that is a hopeless undertaking, but rather, that its aesthetics has turned into aestheticism, into a refined gourmandise. It is just as easy to make an aesthetic fetish out of machines and photography as out of roses and nightingales. The difference lies not in the object, but in the approach to it. ("The Case of the Corpse")[196]

Ležnev assumed that the "dehumanized" world of Left Art was merely another system of metaphoric imagery, initially created to debunk old "humanistic" clichés (the parodistic, polemic strain being extremely pronounced in Left Art), which, in turn, then resolved into an assemblage of clichés. But there exists a more profound "organicist" explanation for this paradox of Left Art: quite conceivably, Left Art, and specifically the poetry of Majakovskij, was actually the expression of an entirely new image of man—"mass man," "man the machine," man beyond history, beyond time, beyond good and evil, and, it was hoped, beyond suffering.[197]

It is significant, in this context, that Osip Brik was highly critical of Fedor Gladkov's epoch-making *Cement* (1925), the prototype of the socialist-realist novel.[198] In *Cement*, a heroic mode (*geroičeskij pafos*) generated by the idea of "building socialism" and creating a new man ("Soviet man") was mixed with all the psychological and sociological detail of a conventional realistic novel. The hero, Gleb Čumalov, was both a "Soviet Hercules," as Brik put it, as well as an ordinary Soviet citizen with his private problems. Brik, was, of course, an admirer of Majakovskij's poetry, in which the *pafos* of building socialism was presented without any petty realistic trappings. Meanwhile, the critics of the Pereval group (such as Ležnev), who persisted in the old organicist tradition, were generally positive about Gladkov's novel, though they, too, found the combination of revolutionary "romanticism" and naturalistic detail (of technology and production, labor problems and management, party organization) somewhat strained.[199] The same critics were, however, highly negative about Majakovskij's poetry.

196. "Delo o trupe," *Sovremenniki,* p. 12.

197. Cf. Lawrence Leo Stahlberger, *The Symbolic System of Majakovskij* (The Hague, 1964), p. 144. Also Victor Terras, "Majakovskij and Time," *Slavic and East European Journal* 13 (1969): 155.

198. O. Brik, "Počemu ponravilsja *Cement,*" *Na literaturnom postu* 1926, no. 2: 30–32.

199. See Ležnev and Gorbov, *Literatura revoljucionnogo desjatiletija,* pp. 89–90. Also,

They also had words of the highest praise for the truthfulness and honesty of A. A. Fadeev's novel *The Rout* (1927), which Brik criticized for its, in his opinion, pointless psychologism and individualization of the revolutionary hero. Here, the lines were drawn very clearly. The Soviet critics who stood for the old organicist tradition, demanding that a work of art be a fusion of the ideal and the real, were also historical optimists, confident that the real, if only grasped perceptively and expressed honestly, would bring out the ideal as well. They did not mind that the soldiers of the Revolution in *The Rout* were presented as ordinary people with human frailties and even vices, or that the novel ended in the rout of the red guerilla detachment as a result of a bad error in judgment on the part of its leader, Levinson.

To be sure, there were some differences of opinion among the organicists as regards the relative position of the real and the ideal. Thus, Gor'kij, who had always leaned toward the ideal, did not find that the characters of *Cement* were excessively idealized, while other critics—Ležnev, for instance—demanded more realism. But fundamentally, there was no disagreement among them. The new aesthetics of Left Art, on the other hand, found any attempt at a fusion of revolutionary idealism and conventional realism false and absurd.

The poets and writers of the leftist avant-garde, as well as their more intelligent opponents, were fully conscious of the fundamental nature of their disagreement, and specifically that the very survival of the old organic aesthetics was at stake here.

RAPP (Russian Association of Proletarian Writers)

The critics of RAPP (Russkaja associacija proletarskix pisatelej), such as L. Auerbach, G. Lelevič, and Ju. Libedinskij, posed a different threat to the old organic aesthetics. Their views represented "contentualism" driven to absurd extremes. To the critics of RAPP, the value of a work of art depended on the degree to which its creator had succeeded in producing an "ideologized" conception of the world in his "artistic images." Critical practice became, for RAPP, an integral part of government policy, fully integrated into the political struggle leading to the victory of socialism. As Miroslav Drozda has pointed out, RAPP critics dealt not so much with man in "real life" as with a flat, one-dimensional world of the ideological functioning of things and people.[200] Clearly, this conception bore a resemblance to that which underlies medieval religious art and literature. In Hegelian (or Belinskian) terms, it meant a

---

A. Ležnev, "O *Cemente* Gladkova," *Literaturnye budni,* pp. 199–208. Very significantly, Maksim Gor'kij, the father of Socialist Realism, came out strongly in support of Gladkov's novel. Cf. Miroslav Drozda and Milan Hrala, *Dvacátá léta sovětské literární kritiky (Lef–RAPP–Pereval),* Acta Universitatis Carolinae, Philologica Monographia, no. 20 (Prague, 1968), pp. 35–37.

200. See Drozda and Hrala, *Dvacátá léta,* pp. 80–81.

disproportionate emphasis on the ideal aspect of life at the expense of the real. In a sense, it was an anachronism—unless one was to adopt a Spenglerian cyclic conception of history in which Russian civilization was passing through its early Middle Ages.

At any rate, the conception of "class art" (*klassovoe iskusstvo*) remained largely a theory. Lenin and the Party hierarchy never adopted it, and preferred to stay with the old concept of a "national literature." An interpretation and classification of all literature primarily as a "class" phenomenon was attempted by the so-called sociological school (V. F. Pereverzev and P. N. Sakulin, among others) mainly in the 1920s. The movement never received official sanction, in spite of some moral support from Lunačarskij, and was eventually condemned as "vulgar sociologism" in the 1930s.

In political practice, the critics and theoreticians of RAPP did a great deal of harm to the cause of free art in the Soviet Union. But as far as organic aesthetics was concerned, they were much less formidable a foe than *Lef* or Formalism. Ultimately, their conception of "class art" was merely another form of social organicism. Only as late as 1930, when Stalin's repressive policies began to cast their shadow over Soviet literature, the critics of RAPP explicitly declared literature the handmaiden of politics, suggested that it be institutionalized, and started to support the notion that it required constant control by the Party. Prior to 1930, the critics of RAPP, in good organicist fashion, believed that an honest proletarian writer's intuition would guide him to a correct understanding of the sociohistorical facts with which he had to deal. Among RAPP slogans, these were conspicuous: *živoj čelovek* ("live man"—as opposed to the allegories and schemes of *Lef*) and *sryvanie masok* ("removing the masks"), which was yet another version of the Plotinian metaphor implying the artist's power of a deeper, more penetrating vision of the world.

The aesthetics of RAPP was, in effect, the old Belinskian aesthetics coupled with a radical political philosophy. Drozda has pointed out the direct influence of Belinskij on RAPP.[201] The creative writers in the RAPP camp (Fadeev, Šoloxov) patterned their art on the honest critical realism of the nineteenth century, and on Tolstoj in particular. Significantly, RAPP critics in the 1920s generally agreed with those of the Pereval group in condemning a budding tendency toward what would become the "official naturalism" (*kazennyj naturalizm*—Georg Lukács's term) of the Stalin era. The critics of RAPP also criticized Gladkov's *Cement* for its mechanical—rather than organic—fusion of revolutionary romanticism and production-oriented naturalism, that is, they, too, saw a "genuine" work of art in terms of an organic synthesis of the ideal and the real.[202]

201. Ibid., p. 95.
202. Ibid., pp. 87–88.

The Pereval Group

The true guardians of the organic tradition during the first two decades of Soviet literature were the writers and critics of the Pereval group, in particular A. K. Voronskij and A. Z. Ležnev, both of whom explicitly and emphatically defended the organicist positions of Belinskij and Plexanov.[203] They considered Plexanov's aesthetics to be a Marxist adjustment of Belinskij's and saw nothing basically wrong with it.

While in full accord with Plexanov's "social organicism,"[204] the critics of Pereval placed less emphasis on "class" than the critics of RAPP. Where Auerbach would seek to remake the world, and literature, in the image of class ideology, Voronskij and Ležnev would try to view the objective world from a Marxist point of view. Both their general and their aesthetic philosophy were emphatically "organicist," "historicist," and even "nationalist."

The organicism of Voronskij and Ležnev was not only conscious and consistent (the words "organic," "organism," "live," "life," and "living" appear as often in their writings as in Apollon Grigor'ev's) but it was also meant to be taken literally. There is a strong dose of outright vitalism about their philosophy, and their arguments and metaphors hark back to the romantic period, to E. T. A. Hoffmann's *Serapion Brothers*[205] and V. F. Odoevskij's *Russian Nights*. The following passage from an article by Ležnev is typical:

> Formalism attracts youth by seemingly revealing all secrets and solving all riddles, by showing a mechanism where an organism was assumed to exist. And there, before the eyes of an astounded public [the Formalists] disassemble

203. For a concise statement of Pereval aesthetics, see A. Voronskij, *Iskusstvo kak poznanie žizni i sovremennost'* (Ivanovo-Voznesensk, 1924). For two manifestos of the Pereval group, see *Literaturnye manifesty,* pp. 272–82 (the manifestos are dated 1925 and 1926). Cf. also Robert A. Maguire, *Red Virgin Soil: Soviet Literature in the 1920's* (Princeton, N.J., 1968) and the book by Miroslav Drozda and Milan Hrala (see n. 199 above). An excellent article on Voronskij is found in Edward J. Brown, *Russian Literature since the Revolution* (New York and London, 1969), pp. 197–208.

204. Like Plexanov, the critics of Pereval always sought to define the social meaning of literary phenomena. See, e.g., A. Ležnev, " 'Levoe' iskusstvo i ego social'nyj smysl," *Literaturnye budni,* pp. 60–88. Ležnev would call Gor'kij's work "an expression of the psychology of those layers of the petite bourgeoisie that were turning proletarian" (*vyraženie psixologii proletarizirujuščixsja sloev melkoj buržuazii*) (*Literaturnye budni,* p. 105).

205. The direct influence of German romantic aesthetics on the Russian Serapion brothers and other Russian writers and poets of the 1920s is an important chapter in its own right. It does not enter the scope of this book. See Hongor Oulanoff, *The Serapion Brothers: Theory and Practice* (The Hague, 1966). Very significantly, Ležnev recognizes that Boris Pasternak is a poet "of the Fet-Tjutčev type and, to go back even further, of the type of the German romantics"—and in the same breath warmly approves of his poetry. See A. Ležnev, "Boris Pasternak," *Sovremenniki,* p. 53. Cf. Victor Terras, "Boris Pasternak and Romantic Aesthetics," *Papers on Language and Literature* 3:42–56.

this mechanism—a mechanism, to be sure, but incomparably more complex than one that is produced by industry. The reconstructions of the Formalists relate to genuine works of art much as an artificially built automaton relates to an animal. (*Literary Weekdays*)[206]

Nor was Voronskij's and Ležnev's organicism limited to aesthetic theory. A certain vitalism and mystic humanism was apparent in their whole thought. Thus, in a necrology to Esenin, Voronskij exclaims in his *Literary Notes:* "But the most disquieting thing about contemporary civilization is that, in the place of immediate human relations, it sets up a fetishism of things and ideologies (*veščnyj i ideologičeskij fetišizm*), a love of things and phantoms. This devotion to things and ideas hides from view immediate human relations."[207]

Voronskij and Ležnev fully endorsed the Belinskian notion that great artists were invariably and unavoidably on the side of historical progress:

> The classics were always abreast of their epoch, and many of them were clairvoyants and visionaries of the future. They were deeply committed to ideas; they were attuned to the highest ideals of humanity in their age. At the base of their creations there always lay emotions of import, love of man, of the oppressed, hatred for the oppressors, for everything misshapen, trivial, dead, wretched. In their minds there lived a yearning for a new, regenerated life. (A. Voronskij, "Crossing Over")[208]

The critics of Pereval were historical optimists even in a more concrete sense than the above indicates. They believed that the progress of the socialist Revolution had no need of Majakovskij's shrill hyperboles: it could well afford to express its ideals and its world view in a simple, objective, matter-of-fact way. "You cannot cheat history," said Voronskij.[209] Plexanov had said that realism was the "natural" style of a young, vigorous class whose period of ascendancy lay before it. Ležnev adjusted this position to apply to a vigorous ruling class, such as the proletariat in the Soviet Union. "Formalist," stylized art, said Ležnev, belonged to social classes who were near the end of their active role in history. Therefore, the critics of Pereval, along with the earlier Russian Marxists and RAPP, were decidedly opposed to all forms of "modernism."

206. Ležnev, *Literaturnye budni*, p. 57.

207. A. Voronskij, *Literaturnye zapisi* (Moscow, 1926), pp. 154–55. Cf. the following passage from Voronskij's article "Art as Cognition of Life, and the Contemporary Scene" (after having told an anecdote about Anatole France, who likened Esperanto to a beautiful doll and then added: "Still, a live woman is better, even if she has no beauty!"): "Our comrades, the Esperantists-Futurists, having forgotten that every language develops organically, keep presenting to us a doll instead of a woman: living speech is replaced by dead, cerebral, labored word-formations" ("Iskusstvo, kak poznanie Žizny, i sovremennost'," *Iskusstvo i Žizn': Sbornik statej* [Moscow and St. Petersburg, 1924], p. 26).

208. "Na perevale," *Iskusstvo i Žizn'*, pp. 80–81.

209. Quoted from Drozda and Hrala, *Dvacátá léta*, p. 125.

This also applied to Freudianism, which in the 1920s was making some inroads even in Russia. Voronskij rejected any extensive application of Freudian insights to literary criticism or scholarship, labeling Freudianism "subjectivist" and "idealist," and suggesting that it ignored, or at least grossly underestimated, the role of objective sociohistorical reality which, he said, had always been and still was the basic motor, and object, of artistic creativity.

Voronskij extended the charge of "subjectivism" to the theories of his left-wing opponents of the *Proletkul't* and *Na postu* groupings (both predecessors of RAPP). The rigid futuristic "goal-directedness" (*celeustremitel'nost'*) of *Proletkul't* and the equally rigid fixation on "class" of *Na postu*, said Voronskij, tended to conceal the facts of objective sociohistorical reality from these poets, writers, and critics.[210] These tendencies, Voronskij warned, frequently boiled down to a subjective emotionalism in art, which in turn "easily blended with idealistic and agnostic theories" (that is, with aesthetic relativism).[211] In another essay, "On Art,"[212] Voronskij explicitly rejects the class-based relativism (*klassovyj reljativizm*) of his opponents, pointing out that it renders an artist useless to all but his own social class. Reasoning strictly along Hegelian lines, Voronskij expresses his belief in objective historical truth which can be perceived from different angles, to be sure, but is still the truth to every genuine artist—no matter whether his sympathies lie with the winning or the losing class.[213] Voronskij simply refused to admit that even in art it is the winner who dictates his truth to the loser.

The writers of Pereval also followed the Belinskian tradition in believing that genuine art had to be "national." Thus, Voronskij juxtaposes Dem'jan Bednyj's "concrete" and "national" revolutionary poetry (of which he says that "it smells of Russia") to the "transplanetary" cosmism of "so-called proletarian poets," approving of Bednyj and disapproving of the latter.[214]

In their polemic with Auerbach, Lelevič, Rodov, and other theorists of the RAPP camp, on the one side, and Constructivism and *Lef*, on the other, Voronskij and Ležnev were defending the autonomy and the traditional—exalted—position of art against the attempts of their opponents to reduce it to an "instrument" (of class struggle, of "building socialism"). This defense of the autonomy and importance of art had to be necessarily centered in an assertion of the

210. Voronskij, "Frejdizm in iskusstvo," *Literaturnye zapisi,* pp. 16–17.
211. Ibid., p. 11.
212. "Ob iskusstve," *Literaturnye zapisi,* pp. 35–36.
213. In an article, "Outside Life and Outside Time," Voronskij discusses some recent works by Ivan Bunin, a nobleman, an *émigré*, and a bitter enemy of the Soviet regime, and asserts that these works tell the truth about the Russian *émigré*—because Bunin is an artist ("Vne žizni i vne vremeni," *Literaturnye zapisi,* p. 119).
214. Voronskij, "O pisatele i čitatele (Dem'jan Bednyj)," *Iskusstvo i žizn',* p. 205.

reality of creative intuition and the cognitive capacity of art.[215] In his article "On Art," Voronskij held up the importance of intuition in the creative process, as opposed to the "constructivist" ideas of *Lef* and the Formalists. The whole article is built from and around quotations from the Mixajlov episode in *Anna Karenina*, a classical statement of the Neoplatonic organic conception of the creative process.[216] The concept of the artist's inner vision is energetically defended, as are the other pivotal concepts of organic aesthetics: intuition, creation, and inspiration. Voronskij quotes a passage on the artist's "inner vision" from Belinskij's early (still Schellingian) essay "On the Russian Short Story and the Short Stories of Mr. Gogol' " (1:286), heartily agreeing with it. Elsewhere in the same article, Voronskij explicitly asserts his belief in "the artist's gift of clairvoyance" (*dar jasnovidenija*).[217]

Furthermore, Voronskij and Ležnev energetically defended the concept of the unity of the work of art in terms of an organic fusion of content and form, of the ideal and the real, and of the universal and the particular.[218] They were critical of naturalism (now called *bytovizm*—which they felt was an unhealthy overreaction against "abstract cosmism and empty propaganda slogans"), demanding that the ideal should never be absent from literature. "We need more of the heroic in our literature," wrote Voronskij, as he expressed his sympathy with the pathos of Gladkov's *Cement*.[219] Simultaneously, Voronskij—as early as 1926, two years before the launching of the first Five-Year Plan—demanded that Soviet artists and writers acquaint themselves with the concrete facts of the country's economic and cultural reconstruction, that they abandon the notion according to which "the opening of new factories, the reopening of a plant, the building of a power station, the struggle on the economic and cultural front are themes of no interest to the writer."[220] Yet Voronskij also takes for granted that the new Soviet literature will fill this "social order" (*social'nyj zakaz*) freely, "organically":

> There is a lot of talk about "social order" these days. Yes, the new class, asserting its rights and its power, issues its "social order" to the artist. But the artist must sense that he is filling this order freely, by his own choice,

215. On the cognitive powers of art, see, e.g., Ležnev, *Literaturnye budni*, pp. 16, 25.

216. Voronskij emphasizes that Tolstoj's description of the nature of art in *Anna Karenina* clashes sharply with his emotionalist and moralist aesthetics in *What Is Art?* Naturally, Voronskij accepts *Anna Karenina,* and rejects the emotionalism and moralism of *What Is Art?* ("Ob iskusstve," *Literaturnye zapisi*, pp. 54–55).

217. Ibid., pp. 10, 46.

218. Ibid., p. 43; cf. Ležnev, "Xudožestvennaja literatura revoljucionnogo 10-letija," *Literaturnye budni,* pp. 254–55. See Voronskij, "Ob iskusstve," *Literaturnye zapisi,* p. 52. And see Ležnev, *Literaturnye budni,* p. 200.

219. Voronskij, "O tom, čego u nas net," *Literaturnye zapisi,* p. 65.

220. Ibid., p. 67.

by his own free will. More correctly, he should not feel at all as though he were filling an order. ("On What We Do Not Have")[221]

In the same article, Voronskij complains that contemporary Soviet literature is either cold, abstract propaganda, or naturalism (*bytovizm*) without an ideal, and expresses a hope that the new literature will create works which will be real, alive, concrete, yet will also express the ideals of the Revolution, "the ideals of brotherhood, unity, and the triumph of the working class."[222]

Voronskij and Ležnev fought tirelessly not only against thoughtless, mechanical schematism,[223] empty rhetoric, and narrow "factography,"[224] but also against outright insincerity and untruth, which were beginning to creep into Soviet literature. The title of Voronskij's article "Dodgers and Toadies" speaks for itself.[225] In particular, many early Soviet critics (including Voronskij) tried to diagnose the insincerity which was then taking hold of Soviet art and literature as a social phenomenon: artists and writers of bourgeois background and loyalties, they thought, were camouflaging themselves as honest fellow travelers of the Revolution and were more or less skillfully adapting themselves to the new situation. The implication was still that an artist needed sincerity, integrity, and an honest commitment to an ideal in order to create worthwhile art. In other words, a work of art had to rise "organically" from life itself.[226]

Belinskij had gone against Hegel in predicting a bright future for art in general and for Russian literature in particular. The critics of Pereval found themselves facing several different groups who were not only predicting, but actually demanding, the death of art, at least in the form in which it had existed before the Revolution. Voronskij and Ležnev rejected this notion and stressed the continuity of human as well as of Russian civilization. Voronskij denied that the new "socialist" art would be created any differently than the works

221. "O tom, čego u nas net," *Literaturnye zapisi*, p. 71. Regarding "social order," cf. Ležnev, "Delo o trupe," *Sovremenniki*, p. 16.

222. "O tom, čego u nas net," *Literaturnye zapisi*, pp. 69–70.

223. Ležnev singles out V. Ermilov as a typical "schematist" and "simplifier" (*sxematik i uproščenec*) who refuses to see literature as a "living thing" (*Literaturnye budni*, p. 45). Cf. this passage from the "Declaration" of Pereval (1926), signed by M. Prišvin, È. Bagrickij, D. Gorbov, A. Ležnev, M. Golodnyj, A. Platonov, A. Karavaeva, and I. Kataev, among many others: "The members of *Pereval* take a stand against any attempt to schematize man, against all simplism, against dead standardization, against any lowering of the writer's personality in the name of petty naturalism" (*Literaturnye manifesty*, pp. 276–77). Cf. also Voronskij, "Na perevale" (1924), *Iskusstvo i žizn'*, p. 85.

224. See, e.g., Voronskij's article "Xudožestvennaja literatura i rabkory," *Literaturnye zapisi*, pp. 101–9.

225. "Prolazy i podxalimy," *Literaturnye zapisi*, pp. 90–95.

226. See, e.g., Voronskij, "O kritike i bibliografii," *Literaturnye zapisi*, pp. 110–11,

of Puškin or Tolstoj. Any talk of "collective creation" he called "leftist child-
ishness" (levoe rebjačestvo).[227]

At the same time, Ležnev and Voronskij predicted that art would be playing
an increasingly significant role in Soviet life as it approached the ideal of a
socialist society:

> Man under Socialism will enjoy a tremendous amount of leisure. The suc-
> cesses of technology will easily replace the eight-hour day with a six-hour
> day, a four-hour day, and perhaps less. This leisure will have to be used for
> activities not connected with production—science, sports, play, and art. Not
> only will the role of art not decline, but it will actually grow immeasurably.
> (Ležnev, "The Case of the Corpse")[228]

Furthermore, the critics of Pereval, much like Belinskij and most of Belinskij's followers before them, were willing to allow some exceptions to the rules
of organic aesthetics. There were times, said Voronskij, when utilitarian art
had to be in the forefront, when it was necessary to write agitki, much as there
were times when every honest writer would have to drop his pen and reach for
his rifle. But this should never become a permanent condition.[229] Obviously,
this line of thought repeats Belinskij's conception of critical periods in the history of a nation and its literature.

Voronskij and Ležnev, along with many other members of the Pereval group,
eventually fell into disgrace, and their opinions were repudiated by the doctrine
of Socialist Realism which emerged from the First Congress of Soviet Writers
in 1934. Their opponents of RAPP, as well as of the Left-Art movement, generally shared their fate. Drozda calls Pereval a future-oriented movement which
anticipated an undercurrent of Soviet literature that was to surface only after
Stalin's death.[230] In my opinion, this is only partly correct. Voronskij and
Ležnev were men of conviction and intellectual honesty, and one can certainly
speak of a partial revival of intellectual honesty in Soviet literature after the
death of Stalin. But this development has little to do with the heritage of
Pereval. Certainly, much of "liberal" Soviet aesthetics, literary theory, and
literary criticism during the post-Stalin era, and to this day, bear many features
which are familiar to us from Pereval. And the charges which adherents of a
more orthodox Socialist Realism will produce in challenging these "liberal"
writers, critics, and literary theorists will be exactly like those directed at

227. In this, as in so many other instances, Voronskij was a poor prophet. Even in his
day, "collective art" was beginning to flourish in the film industry.
228. "Delo o trupe," Sovremenniki, p. 31.
229. See, e.g., Voronskij, "Iskusstvo, kak poznanie žizni, i sovremennost'," Iskusstvo i
žizn', pp. 23–24.
230. Drozda and Hrala, Dvacátá léta, p. 150.

Voronskij by A. G. Dement'ev in a rather hostile introductory essay to a new
edition of Voronskij's writings:[231] "idealistic leanings," overemphasizing the
"disinterestedness" of art, excessive attention paid to the spontaneous aspect
of the creative process, "irrationalism," and insufficient *partijnost'*. However,
the aesthetic theories of Pereval were unoriginal. For the most part, Voronskij and Ležnev merely repeated what they knew from Belinskij, Dobroljubov,
and Plexanov. Their contribution lay in their application of the organicist and
historicist ideas of their predecessors to contemporary literary trends.

Soviet scholars and critics of the post-Stalin era, insofar as they sincerely believe in the Belinskian principles of honest realism, historical awareness, genuine social concern, conscientious psychological individualization, and the unity
of content and form, as well as of the ideal and the real, owe these principles
first to Belinskij himself, then to the tradition of Belinskian thought which permeates much of Russian literary criticism and literary history, and only lastly
to the influence of such "organic" critics and theorists of the 1920s as Voronskij and Ležnev. At least from a Western point of view, Formalism and Left
Art, and not Pereval, were the future-oriented movements in the Soviet literature of the 1920s.

A description of the present situation in Soviet literary theory, criticism, and
aesthetic thought is beyond the scope of this book. As I hope to demonstrate
in a separate monograph, the great majority of Soviet works in this area do not
transcend the conceptual and terminological system of Belinskian organicist
aesthetics.

It is my conviction that it is at least theoretically possible, today no less than
a century ago, to write interesting and meaningful literary criticism in terms of
a Belinskian organic aesthetics. Nor do I think that practical examples to this
effect are entirely nonexistent in our day. I would like to mention the late
Mark Ščeglov as a critic, entirely in the Belinskian tradition, yet capable of
making genuine contributions toward a better and more profound understanding of contemporary Russian literature. Yet by and large, for over half a century now, most of what has been new, original, and stimulating in Russian literary criticism, theory, and scholarship has come from opponents of the Belinskian organicist tradition.

231. A. G. Dement'ev, "A. Voronskij–kritik," in A. Voronskij, *Literaturno-kritičeskie
stat'i* (Moscow, 1963), pp. 3–46.

Index

In the Belinskij entry below, italicized numbers refer to pages on which there are long quotations from Belinskij's works; and following the title of Belinskij's reviews, the year given in parentheses refers to the date of the review, not the work under review.

287

Belinskij, 75, 106, 186–87; in Blok, 229; defended by Pereval critics, 282–83; in Dostoevskij, 224; endangered by ideology in Belinskij, 170; in Grigor'ev, 219; ideology is a threat to, acc. to Volynskij and Eichenwald, 271; redefined by Plexanov, 261; in Schelling, 56; in Utopian Socialist aesthetics, 74–75
Freud, Sigmund, 7, 281

Galič, A. I., 21 n42
Genius: definition of, 47–48, 190–91; national role of, 17, 58–59, 72, 93, 97, 98, 111–12, 190; prophetic powers of, 15, 21 n40, 112, 190
–Belinskij's conception of, 38, 59, 84, 112, 190–91; stands below the collective mind of humanity, acc. to Belinskij, 38; Puškin an example of (in Belinskij), 112, 131
–Černyševskij rejects conception of, 236
–and talent: as a category of organic aesthetics, 7, 13, 23 n48, 190–93, 211, 232, 253, 270
–in various writers: Dobroljubov, 249, 253; Grigor'ev, 221; Hegel, 111; Kant, 47; Schelling, 58–59
Genres of poetry, 19, 30, 45, 55 n32, 64, 117, 125, 163, 170–75, 240; "lowering of genre," 30, 133, 140, 189, 209, 276. See also Comedy; Drama; Epos; Lyric poetry; Tragedy
Gessner, Salomon, 158 n60
Gladkov, Fedor, 276, 277, 278, 282; his Cement, 276, 277, 278, 282
Glinka, F. N., 92, 175
Goethe, Johann Wolfgang von: his cosmopolitanism, 72; his opinion of Hoffmann, 160; his view of poetry, 25–26; mentioned, 17, 19, 20, 32 n1, 35, 44, 45, 46, 79, 81, 84, 112, 114, 138, 150, 164, 181, 183, 196, 201, 249 n114
–Belinskij's opinion of, 33, 40, 41, 51 n24, 61, 145, 186, 195–96, 198, 199; as a German genius, 93, 195; on his "indifferentism," 76, 102, 105, 195, 198, 199; as a son of his age, 195–96
–Faust: as "an apotheosis of reflection," 165; as an example of "philosophic poetry," 114; as an expression of the German national spirit, 79; mentioned, 45, 136 n17, 150, 181
–Hermann und Dorothea, 158–59; Prometheus, 114; Werther, 197–98, 249 n114; West-oestlicher Divan, 73
Gogol', N. V.: his aesthetics outlined,

26–31; an antipode of Puškin, 23, 26, 27, 207, 231; his conception of humor, 28, 177; a creator of myth, 59, 123; and "the negative ideal," 53, 85, 187, 259; not a realist, 134 n14, 149; his view of art, 11, 26–31 passim; his view of Puškin, 96; mentioned, 22, 34 n6, 37, 40, 41, 48, 63 n53, 64, 65, 66, 89, 94, 100, 101, 111, 114, 126, 132, 151, 152, 161, 167, 168, 173, 180, 184, 185, 193, 194, 199, 204, 214, 219, 235, 240, 242, 262, 264, 282
–Belinskij's view of, 17, 70, 78, 86, 115, 116, 122, 125, 126, 169, 177, 179; ceased being an artist when he turned reactionary, 17, 115, 180; Formalists refute Belinskij's view of his works, 211 n2, 273; expressed the spirit of his age, 19, 86; his historical role, 64, 68, 180, 207–8; his humor, 169, 176–77, 178; his literary connections ignored by Belinskij, 115, 125, 163; not a poet of universal stature, 145, 146; not a satirist, 105; his originality, 155; a realist, 133, 135–36, 140–41, 149, 189–90; a social critic, 136
–Černyševskij's view of, 243–44, 246
–Grigor'ev's view of, 216, 221
–Dead Souls: an altogether Russian work, 111; Belinskij's and K. S. Aksakov's polemic about, 63 n53, 184; Belinskij's view of, 86 n24, 133, 136 n18, 159, 193–94; Černyševskij's view of, 241, 244; an expression of Russian reality, acc. to Belinskij, 86 n24, 133; its humor, as seen by Belinskij, 177; its "idea," acc. to Belinskij, 133, 136 n18; negative ideal present in it, acc. to Belinskij, 187; not a satire, 105, 174; presence of "reflection" in it, praised by Belinskij, 165, 193; as a Russian myth, 123; subjective element in it, acc. to Belinskij, 40, 199–200; mentioned, 26–30, 37, 63, 87 n26, 97, 136, 137 n18, 146, 153, 168, 191
–The Inspector-General: Belinskij's interpretation of, 40, 65–66, 133, 152, 168, 173; mentioned, 26, 29, 34 n6, 147
–Taras Bul'ba: Belinskij's interpretation of, 86; mentioned, 133 n13, 148
–"A Terrible Vengeance": Belinskij's negative evaluation of, 161
–works mentioned: "After the Theater," 11, 28–29; "The Architecture of Our Age," 26; "Author's Confession," 28; "Dénouement of The Inspector-General," 28; "Diary of a Madman," 80; "Hans Küchelgarten," 244; The Marriage, 133 n13; "Nevskij Prospect," 30–31, 148; "On the

Ukrainian Folk Song," 26; "The Overcoat," 115, 141, 158, 216, 243, 273;
"The Portrait," 27 n59, 30, 221 n35;
"Rome," 27 n59; "Sculpture, Painting,
and Music," 26; *Selected Passages from
a Correspondence with Friends,* 28–29,
78, 216; "The Story about How Ivan
Ivanovič Quarreled with Ivan Nikiforovič," 85–86, 133, 177, 240
Gončarov, I. A.: his aesthetic views, 234
n67; his reminiscences of Belinskij, 107;
mentioned, 119, 148, 203, 230, 232,
249, 258
—Belinskij's opinion of, 41, 200 n61; an
objective artist, acc. to Belinskij, 37;
"only an artist," acc. to Belinskij, 82
—*Oblomov:* Družinin's interpretation of,
232; Dobroljubov's interpretation of,
249
—*The Precipice,* 119; *The Same Old Story,*
82, 148, 158, 203
Gorbov, D., 275 n194, 283 n223
Gorjačkina, M. S., 257, 258 n138
Gor'kij, Maksim: his alleged "cruelty,"
266; approves of Gladkov's novel *Cement,* 277; as the father of Socialist Realism, 211; Ležnev's opinion of, 279 n204;
a new social type inaugurated by him,
266 n167; his view of art as a catalyst of
social change, 269–70; mentioned, 5, 90,
176, 261, 264, 265, 267
—works mentioned: *The Burghers,* 264;
The Mother, 261, 267, 269–70; *Odd Fellows,* 269–70
Greč, N. I., 187, 204
Griboedov, A. S., 19 n34, 33 n6, 127 n3,
132, 173
Grigor'ev, A. A., poet and critic: his aesthetic views, 168, 214–22; his belief in
the universality of the Russian national
spirit, 96; concerned with the conflict between ethical and aesthetic values, 16;
his historicism, 88, 119, 217–18; his national organicism, 93 n36, 99, 218–19;
sees Russia in the context of occidental
civilization, 18
—as Belinskij's disciple, 34–35, 214, 236;
his view of Belinskij, 36, 214–15; his
view of Gogol', 53, 216, 259; mentioned, 19, 26, 52, 68, 125, 223, 224,
225, 226, 227, 235, 252, 253, 254, 268,
269, 279
—poetry reviewed by Belinskij, 128 n6,
182, 194–95
Grigorovič, D. V., 100 n50, 101, 149, 161,
163, 168, 189, 243; *Anton Goremyka,*
106, 149, 168; *The Village,* 149, 243

Grossman, Leonid, 214 n5, 215 n8, 216
n13, 222 n38
Guber, Eduard, 155, 181, 195
Guizot, François, 44
Gukovskij, G. A., 86
Guljaev, N. A., 43 nn1 and 4, 81
Guyau, Marie Jean, 267 n167

Hahn (Gan), Elena Andreevna, 106, 124,
137, 141
Hamann, Johann Georg, 183 n14
Hegel, Georg Wilhelm Friedrich, philosopher: the absolute in his aesthetic system, 119; his aesthetic historicism, 42,
50, 64, 95, 117, 134, 140, 177; his aesthetics outlined, 59–69; on art and other
aspects of human creativity, 81, 183; art
should be universal, 66; artist's vision directed at the outside world, 13–14; beauty (and art) as a fusion of the ideal and
the real, 12, 52, of idea and form, 202
n63; his conception of the comic, 28,
173; his conception of genius, 111, 193;
concreteness of art, 42, 139; content at
the expense of form, 68, 112, 143, 210;
his defense of Flemish genre painting,
141, 204–5, 240; his definition of the
work of art, 138; his dialectic method,
67; distinguishes between historical and
ahistorical peoples, 64, 94, 117; every
true work of art an absolute, 127 n2; excludes satire from art, 105 n60; favors objective over subjective art, 37; great poetry necessarily national, 17, 66, 125; his
hierarchy of individualities, 91, 125; on
"inner vision," 128 n7; his interpretation
of *Don Quixote,* 118 n78; operates with
identities between ideal and empirical
planes, 169; his opinion of E. T. A. Hoffmann, 160; opposes naturalism, 65; pre-
dicts the demise of art, 49; the real aspect in art's fusion of the ideal and the
real, 57, 65, 88, 159; rejects "art for art's
sake," 82, esoteric art, 66, the fantastic
in art, 79, 161; on romanticism, 65; the
universal above the particular, 87, 92,
146, 208; unsympathetic to folk poetry,
96; his use of the term "pathos," 67, 136,
of the term "fantasy," 154 n51; his view
of China, 97; mentioned, 4 nn2–3, 5, 9,
19, 48, 53, 55, 56, 71, 73, 90, 120, 122,
130, 131, 148, 164, 194, 203, 207, 224,
239, 241, 244, 249, 257, 259–61, 264,
277, 281, 283
—Belinskij on, 33, 34, 68, 69, 85, 88; and
Belinskij's "reconciliation with reality,"
197–98; his influence on Belinskij, 37,